STOCK MARKET SUPERSTARS

SECRETS OF CANADA'S TOP STOCK PICKERS

Andrew,

Good luck in the markets!

STOCK MARKET SUPERSTARS

SECRETS OF CANADA'S TOP STOCK PICKERS

BOB THOMPSON

INSOMNIAC PRESS

Library and Archives Canada Cataloguing in Publication

Thompson, Bob, 1969-
    Stock market superstars / R.J. Thompson.

Includes index.
ISBN 978-1-897178-67-6

    1. Investment advisors--Canada--Interviews. 2. Investments--Canada.
I. Title.

HG5154.3.T56 2008   332.6'0971   C2008-904293-X

The publisher gratefully acknowledges the support of the Department of Canadian Heritage through the Book Publishing Industry Development Program.

Printed and bound in Canada

Insomniac Press
192 Spadina Avenue, Suite 403
Toronto, Ontario, Canada, M5T 2C2
www.insomniacpress.com

To my father, whose guidance, tireless dedication, and willingness to give his time have contributed significantly to my success.

Contents

Acknowledgements

I wish to express my thanks for all the support I received in the making of this book. It was a long task, and it could not been done without each and every one of the following people.

There were also countless individuals who allowed me to bounce ideas off of them, helped me get names for possible managers to interview, and gave me informal advice on the book. For those that I have not mentioned, I truly appreciate all your efforts.

All the managers – I wish to thank all the managers, who gave me innumerable hours of their time during the interview process and supplied me with lots of backup information.

The managers' support staffs – For putting up with our incessant badgering to get performance numbers, pictures, and background information.

My dad – For all the moral support, suggestions, comments, listening to me talk about this book for the better part of two years, and just being a wonderful father.

My clients – For putting up with my talking about this book constantly, and for putting up with my frequent trips to Toronto and other places to conduct interviews.

Ashley Sahota – For her endless devotion to the editing and research process. Without the tireless dedication of Ashley, this book would not have been.

Melanie Yang – For helping tremendously in the editing process. Without Melanie's persistence, this book would not have been published on time.

Andy Tu – For his constructive comments and the increased workload that he maintained to allow me time to spend in the preparation of this book.

Matthias Andruschko – For conducting valuable research on many of the managers interviewed. Without this research, I would not have been able to ask intelligent questions.

Mike O'Connor – For publishing this book and having the faith that it will be a success

Howard Atkinson – For listening to my idea, and referring me to a fantastic publisher.

Preface

I wanted to be a doctor when I started at Simon Fraser University in Burnaby, British Columbia. I was good at science, and the sight of blood didn't bother me, so medicine was perfect. I wanted to be a doctor, right up until my family hit some really tough financial times while I was going to university. Money was so scarce that a dentist chased us for fifty dollars, and my barber, who felt bad for me, said my dad and I could have free haircuts until we "caught up." I finally started at a local grocery store for the grand sum of $11.60 an hour, thinking I was set. Well, that job came to a crashing end, so to speak, when the roof of the store, which had rooftop parking, collapsed. The roof brought twenty cars with it right into the deli counter and book department, all within fifteen minutes of the grand opening. No one was killed, which was a miracle, especially with so many people still in the store. That was the end of the high-paying job and the start of more financial strife, at least for a few more months. More delivering phone books on contract for three bucks an hour, and more money worries ensued.

When the store finally reopened six months later, this time with a rein-forced roof, I was back in the money for $11.60 an hour. After living on next to nothing for a heck of a long time, I wanted to make sure that didn't happen again. I diligently saved, and studied how to make money work. I read that "money makes money" and that anyone could become wealthy if only they were patient, diligent, and, most important, they started young. I was on my way, and investing became my new passion.

Don't get me wrong, I still to this day browse through my anatomy books from time to time, but the financial business was where it was at for me. I don't think I would have pursued a career in finance if I had not gone through these financial woes, and I think in the end it was good for me. You always better appreciate what you have when you have been through some very trying times. As they say, it builds character.

Money was still tight after I started my job at the store, so I went for a student loan. I still remember my shock when the loan officer wouldn't give me the loan I wanted. It's not what you are thinking. I wanted a $1,000 loan, and they said, "No way, the minimum loan you can take is $2,500."

"Excuse me?" I said. "I only need $1,000."

"Hey, kid, it's $2,500 or nothing."

Needless to say, I took the money and decided to invest the difference. I was going to be a value investor. I had done my reading and knew that value investing was the safest way to go. Buy beaten up, unloved, unwanted companies and reap the rewards when they came back into favour. I know you are wondering about the first stock I bought. Well, it was a Canadian institution in business since 1899, with a AAA credit rating, and it was one of Canada's largest financial institutions to boot. How could I go wrong? The stock was a classic value play at $10, having come down from a year high of $20. I impressed myself. I was pretty smart. Well, I dove in, buying 200 shares for a total of $2,000. Easy money, I thought.

Unfortunately, it turned out that the stock was called Royal Trustco, a holding company that eventually went bust going down to below $0.50 per share, finally changing its name to Gentra. I wondered whether the name Gentra was short for "general trash." Who cared? I lost my money. But it was another great experience in the grand scheme of things, as I learned that success never comes easy and learning only comes with a good dose of failure. I redoubled my efforts and invested my extra student loan money more wisely in the future, and I had eventually doubled my money by the time I had to pay it back.

This was my first lesson in the principle that money makes money. I started examining the traits of successful investors from Warren Buffett, to John Templeton, to a momentum investor (a.k.a. gunslinger) named Richard Driehaus. Fast forward twenty years, and here we are, trying to determine the traits, qualities, and secrets of some of Canada's best money managers.

A sad fact is that many, if not most, individuals who have invested with even the best money managers have not made a lot of money in the process. Why? Because most investors, high net worth or not, make the wrong decisions at the wrong time. They sell a great manager's fund because of short-term underperformance, without looking at their portfolio as a whole. Smart money managers don't suddenly become stupid; their style simply goes out of favour for a period of time. Almost without exception, the average investor sells a fund after a period of underperformance, and can be counted on to buy again after a period of short-term outperformance.

Eric Sprott, one of the best money managers in the country over the last three decades, even discussed this in my interview with him. His firm usually loses assets after his performance has lagged for a short period, but the money comes flooding in again, right at the top, after his performance has been spectacular. This is the real reason why many investors get crummy returns from their portfolios. Most financial pundits, being self-acclaimed "champions for the average investor" blame investor underperformance on the high fees that money managers charge and the other evil-doings of mutual fund companies. Being "in the trenches" with the retail investing public, I can say that, generally speaking, this is hogwash. Investment returns are lousy because the average investor makes lousy decisions based on emotions instead of making good ones based on discipline.

Investment management is certainly not a science, and, in many ways, it's not an art—it's a combination of both. The problem is that few individuals have the attributes to be a scientist and an artist, and the ability to balance the two of them. That may be why many of the best don't even have finance degrees. Frank Mersch, one of the best managers in the country with an uncanny grasp of "the big picture," says that his degrees in philosophy and history helped him realize the importance of knowing history and being a non-linear thinker. His thesis in university was to prove that there were angels in the world! His having to learn to think outside the box was an understatement, but it was these experiences that helped him to outperform his peers.

I came up with the idea for this book for a few reasons. First, not many money managers actually do well over long periods of time. There are only a few that are stars in their field. This book, through interview transcripts, will highlight the common traits that some of the best money managers in the country have developed over the years. Second, I had an idea that investors could increase their investing skills through education. Third, I thought investors needed to hear, in money managers' own words, how their strategies, style, and success have developed over the years. Plus, it was just plain fun to sit down with all these personality types, some of whom were very humble and shy, and some of whom were a bit arrogant, and some of whom who were hilarious.

Oh, yes, and before you say, "Why isn't so-and-so in the book? They're better than these jokers," I have chosen all these great managers for a particular reason. They have all done a magnificent job in respect of their stated goals, whether it is beating their respective benchmark or generating absolute returns. I particularly picked managers that had achieved their great returns by varying methods. Some are value managers, some are growth or momentum managers, some are hedge managers, and some can't be pigeonholed. All these terms are defined in future chapters.

Some good money managers come and go with the market cycles. Only a few "great" managers have achieved significant returns in good and bad markets. This is why I chose managers who have been doing it for a period of time with the shortest track record being ten years or so. This time frame still encompasses the great markets of the late '90s; the nasty, atrocious, and horrific markets of the first years of the new millennium; and the good markets of 2003 to 2007. I wanted to make sure that their track records at least covered these varying cycles because money management in many respects is based on adaptability of the money manager to differing times. They have to know whether it is different this time or the changing market dynamics are a trap, like the Internet run up in the late '90s. Nevertheless, the list of great money managers I have missed in this book will be long and distinguished, I'm sure. If you know of some of them, let me know…material for the next book.

There are as many investment managers and funds in Canada as there are stocks on the stock market. It therefore takes as much time and effort to research, pick, and follow a money manager that suits your goals as it does to pick a stock. For those of you who think that profitable investing is easy, it isn't. I read, and read, and read again to get insight into the world as a whole, from investment literature, to research, to the history of World War II. At the 2003 Berkshire Hathaway Annual Meeting, Warren Buffett's famous business partner, Charlie Munger, said, "I have said that in my whole life, I have known no wise person over a broad subject matter who didn't read all the time—none, zero. You'd be amazed at how much Warren [Buffett] reads. You'd be amazed at how much I read."

Will reading this book make you a better investor? I am sure of it, because it will highlight the insights, personalities, foibles, outlooks, and misgivings of some of the brightest minds in the investment world here in Canada. It will help you realize your strengths and weaknesses, and make you aware of what it takes to be a great investor over long periods of time. Remember, however, that the stock market is like a big auction. You compete with all these bright minds when you decide to be a do-it-yourselfer. Do you feel confident to go out and do brain surgery tomorrow? The brain surgeons reading this aren't allowed to answer this question. If you aren't a brain surgeon, and the answer is yes, then give it a shot. You will probably be responsible for someone's death.

Luckily, with your investments, you will only be responsible for destroying your own portfolio.

Last but not least, by writing this book and highlighting the managers that I have, I run the risk of causing overly inflated egos. One of the reasons I have chosen these "stars" is precisely because they are generally humble. This is a tricky subject because you won't do well at investing unless you are confident, but hubris will destroy you every time. Once you hear cockiness, arrogance, and the "I'm always right" mentality from a money manager, it is usually a good time to run for the hills, as this is definitely a contrary indicator of future performance.

Introduction to Investment Management Styles

Portfolio Structure: A Simple Guide to Building the Portfolio

There are many ways to manage money. Since the business consists of more styles, systems, and approaches to the art of trying to make money than you can imagine, this proves only one thing: There is no best way of doing it. If there were an unchanging foolproof system, everyone would use it. The problem is that if too many people use any one system or approach, it will soon be doomed to failure, as no one will have an edge over any other. This is why one of the most important traits of any money manager is adaptability. Even the vaunted value manager Sir John Templeton said that "if you are doing things the same way today that you were twenty years ago, you will most likely not be doing well." Adaptability is also the reason why the cockroaches survived the catastrophic climatic change that happened millions of years ago, while the dinosaurs did not. As with the dinosaurs, size is not that important in the money management business; it is the ability to react and change with varying circumstances.

Now that we are clear on cockroaches and survival, there are actually a few quantifiable ways of managing money. I will discuss them in detail in the following pages, but in summary, there are value managers, there are growth managers, there are equity long/short managers, and there are variations of the three styles. Some very smart people scoff at pigeonholing the various styles, but, either way, if you have a grasp of how different people manage money in different ways, your ability to manage your own money will take a quantum leap forward. I have taken the following three outlines from a piece issued by Synergy Mutual Funds, now a part of CI Investments.

1) Value Investing

Value Stock Picking

Value managers invest in shares that trade below the estimated true (or intrinsic) value of the underlying company. Over time, it is expected that the market will come to recognize the value of the business and the stock price will move up accordingly. Value investors do not pay a premium for a stock on the assumption that its intrinsic value will rise.

Value Portfolio Construction

Portfolio Characteristics – Value portfolios are expected to have a lower than average volatility. The portfolio's weighted average price/normalized earnings and price/book value multiples should generally be below the market average. Dividend yields will vary but are often above the market average.

Risk Management – The portfolio is consistently diversified by industry. By establishing downside risk targets and trying to purchase securities below intrinsic value, a "margin of safety" is provided to somewhat cushion the impact of errors and uncertainties. A quantitative model is used to manage risk factors and will influence weights of holdings.

Sell Discipline – A holding will be sold (1) when its price approaches intrinsic value, (2) to replace with a stock exhibiting better value characteristics, or (3) to improve the risk/reward profile of the portfolio.

2) Growth Investing

Growth Stock Picking

Growth managers invest in shares of companies that are exhibiting secular growth in excess of the market rate. This growth may be in the form of earnings, cash flows, revenues, or volumes.

Valuation parameters such as price/earnings and price/book value ratios do not define growth—underlying fundamentals define growth. Valuations will vary widely among growth stocks and should be a reflection of the predictability, sustainability, and quality of the growth.

Growth Portfolio Construction

Portfolio Characteristics – The weighted average earnings and revenue growth rates of the portfolio consistently exceed the growth rates of the market.

Risk Management – The portfolio is well diversified by industry, market capitalization, and valuation.

Sell Discipline – A holding will be sold (1) when an underlying company stops exhibiting superior growth potential, (2) if the valuation of a security goes beyond its fundamental merits, or (3) to improve the portfolio's risk/reward profile.

3) Momentum Investing

Momentum Stock Picking

Selection Criteria – Momentum managers invest in shares of companies that are exhibiting positive relative and/or absolute fundamental change. To that end, holdings selected for a momentum portfolio will generally display the best combination of the following four characteristics:

Positive Estimates Revisions – Analysts' forecasts for the stock's earnings, cash flow, revenues, production, etc., are rising.

Positive Surprise – Actual reported results exceed market expectations.

Positive Relative Strength – The stock's price is outperforming the market and/or the industry peers.

Positive Acceleration – The company's revenues and/or earnings are accelerating, or declining, at a slow rate.

Momentum Portfolio Construction

Portfolio Characteristics – The weighted average positive change characteristics of the portfolio consistently exceed those of the market.

Risk Management – The portfolio is well diversified by industry and risk factors. A quantitative risk model may be used to manage risk factors and will influence weights of holdings.

Sell Discipline – A holding will be sold (1) when the underlying company's fundamentals exhibit negative relative and/or absolute change as indicated by the four characteristics listed above, (2) to replace it with another stock that demonstrates better momentum, or (3) to improve the portfolio's risk/reward profile.

The styles seem to be favoured by the market in alternating periods of years. In other words, value investing outperforms growth for a period, and then growth investing outperforms value for a period. The key is to mix the two so that your overall portfolio return is achieved with lower volatility than would otherwise happen. Inherently, heightened volatility should not be a problem, as many of the managers say you cannot achieve excellent performance without some significant volatility. In real life, excessive volatility is difficult for all but the most seasoned investors to take.

Let's take a look at some examples. From 1981 to 1986, value outperformed growth investing by a wide margin. Value generated 23 percent compared to growth at 12 percent. If you had invested from 1987 to 1991 based upon what had happened in the years previous, it would have been exactly the wrong move—growth outperformed value 18.9 percent to 11.9 percent. Leadership again changed from 1992 to 1996 as value-generated returns of 18.6 percent and growth-generated returns of 13.2 percent. Many of you will remember what happened next. The tech bubble happened from 1997 to 1999 and, subsequently, growth achieved 32.1 percent compared to value at 14.2 percent. As often happens after speculative blow-offs, market leadership changed over the course of the next few years. From 2000 to 2006, value did well as growth treaded water, but in 2007, growth had its best showing as compared to value in almost a decade. This is typical of peaks in economic activity. Growth often significantly outperforms value leading up to a recession. Both styles have done well historically, but leadership has changed depending on market conditions.

Annualized Return (%)

	Value	Growth
1981-86	23.3%	11.8%
1987-91	11.8	18.9
1992-96	18.6	13.2
1997-99	14.2	32.1
2000	29.5	-13.9
2001-06	7.9	-1.6
2007	-0.17	11.8

Source: Fama & French and Bernstein until 2000; Russell Value 1000 Value & Growth Index from 2001 to 2007.

Logically, the next question one should ask is, "Why don't I just invest in growth funds when they are doing well, and change to value funds when they are doing well?" A good idea in theory—usually lousy in practice. It's impossible to know which strategy will outperform, but we can always see it after the fact. It's like recessions: we never know there will be one until we are already in it. The bottom line is that having a disciplined process and plan is usually much more important than making your investment decisions based on emotions and whims.

Styles Go In and Out of Favour

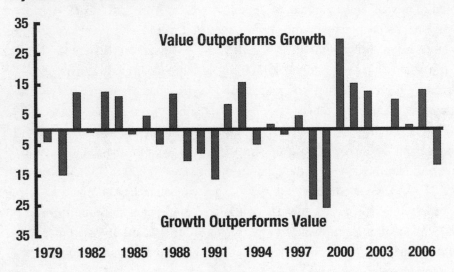

Annual difference between the Russell 1000 Value Index and Russell 1000 Growth Index for the period January 1, 1979, through December 31, 2007. The unmanaged Russell 1000 Value Index contains those securities in the Russell 1000 Index with a less-than-average growth orientation. The unmanaged Russell 1000 Growth Index contains those securities in the Russell 1000 Index with a greater-than-average growth orientation.
Source: Frank Russell Company.

Proper style management has proven itself over long periods of time. By actively rebalancing your portfolio to retain a particular style, you can increase your returns over time while reducing the overall volatility. For example, if, at the beginning of a value cycle, an investor has a 50 percent allocation to value and a 50 percent allocation to growth, that balance may be 65 percent value and 35 percent growth after a year. This would be caused by the relative outperformance of value versus growth. Rebalancing back to the 50 percent value, 50 percent growth model would result in an investor's adding to a position in a style that has recently underperformed. Historically, a style that has underperformed for a period of time will subsequently outperform.

Setting up a portfolio with the following parameters and actively rebalancing can help to achieve better returns with less volatility than either style can accomplish separately. Invest in:

- Funds with a pure, defined style
- Top-performing funds within each category
- Non-correlated funds that bear little resemblance to each other in various market environments

Alternative Asset Managers

In my quest to find some of the best stock pickers in Canada, I knew that this would take me to alternative asset money management. Many great traditional money managers see that they can add value and reduce some downside risk by employing non-traditional strategies. These strategies may include short selling, leverage, or arbitrage strategies. I think that non-traditional investing is so important that I will dedicate quite a few pages to the process of why money managers migrate to the alternative side and how they can add value.

The term *hedge fund* is often associated with alternative asset or non-traditional asset investing. It's funny because when one says hedge fund, the general public tends to think that this is a very risky vehicle. In most cases, this is not true at all. Most traditional money managers who decide to run hedge funds do so to enhance the returns, to have more tools at their disposal, and to reduce volatility.

Market Risk Versus Non-Market Risk

Broadly, there are two types of risk inherent with money management. One risk is called market risk, or the variability of returns that one may achieve that is based on the market. In other words, if the market drops 10 percent, an index fund will drop 10 percent. This is because the index fund returns are entirely dependent on the market. The index fund is exposed to 100 percent of the market risk. As you can see, it is impossible for the index fund to add value over the index. Because of this, investors are unwilling to pay high fees for the service of simply achieving index returns.

Non-market risk in money management usually refers to factors that affect securities that are not dependent on the overall market. For example, what if a broad-based group of gold stocks does well but your gold stock does poorly? This may be because the individual company that you own accidentally dumped a chemical into a river during the mining process, causing environmental damage, or because the company missed its quarterly earnings numbers. This risk was not caused by the market, but by a specific event that happened to a particular company.

Alternative investment managers generally consider themselves to have an edge that allows them to use their individual skill to do better than other managers. Because of performance-based compensation, they generally want their returns to be more dependent on their individual skill than on the market. They can therefore try to take away market risk, over which they have no control, and shift their portfolio more towards non-market risk, where they feel they may have more control. This means that the portfolios may look very different than the underlying index where they invest. For instance, here in Canada, financial service stocks consisting of banks and insurance companies make up a large percentage of the index. Most alternative managers or mutual fund managers who have done a fabulous job over time will not own bank stocks just because they make up a large piece of the index. They will only own them if they feel the prospects or valuations of the companies are compelling. This is the case with all the managers in this book, and this "thinking outside the box" mentality is not coincidental. It is one of the fundamental reasons they have done so well.

Alternative asset managers generally have 80 percent of their returns attributable to their skill and only 20 percent attributable to the market. The opposite is true with traditional money managers, whose returns are 80 percent attributable to the market. This is one of the reasons why many traditional managers have trouble beating the market. I classify the stock pickers profiled in this book as non-traditional even if they don't hedge, as they follow their own reasoning rather than the market index and their portfolio returns are generally more affected by their decisions than by the index. This is the only way you can outperform.

An Introduction to Long/Short Equities
What Is Long/Short Equity Investing?

Long/short equity funds are the most popular type of hedge product available in Canada, with approximately 80 percent of the funds falling into this category. In the U.S., approximately 35 percent of hedge funds are long/short and they also represent the largest category of hedge fund. Long/short equity funds are the easiest of all hedge fund styles to understand because they use equities as part of their investment strategy. Other hedge styles use complex arbitrage strategies, derivatives, fixed income, or a myriad of other vehicles to achieve their objectives. While absolute returns (positive returns) are a common goal of most hedge strategies, the different styles will generate varying risk/return profiles.

Long/short equity fund managers buy stocks they like and sell short the ones they don't like. In many cases, the reason for selling a stock short is to reduce the overall risk in the portfolio, not to make a bet that the stock will go down. The long/short model is based on the premise that using a modest amount of leverage combined with short selling could generate market-beating returns, with less risk than the market.

The returns of long/short equity funds should be primarily dependent on the stock-picking abilities of the manager, and less on the overall return of the market.

Although long/short investing has evolved, the original model, developed by Alfred Jones around 1949, used a modest amount of leverage, short selling for risk control, and some profit generation. The terms listed below are defined in the glossary at the end of this chapter.

Example:

Long exposure:	125%
Short exposure:	75%
Net exposure to market:	50%

In the above example, if the manager can simply generate index returns with the long exposure to the market, he will be generating 125 percent of the market returns. Without the short position, the volatility would also be 125 percent of the market. Hence, the manager initiates a 75 percent short exposure. The short can be used for risk control, in case the market falls, and the fund can generate positive returns on these positions. As can be seen, the net exposure to the market is only 50 percent. If the manager can simply use the shorts over time as a risk-reducing measure, he actually does not even have to generate positive returns on the short. If the shorts break even over time, we can see that the fund can generate 125 percent of the market returns, with 50 percent of the risk, on any given day (125 percent long – 75 percent short).

This is easier said than done, and I have oversimplified this example, as managers have other parameters and risk controls they look at, but you get the point.

Long/Short Equity Style Differentiation

To consistently accomplish their goals, a long/short manager must be a good stock picker, have a defined investment philosophy, and have a method that is sustainable. A manager can achieve these goals through various measures. Below are several methods employed by long/short equity managers:

Pairs Trading

This style is commonly used to reduce the market risk of a particular trade. An effective pairs trade is very dependent on the manager's stock-picking abilities. Given the two main types of risk—market risk and non-market risk—a manager may be a great stock picker, but if the overall market declines rapidly, the stock may still fall simply because of overriding market factors. Also, the stock may fall because an entire industry is falling. For example, if the aerospace sector falls out of favour, this will likely cause a precipitous fall in airline stocks.

On the other hand, stock-specific risk can be attributable to situations where individual stocks are falling even though the market is rising. This can occur for a variety of reasons, including poor earnings, bankruptcy, lawsuits, fraud, etc.

A manager will employ pairs trading to reduce the effect of market risk on the portfolio. The return of the portfolio will be entirely dependent on the stock-picking ability of the manager rather than the specific industry represented by the equities.

Example:

After events such as September 11, 2001, certain sectors fall out of favour, as happened then with the hotel industry. A long/short manager may see value in the sector but is worried about the prospects for the entire industry in case people stop travelling. In this case, by buying a stock, or "going long," the manager is still exposed to the hotel industry. The risk is that a great stock can still turn out to be a lousy performer.

To offset this risk, the manager will short a stock deemed to be of lesser quality or which has low chances of appreciation. If the long and short positions are of equal value, the industry risk is reduced and the return is solely dependent on the performance of the stocks relative to each other.

Long:	ABC Hotel
Short:	XYZ Hotel
Net Exposure	0%

Possible Outcomes:

I. ABC rises   +30% (for illustrative purposes)
    XYZ falls   +20% (share price fall = capital gain)
    Total return +50%

II. ABC rises   +30%
    XYZ rises   -20% (share price rise = capital loss)
    Total return +10%

III. ABC falls   -30%
     XYZ rises   -20%
     Total return -50%

IV. ABC falls   -20%
    XYZ falls   +30%
    Total return +10%

Clearly, the third scenario is the alarming one. A manager can reduce the risk of this example by several methods. First, the manager diversifies with many different pairs trades. Second, an active stop-loss program can be used that will eliminate the position if it goes offside by a predetermined amount.

Industry or Sector Rotation

Some long/short equity managers tend to take a "top down" macro view of the economy. Based upon their analyses, they will make sector bets. Sectors that are perceived to benefit from the macroeconomic outlook will have long exposure in the portfolio, whereas sectors that are perceived to have a negative outlook will be shorted. Individual stocks are then picked in each sector according to the manager's stock-picking parameters. Equities may be selected on the basis of their growth or value attributes. This type of fund may have a higher volatility than a fund that strictly does pairs trading, but the returns can be very high if the manager is correct.

Example:

Specific or general economic events may cause some sectors to come into favour, while others will fall out of favour. With this set of certain circumstances, it can be highly profitable if a manager can short one sector and go long in another sector. The following would have worked well during the 2001-2002 bear market.

Short: Technology
Long: Gold

There are two ways to execute the trades. A manager can use index products as a proxy on the sector or, of course, execute trades in the underlying stocks of the particular index. As with the previous example of pairs trading, managers can use various means to manage the risks arising out of several outcomes.

Special Situation or Opportunistic

Some long/short managers use an approach that is opportunistic in nature. They may take advantage of short-term mispricing of securities or extreme value situations based on market perceptions. This is usually very stock specific in nature and may not be hedged with other investments. The manager may also use a combination of this method and other long/short strategies. This type of trading may be more non-market dependent in nature than some other management styles because returns are more event driven in nature.

The strategy is highly dependent on the manager's ability to identify opportunities, and may involve the need to be very active.

In other words, the manager may be in and out of positions quickly, maybe on a week-to-week or month-to-month basis. For this reason, liquidity is paramount. The manager may want to limit the size of the fund and pay attention to how many shares of a particular equity are owned in comparison to the average trading volume of that stock.

Example:

A stock picker buys a security such as a closed-end fund that trades on the market, knowing that the security is redeemable at a point in the future for its net asset value (NAV). The security may be purchased when it is trading at a 10 percent discount to its NAV based on the premise that it can be redeemed or "cashed in" in three months at its NAV. In this case, the only risk that would be involved is that the NAV of the security would go down. However, in any scenario, there would still be a "cushion" of 10 percent for the hedge manager. This style of long/short can overlap with some other hedge styles, such as event driven or arbitrage.

In the above case, if the NAV is stable, a manager could achieve a low-risk 10-percent return over the period of three months if they execute it properly.

The goal of most long/short equity funds is to achieve equity-like returns with less risk and volatility than the market. As measured by the Credit Suisse/Tremont Long/Short Equity Hedge Index from January 1994 until March 31, 2008, the index has been able to achieve annualized returns of 11.6 percent per year. On the other hand, the S&P 500 over that time frame has generated returns of 9.5 percent per year. Further, the Long/Short Index has achieved the better returns with only about 70 percent the volatility of the S&P 500. To achieve their objectives, long/short managers can use a variety of tools including selective use of leverage, short selling, and option-based hedging strategies.

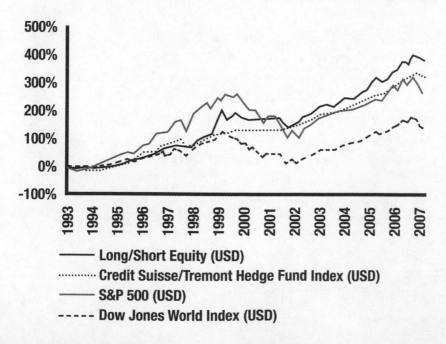

───── Long/Short Equity (USD)
············· Credit Suisse/Tremont Hedge Fund Index (USD)
───── S&P 500 (USD)
─ ─ ─ ─ Dow Jones World Index (USD)

An investor should understand the statistical measures associated with the long/short fund in order to properly analyze it in the context of the portfolio. Alternatively, and more practically, a prospective investor should rely upon an individual who understands the long/short strategy and can give proper advice within the context of a portfolio approach.

In the course of these interviews, several managers were long/short equity managers, including Eric Sprott, John Theissen, Frank Mersch, Randall Abramson, Peter Pucetti, and Rohit Sehgal. Given the choice of putting their own money in their long/short equity product or a long-only product, most of the above managers choose the long/short because of the added flexibility.

Long/Short Equity Glossary

Long/short investing is relatively simple to understand. Most managers use variations of the basic principle of buying stocks they like and shorting stocks they dislike, or at least dislike relative to their long holdings.

Short selling – We won't get into all of the dynamics of a short trade; however, the basics are important. Shorting a stock consists of borrowing a stock that you don't actually own, and then selling it with the hope that it can be bought back at a lower price. The difference between the stock's selling price and the lower buyback price is your profit. On the other hand, buying the stock back at a higher price than what you sold it for will generate a loss.

Leverage – Many long/short equity funds use some leverage in the investment process. Leverage is simply borrowing against existing holdings to try to enhance returns over what would normally be possible. In other words, an investor borrowing $0.50 for every $1.00 invested would have $1.50 invested. Thus any gains would be on the $1.50, and the only cost would be the borrowing cost of the $0.50. Of course, leverage can work against you, resulting in a larger loss than would be normal if things go awry.

Gross exposure – The combination of adding the stocks that are owned by the fund (long positions) to the stocks that are shorted by the fund (short positions). For example:

Long positions	125%
Short positions	75%
Gross exposure	200%

Net exposure – The difference between the long exposure and the short exposure of the long/short equity fund. For example:

Long positions	125%
Short positions	75%
Net exposure	50%

Market risk (systematic risk) – The risk associated with owning securities in a particular market. It is that part of a security's risk that is common to all securities of the same general class and thus cannot be eliminated by diversification. The measure of systematic risk in stocks is the beta coefficient.

Sharpe Ratio – A number measuring the reward-to-risk efficiency of an investment, used to create risk-efficient portfolios. In other words, the Sharpe ratio measures the return of an investment per unit of risk. The mathematical formula is listed below; however, the number is readily available for different investments and it is not required for the individual investor to calculate it.

The definition of the Sharpe ratio is:
$$S = (r_X - R) / StdDev(x)$$

Where:
S is the investment;
r_X is the average annual rate of return of x;
R is the best available rate of return of a risk-free security (e.g. cash);
$StdDev(x)$ is the standard deviation of r_X.

Practically speaking, the higher the Sharpe ratio, the better the investment, based on a return-to-risk measure.

Tim McElvaine
Dealing in Nightmares, Not Dreams

**"I make Homer Simpson look active
because there's not that much excitement happening in my office."**

As the ex-chief investment officer for Peter Cundill's company, Tim McElvaine is all about deep value investing. If you wondered what the definition of deep value investing is, it is buying the equity of companies that are beaten up, unwanted, and unloved. Even hearing their name will sometimes make you cringe. As Tim says, "We deal in nightmares, not dreams." So why would you buy nightmares, you say? Well, because if you pick the right ones, you get a great bargain on the purchase price, and this is how Tim says he makes his money. With a 20 percent annualized return (16 percent net to investors) for the last ten years until December 31, 2007, "nightmares" have turned into dreamy performance for Tim's investors.

As a value investor who is strict in his style, he will build up the cash when he can't find bargains. Surprisingly, he has been able to achieve these returns while holding a lot of cash over the years. In 1997, the average cash position in the fund was 59 percent, and at various times over the last decade, the fund has averaged 20 percent-plus in cash. What even makes the performance more remarkable is that there are hardly any resource stocks that have accounted for the performance. Chances are, you won't have heard of many of the companies that Tim has owned over the years.

Buying stocks with a margin of safety can also help to reduce your downside and can result in amazing consistency. Tim is one of only a couple of managers I can think of who have not had a down year in the last ten years. Other than a drop during 2002, and the recent drop at the beginning of 2008, the chart for the McElvaine Investment Trust has generally been a nice upward sloping line over the last ten years with very few bumps along the way. Even in 2007, in which many "value managers" were beaten up, he squeezed in a positive return by the tightest of margins. The style has been pretty easy on the nerves over the years, and it proves repeatedly that to make a lot of money over time, you just need to avoid the big drops during the bad times.

Known for his witty and self-deprecating humour, it is always fun to chat with Tim. Putting yourself down in a fun way I think actually helps people to stay humble, which is one of the traits of the most successful investors. I actually had to convince him that he should be included in this book. When I asked him why he developed a value philosophy, he said, "I am not as bright as growth managers, so it was logical for me to do this." When asked why he tends to hold stocks for so long, he says, "Because it takes so long for them to go up," referring to the fact that many value managers get into stocks a bit early.

I first met Tim in 2006 after doing some research on value managers. The McElvaine Investment Trust had one of the best and most consistent return profiles going, and upon further examination, I found the results and process to be very repeatable. I called his office in Vancouver and arranged a meeting to sit down and talk about his philosophy. We had to book a meeting a couple of weeks out because Tim is only in Vancouver every so often, living full time in the beautiful city of Victoria, B.C.

What I love about many of the Stock Market Superstars profiled in this book is that most have small unassuming offices. Tim is no exception. With only a few people working at the firm, including Kim and Di, who Tim constantly praises in his updates, the office in downtown Vancouver is very small. We chatted the first time in Tim's office, which was about as plain as could be, with simply a laptop on his desk. I interviewed him a second time in his room at the Four Seasons Vancouver in May 2008 just after one of the more brutal drubbings for value stocks in years.

Bob:

You were the CIO at Cundill. How did that come about?

Tim:

At the time, I was working in Bermuda for the Bank of Butterfield taking my CFA. I wanted to get more involved in the investment business, and I went through a list of people who I view as mentors. John Templeton was on the list, Peter Cundill was on the list, and someone from Trimark, what was his name?

Robert Krembil?

Krembil was on the list. This was in 1989, 1990, which was not a great time for stocks and not a great time for hiring. Out of them, Peter showed the most interest, so I hounded him. He had to either change his fax number or hire me. Thankfully, he hired me, so I moved to Vancouver and started working with him, and that would have been in March of '91.

Nothing like persistence, then?

Nothing. Yeah, persistence. Companies get lots of resumes, but people who send resumes who obviously know a little bit about what you do I think is so important. So when people say they're looking for a job these days, if they can tailor the package they're sending to the person they're sending it to, it goes a long way.

Mark Holowesko used to run the Templeton Growth Fund. He called Templeton at 27 years old, or 25, and said, "I want to work for you," and Templeton said, "Go get your CFA and then talk to me."

He went back a few years later with his CFA—three years later or whenever he finished it—Templeton said, "Sure." I think he gave Mark the Templeton Growth Fund at 27 years old, right? The people at Cundill today are fairly young when you look at them. Is that something that Peter did, is he'll bring somebody young in with not a lot of experience and say, "I'll teach you the value way"? Or did you have a lot of experience before you went and saw Peter?

No, but Pete's a value investor. They're cheap that way.

Right, right. So they run their businesses that way too.

No, I didn't. What I did do is send Peter a lot of very specific ideas, so I think he had an idea of how I thought. Then when I went to start to work with him, it was kind of just working, how I always approached stuff and how he approached stuff.

How long did you work for him before you were a CIO? It was pretty quick, wasn't it?

The advantage was there were only two of us, so [laughs] I didn't have to climb to the top of a ladder. We had fifteen people in the firm, but there were only two on the investment side.

How much money did the firm manage?

Probably about $300 million, give or take a little bit, and going down because it was 1991, so things weren't going too well.

You have an accounting degree and a CFA. A lot of people have CFAs and a lot of people don't have either one and do fine. So which one do you think was better, as far as helping you with what you do?

I didn't have the personality to do your job, so that meant I became a CA. It's a language thing. A CA is like learning French—there's nothing magical there, but it makes you quite comfortable with the lingo and mostly with the BS that people toss out. Then it also makes you understand how divorced accounting sometimes is from the reality of the situation. So you're not in awe of it; you say, "Well, that's crap." What they're doing for accounting is whatever the CAs or CPAs want, but that's not what's happening in the economics of the business. The CFA—and God bless the CFA because as long as they keep that program, there won't be very many people doing my thing in the business. So the CFA was interesting to me because it's where I wanted to go, but there's an awful lot of stuff in it that doesn't apply to what you or I would do on a day-to-day basis.

My accountant who's a CA told me this. He said, "What do accountants use for birth control?" I said, "What?" He said, "Their personalities." [Laughs] That came from my accountant. That wasn't me. Obviously, you said you sent Peter some ideas. You were a value guy before you met Peter Cundill. How did you evolve into that, rather than a growth investor?

Well, partially given that I was a CA, I obviously had low self-esteem, and when you have low self-esteem, you work towards value stocks. If I really thought I was that smart, maybe I would have been a growth guy. That's kind of what got me towards it. In the '80s, I had read a lot of stuff about Buffett and Ben Graham and John Templeton. I had been to a number of John Templeton AGMs in Toronto in the early '80s, so it felt like a better fit to how I thought about the world.

Do you remember the first stock business experience or when you became interested in the stock market, or when you started buying stocks?

My first experience—other than the lemonade-stand-on-the-side-of-the-road-type stuff? My first experience in business was probably when I was about 12. We lived on a farm. I decided, with certainly my parents' "encouragement" so to speak, to produce eggs and sell them to the neighbours. I ended up getting twenty chickens or something like that. We built a coop. My dad put up the capital cost and lent me the money to build a chicken coop and the wiring to buy the chickens. Then my theory was the chickens would lay the eggs, and I'd sell the eggs to the neighbours, and we'd pay my dad and then make some money for myself, and this would be my enterprise. So I had visions of being the chicken king of Kingston, Ontario.

Well, you know, agriculture is a tough business. First of all, the chickens' eggs kept breaking, so I had to change their feed. Then the foxes came by and ate the odd chicken, which doesn't do very good for production. Then winter came and the eggs would freeze before I came home. Finally, for the poor egg that made it from the chicken into my fridge, sometimes my mom took them without telling me. I quickly moved into bankruptcy in my chicken business. We ended up selling them to the farmer across the road, and he slaughtered them. After that, I decided I didn't want to do anything in agriculture, and picking stocks seemed a heck of a lot easier than taking care of chickens, so I kind of worked towards that.

You had seen a business go through a rough time, so you're familiar with that.

As well as the liquidation value; I was quite familiar with it.

You were a value trap, weren't you?

Yeah. Yeah.

You wouldn't buy your business even at a cheap price?

No, it was not a good business, but I think like my early stocks, like everyone else, I was kind of lurching around trying to figure out how to do this. I looked at technical analysis. I tried to think about growth stuff. I think I had some Wardair and some Pop Shoppes International at one stage, and I think Wardair made some money and Pop Shoppes went to zero. Sometime around that area I kind of bumped into Buffett and then Ben Graham and I thought, "Okay, well, that makes sense. Here's more of a framework that makes sense to me."

Your personality has a lot to do with how you invest money a lot of times. Some of these growth guys that are out there, they're cocky. You could look at somebody and say, "That's going to be a growth investor." Somebody else can say, "That's going to be a value investor," because value investors seem to be more conservative in their personal lives. They're softer spoken.

Yeah. Yeah, I guess so, meaning if you want to party, find a growth guy. I think that's what you're saying.

Yeah, maybe. But none of the growth guys are as funny as you are, and you don't even know it. Now, were there some lessons that you learned from Peter?

Yeah. The two biggest things are, when you have the courage of your convictions—if you're right—then don't worry about what other people think. The second thing is it always takes longer than you think for stuff to work out. That would be the two I recall at this moment.

Your average holding period is a long time with stocks, right?

Yeah. We own stocks for a long time quite simply because it takes a long time for them to go up. If they went up quickly, I'd love to have high turnover and sell them quickly, but it'd take a long time to go up.

There was a poster that you saw a long time ago that you read ...

Oh, yeah. Yeah.

How did that affect you?

A lot of people who come into the business want to do something. They like the activity, I think it comes a little bit from—our business today is like Xbox on steroids, right? You can get the game in front of you, you see the lights flashing, you can hit a button and buy and hit another button and sell. There's lots of adrenalin; it's exciting. So for me, I kind of operate at a completely different spectrum. I make Homer Simpson look active because there's not that much excitement happening in my office. I can go to the bathroom and not worry that I missed making a million dollars because of a portfolio decision. So my sister had this poster up that said, "Sometimes I sit and think, and sometimes I just sit." That kind of summarizes a day at the office for me.

In other words, if there's nothing to do, nothing to buy, then don't spend the money.

Then don't do it. Yeah.

One of the best hedge fund managers of all time, George Soros, the big macro guy, said exactly the same thing. He said, "I sit there…I do nothing…until if I see a big pile of money in the corner, then I'll go pick it up, and I'll bring it over." And then he said, "I'll sit and do nothing for a long time until I find another big pile of money." It's interesting because he has a totally different philosophy from what you do, but he was really saying the same thing.

Yeah, it's kind of like….

You don't feel the need to always be busy.

Yeah, Buffett talks about how you don't have to swing at every pitch. It's kind of like value investing. Certainly, maybe investing in general is really boredom with moments of pure panic in between. A lot of time there's nothing to do, and then all of a sudden there'll be those moments where there's something to do. You need to make sure that in the boredom times, you are getting yourself ready to act when you need to. But you don't need to do everything every minute. I think that's the most important thing I learned.

Do you think most people have the ability to be as patient as you need to be? It certainly doesn't seem like it because you have to be extremely patient. You've owned stocks for years before they go up, and then they'll go up 50 percent in three months.

It's helpful to be somewhat challenged, so time passes and I'm still thinking well of stuff. I think if you're confident with what you're doing and you see the value building over time, then you don't mind waiting at all. It's a lot easier to do than you think. The important thing is not to get distracted by greener fields, because every day you come in there'll be something over there that looks like it might be more interesting. It's kind of like with a girlfriend or a boyfriend, and for sure if you're on a diet you can look at the menu, but you'd better not go and start sampling unless you've decided you're no longer on the diet. Same thing with investing, for me at least. It's fine to go and look at all these other stocks to see because they look interesting. To actually make the purchase and sale decision, you have to be really careful because the only thing we control in this business is when you buy and when you sell. That's the only one thing I can do. I can't make the stock go up or down.

Frank Mersch said the one thing he could do better is to be more patient. He said that he owned 30 percent of Canadian Natural Resources, of the entire company, at $0.10 a share. He said that he got bored with it and sold it. He said, "Can you imagine?"

I had over 10 percent of Denison Mines at one stage. It went up a little bit, and I thought, "Wow! Ooh, ain't I bright?" So I think I sold it for $0.15 or whatever. The interesting thing too is quite often the ideas you're most focused on will languish and the one that you've kept in the portfolio because you think it's cheap but you're not expecting anything out of it this year...suddenly something happens. So, yeah, it's kind of funny that way. You start a year and you never know exactly where your gains are going to come from, at least in my case.

What are the three things that you look for when you assess a stock?

There are actually like three and a half, and the half thing I'm a little bit reluctant to talk about because most people think I'm dumb when I mention it, but, regardless, I will. First thing is, "Does it trade for less than it's worth?" which you know every person will say that. So you figure out what you think the company is worth, and we go through a four-step process to do that. We look at liquidation value. We look at kind of a break up value. What would a private market buyer pay for it? We also look at what happens if things go the way we think. I try and model out three years. I don't try and go out a long period, but try and go out a couple of years and say, "This is where I think they're going, and if they're going in that direction, what does it mean the company will look like in three years?" What will happen to cash primarily? Not so much worried about earnings, but what will happen to cash over that period? A fourth one is a kind of discounted cash flow, but there are so many things you can play around with when you go out longer term. I'm really careful not to let the Excel spreadsheet rule me. In fact, I much prefer analysis that you can do with a pencil and a piece of paper to one that's very elaborate with multiple spreadsheets. That's the first thing. Does it trade for less than you think it's worth?

The second thing is, "How volatile is that estimate of what it's worth?" Think of the story of "The Three Little Pigs." If you take an example of a straw hut, at the first sign of difficulty, the first time a wolf comes around, it'll get blown down. Then, perhaps a comparison to that is Nortel. When Nortel was a hundred bucks, the winds came up and the company blew up essentially, and the valuation was way too high. So that's a straw hut. I kind of look for brick houses in the three little pigs lingo, and what I mean there is you feel like you have a strong foundation in what you're buying. Because I'm a value investor, your brick house won't look like a beautiful waterfront property on Lake Muskoka or West Vancouver. The roof might be damaged, the window might be missing, it might need a paint job, but "the bones" in real estate lingo are good, and then that gives you your foundation.

We owned shares of a company called Sun-Rype many years ago, and even if Sun-Rype may be no money for a number of years, I felt comfortable that its presence, its position in the marketplace, had an intrinsic value, that no matter what I could get our money back. So that's what I mean in having a firm foundation. Going back a step, the first thing was, "Does it trade for less than it's worth?" How volatile is that estimate? The volatility you want is on the upside and not on the downside.

The third thing is to determine whether management is for or against you. Basically, are they in the same boat as you, the management and the board? Many times, a good board has saved us from a difficult situation.

The half, as I call it, the three and a half thing, is I try and look for situations where the sellers don't care about price. What I mean there is when you're buying a stock, if the seller is thinking carefully about whether or not they ought to sell, then it's a tougher decision to buy because you're basically betting the buyer is wrong. I prefer situations where people just want out, and that can happen. There are a couple of reasons. One is it's an area people don't want to be involved in, meaning there's really bad news. It can be specific to a stock or it could be an industry. An example might be newspapers these days. People just don't want to be involved in newspaper stock, so they sell them. That'll lead to depressed valuations. A second reason is if there's some type of constraint that prevents them from buying the stock. For example, with a bond, because I do distressed too, I would ask if there was a bankruptcy filing, then you might have someone sell the bonds because they can't own those shares in their portfolio, or those bonds in their portfolio. The third reason, and the one I tend to use the most, is a corporate event. For example, a spinout, a rights issue, something happens like that. An example there is we own some shares in a company called Citadel Broadcasting, the third largest radio broadcaster in the U.S. It suffers from two things: one, people don't like radio, so they're not particularly interested. Secondly, it existed before, but primarily a large portion of it's float, or a large portion of the shares that are currently out-standing came in June of last year when they acquired ABC Radio from Disney. They gave Disney shares in Citadel, and Disney then spun those shares out to Disney shareholders. So very roughly speaking, if you had $5,000 in Disney, today you'd have about $40 in Citadel stock. The inclination then is I don't even want to look at the Citadel. I'll just sell it because Disney is the company I bought. That's what I mean as a spinout, someone just wants to get rid of the security without thinking about price, and that's when we like to get involved.

That was the situation with TELUS bonds a few years ago.
TELUS was the same thing. I actually didn't end up buying them, so I missed that one, but I looked at them, that's for sure.

They went down to $0.50 on the dollar.
Yeah, yeah.

When did you take over the Cundill LP? Is that what it was called at the time?
At that time, I was living in Ontario. I came back to Vancouver to work with Peter on Value Fund. I acquired Cundill Capital Limited Partnership at that time and changed the name.

Peter, he had a lot of his own money in it at that time. Does he still?
No, Peter has been very generous with me, not only allowing me to set up

my own business many years ago, but also being a large investor of mine over the last eight years in the case of the LP or twelve years in the case of the trust. He owned part of my management company for a number of years, but when he sold his business to Mackenzie, they had a non-compete, so I bought him out of that. In typical Peter fashion, he did it on a generous basis to me.

I find it incredible that Peter Cundill, one of the gods of value investing, entrusts his net worth to you. He obviously must have a tremendous amount of confidence in what you're doing for him.

Maybe he has a tremendous amount of money too. [Laughs] He says, "Aw, I can afford to give him a little bit."

What is the difference between the trust and the other fund?

Yeah, it's now a corp.

Right. It's the same now?

Yeah. On investments, I always believe strongly in simplicity. For example, if you hire an MBA or a CA or even just someone off the street and say, "Can you tell me ten reasons to buy a stock?" It's easy to come up with ten reasons. It's hard to say instead, "Can you tell me the three key drivers that we should be thinking about, but only the top three?" That's a lot tougher, so it is the same thing with valuations. It's actually very easy and comforting to do a big Excel model because you feel like you're active, you have all of these numbers, and it feels good that you're putting something together. It's very hard to sit there with a pencil and say, "What do I really think? Define how this company should be valued." The same thing with my business—I try and keep everything simple. We outsource as much as we can to RBC Dexia, as far as doing valuations, record keeping, and trade settlement. We try and do all of that outside so that the people inside are focused on client relations and investment. We had two funds. To the extent that I can get them together and make it one fund, I'd be happy with that and keep everything very basic, very simple. I don't want a family of sixteen different funds.

I think one of them was more foreign?

Yeah, originally it was set up to be foreign. I ended up getting a lot of calls from people. Someone would come to me as an investor, and they don't come because they think I have a brand or they want my Far East Asian Fund or my mining fund or something like that. They come because they like the fact that I have all my money in our funds, and they want to be a partner. So having two funds actually complicated that process because instead of saying, "We're interested in the foreign fund or Canadian fund," just said, "Well, I don't care. Where does Tim have his money?"

Right, right.

That was part of the impetus behind combining everything, keeping our business very simple, and keeping my focus very simple.

What funds at Cundill did you run?

I ran Cundill Security Fund from June '92 until June '99. Then I was involved in Cundill Value Fund from 1999 to 2004. I co-managed Value Fund with Pete, and I managed Security Fund by myself, primarily out of Ontario where I was living at that time. I came back to Vancouver to work with Peter on Value Fund in '99 or 2000.

Cundill has been kind of famous in the last few years for having a massive amount of the fund in Japan. A lot of people just didn't see what you saw in Japan. I think the Japanese market was going down and down and down, but you were doing great. I think the stocks, generally speaking, were doing fine.

We had a good group of research guys at Cundill on Japan, but I think it suffered. Even if you look at the period from 2000 onward, it was a pretty good period for value investors in North America. You had a lot of stuff in Japan that had bad balance sheets but high valuations, so that stuff just kept going down. You had stuff with good balance sheets and low valuations, and that kind of percolated up a little bit, so it was a little bit of a two-tiered market.

Have you ever shorted stocks? Peter did, I think.

Yeah, we used to short indexes for a little while. I bought puts on stocks in 2000, and in typical fashion, the puts expired. I had puts on GE, CIBC, and some others as well, but they expired in January of 2000. Then I didn't renew them because I was so tired of losing money, and then all hell broke loose in March of 2000. So other than a good tale, I can't say I profited from it, but that's about the closest I ever got to shorting.

Last year in Omaha, Nebraska, somebody asked Buffett about silver. He said, "Oh, yeah, we owned a lot of silver, and we bought it way too early, and we sold it way too early, and we never made any money. But that's what we always do, so that's okay." So he said to Charlie Munger, "Well, what do you have to say about silver, Charlie?" Charlie said, "That'll just about cover our expertise in commodities." How is running what you run now different from the funds that you ran at Cundill? I think one of the things I'm thinking about here is size. I think it helps to be smaller generally.

When I got involved with Peter in '91, the Value Fund had 400 stocks. I think it shrunk down to about 150, 100, 125 when I got involved in Value Fund again in 1999 or 2000, and then we worked it down to about 30 stocks after that. I think my predisposition has always been to have a more concentrated portfolio than maybe the average traditional value guy. I think Ben Graham certainly espoused having a large number of securities, and that's been Tweedy's approach as well.

Templeton's got a ton of stocks too.

I'd say that's a difference. The second thing is I do sometimes get involved in the securities, for example, go on the Board. That would be different from Cundill. Finally, I don't mind looking at small stocks or big stocks, and when you're running a large mutual fund, as much as you'd like to, you can't spend your time working on small companies.

Do you look for stocks a lot of times that are undercovered by analysts, or analysts don't even cover them at all?

There are two ways that they get undercovered. One, of course, is if they've collapsed. There's a certain…I don't want to be cynical about it, but you see it happen with some regularity where a stock may be $20, and a broker will have a buy on it with a target of $30. The stock falls to $10, and a broker will go to a hold, and then the stock falls to $5, the broker will go to a sell. The stock falls to $4, and the research analyst will suddenly no longer be working there. That is, I'd say, not an unusual pattern of some of the stocks we get involved with. Then over time, the analysts will come back in and they'll get covered again, or sometimes the stocks just weren't really covered from the beginning. That is the case with even something like Citadel Broadcasting, which used to be a billion dollar type company, but now is maybe $300 or $400 million in market cap. Because of all of the changes over the last year, there's a very limited amount of analyst coverage, and that works to our advantage, of course.

Right. It creates the inefficiencies.

Yeah, it creates inefficiencies, so I agree. An undercovered stock $15-something that we're quite happy to get involved with.

I think a value investor believes that the market is very inefficient in the short run, but you're banking on the fact that it's efficient in the long run or else you're never going to realize the value that you think you should have. Is that true?

Yeah, for sure. I joke that there are two types of investors out there. There are the people who approach life saying, "I'm smarter than everyone else because I think I can figure out," and this is my comment about that. I think that's great. They think I can figure out why the stock is cheaper and therefore will go up more than people realize. That would typically be a type of growth manager because he's saying, "My cousin's best friend's housekeeper works also for the CEO of Research in Motion. They tell me the number of units shipped is going up; therefore, I think I have an inside edge, and I want to buy that stock." Once again, their analysis is all based on the fact that they think they know something the market doesn't, or they think the market is wrongly valuing it.

On a value basis, I suggest that value managers are much dumber than growth managers, but at least they know they're dumb. When I'm buying a stock, I don't think about all the wonderful things that could go wrong. I just try and think about all the things that are going wrong and whether or not they're really serious, so that means a couple of things. First, it means if the market thinks things are worse than they are, then you'll get appreciation—the relief, so to speak—because things weren't as bad as they thought. The second thing is it usually takes some time for the stock to turn around, so that's why your holding period is a little bit longer.

A lot of stocks that you own are very illiquid, but you own big chunks of the company. How do you get the liquidity you need to either buy or sell when they trade 500 shares a day?

What always happens is you see a stock and you say, "I like that idea," and I try and have my positions between 5 and 10 percent. Let's assume I buy a 5 percent position in a stock, and the broker says, "Tim, this is part of a cleanup. This is a guy who had a million shares, and he can't get a bid on this somewhat illiquid stock, and there's bad news on it. Are you interested?" So I'll end up buying some, and I'll think, "All right, we got a somewhat illiquid position but it has a good story." The stock will promptly fall by a third and then, lo and behold, if the broker doesn't phone back and say, "Actually, it wasn't a cleanup. There's another block of a million shares available. Are you interested?" I end up saying, "Yes." Then, over time, I end up with these relatively large positions in stocks that don't trade all the time. The situation usually changes a little bit, and either there's a takeover or pick up of research coverage, and we're able to sell into that.

So you got liquidity?

So we get liquidated that way. You have to be a little bit careful, and I'm guilty of this a couple of times. When the liquidity comes in on some of these stocks, it's usually because there's good things happening. It would be easy, then, to say, "Oh, maybe I should hang onto this for a lot longer because maybe I was too pessimistic." When you see liquidity start to come in, one of the things I'm very conscious of is, I make the easy decisions when there's no hope, and then it gets some hope. The person who's coming in and trying to value how much that hope is worth has a much tougher job, and I'm better off to sell to them and take my money and go and find another hopeless situation.

I don't know if you ever read this, but I found it very interesting. Benjamin Graham set up his office down the hall from Tweedy Browne, and they were the broker, and they'd accumulate the stock that nobody wanted and then he'd buy it. Tweedy Browne looked and said, "Well, he's actually doing pretty well on these crappy stocks, the ones that we're dumping off to him." So they became a value money management firm themselves. Many great stock pickers have a team of analysts working for them. I've been to your office in Vancouver here, and it was an empty office with a laptop. How do you find ideas when you don't have a bunch of people looking around for you?

The first thing is, I worked with a good group at Cundill, and without a doubt, a lot of them were brighter than I. The important thing in the investment business is that you have someone who the buck stops with—so someone who feels responsible for the fund or for the portfolio. When you have a lot of people working with you, you can spend a lot of time getting into elaborate discussions over what you should and shouldn't be doing. That can be quite helpful, but it can also be quite distracting. I get involved in messy situations, so I feel quite comfortable with how I'm approaching it. It can be good to have a sounding board.

It's kind of like the song by Sony and Cher.

Oh, "You've got me, babe." Yeah. With my funds, my name is on the door—You got me, babe, so to speak—and unfortunately, I'm the only one. I'm working now with another guy who's helping me with some structural stuff as well as the investment portfolio, and it's a bit of an experience for both of us. I do think that having people working with you that help generate ideas lets you cover more ground. The only question is, how distracting is that to the decision making process?

Peter Puccetti told me he has a good friend who just watches what Peter buys. He says, "I'll just watch what you buy and then two years later, I'll buy it." When you get into something, does the news usually get a bit worse? Is it catching a falling knife?

Well, I think for sure every time I buy a stock, it tends to go down by a third after we buy it. Every time I buy it, I'm pretty sure this one won't go down by a third. So the answer to your question is yes. The neat thing about value investing is if you think a company is worth five and you're paying three, you have a margin of safety. If the stock falls to two, and you still think the company is worth five, it's actually a better deal. You have a larger margin of safety. Unlike a growth guy, the second the stock may start to go down, they worry that it's an indication that they've missed something in the valuation and the smartest thing to do is sell. Quite often with a value stock, if you're confident that your analysis is correct, a stock going down is really the opportunity to keep adding money to it. So averaging down is a fact of life, and I think probably the thing that tests your judgment the most is if the stock falls by half, would you still be interested in buying more? If you say yes from the beginning, and you're able to do that, then I think that says a lot about your discipline as an investor, certainly a value investor.

You said once that you tend to own cheap stocks—stocks that everybody agrees are cheap. I think your idea is to take out the *but*.

Yeah, it's the same thing, I would be a great golfer but for the fact that I can't hit the ball properly. So that *but* is a pretty big thing in life. I'd look like Fabio but for the fact that I'm thirty pounds overweight and bald, so *but* is a pretty big word in stuff, and it's certainly a big word in investing. So people will say, "You own some shares in…." Let's take Citadel again because I talked about it, "…but it'll be a couple of years before they execute on their plan, but it's in the radio segment, but there are a lot of sellers." You just look at what's behind the *but* and say, "Does that really matter to me? Does it matter that it might take a couple of years?" No. One of the things I think we do as investors is trade time for price. Does it matter that it's in the radio business? No, because I think the price I'm buying at is attractive enough. So, yeah, we try and take the *but* out of investing. It sounds like a bad joke, but that's the way we do it.

Right.

The other thing that is related is quite often I think people mix up uncertainty and risk. I can say without a doubt all of the stocks I get involved in are uncertain, and by uncertain I mean you don't know what's going to happen over the next quarter, over the next six months, maybe even in the next year. But I measure risk as: What's the chance that we'll actually lose money on the position? Whether or not it goes up and down in the stock market, whether or not I know what's going to happen next quarter, isn't a risk to me. As I said, risk is: What's the chance in permanent loss of capital? So when someone looks at a stock and says, "I'm uncertain about where it's going," I think that's fine.

If you're wrong on a growth stock, and you hold it, you can have a permanent loss of capital. If you're wrong on a value stock, other than being a value trap, you don't normally get a permanent loss of capital?

Yeah, let's face it, value portfolios look ugly. I think the best example is I remember I used to take my kids to Stanley Park when it had a penguin exhibit. When you were just entering the area, you were maybe a hundred yards away, you'd see the penguin exhibit and all these penguins are splashing and dancing, and you go, "Oh, ain't that cute?" When you walk up within five feet of a penguin exhibit, it stinks like heck, and you say, "This thing is awful, like let's get away from here." So it didn't matter how picturesque it looked from the distance. My portfolio is like that. From a distance it's a beautiful work of art. Up close, someone would say, "You own twelve duds." I guess that's what I do for a living.

Own duds?
Own duds.

How important is the qualitative side of it? Do you get to know the management? Are these guys honest? Are they going to execute properly? Is that why you get on the board of companies?
Well, let's try and pull that apart. The first thing I think is running the numbers on the stock doesn't give a reason to buy it. The things I'm looking at are the qualitative stuff. What can go wrong? What can go right? Where are the incentives for the group? What's in it for the managers? I think that's a very important part. Of course, it's always nice to see insider buying. That's a well-known thing. Sometimes at moments of crisis, though, insiders may be restricted from buying, or they're unable to for a number of reasons. So you have to be a little bit careful with insider buying.

What I look for is, as I said in the beginning, is management in the same boat as you or not, or is their compensation, or preferably, their ownership such that in a moment of crisis when they're dealing with shareholders' money, will they make a decision in the best interest of the owners, or will they make it in the best interests of the managers? That's the main thing I try and think about. What are those crises occurring? How damaging are they to the company? How will management make a decision when they reach that position? Now, in a couple of cases, three in particular, I've gone on boards, but I don't go looking for a fight. I'm a lover, not a fighter, so I don't like doing activism. I don't say, "I'm going to buy that stock," and agitate. That's not our way. It's more like I've got backed into a corner, and I'll get involved because I have to be. Once again, in all of those cases, I can say without a doubt I've never met a board member who wasn't honest and had the best intentions, but as a shareowner of a company, you have to try and evaluate whether or not their intentions are really in your interest. An example of that might be where someone is making an acquisition that they believe will make the company stronger in aggregate, but on a per-share basis, it is not. The best example of that would be oil and gas stocks. They may feel that they want to buy more reserves when the price is high because it'll make the company stronger. If you measured reserves per share, you might figure that it's a dilutive deal for each of the individual investors. So that's what I'm talking about when I say I am trying to fig-ure out where the incentives are.

One of the biggest shareholders of Sun-Rype was the Jim Pattison Group. I think they still are one of the biggest?

Well, yeah, I think if you have a choice of investing with a billionaire or in-vesting with a pauper, you're probably better off investing with the billionaire.

The billionaire. There you go.

Certainly, we've sold a large portion of our Sun-Rype position to the Pat-tison Group. I was on the board with Mike Korenberg and Don Selman from the Pattison Group. I was always very impressed with their honesty and their integrity but also how they looked at stuff. They were focused on return on cap-ital. They were focused on cash flow; everything that you and I would think about as a value investor, they were doing from a business perspective. I think that's a tribute to Jimmy and the culture he's put in place there.

Everybody kind of says the same thing about how they look at a stock, but why have you generated 20 percent a year for the past ten years before performance fee and hardly anybody else has? What makes you different? Is it the smaller base of money? Is it the different ways you look at it?

The bizarre thing in this business is when you meet someone and they say, "The stock's going to $30." You can't control that part of the business. Where I sit, you really can't. Sometimes if you get involved in the board, you can do stuff that will further it, but, nevertheless, you can't control what the market is going to do with the price each day. The only thing you can control is when you can buy and when you can sell. I've been fortunate in that I've been re-ally involved in a number of hopeless things that became not as hopeless as people thought, and that's been a large part of the performance. Unlike some of the other investors that you talk about in your book, some people make overall projections and then find stocks that'll fit in. I have enormous respect for people who do that, but that's not where I am. I'm really looking for com-plete despair and protecting the downside and knowing that when the turn comes, it usually comes back, and it's a lot better than you expect.

I think Benjamin Graham said that he would definitely buy a crummy business as long as it was at the best price, whereas other people have said,

"I'm going to buy a great business at a good price but I'll never get a great business at a fantastic price."

What I've tried to do is stay away from the really bad stuff and realize that whenever I think a really wonderful business is at a good price, it's usually me who's confused about the quality of the business, not the person selling. So what I've tried to do is say price is important and cash is important, meaning cash flow. I'll try and stay away from the stuff that consumes cash. What I ideally like is a mediocre business, so to speak, that each year will be worth a little bit more primarily because of cash flow. If the stock prices stayed the same, your margin of safety over time inches up. That's where I've had the best luck. If we take Sun-Rype, for example, I think we bought our first stock at $2.10 or $2.20 or something like that. We got $1.50 in dividends, and we sold our stock to Jimmy for $11.50. When we bought it, we definitely did not think it was worth $11.50, but over the years, the value kept compounding. The return on invested capital within Sun-Rype was very, very high, and it doesn't take very many Sun-Rypes in a lifetime to have a good outcome.

How do you avoid a value trap? A company is really, really undervalued because it's going to zero! Have you ever had a situation like that?

Well, yeah, sure, you get them all the time. I don't mind buying situations that are challenging at the moment, but I'm not a dumb contrarian in that I'll buy situations that there's no hope of winning. For example, if I go and box against Mike Tyson, I'm not going to win. So if I'm going to get into a fight, which I don't want to, I want to make sure it's a fight I can win. Same thing with a business. If it's losing money, losing cash, and the value is staying constant or declining, you have to be really, really careful what price you pay. The value traps I've been stuck in tend to be where the net asset value has stayed about the same over the period and the stock price hasn't gone anywhere. The best situations for me have been where the value of the company has grown. It can be quite slowly over time so that my margin of safety is getting bigger, and that gives you the large return. I try and avoid stuff where I think it's going to be stagnant. I'm talking about the underlying value, not the stock price, so I'm really careful about what you pay in those circumstances.

You said you're the only guy in Canada who missed the entire oil and gas run in gas and minerals.

Yeah.

Have you ever had resource stocks in a portfolio? Cundill had Canadian Natural Resources for a long time.

You know, I never had that.

Have you had resource stocks? How do you analyze a resource stock versus a retailing company because it's a totally different business?

I've been in all of the hottest sectors. I was just, like, five years too early and sold three years too early. We owned real estate, closed-end funds, and sold them before they became very popular. I think we owned some oil and gas trusts, and I owned some gold mining stocks and Teck, which then became Teck Cominco. I owned Denison Mines, I owned oil drillers, and I bought them when there was despair, meaning people felt they didn't have any hope. Then the stocks go up somewhat and you sell them. I could definitely be faulted on selling early, but that's okay. What I said before was I try and make the easy decision that things aren't as bad as people think. I have protection in the price, and when it gets up into the area where you're debating what type of multiple should be put on it, then I'll let someone else make that decision. Paraphrasing a little bit the Rothschild quote, "I buy on assets or I buy on intrinsic value; I sell on earnings." That's kind of what I do. I don't try and figure out what the multiple ought to be—that's someone else's job—or where the growth rate is going to be. They're difficult decisions, and I'm happy to leave them to someone else.

To give you an example of that, we had a large position about five years ago in a company called Sask Wheat Pool. It actually first was a distressed debt position in that there were some concerns that Sask Wheat Pool was going into bankruptcy, so we bought some debt, and that got resolved. We made some money on the debt and sold it. Then Sask Wheat Pool did a rights issue at about $5, and we stepped in and bought a lot of the rights, which then led to stock. That's how we got a large part of our Sask Wheat Pool position, or really nearly all of it, is around the rights issue. At the time, people said Sask Wheat Pool had been through a couple of years where there had been not very much production on the prairies, so it was a business that was going to be impacted by global warming. They had too many fixed costs in that business. It was controlled by the railways because they did all of the shipping, and there was generally despair. Now, today, with the stock almost three times higher and with many, many more shares outstanding, people are setting up agricultural funds to invest in stuff like Sask Wheat Pool, which is now called Viterra, because they feel that the outlook looks bright.

Without a doubt, I did not make any prediction when we were buying the stock that agriculture was an important place to invest. I'm not that smart at all. It was just that Sask Wheat Pool was cheap, they were doing some smart stuff, and they had a very important presence in the industry. That's why we bought it, and, of course, we sold it too early. I think I sold at $10 or $11 or something like that. It worked out very well. We got very high rates of compounding because it came off such a low base, and that's kind of what's helped the numbers.

A stock like Potash used to be a value stock that nobody in their right mind would ever own.

Exactly. I didn't buy it, but I was aware of it, yeah.

Now it's only growth momentum managers who own Potash. How does the baton get passed when a value manager sells their stock to a growth manager?

We buy stocks when they're burned out, and then they start to go up a little bit, and we sell it to maybe a GARP (growth at a reasonable price) manager who then might sell it to a momentum guy. I don't know who he sells it to, but he sells it to some poor person, and the stock collapses and comes back.

It's like passing the hot potatoes.

[Laughs] Yes. It's a good thing about getting older in this business. Some of the stocks I used to own come back. It also shows you have to be a little bit careful that you don't believe that all trees grow to heaven.

I've heard some value managers say the biggest mistake you can make is extrapolation. They say, "Well, this has happened for the last five years, so if this continues to happen into the next ten years, it's going to be massive." It never seems to work that way.

I'm also a little bit careful on reversion to the mean. People who say, "Well, they had 30 percent margins two years ago, and they only have 5 percent margins now. If they go back to 30 percent margins, I'll make this much money." That's always a big leap of faith that I think you have to be careful about making.

My dad moved to California in the early 1960s; I always remember this story. There was a weatherman speaking on TV, and the way he said it everybody knew it was a joke. There was a huge influx of people into California at the time, and he said, "Now, I've calculated that if this number of people continue to move to California, then twenty years from now everybody in the United States will live in California." Everybody laughed because everybody is not going to live in California. However, if you extrapolated that, that's exactly what it would show, right?

Yeah. If you're playing poker and you don't know who the patsy at the table is, then you're the patsy. It's the same thing a little bit in the investment business. If you're looking around and you don't know who the sucker is, then it's probably you.

In poker, I think a good poker player will make most of their money on a relatively small number of hands. Is it the same in the stocks? Do you make most of your money on three stocks out of ten that you'll own?

Well, I run a pretty concentrated portfolio, so I agree that I'm always surprised with which of those stocks go up in any year. I think what I also try to do is not make too many bets but just wait until the odds look definitely in your favour, and then bet significantly. As we talked about before, I think it's human nature to say, "Well, that looks kind of interesting, so I'll buy some of that. And that one looks kind of interesting, so I'll buy some of that." Then you soon end up with a hundred things that look kind of interesting. I much prefer to sit and wait for something that looks really interesting, and then go into it very significantly.

Go big or go home.

Yeah. So in your poker analogy, you wait until you've got a really good hand, and then bet strongly. Now, of course, in poker, when you do that, if you've been quiet all of the previous five hands, the second you do that everyone else is going to fold. In the investment business, that doesn't happen, so that's a huge advantage you have in our business versus playing with a group of poker players.

To get more understanding of your philosophy, let's go through some individual examples, like Humpty Dumpty Foods.

Yeah, we....

What attracted you to that stock? How about Indigo?

Yeah, the good, the bad, the ugly. We talked about Sun-Rype, and that was clearly a good. A bad one, to some extent, would be Humpty Dumpty. I got involved in it—I don't remember exactly when—but it was an IPO. They acquired a private brand business, I think, from Cott for chips, so there was a growth idea. They thought it was going to do really well, and I don't know if it got as high as $10 or $8. Then the stock collapsed to $2 or $3, and that's when I started to buy it on the basis that they were the second largest potato chip manufacturer east of Winnipeg and their competition was Frito Lay. They had got into a price war with Frito Lay, and management owned a significant amount of stock. I learned a lot from the Humpty Dumpty experience. I eventually ended up going on the board as part of a proxy fight and we replaced management, and then closed the facility and ended up selling the company to Old Dutch, so it came out as a save at best.

But I learned a lot about business being on the board, as I did at Sun-Rype, and as I do on Rainmaker. I think that's made me a better investor. The type of things you think about are a competitive situation and cash flow and business model. In the case of Sun-Rype and Humpty Dumpty, in a different fashion, in the case of Rainmaker, there was a focus on doing volume perhaps at the expense of margins and cash flow. This gets back to my earlier discussion. Even in my own business, I'm just trying to keep things simple. Activity doesn't equal success or profitability. I think that's what was a bit of the issue with Sun-Rype and Humpty Dumpty. But Sun-Rype resolved it quite successfully, and Humpty Dumpty, as I said, was at best a save.

That was a criticism people had about Japanese companies. They weren't shareholder friendly and they didn't really make a lot of money.

Oh, for sure. When I look at a company, there are lots of wonderful companies run by great people. It doesn't mean that you have to buy them. That's the great thing about being a value investor. I can benefit from the RIMs of the world who are doing things like the BlackBerry, although I actually don't have one. That's too much connection for me. I don't have to put my money into that type of situation. I wait. When I really think I have an advantage on the investment, on the price, then I act.

I've always found when stocks go into the index, they've already gone up a tremendous amount, so the index is momentum based. Microsoft and

Intel were put into the index in 2000, right at the top.

Yeah, I think it would be fair to say, because as a value guy, I do look at when the index changes come out. It's not because I'm thinking about the weighting of my portfolio, but it's quite simply to see what's being deleted because, once again, I like ideas where the seller is not caring about price. You get a certain amount of selling after an index deletion that might be interesting, but it hasn't really been a source of great ideas. But who knows? Maybe tomorrow.

If you look at the past ten years—and it's been a rough year for value in the past year—you've still generated before the performance fee 20 percent a year, 16 percent net to investors, which is right at the top. You've had great returns while maintaining pretty high cash positions along the way. I think at the end of '97 you had 59 percent cash. You've had less cash recently, but I think 25, 27 percent cash has been common. How did you generate those returns with that much cash?

This gets back to a comment I made before: I try and only act when I think there's something to do, and I don't care what the portfolio looks like relative to the index. If there isn't anything to do, I'm quite happy to sit on my hands. That's what cash ends up being. It's not an asset class in my mind, it's the residual. If there's nothing to do, we'll just sit in cash. If there's something to do and it's really good, then let's spend the money. As I said to you before, when the year ends and you look back and say, wow, I was up whatever this year, sometimes I'm as surprised as the next person. I can't say how it happened that way. All I know is I try to be disciplined on when to buy, and that's worked to our advantage.

Back to distressed securities. The Loewen Group bond—did that work or not?

Yeah, it did. Yeah, I like doing distressed debt.

It's the same thing as buying distressed stocks, really.

It's just a different part of the capital structure. There hasn't been as much stuff to do recently, although I have to say in the last six months, we've started looking at the distressed again, and we're quite close on at least one idea to buying some of the debt. The advantages to distressed debt are twofold. Sometimes you get a coupon, sometimes not. Secondly, there's usually an event that comes along—a restructuring, an emergence from bankruptcy, or something like that—that allows the position to turn over naturally. You're not dependent on waiting for the business to improve or analysts to get coverage or liquidating to come in. There's usually an event with distress that gives you liquidity. It's an interesting place to invest. We do not buy bonds unless they're significantly discounted from face, and that's the only time we would do it.

Can you pinpoint one thing that has helped you to do well?

As I said this to you before, it would be trying to emulate Homer Simpson in my daily investment activity. I'm always amazed with the people who get on television and people ask them stock ideas, and they know something about every stock. My brain can only hold so much information. If it's not something that I want to focus on, then I'm not going to spend a whole bunch of time thinking about it. If it is something I'm interested in, then I'll focus on it, and if it's attractive, I'll actually do it. So not feeling like I come in every day having to make a decision but being focused on waiting for what I think are the right decisions and being confident when you make them. I think that there's some advantage to dropping your children on their head at an early age because I think that's what happened to me. Send them into the investment business if that happens.

There was a study done where they gave investment problems to sociopaths in prison, and they did much better than the average population. They had no conscience. They didn't care. They just made logical decisions without any emotion.

At times, my performance has been compared to everything from sociopaths to primates, so if there's any day you're feeling like you're a bright person, don't worry. You can find someone to tell you you're not. So it keeps you humble.

Why did you make the insignia for your firm a toad with a prince's crown?

Well, I guess all of our stocks have warts on them. We have to kiss a lot of frogs to look for the prince, so quite often I think that if I needed one investment tool in this business, it might be LypSyl and not a calculator. That's how the frog came into being.

Does one stock kind of stand out in your mind as being your biggest win and your biggest multi-bagger?

Your mind is always drawn to most recent stuff, so Sun-Rype was a great win for us. I probably overstayed by a couple of years. I could have sold it earlier. Glacier Ventures is one of the largest publishers of community newspapers. I think we bought our first stock at $0.70 or so. That management group, Sam Grippo and Jon Kennedy, have been wonderful at creating value over the last five years, and the stock's roughly $4 give or take a little bit. What I found, is when we look at a stock, I'm not looking for a 20 percent discount to what I think it's worth. I'm kind of thinking if things go right and we wait three or four years or five years can the stock be a double or triple, or quadruple? Thankfully, we've had a number of those and that's helped the performance a lot.

You seem to find a lot of stocks that are under $5.

It's quite often not before I buy them.

Indigo Books, what drew you to that? At the time Indigo was a dog with fleas.

I go back to my joke earlier about penguins. It's certainly like that when you go up and you look close at each individual idea. There's usually some significant part that stinks. What happened in Indigo was that they bought Chapters, and the stock essentially had collapsed.

Heather Reisman was involved.

Yeah. Heather Reisman had formed Indigo, but she was the person behind the merger with Chapters, because Chapters had gotten into some difficulty. They were doing a rights issue. I just was scrolling through the paper, and I saw, "Oh, Indigo is doing a rights issue." As I said before, I try and look for situations where there's an event going on. Following that up, I noticed that the rights issue was backed by Gerry Schwartz. Now he is Heather's husband, but he's also one of the most successful businessmen we have in Canada. I have a partner as well, but I know she's not going to put money into something that I'm doing, into my fund if she thought it was a losing proposition. I think Gerry approached life the same way.

What you had there was essentially insider buying, so that got my interest. I got the documents and said, "Well, what's interesting about Indigo?"

First, they have an important presence in Canada. It would be very hard to come in and compete against them. Chapters and Indigo are a large, large network of stores, both in the malls and the superstores, so they have a competitive position. Whether it's worth a lot of money or a little bit of money, it's there. The second thing is the book business is extremely cash generative compared to a lot of retail. The furniture and fixtures are not as significant as you'd expect, so there's actually a fairly high return on invested capital. The business is seasonal. Thirdly, their margins were significantly below similar companies elsewhere in the world. That was basically the four key things. Gerry was putting in money to backstop it, they had an important presence in the industry, they could produce free cash flow, and there was the opportunity for margin expansion. Then from there, I talked to the company—I tried to figure out what might happen over time, and they worked out okay.

You bought it at $4.50?

Yeah, something like that. It got as high as $18 and it is now about $12. Having a stock go from $4 to—let's average those two and say $15 or $16—that's quite helpful to performance.

When you take a stock on, is it always less than 10 percent of the portfolio at cost?

Yeah, it's like say 5 to 10 percent. In the case of Indigo Books, I think it was like a 7 or 8 percent position, or something like that. If it doubles, it's extremely accretive to performance; if it doesn't, that's where it's painful. That's why I try and only invest in stuff I feel confident in, because when you have a 5 percent position in the portfolio or a 7 percent position in the portfolio, you hate to make a mistake on the easy stuff. There's always going to be stuff out of the blue that hits you, but you hate to make a basic unforced error, as Warren Buffett would call it, on the analysis.

There's a difference between patience and delusion. The important thing for me in Indigo was hearing that management thought margins could expand and seeing some progress towards expanding margins. If that didn't happen, then you have to get out of the position because it's not becoming what you thought it would. I think that's important to understand. You have to be patient for stuff to happen, but you also have to be realistic where you think they're going and test the company against that.

How much money do you manage now?

About $160 million give or take a little bit. I enjoy my goal in this business: to make my partners a respectable return and enjoy the relationships with them and have fun. Although I'm an accountant, so it's not the same as a growth guy, as I said before. My objective isn't to have a $10 billion fund. My objective is not to have a family of funds. My objective is over time to compound at a respectable amount of money. I have all my money in the funds, so I can look people in the eye and say, "I'm in the same boat as you."

How many investors do you have approximately?

Probably about 500, give or take a little bit.

I think you try to treat them, like you said, as partners. You did something a few years ago where you got their pictures?

Yeah, what I said to people was, "Why don't you send us your picture—you doing something fun, not your passport photo. With 500 people, it's unrealistic to know all of them. The people broke into three categories: those who just didn't respond, those who sent pictures of themselves doing fun things, and those who just thought I was some psychopath wacko who wanted a picture of them to post on my bathroom wall.

Didn't they get bonus points if they were holding products?

Yeah, if they sent a picture holding a product of a company we owned in the portfolio. Now at the time, we had Loewen bonds, which was a funeral home, so I wasn't really looking for someone sending that along. We had Molson too, so if they sent a picture, drinking Molson or eating Humpty Dumpty chips or Sun-Rype, that was fine. As I said, not an insignificant number of people thought I was some type of warped psycho. We haven't done that recently.

What's your biggest mistake? Is there something that stands out that you just wish you hadn't have done?

I make a fair number of them. The one that I make consistently is buying too big a position too quickly. Every time I do that, I vow next time I won't, and then I do it again. That's always one of those kind of "I should have known better" things. It doesn't mean that I think I was wrong with the initial position. It was just I went in too early, thinking this time it won't go down by a third or half or more, and then they always do. So one of these days I'll figure that out, but I haven't yet.

What did you learn from your biggest mistake?
Well, I was hoping to learn.

You haven't learned it yet, but you're still working on it? [Laughs]
I think that's getting into my brain. The other thing is, if I kind of look back over the ten years, it always takes a little bit longer than you think in a value stock. You get in there and you think that it's a two-year turnaround, and it ends up being a three- or four-year turnaround. Sometimes it can take more money that you think, but sometimes it goes up more than you think. I never once thought that Indigo would ever see $18 when we bought it. The second thing is being invested with good people has always made a difference to me. I've been fortunate enough to understand the incentives or where people are coming from. I'm talking about primarily the board here. That's bailed me out of many a difficult situation. I think more about that now than I perhaps did when I first started in the business in '91.

Management is the key?
Not so much management; it's having directors. I've seen companies with the largest compliance manuals on earth, but I'd rather take a director with common sense and $200,000 worth of stock over the best compliance follower in the world. I think having some skin in the game makes a real difference at the board level because the board then sets the goalposts for management.

I think sometimes you have warning labels on your reports. What are those all about?
You always say, "What I did yesterday doesn't mean that I can do it again tomorrow," so that's a big thing in the investment business. Conversely, I would say that if you invest with someone, whether it's Eric Sprott or Warren Buffett or George Soros or whomever, the first thing you want to do is understand how they invest and whether or not you're comfortable with it. Then, from time to time, check and make sure they're still investing the same way they said they would invest. People are going to have good times and they're going to have bad times, but I think the best investors have been ones who are disciplined and consistent in their approach.

I think that's why a lot of these guys that I've interviewed for the book work for themselves, because they can be free thinkers. You can afford to think outside the box when you work for yourself.

What you do is you get people who come in and say, "You shouldn't own this, you shouldn't own that, you shouldn't own this," so you end up succumbing to the pressure from others. With your own business, you answer to your investors, of course, but also to yourself at the end of the day. A lot of my investors are friends or family or people I can put a face to, which means I do feel quite a responsibility to them with every decision I make. My reputation is really all I have, so without a doubt I can make mistakes, but I'm not going to do anything that disadvantages my investors.

The McElvaine Investment Trust ("The Trust")

1. Highly satisfactory longer-term performance can be achieved by focusing on companies selling below net asset value.
2. Given the size of the Canadian market, a small investment fund has a significant competitive advantage.
3. The purpose of an investment vehicle is to make money, not to own stocks. This is an important distinction because it means the Trust will only invest when presented with an attractive situation.
4. As there are few good ideas, there are times when concentration may be helpful.
5. An incentive fee structure rewards performance, not asset growth.

Wayne Deans
Buying at the Right Price

"I think the single biggest weakness with most investors is that their time horizon is way too short."

It was another dreary Vancouver morning as I walked from my office at Canaccord Capital to Deans Knight Capital, just a few blocks away. Although convenient for me, Vancouver is not a Mecca for great money managers. A 23 percent annualized return since inception in 1993 sure qualifies Wayne Deans as one of the best in the country, however. This basically crushes the Nesbitt Burns Small Cap index return of around 9 percent over the same period or the S&P TSX composite return of around 11 percent, and proves you don't have to be on Bay Street to excel.

I first visited Deans Knight in 1997 after a conversation that I had with a local newspaper. Wayne Deans had just won the 1996 "Fund Manager of the Year" award. Everyone was talking about his blockbuster returns. Greed was firing on all cylinders among the investing public. At a financial forum during RRSP season, I was approached by a newspaper reporter after he heard that I was an investment advisor. He wanted my insight on the topic of the day: Wayne Deans and his outsized returns.

"How does he do 40 percent a year?" this guy asked.

I think my response burst his balloon, but I was happy to do it. "Wayne is a great money manager, but he would be extremely happy if he could average 15 percent per year over a long period of time," I quipped.

A few days later, I received a call from Mr. Deans. Thinking he would not be happy with my remarks, I was surprised to hear him thank me for trying to bring investor expectations back in line. I went and visited Deans Knight for the first time and saw a small modest operation, typical of successful money managers. Actually, there was a bit of disarray, as the decision had just been made by the firm to expand the operation and take over the space next door.

Fast forward about ten years. As I was waiting for Wayne in an area that was at the side of the trading and analyst space, the mood was calm. There was not a lot of high pressure trading going on. Wayne was having a discussion with one of the many companies that come rolling through the office, pitching their story. There are only a few with whom Deans Knight chooses to entrust their clients' money. Another clue that told me that this was an investment firm, and not a trading firm, was that our interview was scheduled for 9:00 in the morning. In Vancouver, the market opens at 6:30 a.m., so we were well into the trading day. Needless to say, I was surprised to meet Wayne during market hours.

The operation was basically one big space, with traders, analysts, and administrative staff all in the same area. The office was neatly decorated, with heavy black framing around all the doors, which gave an air of quality. The boardroom was adorned with beautiful framed maps of the New World and other places of significance of the day in the 16th century, along with some great shots of the Deans Knight sponsored racecar. I had to ask him about that.

A self-proclaimed "opportunistic investor" instead of "money manager," Wayne was raised in Montreal with no financial background in his family. His father was a dockworker, and Wayne decided to get a degree from university. But getting a job with the "white shoes of Bay Street" was a different story. After sending out dozens of resumes and getting shunned by everyone, he had to do something different. In the early '70s, Bay Street was a closed shop, being exclusive to the "old boys' club." He went to McMaster University in Hamilton to get an MBA, thinking it might help. This is where the Bank of Canada came calling.

What did he learn at the Bank of Canada, and how did it affect the way he would manage money? Not what you would expect, I'm sure. Speaking with Wayne was not only enlightening, he also had the best stories of all the Stock Market Superstars. His insightful and hilarious stories were riveting, especially the one about his experience with Bre-X Minerals. He certainly didn't fit the mold of a dry, boring, accountant type, that many money managers are known for being. After the hour-and-a-half interview, we wrapped it up because Wayne had a meeting with the legendary investor Bob Disbrow.

Leaving the office, I ran into Wayne's business partner, Doug Knight, who in his own right is one of the best high-yield bond managers in the country. I thought, "I'll have to come back and chat with Doug a little more in the future."

Bob:

You won an award in the mid-'90s as "Fund Manager of the Year." Isn't that the death knell for future returns?

Wayne:

It's not the award or the recognition that causes the returns to go down. It's what causes the recognition that causes the returns to change.

For instance, I guess our returns since the year 2000 now, looking in the rear-view mirror, we're probably annualizing somewhere around 30 percent. That's simply because there were so many phenomenal investment opportunities available six or seven years ago. They're not there today.

For twenty years there was no capital expenditure in the resource sector?

Yeah, you know…we looked rather silly…because we were investing heavily in some oil stocks back then. Oil was $11 a barrel. At the time, it doesn't make you look very smart. But, you know, there'd been a significant underinvestment in the sector essentially on and off, for pretty close to twenty years. Oil peaked in 1981 and there was pretty much a steady decline in oil prices from that period of time until '99, and underinvestment. So here you are today. We've eaten through a lot of that excess capacity that existed and there hasn't been a whole lot of investment in productive capacity, and now you've got a demand/supply imbalance which is going to be difficult to rectify.

Are you a believer in the peak oil story?

Well, we've read all the books…Hubbert's peak, Matt Simmons' book *Twilight in the Desert*. That's pretty dramatic. I mean, I'm not a geologist or reservoir engineer, but it seems to make some sense that oil reservoirs have a peaking cycle in them. Oil's brought to surface because of pressure and the more you drain the reservoir, the lower the pressure in the reservoir, the less you recover. Sounds reasonable to me because….

Because you've got to start pumping water in, in order to bring it to the top….

You bet, you bet. It's more and more difficult to recover, and it does peak, you know. You could prolong a process with technology, but you can't prolong it forever. Now, I think we said a few years ago we're not running out of oil, but we've certainly run out of $20 oil. And where are we today? Man, I really don't know. Are we out of $50 oil? I don't know the answer to that. I suspect that we're in a different pricing environment long term for oil.

Matt Simmons said that people don't really know what a barrel of oil is. Bring it down to a pint. He says that it is $0.18 a pint. At $60 a barrel, it makes it one of the cheapest liquids in the world—$0.18 a pint that's ridiculous! At $120 a barrel, it is $0.36 a pint.

Absolutely. It's way cheaper than bottled water by a long shot.

Sure, sure. Beer costs $4.

And it's very expensive to find—increasingly expensive to find and increasingly expensive to produce.

Were you parents involved in the market? Or what did they do?

No, I grew up in Montreal—my father worked on the docks in Montreal. I didn't come from a financial or even a privileged background. I went to high school in Montreal and went to undergraduate university in Montreal—at a school that's now called Concordia, but it used be called Sir George Williams University—and graduated with a B.Comm. For the last two summers, I had a summer job working at the Royal Bank, which really was headquartered in Montreal in those days. I worked in various branches, gaining experience in all the jobs you do at a bank branch. So when I graduated from school, I went to work for them full-time. I started working in the branch network around the Montreal area and eastern Ontario and then wound up at head office. They taught me how to be a computer programmer, and those were the days when they were computerizing or beginning to computerize all the branches so that they could centralize all the branch banking accounting at head office. That was the beginnings of it. In total, I worked for the Royal Bank for about a year and a half after I graduated. I decided that I really wanted to be in the investment business, so I tried to get into the Royal Bank's investment department. But everybody else wanted the same thing so I decided that I was going to get an MBA.

I graduated in 1970 from McMaster with a MBA. I must've sent out, I don't know, fifty letters or more to stock brokerage firms on Bay Street, and St. James Street in Montreal, but I couldn't get a job. If you recall, back in the '60s and maybe even an early part of the '70s, the investment business—Bay Street, St. James Street in Montreal—was really a white-shoed business. You needed to know important people to get jobs at important investment firms. It was all about those old relationships. I was a kid from nowhere. Why would the venerable Athey, Aims & Co. bother hiring me? They hired the sons of friends of theirs that lived in Forest Hill, Westmount, and things like that. That's just the way it worked. So when I graduated, I was destined to go back to the Royal Bank.

I went to one on-campus interview and it was the Bank of Canada. You studied economics in business school and here comes the central bank on campus to interview for people. I went to an interview, and I thought this is kind of neat, you know, working for the central bank. So they asked me to come to Ottawa for another interview and they offered me a job. So I said, "Great!" Ten grand a year! That's what it was. That was my starting salary. So I moved to Ottawa and started working for the Bank of Canada. In those days—that's thirty-five years ago when I started there—it was a very small institution, nothing like what it is today. Everybody knew everybody, and there was a lot of overlapping of what you did. You needed multitasking skills.

Sure.

I started in a department called the Securities Department. There were two main departments, one was the Research Department, where all the gurus and propellerheads worked. Those guys built economic models. And there was the Securities Department, which did the day-to-day stuff that you read about in textbooks that central banks do. We bought and sold T-Bills to affect interest rates; we set the bank rate; we banked dealers' approved inventories at the end of the day if they couldn't get banking in the commercial banking system; we affected the level of excess reserves in the systems to influence interest rates—all that stuff. We were the fiscal agent for the government. What me and a few other guys did in our spare time was manage the bank's pension plan.

Wow, right off the bat?

Yeah, none of us knew anything about what we were doing. I think when I started there, we might have had $30 million in the bank's pension fund, and we had about 60 percent of it in bonds and 40 percent in common stocks. Every time that we wanted to buy or sell something, we had to write up the recommendation and go to one of the deputy governors of the bank and convince him to let us do it. It was a pretty Mickey Mouse operation, but that was my introduction.

Did you invest in any stocks yourself at the time? Or when did you start doing that yourself?

In college, but I didn't have a clue about what I was doing. I'd invest in whatever was in the headlines in the newspapers, whatever was getting hyped, right?

Do you remember your first stock?

The first stock that I ever bought myself—and remember that we're going back into the late '60s—it was called New Providence and they were real estate developers in the Bahamas on New Providence Island.

Exciting business?

I think that the company disappeared within two years of me buying shares. One thing that I've learned, for sure, in this investment business is that you learn way more by making mistakes than you do by getting things right.

Right.

If I was giving my money to some guy to invest for me, it's likely going to be someone as old or older than I am. I know that if they've been around that long, they've made a lot of mistakes and they've learned a lot from making those mistakes. The younger guys are as smart; they just haven't made enough mistakes yet.

Why did you move to Vancouver in the first place? A lot of people on Bay Street. say that you're not in the loop here in Vancouver. I was talking to this guy the other day and he was talking about a money manager in Burlington, Ontario. He said, "I don't know how anyone can manage money in Burlington. I mean, it's way out in the boonies; you've got to be in downtown Toronto."

I don't think so.

Exactly.

The reason I came here, by the way, was that the Bank of Canada sent me out here in 1976. They used to have an office right here. They sent me here in 1976 and I was 29 years old. My job was to act as the eyes and ears for the central bank in Western Canada. You know, I'd report back to them on a regular basis on what was going on out here. Not only in capital markets but also what was going on politically and economically in this part of the world. I came here and liked it here. After that, they transferred me back east in 1978. I always longed to live here because I liked the lifestyle. Other than the rain, I liked the climate and the geography. After ten years in central banking, in 1980, I decided that I had enough. The deciding factor for me was when I was 30 years old, I was making $30,000 a year. Someone said to me that that was the benchmark for success. If you can earn your age, then you've got it made. I was thinking, "Holy Shit!" There's got to be more to life than this, so when I'm 60, I'm earning $60,000? That's it?! Then I can't make a million dollars?

That's your upside.

That's your upside. So I left central banking after ten years. It was a great education. It taught me a lot about how central banks work, and that's unique because I don't think that a lot a people understand how central banks work.

That was actually my next question. What did the Bank of Canada teach you about investing in stocks and making economic calls?

Well, actually, it taught me not to do that, not to make any economic calls. Central banks aren't proactive; they're more reactive. Their job is to create stable climates for economic activity, to foster it. For instance, if you look at the charter of the central bank, the most important thing in there is to protect the purchasing power of the currency. So what they do is they lean against trends that they don't like and they try to encourage trends that they do like. They don't actually create anything. I don't know if it's true today, but certainly when I was there, they had the biggest investment research team in the country—brilliant people—with the model that they built. But the predictive ability of the model was no better than anybody else.

All the economists of the world still can't reach the same conclusion. That sort of thing, right?

Yeah. They'd come up with predictions, but they weren't always that accurate. Secondly, to an investor, should it matter whether you know the Canadian economy is going to grow by 3.6 percent or 2.6 percent in the next twelve months? What I learned was those things that the central bank concerned themselves with are not always important things to know when you're investing money. It taught me a lot about ignoring a lot of what people are paying a lot of attention to. I think that it's important—it's the most important lesson that

I learned in central banking. But they sent me here and I liked it and I came back here and I started working for Wood Gundy.

What do you think of the quality of the financial press?

Well, you know, the job of newspapers is to sell newspapers. The higher the circulation, the higher the advertising rates, the more money that you make, so one has to keep that in mind. The quality of reporting varies. I think, as a general rule, newspapers tend to sensationalize things and it does a disservice to the average investor.

That's why I was ecstatic when the paper asked me to write. I am somebody who is in the industry and knows retail clients and knows money managers. I was ecstatic to write practically on the subject of alternative investing.

The columns tend to be better than the general day-to-day reporting, right? You know, I read three or four newspapers a day because I'm interested in what other people are saying. But, generally speaking, I think that they sensationalize things. They provide opportunities for really professional investors to take advantage of the public's overreaction to things.

That's a good way of putting it. I've always thought that the market would be more efficient when you had CNBC and all that, right? But it creates more inefficiencies.

I think that the markets are incredibly inefficient. When I went to school, I was taught the efficient market hypothesis, and that is still being taught at schools, and it's absolute nonsense, right? If markets were efficient, how do you explain, in the year 2000, the market valuing Nortel Networks at close to $400 billion and then, less than two years later, the same market says that the same business is worth $10 billion? That is pretty bloody inefficient, if you ask me.

On that, why do you think that most investors don't do well in the market? I've written a lot on behavioural finance and I guess it's emotions that destroy you, right?

I think that the single biggest weakness with most investors is that their time horizon is way too short.

They have a long-term time horizon until their monthly statement comes out!

The value is not always created overnight, or, if you're a value investor, value is not always unlocked or realized overnight. I mean, you've got to be patient. Somebody once said—and this is absolutely true in my opinion—that the stock market is a voting machine and the pretty girls get all the votes. The pretty girls are all the ones going up in price. In the long run, let's say ten years, the stock market becomes a wave machine. A lot of people aren't prepared for that. They'll look at it as a wave machine and they play it as a voting machine and they're way too short-term oriented in terms of their expectations. Going back to newspapers, when you read newspaper headlines, they're always short-term focused, "Oil prices plunge 60 cents."

Right.

But the long-term trend in oil prices was up, so what are you talking about?

Yeah, you've got to find a story every day.

Exactly.

I guess just a little bit about the firm. How does a small-cap guy get together with a high-yield bond guy and start a firm?

We were together at another firm at the time. We worked for a guy named Milton Wong. We were called M.K. Wong and Associates. And, uh, Milton fired me in 1992, right?

Right.

Doug asked me what I was going to do? I said that I was going to start my own firm. He said, "Well, can I come with you?" I said, "Sure."

Nothing like opportunity being created for you, right?

Yeah, exactly. So off we went, in late 1992, and set ourselves up. It wasn't that I was a small-cap guy. What I was looking for when I was investing was to buy a business that was not well understood and as a result of that might be mispriced. You tended to find those opportunities in smaller companies because they were less followed by the rest of the universe. We kind of had that reputation of being small-cap guys because most of what we bought was under a billion dollars in market value when we bought it. The other philosophy that we always had was that it was very difficult to add value if you're buying government bonds for people.

Definitely. A government bond mutual fund charges 1.5 percent. The rates are 3.5 percent.

We did this study when we opened our doors: We went back for thirty years and we used publicly available data about mutual funds and data available from performance measurement companies. We showed that over rolling ten-year periods, there were hundreds of periods of these thirty-year time spans, that the rate of return before fees in each ten-year period was roughly equal to what the coupon levels were at the beginning of the ten-year period. In other words, if you're buying government bonds or trading them or managing them, essentially, whatever you were doing wasn't adding any value. You were essentially earning your coupon, and that makes sense, right? To be able to earn more than the coupon, you would've had to be able to predict short-term changes in interest rates and be able to buy and sell the bonds for capital gains to add value to the coupon. So we said, "Okay, for our customers that needed a steady income stream, why don't we try to do it differently for them. We got involved in corporate bonds—particularly in corporate bonds that aren't well-priced and mispriced. That led us into the high-yield bond market.

A high-yield manager is like an equity manager because you have to do the same analysis.

Same thing. So that's why we're not two different groups any more—we're all one. Whether we're buying a bond that we think is mispriced or a business ownership that we think is mispriced, it's the same way of thinking.

There is still the impression out there that high-yield bonds are junk bonds. Those are risky. I mean that you can go buy Hudson's Bay stock on the market but don't buy Hudson's Bay bond.

Well, that's the inefficiency in the market created by pension fund concerns. They write these policy guidelines for pension plans and they'll prevent pension plans from buying debt in a company, but it'll allow them to buy the equity in a company. Makes no sense to me.

A high-yield bond trader said that when he worked at TD, he used to phone up all these pension plans and say, "I see that you own Rogers Com-

munications stock in your portfolio—the bonds are paying 9 percent." And they'd say, "No, no, no. We don't want to invest in high-yield bonds." But he'd say, "But you own the stock in your portfolio?! This is less risky because it's the bond." "Ah, no, we don't do that." So, obviously, like you said, it creates inefficiencies.

We went to the Rogers pension plan and said that. Your own pension plan can't buy your own debt?! Yet, you want other pension plans to buy your debt?

On that, I see that you have about a third of your business is pension/institutional, about a 42 percent mutual fund and about 25 percent in private clients.

Probably a little more than that in private clients now. More than half our revenues come from private clients. That is the thrust of our business. That is the client base that is best suited to the way that we invest. We do have some pension business that we've had for a long time.

Let's talk a little about the performance and about your investment discipline and style. You have more than double the performance of Nesbitt Small Cap Index over the last ten years.

That's using the Northwest Fund as a benchmark?

Uh, the Deans Knight Equity.

Ok, the equity pool.

Throughout that time, there's been some good times and some bad times. Were you happy with your performance? What were your biggest mistakes?

Absolutely. You know, when we started the firm, people asked us, "What are you trying to achieve in terms of rates of return?" The honest answer to that is we didn't know. We don't know what opportunities the market is going to present us with at that point in time. But we said if, ten years out, we look back at the history of our firm and we have delivered a rate of 10 percent per annum, I think we'd be satisfied with that. So that was our goal. As it turns out, over the twelve or thirteen or fourteen years that we've been in business, we've annualized 20 percent, so double of what we thought we could do. That's because of extraordinary times. But when we started, it was a pretty decent mining market, right? We were involved, but not to as great as an extent as people thought.

I guess the first big win in the mining business that we had was Diamond Fields Resources in 1994. That taught me a lot. First of all, it taught me that sometimes the market ignores important information for all the wrong reasons. The key to Diamond Fields was that it was run by Robert Friedland. He had previously gotten some really bad publicity because of his mine down in the United States. They called him a bad name, he polluted the environment, and he just had a bad reputation. Whether he was a dishonest individual or not is a different question. But because of his reputation, people refused to look at the information that was being released by the company, Diamond Fields. I knew some people that knew a little bit more about the mining business than I did, and they convinced us to look more seriously at what was being released. It occurred to us that the deposit didn't know who owned it. So forget about who owns the deposit, just concentrate on the deposit, and you'd make the right decision. There was huge value in the deposit and it just kept getting bigger and bigger and bigger. Lo and behold, Inco ended up buying it for a lot of money and everybody made a lot of money, including ourselves.

We also diddled around in a number of other juniors in those days, and with some of them we made really good money. When we made really good money, it was because the people that ran the junior companies actually discovered commercially viable deposits that actually became producing mines. That's the key, right? I mean, there's a lot of shit going on in the junior mining and the junior oil and gas business. There is a lot of promotional stuff—a lot of people in good times that trot out deposits and market the hell out of them and they never become mines, at least not commercially viable.

Right.

So we made a few mistakes along the way too, but we had some big wins, you know. International Musto Explorations is one of the biggest copper mines in the world today. Catherine McLeod's Arequipa Resources was bought by Barrick, and it's a producing mine today. So you learn to be very, very selective if you're going to invest in the mining business. It's all about the quality of the assets and the quality of the people. Some of the things that we looked at in those days, and even some of things we invested in, never became commercially viable mines and you lost your money. If you have enough wins like Arequipa, Musto, and Diamond Fields, it covers up a lot of the mistakes that we did make over that period of time.

It's always the same: A fairly small percentage of your picks are huge wins.

Exactly, exactly. But we were doing other things. People thought that we were just mining experts. We certainly weren't. We weren't experts in mining, but we made some money there. We were investing in lots of different things that we did well in, in the early to mid-'90s.

Do you consider yourself to be a value investor or growth investor?

Yeah, I think that most successful investors are value investors of one kind or another. *Value* is a pretty big word. There's a Cundill extreme and there's another extreme. I guess we're somewhere in between. But you're always trying to buy something for less than what you think it's worth today or what it could be worth with some added ingredients in the future. When it comes to a resource company, it gets a little more difficult, right? Fundamentally, one thing is true: You're better off investing in resource companies when resource prices are low. For example, more money was made buying good quality nickel producers when nickel was $1.75 a pound than what you could make when nickel is a lot higher.

LionOre Mining, I think you bought.

As low as $0.36, right, when nickel was a $1.75. What happens at the bottom of a cycle is that mines shut down, exploration ceases because nobody's got any cash flow. Who needs any new mines anyways? Eventually, when demand does pick up again, there's not enough supply, right? The price of the metal rises and you make a lot of money. So that's the value proposition in a resource play. First of all, it has to be a producer so you can place some value on what they have. You want to know the reserves, and they should be a low-cost producer so they stay in business at the bottom of the cycle. The value proposition is that nickel has to one day be more than a $1.75 a pound or 90 percent of all the producers are going to shut their doors because they can't make any money. The same thing is true with oil and gas. When oil was $11 a barrel and the *Economist* magazine was telling everybody that it was going down to $5, if you knew anything about oil, you knew that was not likely going to happen. If you talked to a producer and it's costing them $10 a barrel to lift it and you offer them $5, then they're going to cap the well. So, that's the value proposition in oil.

It's interesting that you mention that because I think that commodity cycles are very, very long. Obviously, when you have prices so low and demand starts to ramp up, it takes years in the commodity business for that supply to come online.

Absolutely.

Is that why the cycle lasts so long?

That's exactly why the cycle lasts so long. How are you going to find a commercially viable nickel deposit and get the mine built and get the mine producing in a year? I mean, you can't do that, right?

Voisey's Bay has already been twelve years now and it's starting to….

Yeah, longer than that actually; it's been fourteen years now. Well, thirteen years since discovery, and it's now beginning to produce. So, yeah, that's the problem. There is years and years of underinvestment, and demand is still growing, and you're eating away at stockpiles. Then suddenly you've reached a point where there is not enough being produced to meet demand, and cash flows rise, which is what's happening now. Inco was recently throwing off a billion a year in free cash flow. So they go out and buy another company to try to get production up for themselves and the cash flows eventually wind up creating new mines. I mean, it takes time.

I would think years and years. Does it make sense that, as commodity prices move up, that's going to hurt the average non-commodity company's profits? Is that why it seems that commodity cycles and stock market cycles are completely different? If the price of grain or corn or whatever goes up, Kellogg's going to be in trouble. You can't pass that on to the consumer, so the profits get squeezed.

Right, that's happening now. We own a lot of Canadian manufacturing companies whose margins have been hurt: Well, twofold, the dollar is going up because commodity prices are going up. Also, because commodity prices are going up, the raw materials costs are going up. Packaging is going up because a lot of it is petroleum-based. They can't price increases through as fast as their cost base is going up, but they will get those price increases through one day. Suddenly, we're going to wake up one day and say that inflation's back.

How can you get all these rises in commodity prices and no inflation?

There's a convenient excuse that everybody's using today, that China's exporting deflation. Well, that's a crock of shit, you know. In the long run, that's not going to wash, or otherwise a lot of our companies are going to be forced out of business. Then, where am I going to get my dog food from? I've got to have dog food and you just put the dog food companies out of business because you wouldn't pay more for the dog food. Ultimately, we'll pay more for the dog food, right?

Well, that's extrapolation: China's done all this, and in twenty years, they'll produce everything in the world.

It's not going to happen. They may consume everything in the world, but they're not going to produce everything in the world.

What's the most important thing to you, qualitative research on companies or quantitative research on companies?

I guess, to us, the balance is tilted towards qualitative research. The single most important decision we make, ever, is the price we pay for a business. So it's a mix. There's got to be some quantitative stuff, but there's an awful lot of qualitative stuff that goes into what we do.

All managers—money managers—say pretty much the same thing: We try to buy undervalued companies. So why has it been that you have been successful in that and they aren't?

Well...first of all, we don't think we're money managers; we think we're opportunistic investors. I don't think that most investors, professional or otherwise, really do try to buy undervalued companies. They think they do, but they don't do it. They're more concerned with momentums and trends than buying a business for hopefully less than what they think the business is actually worth. I think that's why they don't get good results. Overlaying that, I think, the most important factor that results in poor investment returns is performance measurement. That shortens the investor's time frame down. Really, you can't buy anything unless you've got a five-year time horizon, and that's even short. Most money managers, which we don't consider ourselves, are measured by their monthly or quarterly numbers, and it affects what they do. Like oil stocks—shit, I got to get off my oil stocks because they're not having a good quarter, and come December 31st, if I have too many of them and they don't do well, then I've got some explaining to do.

It's so interesting that you say that because I was talking to Ned Goodman. Ned says that back in the '60s, he used to manage money the way you should manage money. He tried to make money any way he could, and then he said the consultants came along and told us no, no, there are things called tracking errors and relative performance. He says, "So what do you expect today? Everybody gives you index performance minus the management fee."

That's what you get, and now you got this huge growth in the hedge fund business and the way hedge fund managers are compensated shortens their time horizon down even more because they are paid quarterly based on rate of return. And if they exceed a hurdle rate, they're going to make a shitload of money, so their time horizon is just compacted. It creates volatility and creates opportunities for people to take advantage of what's happening out there.

That's a great point. Like you said, it creates more volatility.

I hear this from brokers that we deal with: "A lot of guys—professional managers—buy and sell companies when they don't really know anything about the companies." They don't really know why they bought it. I hear this expression lately, "Give me a nickel play." "Because I think nickel's going up this quarter, I'll need a nickel play." Is that crazy or what? Or, now, for instance, energy's popular, and uranium's popular, because now we're building nuclear power plants again. So the market is feeding the portfolio managers' desire for uranium plays. That's crazy, right?! You're supposed to go buy an undervalued uranium company, not go buy a uranium play. If you can't find one that you think is fairly valued or undervalued, then don't buy one.

On that, have you ever wanted to short companies that you've considered to be extremely overvalued, or that have held deteriorating fundamentals?

With shorting, you can be dead right and go broke trying to prove it. You can be right and your clients don't have the patience to see it through with you. So, Christ, I would've shorted Nortel at $40 and I would've busted by the time it hit $125. I would've been right in the long run, but out of business in the short run.

I've found that many people who successfully short say they never short based on valuation because you would get killed. You short based on deteriorating fundamentals.

Yup.

So, a lot of your performance attribution over the years has been in the resource sector, or has it been pretty mixed?

It's been mixed, you know; it's been all kind of things. In fact, we just did something for a potential customer recently. This is a high net worth family that came to see us; "Show us, give us an idea, where all your money's been made in the last five years." Really, the question that they're asking is, "We bet that you made all your money in oil, so show us." It's not true. We looked back to the year 2000 and we picked our ten best investments that we've made. Two of them were oil and gas stocks and eight of them had nothing to do with resources at all or oil and gas. There were two mining companies, a steel company, oil and gas company, a health care company…it was a mix of all different kinds of things. We're not there to play a cycle; we're there to buy things that are cheap. We happened to buy two mining companies and some oil companies we liked— we thought were undervalued in 1999 and 2000—and they went up a lot. But there was lots of stuff that went up a lot, you know. We bought Unican and sold it to Cobalt Holdings for twice what the market said it was worth. Western Star Trucks was sold to DaimlerChrysler for three times what the market said it was worth. We had tons of those non-resource related companies that produced enormous returns for us over the last few years.

Why does the market sometimes favour small caps and sometimes favour large caps? Do you think when foreigners come into the market, they are going to buy Encana before they go into a small cap ?

Probably, yeah. Big fund managers have difficulty moving large amounts of money around in smaller capitalization companies, and that's true of Canada. People often say to us, "Why are most of your great investments made in Canadian-based companies?" Well, the simple answer to that is the opposite answer that most people give about Canada. There was an article in the paper yesterday about Canada being only 3 percent of the world capital market, so who cares? Well, that's the whole point—nobody cares. I can buy things cheaper here than I can in the U.S. market. I could up until recently because Canada was being ignored, right?

That brings up the next question: What do you think that the capacity for your style is?

It varies, it varies….

It varies on the market and liquidity.

In 1999/2000, our capacity was unlimited because there were so many great investment opportunities. But as you pointed out earlier, people were taking their money back. They were taking money out of us when our capacity was unlimited. Now, people want to give us money at a time where our capacity is way more limited. Our business plan calls for shrinking our asset base over the next five years.

I think it's kind of important in Canada to manage a manageable amount of money.

Right. It's much easier if you have smaller amounts of money, and we're very cognizant of that. So we can't really grow our business. What we do is we have resigned in the past some pension mandates that we did not think were a good fit for us. There may be some more of that happening in the future as we go forward.

Whenever you tell people that you don't want their money, they always want to give you more.

Yeah, we had one pension fund that we resigned recently and they treated us like shit for ten years. Every time we had a bad quarter, they beat the shit out of us. I had to go to Toronto. "Why did you underperform the index or benchmark?" I'm going, "Get a grip!" Ten years later, we resign, and they're begging us to stay. You kicked the shit out of us every three or four years, what are you talking about?! They said, "You're our best-performing managers. You've given us 20 percent per annum and you double the benchmark." "But the first bad quarter that we have, you're going to give us shit?! And you're only paying us 30 basis points and our private clients want to give us money at a 125 basis points!" So what's going to happen is that the best investors aren't going to be available to the pension plans or the mutual fund market at some point in the future. What's happening is that you don't get paid and the regulations are insane, right?

I read a whole piece on the institutionalization of money management. It's not a great thing. No wonder all the pension funds are going to index funds, because that's what they wanted. They wanted a money manager to beat an index fund but not stray from it. I mean, how do you that?

Another interesting point that people don't realize is that the financial health of the Canadian pension funds is not that good. I mean, as a group, together, pension plans are seriously underfunded. The main reason for that is their investment policies. It's not a question of whether they're making the right contributions. They haven't been making the proper returns. They haven't been making the proper returns because they've got these stupid consultants that design investment strategies when they don't know a thing about investing money. As a result, lo and behold, pension funds don't have enough money to meet their obligations. That's nutty! It's even getting worse now because of liabilities, right? The liability that they have makes it so they can't afford to be wrong.

Do you use analysts' reports at all?

Not very much because there are some serious biases, particularly with the bank-owned dealers. It's almost impossible to eliminate those biases, and you have to recognize that they're there. The analysts that we tend to use are older guys; they don't give a shit about whether they'll get fired or not, and they work as an analyst so that they'll have information flowing that'll help them run their own money. They don't care whether or not they get paid a big bonus. They're there for information flow. So we talk to a handful of those guys, but, otherwise, we prefer to remain independent and make our own decisions. But that gets us back to....

We've never answered that question on how you could manage from Vancouver when you should be on Bay Street?

Let me tell you a story. We got a call a couple years back from New York. There were some people in New York that represented some very wealthy non-American families. "Would you come and see us?" So we go and see them. Nice offices, midtown Manhattan. They represent some very serious big money. "First of all, why did you call us?" "Oh, you have a customer that we can't name that gave us your name." Okay. But you're midtown Manhattan, the centre of the universe, why would you consider dealing with a couple of guys sitting way out there in Vancouver, B.C., when you've never even been there? "Let me tell you something. We're dealing with a half a dozen investors, none of them are in New York. They're in a small town in Pennsylvania, one in the Midwest, we've got one in Florida, and now you guys on the west coast." "So why's that?" I say. "Everybody in New York—they think the same way. We all drink the same bathwater—no independent thinking is going on here."

You can't make money, in their opinion, unless you think and act independently. I think that it's much easier if you're away from Bay Street and Wall Street to think and act independently. Lo and behold, we do get caught up on group thinking as well because we're only human, right? But it's much harder to get away from that if you're sitting on Bay Street. You really have to work at being independent because you go to the same lunches, you see the same analyst day after day, the same conferences. We don't go to conferences unless we really want to go skiing somewhere.

Right, right.

I go to one conference every two years and I go not because I like to sit in presentations. It's because I like to corner a CEO of a company over dinner and drinks somewhere at a bar and really get to know something about his business. But none of our guys ever go to conferences.

What was your biggest stock win over the years?

Yeah, the biggest win was Algoma Steel.

Okay.

We sold it all a couple years ago, but we bought the stock as low—this is five years ago now—as low as $1.75. It had been as low as a buck a share. It was emerging from Chapter 11 for the second time, the steel business was in disarray, plants were closing all over North America and the new CEO of Algoma Steel was a forest products guy. How bad could it get, right? But at a dollar a share, there were thirty million shares outstanding. They were doing $1.2 billion in revenue, and you could buy the whole company for thirty million bucks, right?

Right.

We got to know Denis Turcotte, the new CEO, well. He told us what he was going to do with the company—not insider information. He said, "Look, I've got to lower the wages and the cost of production. First and foremost, I've got to trim back people. To do that, I've got to get the unions to play ball with me, and I think that I can do that." He said, "Plants are closing all over North America. That's a good thing because there's overcapacity in North America and we're rectifying that." He says that, "Because we've come out of Chapter 11, we do have a cost advantage over some of our competitors. We've renegotiated our debt. We've got pension obligations that have been taken off our books and looked after by the government. So if there's an improvement in steel pricing, we are going to be the biggest beneficiary."

It made sense to us, right? The book value was like, I don't know, eight bucks a share and you could buy it for less than two bucks a share. Was it really worth eight bucks a share? We didn't know for sure. Only time would tell, but at least you weren't paying a multiple of book value. We also looked at Stelco and came to the conclusion that it was just a bag of poop. It was badly run, they caved to the unions, they were going to get themselves into serious trouble. Algoma was going to benefit. So we bought 10 percent of the company. We invested $3 million at roughly $1.75, $2.00, and we sold the last of our stock in February or March 2005 at $38.50.

Twenty-bagger.
Shot that right out of the park! Home run!

[Laughs]
Now, those don't come along very often, but we've had a number of ten- and twenty-baggers over the years. That one was the most dramatic because it happened so quickly. Like it was the perfect storm, right? Right after we bought it, Bush put up trade barriers. We have a free-trade agreement with the United States, so they put the barriers around North America and forced up steel prices. Steel went from $200 Canadian a ton, when we invested, to $1,200 Canadian a ton. A company that was worth $30 million in the market, the voting machine, two years later was cash flowing $500 million! Out-of-the-park home run!

You said you're a lot better as a money manager because you've made a lot of mistakes. What mistakes have you made over the years that you've learned from? What was your biggest mistake?
The biggest mistake…. There have been lots of mistakes, by the way…but the one that has taught me the most is International Wall Coverings. I'm try-

ing to remember the time frame. It was in the late '90s, and we got involved because of the guy that essentially created the business.

Right.

International Wallcoverings was part of a British chemical company, and it was a division that made wallpaper. The guys that ran the division did a management buyout because Wallcoverings was a small part of the chemical company and it became International Wallcoverings. I got involved because he was a really good guy and really knew the business, and he gradually built it up until it became the largest wallpaper manufacturer in North America. It looked like a pretty good business; aging population, reno markets improving, and it was going to stay that way. You know, wallcoverings are a fashion item, and a stable growth business. Anyways, he got cancer and he had to withdraw from day-to-day operations of the business and he took the CFO and made him the CEO, but he was not competent. The stock got as high as, in the late '90s, $20 a share and Gundy did a financing for them at $19, $20, but we didn't participate in that. Then business started to really deteriorate, we got a little bit concerned, and I got together with two other guys that owned a big part of the company. One was a guy in Toronto that was private and he was in the wallpaper business. The other was a well-known private guy here in Vancouver, and the three of us owned a big chunk of the company together as it turns out. So we went and challenged the management and the board of the company. We actually went to a board meeting and said, "What's going on here? Business has deteriorated." The board up and resigned! They had an advisor from Gundy that they were paying a quarter of a million dollars to help them run the business.

Did you give the Gordon Gecko "Greed Is Good" speech from _Wall Street_?

So, lo and behold, we went on the board. We had no choice now. To find out what was going on in the business, we brought in KPMG, the forensic guys. They did an audit of the company and told us where we stood. Well, they came back and said that you're bankrupt.

Right.

Here we got KPMG. Here we got a prospectus, with a time difference of three months. It was black and white. Totally opposite! With that, I resigned from the board, we sold our remaining stocks for like a buck a share, put the company into receivership, and the assets were sold off. What did I learn from that: Number one, don't believe what you read in a prospectus; it could be bullshit.

Right, sure.

Number two, don't trust greedy investment bankers. Assume the board is incompetent until proven otherwise, right? Don't go on a board. So we lost a lot of money. It took six months out of my life in meetings, trying to sort this out and to try to extract the last bit of value for our investors. The whole thing was a nightmare! Boy, did it teach me! I learned a lot, right? I guess that was 1998.

I guess that brings up a good point: Are there any rules that you can lay out that you go by when looking at a stock?

Yeah, first and foremost, you got to trust management. Essentially, people entrust their money to us and we, in turn, entrust that money to a management group to run a business on our behalf or on the clients' behalf. They have to be totally dead straight with you—totally honest, right? That's first and foremost. Then the most important decision you make is what you pay for that business, right?

Price is very important?

You've got to trust what you're looking at. Those are the numbers, and they're not fudging the numbers and they're accurate. They accurately portray the state of the business. Now, what am I willing to pay for that business? If price isn't right, you've got to walk away from it. We were in a meeting today, those guys that just went out. They're telling me about their company, and I open up their annual reports. I always open the back first, because that's where they usually have the directors, who's managing these guys. Then I get to the next section, the notes to the financial statements, and then I immediately go to the stock options and see how many options are outstanding. The guys that were in here were talking about their business, and I thought it was very interesting. Then I looked and thought, "Holy crap! You gave away 20 percent of the company to yourselves!"

[Laughs]

Right? 20 percent of the company is under option at prices at a fraction of where the shares are trading today. These guys are exercising options taking millions of dollars out of the business, and you want me to put my clients' money in?!

Right, are you interested in making money for yourselves or building the business?

It's a showstopper! Right there—it's a showstopper for me! Your gut tells you that if you're not comfortable with the management group, just don't go there.

One of the biggest financial fiascos in Canada was Bre-X. How could somebody differentiate that problem...other than going to that site?

They did a great job of hoodwinking people. I was very involved in that story. We made some money, actually, by sheer luck. I'll tell you how I got involved, and, again, I learned something from that fiasco. Somebody called me and said that the Bre-X management team was in Vancouver. "Would you like to meet them?" and I said, "Sure." So I went to this guy's office and they were doing a presentation. I walked in and sat down and I knew that I was meeting the CEO, David Walsh, but I didn't know that it was the same David Walsh that I had known for twenty-five years. He was a portfolio manager at Canada Permanent Trust company in the early 1970s in Montreal when I was there. I walked into the room and he said, "Hey, Wayne!" I said, "David Walsh!" You know, he was big as a house, and he had a brownie and he had chocolate sauce all over him. Then they had Felderhoff, who did the presentation. He had impeccable credentials as a geologist. Then they had a fellow who used to be executive vice president of exploration for Barrick—I forgot his name. These four were impressive guys, so I better take note of this thing. I couldn't get over the fact that David Walsh kept nudging me, "Wayne, do you realize how much money I'm making?!" I'm like, "What's going on here?"

[Laughs]

Anyways, I'm listening to this story and the analyst from Nesbitt is hounding me to buy some stocks. I go, "Well, if the numbers are right, this is another Diamond Fields, right? Nobody's paying attention because this buffoon, Walsh, is the CEO of the company." So I bought a bunch of stock, then we sat down one day and said, "You know what? The market cap of Bre-X, who has-n't produced one ounce of gold, is greater than all the market caps of all the other publicly traded gold companies combined." I said, "We've made a lot of money because the stock has gone up. We're just lucky." We sold half our stock and walked into a gigantic profit. Then I went to East Kalimantan. Be-cause I had been involved in Diamond Fields with Robert Friedland, he in-vited me and some other guys over there because he had a mining lease adjoining the Bre-X property. I thought, here was a good opportunity to see it.

Yeah, Indochina Goldfields.

So, I went over with Robert and some other guys and we go to this god-forsaken place. It was the worst place in the world that I've ever been to in my life, and we tramped around in the jungles with these guys that were carrying our lunches and our equipment, with bones in their noses. Like, this is way out there; this is really primitive, right? This is a God-awful place and I talked to Robert about it. Down the road, there was Bre-X, and he was like, "What is going on here?!" Because there were rumours of a salting scandal at that point. It was just before or just after, Mike de Guzman jumped out of the chop-per and he said, "Wayne, we're in the middle of nowhere! Nobody can come here to do due diligence because they're going to get killed here by all these natives!"

[Laughs]

They have these wars there! I got back to Australia and I got on the phone to the guys here and said, "Look, whatever Bre-X stock we have, just get rid of it." They said, "Why?" If you were going to…I didn't know that they had salted the core…but if you were going to do something like that, this is a place in the world that you could get away with it. You couldn't do it in Nevada be-cause there're too many people looking over your shoulder. There was nobody looking over your shoulders here! It was a corrupt society in a very, very dif-ficult region, and I said, "Just get rid of it." We had already made a whole shit load of money; toss the rest out the window. That's what happened.

Good story!

Rohit Sehgal
Trends, Themes, and Tactical Trading

"Don't be in stocks where earnings are being revised down. I am not going to fall in love with anything."

Revered by other Stock Market Superstars as "one of the best traders" they know, I first interviewed Rohit in Tucson, Arizona, at an investment conference, with a subsequent interview in Hollywood, Florida, and yet another in Toronto. It was during the second interview in Hollywood, Florida, while sitting on a patio overlooking the beautiful Atlantic Ocean that I asked him in-depth questions about the fund that has made him legendary, the Dynamic Power Hedge Fund. Just in case you don't know who Rohit is, you should, because *Barron's* magazine does. In early 2008, his fund was rated by *Barron's* as the number two hedge fund in the world over the three preceding years, with a market-crushing 60 percent annualized return. The fund has actually averaged about 55 percent per year, net to investors, since inception in 2002. Just in case you need help with the math, this equates to what we call in the investment industry a ten-bagger. Think about that. Ten times your initial investment in less than six years. There are hardly any stocks that do that, let alone diversified funds!

Coming from India about forty years ago, it was tough to land a job, but ending up at London Life finally, Rohit traded bonds, a job that most equity people are not exposed to. Why bonds? Because at that time, London Life did little else. Bond guys have to know the "big picture" macro environment, and this is where Rohit started to develop his top-down expertise. He had to figure out a way to do it better than the rest, and prove himself to be unique. Why? Well, lots of reasons, but one reason was because he was from India, and suffice it to say that you had to be better than the rest just for people in Canada to give you a shot at that time.

Rohit is the only stock picker I interviewed from a big money management firm, as this type of culture does not usually give managers the flexibility to "step out of the box." Dynamic is different, however. The company has developed an entrepreneurial culture, where many of their managers have excelled far above their peers in Canadian money management. Rohit, as chief investment strategist since the late '90s, has helped lead the charge.

When I asked him what the one most important quality was to being successful, he said, "To stay humble." When I asked him some of the secrets to his success, he said, "I identify trends and themes early, and have an extraordinary trading instinct." This is putting it mildly, as he is not just accomplished at running his concentrated and highly industry focused hedge fund, but he has a longer track record than any of the other Stock Market Superstars I interviewed. Going back to 1981 with his regular mutual fund products, he has had twenty up years and only seven down years, with a compound rate of return of about 14 percent. Now, only seven down years isn't what you would normally expect from an aggressive "growth," volatile manager such as Rohit. With his defined style, he controls risks and losses by not being afraid to take losses—quickly, if need be.

Most successful longer-term money managers generally describe themselves as more "value" oriented. To be this good, for this long, as a pure growth manager, is simply extraordinary. During our latest interview, he pointed this out to me, saying, "My style of investing is hard on somebody, but if I retired, I would get bored in about two weeks. It's what I do."

Bob:

I guess we'll go right back to the beginning. I think you're probably the kind of guy that started this very young. Did you start when you were in university?

Rohit:

I finished my university in India and I came here via Europe in 1969. I ended up with a job at Moss Lawson, basically as a stock analyst trainee. I think I was 21 or something. It was sort of an accidental entrance in the market. I hadn't really had any plans to be in this. My educational background was economics, so it seemed like somewhat related to it, and beyond that, I had no experience in Canada. So I was really green. They asked me whether I wanted to be in sales or research and I said, "Well, I'm so new here, I'm not going to know too many people. So research seems like a good idea."

A year and a half later, or two years later, a lot happened during that period, of course. I met my first wife here in Toronto and got married. I had an opportunity to go to London Life because London Life at that time was a very, very conservative company, and their investments in equities were almost nil. It was more of a bond shop—coupon clippers. They were doing fine because all they were doing was matching assets with liabilities. Somebody referred me to them and there were two or three guys who were sort of aging and they wanted some young blood. So I got my foot into that at a very, very low— lowest of the low—level. They said, "Okay, here you are. You're sort of Joe Boy and now you have to prove yourself." That was 1970.

In 1974, one of the things they wanted me to do was to do the CFA, so I did it in '74 to show commitment that I really wanted to be in this field. But it was not until 1981 that they gave me my first portfolio. So even though I joined the business at earlier stages, the first portfolio I had which was mine was in 1981 and it was called the London Life Equity Fund. It was $50 million and it grew up into a multi-billion portfolio, both through performance and through new money. At one point at London Life, I was managing, I think, in excess of $3 billion, and an interesting thing was, they let me develop my own style. This was so uncanny for a conservative company like London Life. Some people say I had the first hedge fund in the country—a multi-billion dollar hedge fund—because it was really actively managed. So sometimes strange things happen. Nobody would think that London Life would give you an environment where you could do things other than sort an index fund and so on.

Were you a fixed income analyst for a while?

Well, you know, when I joined London Life, they didn't really have any equity exposure. I was basically doing private placements in the fixed income side. I was even doing a little bit of a bond trading, basically switching, you know, from low coupon to high coupon and adding up yields. That was day-to-day and then gradually equities really fascinated me the most and so I would just, on my own, do strategies and stick it in front of them. You know, I hoped somebody would notice it.

Do you think from being in the fixed income area, which is more of a macro sort of job, it had some....

Exactly, exactly. That's where I started getting the feel that I realized was important. Some people invest bottom up and don't look around at the big picture. I don't believe in that at all. You know, you want to know the big macro trends. It's like a farmer. He's looking at the weather before he starts putting the seeds in the ground. If there's a thunderstorm, he's not going to do anything. That's where the top-down thing became sort of more important to me.

Interesting. Did you ever invest in stocks just for yourself in India?

No. I never had any money. [Laughs]

Was there anything to invest in India at the time?

No. I think the stock market was not really a big deal there. I had no personal experience at all, even when I came here with London Life. I didn't have any money to invest in the stock market, but I was a very keen student of the market, and I did more reading than anybody would do. Plus I had to prove myself because I came from a foreign land. During those days, I was a visible minority, so I was probably not really given the same chances. Not as much as maybe somebody else, because I spoke excellent English and adapted myself very well. But I think that was another reason I had to prove myself, so I really did have to work harder than the guy next door; there was no doubt. That has been a big plus.

I was going to ask that. Was coming here as an immigrant responsible for you being as successful as you are?

I think so, because you do develop a very strong work ethic, coming from that environment. In places like India, you are basically on your own and you have to prove by what you can deliver, you know. So work ethic has become very important. I was very competitive and I wanted to succeed. So it was part personality, part cultural background, and part environment that were responsible. It was a combination of it all.

I always wondered why you stuck around at London Life for so long. Was it because they gave you free rein to do what you wanted to do?

I think that was so important. As Ned Goodman was saying and we talked about, with most of the managers, all that was expected from them was to track the index, plus or minus or whatever. Firstly, insurance companies were typical for that. They considered risk as deviating from the index, which to me is a crazy way of looking at risk. That was part of how I developed my style, and they encouraged it. They saw the results we were producing were so enormous, but, of course, on the other side of the equation, how do you manage risk? Lo and behold, we were managing risk very, very well. One of the ways was to manage the volatility through trading. You know, we take profits when things get overbought and so on. That became part of that process or style. It's just tempting you to evolve, and also I had to prove that I was much better, right? The only way I could prove that was to have a different style.

Inherently, if you do the same as everybody else, you're all the same, and you won't outperform.

Yeah, so then you are not much better, right? I think the same thing could apply to Eric [Sprott]. He wanted to succeed, so he developed creativity. When you want to succeed, you become more creative.

It was funny, because Eric said he was purely a bottom-up stock picker at the beginning.

Yeah, it's a combination, of course. Eventually, you buy the stock, right? It doesn't matter where interest rates are going. So that's where the end result is—picking the right stocks. But it does help to be in the right sector at the right time with the right stock. That's when you get the two- or three-baggers you know, so….

Do you remember the first stock that you bought for yourself?

Yeah, you know, I have to go back. I was trading pretty actively for myself and I did well. You know, we had a lot of constraints. Personal investing becomes very hard because there's so many hurdles they put on you. First stock. Let me think about that. It goes back so far that....

What clued you in to look at the big picture? Was it the fixed income analysis?

Macro sends a lot of signals in terms of what sectors you want to be in. Talking about banks, there's a certain environment where banks do very well. I was getting a lot of guidance from following the big picture, then looking at the stocks within that sector.

So would you regard yourself as a sector rotator in a way?

No, not necessarily. We've been through a lot of different types of business cycles. I can remember, back in the '80s, business cycles had a sort of finite life—every three or four years—and within those, you knew when to get into the financials, when to get into the deep cyclicals, and so on. We played that game as well and that probably makes you a sector rotator. Business cycles recently have not been the same. In fact, if you look at the last ten years in terms of the cyclicality of the economy, it's not been accurate. I can't even remember the last time when we had a serious recession. Even when the market crashed in '01, '02, we didn't really have a serious economic recession as such. It has been a very different environment than we were in the '70s and '80s. We are talking about very extended cycles, like the super cycle sectors that we are in. In the last five years at least, our strategy in terms of sectors, has been pretty consistent. We were very early in resources—extremely early—and, in fact, if you go beyond the four, five years, we were probably the first guys who made a big bet on natural gas. When natural gas was $1 or $2, it had nothing to do with the oil price or resources. It just seemed that we were in a made-in-North-America natural gas pricing problem, so we made a very early call on natural gas. Five or so years ago, we anticipated what was going on in a sectoral basis in the resources area and we haven't changed that. We haven't been a sector rotator for the last five years. The macro picture is not suggesting that you do that.

It's interesting because you've always kind of been regarded as a growth manager. However, when you're getting into industries, very early, some people would say that you're a form of value manager.

The most uncommon thing in our business is common sense. That's fine, so why shouldn't we do that if it's going to add value? Why shouldn't we anticipate although we like the quant models? But it's not a black box, because by the time you see that in the quant, in the numbers, it may be too late. That's where your own intuition or your gut feel or your own understanding of the market comes in. This is very hard to quantify and put it on paper. How could you have, for instance, five years ago, made the bet that we did? The quants were not telling us—the earnings were not yet responding to those things. So we were early. You know, I'm very good at that. Two years ago, we took our energy—natural gas, really—down huge. Just in two days, I took $200 million out and put it in base metals, in copper and so on. That was a huge bet. That was a huge contributor to the performance of all my funds, including the hedge fund. So it was not in the numbers yet, but we're just saying, "Hey, in January, there's nothing left in the winter, it's gone. These guys are going to have a huge problem because they already had the capacity right to the top." So you were basically finished for the next three or four months and you're going to see these prices coming down and there was going to be a lot of revisions in the cash flow. We anticipated it for sure. Don't be in the stocks where the earnings are being revised down, but if you can be early, that's great. So we got a double whammy. So that's, I think, another reason why we are more successful than the other guys.

If you had to pick one thing that has been the reason for your success, what would it be?

Absolutely, we are making a big bet on commodities because we have become a contrarian in the sense that we think that this thing is going to go on for a longer time. However, we are seeing more and more volatility, and it's scary. You tend to second guess yourself, but everything we are looking at from the macro level is suggesting that this thing is going to go on for a while. So we are sticking by our strategy.

Everybody thought you were crazy for going into uranium a few years ago.

Yeah, well, there are a lot of managers that have been underweight in these things. The funny thing is that people who miss the big moves are the ones who are most critical of the type of strategy that I have. It's no doubt, whether it's media or whatever. You just have to be steadfast and believe in your convictions but we keep on revisiting our strategy. I'm not going to fall in love with anything. I'm not going to be a cultist. I don't believe in conspiracy theories. I'm not a gold bug that I would blindly go and buy gold, saying it's the end of the world. No way. I mean, if the resource thing is over, or we think that there's no longer growth, we will move on. We maybe would buy technology or health or whatever.

Do you use technical analysis at all?

No, but, intuitively, we all know where these stocks are trading. They tend to, from time to time, move to the fifty-day average and so on. So you want to know how far you are. You still want to know whether the trend is intact. That'll be not the first thing I'll be looking at, however.

It's kind of an entry point or exit point to help you?

We may do that, but to be very honest, it's not a central theme. There are the times I'm so confident with my decision that I don't pay as much significance to the technical factors. There are times when I do; there are the times I don't.

In the past few years, you've increased the foreign content in the funds. Just to look at the process, do you look at the big picture, the top-down picture? Then do you select countries that you think are going to be rewarded and then a sector and then specific stocks?

We went into India in the early stages and there are a lot of reasons for that. I have probably a little bit of an advantage when it comes to a country like India, because I'm from there. More importantly, some fascinating things were happening. We saw that there was really a very deep commitment from the decision makers to make changes in the way they think. They all became pro-growth, and then, luckily, the people who had started the whole process back in '91, in opening up the economy, are now in the positions like the prime minister or the finance minister. The same guys who started the process were at the helm of the decision making. But that just happened a few years ago. But even before that, the process had already become very well entrenched. So we looked at China, and how well China was doing, but China was not investable. What China provided to us was the opportunity to invest in companies, like the energy companies in Canada or the resource companies who were selling products to them. It could be iron ore or copper or so on. That's how we played the China game because China was still not transparent. There was no business structure or physical structure.

On the other side in India, they had already a very well developed business infrastructure. They had the legal systems with the democracy. Not perfect, but the basic foundations were there, because the businesses had been slapped around and there were so many hurdles put in front of them from the past policies. They became really savvy, and became very efficient. Even given the environment they were in, they became extremely clever. The management skills are far, far, far superior to the Chinese because they had Western education and English language and a lot of them were trained abroad. The market provided four thousand companies in sectors which were like the U.S. You could get in the banks, you could get in the oil companies, and you can get in the steel companies. So if you really believed in the emerging middle class, what an unbelievable opportunity. We bought the banks, and these banks were now well regulated. They had good transparency, and the auditing system was even tougher than Canada. So all these things were cheap because, after '98, everything sort of crapped out. Also, there was very little risk of currency devaluation, because they had started building their own reserves and inflation was well contained. So all these things got me into that market very, very early. We were very well rewarded for that.

A lot of managers say that the buy decision on a particular stock is a lot easier than deciding when to sell. Would you agree with that, and how do you decide to sell?

I think the most difficult time is when things don't work out. How do you respond to that? Again, I think the discipline I developed was not to fall in love with any stock. Sometimes, you get carried away because you get to know the managements well and so on. You just say, "Oh, the guy's going to feel bad," or whatever. So if things are not working out, there could be several things involved. One, the fundamentals could deteriorate and are just a temporary setback for whatever reason. Secondly, you made a mistake. You made a mistake in understanding the real fundamentals, and the reality is you were wrong. In that case, we'll move on. We'll sell the stock. There'll be a lot of signals to us, like earnings disappointments or management telling us something and doing something different. They may deliberately raise the expectations and not meet them.

There is a hedge manager I know named Nandu Narayanan. He is originally from India. He's a hedge fund manager in New York, and it was

interesting because he said, "I can be right 50 percent of the time and wrong 50 percent of the time and make a lot of money for you. If I make $3 when I'm right and lose $1 when I'm wrong, I'll make a lot of money and I don't even have to be right more than wrong."

That's a good analogy, yeah. We don't have to be superheroes. I don't know if it's 50/50. About 60 percent of the time, if you're right, you're going to make a lot of money. But you have to know when to fold, and I guess that has been my strength. I'm not too concerned about selling things if things don't work out. Hopefully, it doesn't happen too often. You don't want to be wrong again and again and again, or that means your whole process is flawed, but it's absolutely going to happen. I mean, if somebody says they never make mistakes, they're lying.

So cutting losses quickly if you're wrong is a key?
Yeah, cutting losses.

Which is not inherent in human nature. They want to hold on to the losers instead of sell them.
True. I think somehow value investors justify the fact that they average down. To me, that's fatal. That's the worst thing you can do is average down. I'd rather average up because, most of the time, things are looking pretty darned good. So I differ from value investors there.

Are you familiar with Richard Driehaus in Chicago, the father of momentum investing? Buy high, sell higher?
Right, but he blew up though at some point.

He blew up in 2001, 2002 because he took a huge bet when tech went down and he loaded more money into it and then it got hit again. Yeah.
Well, the lesson to be learned is: Sure you can be very smart, but never take your eye off doing your proper fundamental analysis. If things are getting too far, companies which keep on going up are going to blow up.

If you disliked an industry for a macro reason, would you sell a really good stock in that industry that you had bought before?
Very rarely I will be in industry where I don't want to be. Technology is an example. It's not that there are not too many good technology companies.

There's a lot of reasons. I just inherently am very weak in technology to begin with. Secondly, I do believe that, to me an interesting thing has happened. Commodities used to be so-called cyclical stocks and had no growth, going back twenty years, because we had been in a bear market for so long. Everybody said technology stocks were the growth stocks. Now I think you are seeing the reverse. Commodities are so scarce, and because it's so hard to replace them, you're getting more and more pricing power. With the pricing power you get the earnings and cash flows and so on. With technology companies, they're becoming more and more commoditized. Of course, you'll have periods where these guys will make a lot of money, but that time span is shrinking. So there's a big risk in technology, just from that point of view. I mean, you've seen that in television sets, with the flat television screens. I bought Fujitsu a couple of years ago—top of the line—for $10,000, and I paid too much. It's now $3,000. Now, look at energy. It's very hard to replace what you're taking out. To me, that's uncanny how the world has shifted.

In technology, you can do a lot more volume, but your profit is being cut dramatically.

Yeah, exactly…exactly. Like your prices are just getting knocked down. There will still be companies which will maintain their superiority, but it'll just be for a short period.

Obviously, in the last few years, you've made a lot of the money in commodities. How did you do it in the '70s, '80s, '90s? It's interesting to see how it changed over time.

The only time I had some technology in Canada was because Nortel became a 30 percent index weight. I will lie to you if I say I never owned Nortel. I did own Nortel. I don't think we lost money, but it was never probably more than 4 or 5 percent of the portfolio. Given the TSE, we were still way underweight. In that period, I think we did have technology stocks like the Celesticas, three or four names in Canada where we made a lot of money. I had some involvement for that period, but prior to that at London Life, it was very, very small.

How would you make money in the early '90s?

Well, we had some very strong growth companies. Loblaws was a growth company. Canadian Tire was a growth company. To some extent, banks had their periods where they would show some good growth. Companies like financial conglomerates, Power Corp and the mutual fund companies were also examples. Those were all growth companies then and we were heavily involved in those.

What were some of the growth companies in the '80s in Canada? Do you remember who those were?

Thomson was a growth company. Now see how the world changes. Moore Corp was also a growth company.

I think 70 percent of the market was resources in the '70s, in the Canadian market.

In the '70s, yeah, yeah. I started actually having the fund in 1981. I was a student of the market, of course, and those were, I tell you, terrifying years. That's when you saw the interest rates in Canada went to 18 percent. There were 18 percent bonds out there!

How do you make money in stocks in those years? It's got to be very hard. Why are you ever going to invest in stocks when you can get 18 percent in bonds?

So I guess I lucked out in the sense that I came in '81 when most of the dreadful stuff had already passed. But still, it was a volatile period, you know, when we had the '87 crash and so on. I did very well during all that period.

Do you remember, just for fun, what some of your biggest stock wins have been over the years?

More recently?

Well, sure or throughout the past. Any that have stuck out in your mind?

Oh, yeah, yeah, we had some—I made some brilliant trades. I have to go back and think. What was the stock? Not Kinross, oh gosh, yeah. These guys had a mine up in the northwest—Echo Bay. Echo Bay went to $19. That was the top and I sold so many million shares. So I've done some brilliant trades in terms of percent gains. By the way, I think that's something I am good at, which not too many managers are. The timing of some trades has been very, very good. So in terms of stocks, the big winners—more recently, of course—

are all in resource. With First Quantum, I did a financing at $3, and it ended up at $60, but I should tell you, I sold most of my stock at $28, $30. I was very happy, but sometimes we do sell early.

Paladin?

Paladin, of course, yeah. From $0.30 to $9 when we sold. In the bigger fund, you can't have the emerging type stocks. Paladin did go in there once it became a reasonable company at $1 or something like that, so I had a four- or five-bagger in that. If you talk about the other funds, we had so many five-, six-, seven-baggers, but they were all sort of emerging companies. Equinox is another example, you know. We were in there at $0.60 and now it's $4.

Profico, well, we were long in all the stocks earlier.

Okay, fantastic. What's the biggest mistakes you've ever made that has lost you the most amount of money? Was there anything you learned from that?

Oh, lots, yeah. Well, biggest mistake most recently was a gaming company and a coal company.

Great Canadian?

No, no, the same group. Grande Cache Coal was a big mistake and one mistake we made was that we didn't see the management. We were so excited about that area and for good reasons. They had infrastructure and everything given to them basically. But I saw the management and it was just unbelievable. They were so bad, so I lost a lot of money on that stock. I got caught in that whole thing. It's partly stupidity, partly just not doing your homework properly. You know, we do get carried away.

[Since the interview, Grande Cache has rallied again on positive fundamentals for the sector.]

I guess that's about experience. You've been doing it for thirty years, which means you've probably made more mistakes than somebody who's been doing it five years, which means you've learned a lot more.

The lesson is that the people are so important behind these companies, especially with the young companies. If the management is not capable or skilled, then it's going to hurt. Back to winners: Wheaton—what was the name before Silver Wheaton?

Wheaton River?

Wheaton River, yeah. So they all became five-, ten-baggers for us. We were early, because we had trust in that area. We did very well in the oil service companies, and Cameco has been a huge success.

I remember Cameco just languished and languished for years, and people said what a lousy company and business it was. Potash, you know, was another one. Now we've talked, I guess, a lot about the big picture, but stock specific, when you're looking at a stock, what do you look for?

If you do the quant in our portfolio, we want that portfolio to show very high earnings growth compared to the overall general market. Currently, it'll show earnings growth from this year to next year of around 25 to 30 percent. We want to make sure that the stocks that we have are continuing to show their earnings momentum. So we look at the quarterly earnings. We want to make sure they're not giving you negative surprises, because that concerns us. Usually, if you have one, you have to be careful there are not more, and once that happens, the stock cannot outperform. So our portfolio always will have high earnings growth. Its earnings and cash flow would look very, very strong.

I would not own Google because of that reason. If you buy a stock—a high growth stock which is priced at perfection—you know you're going to lose money. Maybe not in three months or maybe six months. All you need is a small little negative surprise and boom!

That's right, you see a stock that has 50 percent earnings growth and the stock tanks. It's because the market expected 70 percent earnings growth.

If it's trading at ten times earnings, I don't think it will tank too far. Then maybe we'll buy more.

Do you have to change your parameters for mining stocks or oil and gas?

For emerging companies, that's always been a hard one to explain because I've been in companies which have no earnings. The only way I can explain that is to say we are confident in their future. FNX is an example. They may have now a deposit of eighteen to twenty million tons right in Sudbury, Ontario. It has a huge profit margin and the grades that they have come out with are just unbelievable if you do the calculations. Of course, when all this happens, your earnings are just going to go straight up. That's part of the anticipation. We are so confident that it'll be there that we are willing to stick our neck out. This is even though it doesn't 100 percent follow the growth criteria, which means that you have to have earnings. It doesn't mean that you have to have earnings now. That's how we justify it. It doesn't necessarily mean that it has to be earning now, but it is going to be there.

I guess to talk about particular areas, do you think we're in a commodities supercycle that's going to last for eighteen years?

We do. That doesn't mean we will not have corrections. The market does tend to overextend itself from time to time. There will be a lot of scares. People will be focusing on even the minutest signal that things are slowing down somewhere and that can create some havoc in the markets. Beyond that, the fundamental trend is still very strong. We are in an environment where demand is going to be much higher than what the supply is going to be for a lot of commodities, so you can call it a supercycle.

When you look back in history, this has happened many, many times.

Well, there's lead and lags, lead and lags. It's because it took awhile for analysts to recognize that the oil prices are going to stay high. Until a year or two ago, they were still using $25 or $30 for oil, and now maybe the pendulum is moving too far, I don't know. In the case of metals, it's still way below where the spot prices are. So you're going to see more and more earnings in the upside. So as long as that's happening, as growth managers, that's a great attribute to have.

I always found it interesting that analysts seem to be lemmings: followers rather than leaders.

Of course, of course, absolutely.

Why is that? I mean, they're very smart people, I imagine.

Oh, you know what? It's the same thing like indexation. They are not going to be fired if they stay close to a consensus, even if it doesn't make sense. It's the same analogy as the typical fund manager who basically is a closet indexer, but the good ones will take their own stand. That's the way I can explain it, I think.

Let's just talk for a second about the hedge fund. Why did you start the hedge fund and what's the goal for that?

What did Eric say about his hedge fund? We are very competitive, you know.

He said, "I started the hedge funds in 2000 because I thought we were entering a big bear market and I thought I could make money doing that." He has a totally different philosophy in that respect.

Exactly, yeah. No, that was not the reason. I had a different reason. There are a lot of things we cannot do in the mutual funds, as you know. It allowed us a lot more flexibility and to get into areas very early, which the big funds do not allow us to do. I was just very, very confident that I would be able to raise money because I had a good record. I will tell you, I never, ever thought that we would have such good performance. It has been a ten-bagger, and, of course, I'd be dishonest if I didn't say that it was one way for me to catch up with all the other guys. You know, at London Life, you never had the ability to get the kind of compensation that some independent money managers did. This allowed us, only if we performed, to catch up. We only get paid if we perform in these funds.

I'm taking more risk and getting bigger returns. You know, in fact, for every incremental unit of volatility, the return increase is quite steep. The volatility will be high, but so will the return. This is why we have a big high entry level in this thing, you know. That's one thing I was scared of. If we have good performance, the people are going to be coming in. We wanted to make sure investors understand that this is something that you leave for a long time to make it work. In the meantime, it worked much better than I expected. The strategy is the same, except here we take leverage. We go into companies which are at a much riskier stage, then let them become mature, as Paladin did. If I didn't have that kind of outlook in my mind, I probably would have missed it. I probably would have just stuck with Cameco. The hedge fund is allowing me to look at companies at a much, much earlier level, which gives us the opportunity for two- or three-baggers.

Your hedge fund has prompted you to look at other ideas which can increase the performance of your other funds too?

Absolutely. In fact, Alex Lane is doing the small cap. I handed it over. That was performing as well as the hedge fund, with no performance fee. Nobody ever noticed. So they said, "Have you noticed that this fund is up 70 percent and there's no performance fee there?" Nobody cared.

Now you have a lot of extra tools you can use in the fund. What type of market environment would you use for shorts?

I have to be honest. I'm really a long manager, okay? It's nice to have the ability to short, no doubt, if you can manage volatility from time to time. We have done that in some cases. But I would categorize it more as a long opportunity fund. I think shorting stocks is a very different skill. It requires a very different skill set and I'm not sure whether that will be a big contributor to my overall performance.

I think I know the answer to this. You wouldn't do anything like pairs trading or shorting the index against your long positions?

Well, that's a different ballgame, you know. That's for different funds which are market neutral. I don't want to be trying to do everything. I just tell people, "Listen, this is an opportunity-driven fund; that's why it's risky." So if you want to be there for three years, just put ten percent of your total assets in and it'll do wonderful things. I don't want to change that very much, knowing that there are times when we will have to manage volatility on the markets. Beyond that, I think it'll remain as an opportunity-driven long fund.

You've mentioned a couple times in your reports that you're looking at reducing the volatility in the fund. I, for one, hope you don't do that because you can give up returns, right?

Yeah, hopefully not without the returns.

I think you can always still reduce volatility by following certain procedures. Our first discipline on the sell side is to take your losses early if you're wrong, but we can still do a better job. We always strive to make improvements on that equation.

I'm not a big fan necessarily of statistical analysis, but your documentation says you have an R-squared of 0.49. This means that only half of your return is attributable to the market and the other half is attributable to stock picking ability.

Well, we are creating huge alpha. Yeah, when you buy stocks like FNX, that's all alpha. It's got nothing to do with the market, or very little anyway.

What has been your biggest mistake in the Power Hedge recently?

In the Power Hedge, we got into Internet gaming. Luckily, it was not a big investment, but we basically lost all of our money in that because the government changed the rules. I had a lot of hopes for that company. The people behind it were pretty sharp, and they were U.S.-based guys. That was a disaster.

How many stocks do you own in the Power Hedge? I see it's pretty concentrated.

Yeah, it will always be concentrated. The top twenty names, I guess, basically explain the performance in the fund.

With a concentrated portfolio of small cap names, liquidity is important. When that stops, it usually stops pretty fast and bids dry up.

Yeah, liquidity can work both ways. It can also create bubbles. We saw that in the Shanghai market because it was clearly a bubble and people buy stock just based on how many eights they have in the symbol. Eight is supposed to be an auspicious number for the Chinese. It's a closed-in market— there's no outlet. You probably will see that in other areas of the market too. However, this Chinese position on Blackstone suggests that you are probably going to see more exposure in equities.

A different type of liquidity is the liquidity in small cap stocks. It dries up dramatically when it dries up. Have you looked at that and what percentage of companies you own and how liquid they are for you?

We have done a very good job of managing liquidity. One way we manage that risk of making big bets on small cap names is just to make darn sure that we know those companies well inside out—the fundamentals. For instance, in September of '06, one of the stocks we had, Dynatec, came off sharply and we had a big holding. We did our homework and we bought twenty million shares at $1.40. Guess where the price went? It went to $5, so it works both ways. I think if you manage properly for that kind of volatility, it can create huge opportunities in the kind of names that we own. We'll only take a big position in companies that we are absolutely convinced are big winners. Equinox was another example. The stock hit $1.40 and we were the biggest buyers. It went to $5. So to us, that's an opportunity. We have to make darn sure we know the company well. We spend a lot of time making sure that the names that we have we know inside out.

Why does this volatility happen in the market?

You've got a lot of hedge fund managers who are running around trying to perform by trading mindlessly. On any bad news, they all run for the exit at the same time. So that's part of it. But again, for people like us who have done their homework, it's an opportunity.

It's interesting because the economy can do well over periods of time and the stock market doesn't do well at all. In 1966 to 1982, the economy grew in the U.S. by four or five times, but the stock market did nothing.

That's a very good question. I think the obvious answer for that would be what the interest rates were doing and what the overall inflationary environment was. What was the overall environment for earnings? Economies can still grow, but if you have very high inflation and it's moving higher, like a stagflation type of environment, that is a problem. Stocks don't do well in a stagflation environment. I think that period can be described as a stagflation. One of the things that the market is concerned about now is that we may be going through that period because we're concerned about commodity prices telling us something. I would refute that. It is not the case. But that's one of the reasons why we are seeing a little bit more volatility. Inflation is going higher and we may be entering the same type of period. So I think in that environment, equities will have a hard time because your P/Es are going to get compressed.

Right, so the market revalues itself based on interest rates.

Yeah.

I think you're of the belief that oil's going to stay relatively high in price. Is that because of the increasing demand from China and India and the supply going down? In other words, have we reached peak production in the world and we're not going to be able increase production rates for the demand that's out there?

Well, we will be producing more oil from probably different areas. Russia probably will be able to increase production. Saudis may still have incremental capacity of maybe two million barrels. In other areas, like the U.S., production has been going down. The Gulf of Mexico is the only area where the production's going up, but the hurricanes take care of that. I think the bottom line is demand will grow faster than the supplies, so it'll get reflected in the pricing.

The economists and the naysayers say supply always catches up with demand, so it's only going to be for a short period of time and then oil prices will go right back down again. That isn't necessarily going to be the case this time?

It'll catch up, but it depends on what time period. In the meantime, it will create huge opportunity. That's becoming a very big thing for us. Not just the oil sands production, but they're spending a $100 billion on the whole infrastructure. Can you imagine how well some of these little companies will do?

You ever looked at Connacher Oil and Gas?

I don't own that, but I know a little bit about the company—but I don't own that stock. I own Producers—I own Flint and companies like that.

What's your average turnover, do you think, in the portfolio?

In the big fund? It's above average, no doubt. I don't sweat too much about it. I know traditionalists want a low turnover, and a lot of managers make a point of saying that our turnover is less than one and so on. We do trade around our core positions, which adds to the turnover. So our turnover will be more than one, probably. Somewhere between one and two or even as high as three from time to time.

It depends on the market, I guess.

It depends on the market and it also depends on flows. Surprisingly, the turnover in the hedge fund is not going to be very high because I always have new money coming in, so I'm not forced to sell. In the bigger funds, I don't have those kind of flows. With the big mature funds, it's not very easy to count on new money coming in, unless you were at London Life. At London Life, we had no problem. Every month there was a $100 million coming in. So yeah, the turnover will be above average.

You've talked about the fact that India and China—or India and Asia—are going to be huge growers over time. Doesn't it seem that Canada's resource market is the way to play that in a lot of respects? Or Australia?

Yes, for resources, you are right. But you can go a step further and say, okay, China and India are where America was fifty, sixty years ago. People were buying cars after the war, as an example. We had the emergence of a middle class—call it a boom. That's exactly what's going on at a much larger scale.

So you can participate in that. Retail in India is still not there, and imagine once they start building that out. It's there, but it's all ma-and-pop, so once that gets consolidated, watch out.

Wal-Mart isn't in India yet?

Not yet, but they are looking at it, yeah. I think the Indians are very smart. They will probably beat them to the punch. They will start their own Wal-Mart. So that's what's going on. So it's a huge opportunity. You're investing in what Canada was many years ago. Then we were buying Canadian Tire, plus you have technology and you have health and pharmaceutical.

I've forgotten his name—he's the Bill Gates of India. He's a very wealthy software guy.

Yeah, the guys are from Infosys.

They were interviewing him a while ago on TV and they said there's a technology school in India which is extremely difficult to get into.

IIT.

They said, "We understand that your son wasn't accepted to the university." And he said, "That's right. My son's marks weren't high enough to get in." They said, "Where's your son going instead?" He said, "Instead, he took a fully paid scholarship to MIT." He got in there, but he couldn't get into IIT.

Oh, yeah, that's so true.

I mean, if one in a thousand get in, you can imagine the quality that must come out of there. What other industries, for the next few years, are the industries to be in?

Yeah, but the infrastructure is going to be huge. When I say *infrastructure,* I use the term very loosely. That could mean anything. For example, we own United Technologies because they make aircraft engines and they make Otis elevators. They are into cooling systems, and things related. Those kind of business give them a window to participate in what is happening in Asia at the same time too. So it's all related to infrastructure. Transocean is an oil service company we own, which is building these huge platforms. They are booked for the next ten years, so they've been raising prices every three months. They started at a hundred thousand a day; now it's five hundred thousand a day and there's still a line up. That thing is not going to stop. There's huge commitments, and the big guys, they haven't been able to grow. So that's part of infrastructure. Of course, there are roads, bridges, airports, and power plants. There's so many ways to participate in those. Even our Canadian company, SM—I'm sorry, the guys who own....

SNC-Lavalin.

Yeah, SNC-Lavalin. I won't buy it. It's expensive, but it's sort of in that category. In the U.S. there is Fluor and Emerson. I think that is going to be a huge area. Alternative energies are talked about, which would include ethanol, and, well, uranium is part of it.

Have you made money, and participated in gold stocks in the past? Gold is something that's different because it's not used for anything other than jewellery or a store of wealth. People panic and buy gold if things are going badly.

I have made money, but my timing has not been perfect. I was very good at getting out. I go into gold stocks reluctantly, I have to admit that. Their return on capital is crummy. It's only now I think they have started making some decent returns. Compared to what copper guys can do, it's not there. People buy gold not for the economic reasons, they buy gold mostly for investment reasons, or they buy because of fear and currency hedging or a hedge against everything else in the world. In fact, if we are all going to die, then what good is gold?

There's been a lot of times when gold has done really well in price, but the stocks haven't. In 1987, gold stocks dropped 25 percent in value with the market, but gold went up in value. So the gold stocks a lot of times don't necessarily give you the hedge that they're supposed to.

I think it's just because there are times when people just don't like any paper. They just buy the commodity. Then you will see the stocks lagging. There are other times when earnings are not keeping up with the gold price. When gold was $280 or $300, none of these guys were making money. The only way they could survive was by going into the best, highest grades. Now, number one, the grade's a lot lower, and secondly, they had to buy back their hedge positions at a big price. They're doing it, which is fine, but it affects their profitability. The point I was making is it's been very difficult for gold companies to actually make money.

They have had rising commodity prices too. Energy especially?

Yeah, that was also a factor. Glamis we own. Barrick seems like they're getting their act together. So it's looking more interesting, and if you think gold could stay over $800 or even higher, these companies will make a lot of money.

Some value guys loaded up on Glamis when it got hit in price.

Yeah, we all do that. I don't know why value guys think they are the only ones to do these things.

You use a lot of common sense and are opportunistic, right? Are you ever going to retire from this?

You know, I am over 60 years old. It's a very trying business, especially the way I manage money. It's tiring.

Out on the golf course, I've seen the value guys were all playing golf having fun and you're on the cell phone calling in to the market. It's a lot more active, right? It puts a lot more stress and strain on you.

I'm probably very hard on myself too because I have the competitive juices. I still always want to be at the top of the take. It's a very high-pressure game to be always at the top.

I read an article recently in the _Forbes,_ billionaires in the world, and the interesting thing was that there were three things that they all had in common. First, they all became rich by owning equity. Obviously, none of them ever got rich in bonds. Second, they're usually older, unless they inherited it, which makes sense. But the third thing was that most of them still worked, whether it's Jimmy Pattison in the west or Bill Gates. They have a passion for what they do.

Of course, yeah. If I don't do this, I have no idea what the hell I will do. For two weeks—three weeks, maybe—I'll say, "Wow, this is so good." I'm sure after that I'll miss it.

I don't know if you've ever quantified this, but if you could put three rules down on paper that you never break, what would they be? You talked about not falling in love with a stock. You've anticipated very, very well. You cut your losses quickly. You're good at timing, and management is important in the stocks that you own.

No, they are absolutely part of it. The list could go longer—much longer—but those are very important prerequisites, yes.

If you could think of one key to your success, what would it be?

Stay humble. Please, stay humble. Never think that you know it all. One thing I probably should say is that people try to emulate others. I never do. I admire a lot of people—I have a lot of respect for them—but you have to do your own thing. When people say that I do what Warren Buffett does, you can't say that. To me, it's become a cottage industry to say that you are Warren Buffett. I think to be successful, you really have to develop your own process. You can't follow. You can't copy others, because you don't know what those guys are thinking.

Throughout your thirty-five years, you haven't always been playing resource. What do you see is the next thing for the fund? Is it biotech or tech or another area?

We always had interest in those areas. With biotech, it's hard to find a company where they're actually going to make money. The cash flow that we are seeing is in the energy and resource area, but we have diversified, including in the Power Hedge. The infrastructure area is becoming a more interesting theme for us. Agribusiness in the middle of '07 is becoming a little more interesting theme for us. With resources, we still see that as being in a super-cycle. We don't think there will be lack of opportunities there. We still like that area a lot.

I guess it gets to the point where a stock like Cisco Systems has doubled or tripled their earnings in the last seven years; however, the stock is still down 70 percent. When do stocks get to the point when they're way overvaluing their future earnings growth, even though their future earnings growth will be good?

Well, in the case of commodities, that's not the case whatsoever. We're beginning to see the re-rating of these companies because I guess they are no longer using historical prices as the long term. Analysts are late in the game, and are only now raising their forward-looking commodity price targets, like for nickel and copper.

You mentioned this would happen when I saw you in Tucson. You said analysts are going to start raising their estimates in their commodity price forecasts, and that's going to raise the stock prices. I guess that's what's happened.

Look at Alcan, even after the big run, after the takeover, it's only eight times EBITDA? Given where the interest rates are, these stocks are still very cheap.

[Alcan turned out to be one the best stocks on the market in 2007 and was purchased by Rio Tinto.]

Now, you're originally from India. Tell us again about what you see in the Indian market.

I'm hugely, hugely, hugely optimistic on that. I think India is still not fully recognized. The next five years, I think, it will become even more interesting because now you're going to see the beginning of a catching-up with the Chinese. They're pretty determined that they want to do that.

You have a nice house there too.

I don't have a nice house now. I have a small place that's being built in Goa. That'll become our satellite office, if you want to call it that. I think the whole region will be what's going to drive the rest of the world in terms of where the opportunities are.

China's been mainly where the manufacturing has happened, and India is where the service companies are?

Yes, not just service, but you're right. Compared to China, IT-wise, they're the leader. They're spreading into some very interesting areas. You saw some of the acquisitions now being made by several steel companies and so on. Even on the manufacturing side, I think you're going to see opportunities. So it's becoming much broader.

You cut your position back by half in India, I think in early '07?

Yeah, it was more valuation. We found that some other regions like Brazil were more attractive. In the names that we have, we are very comfortable with the valuations. But we will reallocate our exposure to different regions depending on where the best valuations are.

Mathematically, you're doing exactly what somebody should do managing a fund, but it's very hard on the nerves to increase leverage when things are going down.

Yeah, it is nerve-wracking. You're right, yeah.

Explain, maybe, the process of doing that.

I think to us, that really is big. It helps to manage the volatility and the risk part of the equation.

In May, June, and July of 2006, did you increase the leverage in those months?

Yeah, I think we were increasing our leverage during that period. In September, we did certainly. The example I gave, with the stocks that we were buying, was part of that process.

Right. I think you've been doing some planning as to how to hedge out risk of things going in the wrong direction. Is that something you can talk about?

One thing that comes to your mind is the geopolitical environment. For instance, what if you have a terrorist attack in places like New York? God forbid it's something like a nuclear device. That would be devastating. Markets are not going to respond well in that environment. How do you protect yourself? It's very hard. In terms of macro shifts, inflation is probably one of the big factors. We worry about what's happening on the agricultural side—the food crisis, for instance. A lot of that, unfortunately, is induced by wrong policies in the U.S. They're promoting ethanol at the expense of anything else. They can get it at half the price from Brazil, in the form of sugarcane, which has got a higher octane. They won't do that, but they want to promote farmers because it brings them some votes. I'm sure politics are involved in some of the decisions.

It takes more energy to create ethanol from corn, right?

It takes more energy and it also creates inflation in other areas. That worries me a lot. What worries me is this strife that's going on in China and U.S. in terms of trade barriers. One thing that has helped the whole globalization is bringing the trade barriers down, and it's created a lot of wealth around the world, everywhere. You don't want the barriers to come in. That worries me. We talked about excess liquidity and how it creates bubbles here and there. That would create more volatility, so that does worry me.

The index is becoming narrower and narrower as companies continue to get taken out. Just back to shorting again, can you even short in markets like India and China?

You can short in the Indian market. In fact, the derivative market is pretty robust and it's very active. But we haven't really done very much of that, no. We are more interested in the long-term. Like I said, we will reduce our exposure if we think there's relative attractiveness in other regions.

In the past and in the future, most of your returns are going to be made in smaller stocks that have higher growth rates. Obviously, you can double your earnings in a small company, but Petro-Canada can't double their earnings next year very easily. Will you go to large caps if you see more upside there? Small caps become overvalued at particular times.

Yeah, true. Then we do sell them. If you look at the top ten positions today, compared to a year ago, some of them were taken out—Dynatec and a few others. In Paladin, we sold all our position. We had such a big position, but we sold it all. What we like to see is, if I buy a stock in the Power Hedge given the type of risk we are willing to take, we would expect at least a 50-percent return. If we can get it in a large cap stock, we will buy it too. Alcan was a good example.

The stock that I hang onto myself is UEX. I've owned it a long time. I saw it in your top ten. When you look at its valuation, it's valued higher than most of the uranium stocks for how much they have in the ground. Is that right?

It is. But it's the only real deposit in the world. If you look at the grade, it's just unbelievable. It's part of the whole Athabasca Basin. There's more to come. There are associations with companies like AREVA and Cameco and that is a big plus. It's a matter of time, I think, before somebody's going to take a shot at it. If they do, the stock will be a lot higher than where it is now.

Right. I guess it's going to be a few years before they get any uranium out of the ground, versus companies like Energy Metals and some of the other ones that produce in the near term. That's a risk if uranium prices drop a lot five years down the road. That's going to be a risk to the valuation of the stocks.

Yeah, well true. Related to UEX, even if the prices drop, they've got such a huge margin. It's such a rich deposit and it's deep in the ground. I think in terms of what their cost is going to be, even if you're looking at a $20 cost, it still provides a huge margin.

I think in '07 you started looking at natural gas stocks again?

Yeah, we went back, and I went to Calgary and saw the companies that I had an interest in, mostly mid caps, companies like Proex and Crew. We also saw Kereco. We were shareholders of all these companies a couple years ago. They were all very well managed companies, except the gas price came down pretty hard. It was the perfect storm for them. Not only that, the cost went up too. We thought that would be a good area, and these stocks began to perform as the gas prices recovered.

In the last five years, when oil and gas hasn't done well, mining has done well. When mining hasn't done well, oil and gas has done well. If neither one of those did well, gold did well.

Within the resources, you always have these opportunities, you're right. I don't know about gold though. Gold is one area that I'm a little confused about. At higher prices, they're making less money. They're disappointing on the earning side, unlike the metals and some of the energy companies. I think if you pick smaller junior companies which are doing exciting exploration, you'll be fine because they will be taken out by the bigger guys. So that's where the attractiveness is.

When you look at the M&A, the reason that the big companies are taking out the small ones is because they find it cheaper to do than to go explore for themselves.

True. Also, it's part of their risk management. They let the little guys go and take the risk. Once they have come out with a discovery, they'll go in there. They would rather pay up a little bit rather than take the first shot.

What are your thoughts with regard to a lot of these countries nationalizing?

There's a reason to worry, but I believe, as we see the prosperity spreading to the rest of the world, that common sense will prevail. It is easier said than done, I know. We would have never gone to Congo, for instance, if we were worried about the political risk. I think this globalization will bring the overall risk down.

It's happened with Ivanhoe, Western Prospector, Aurelian, and Khan, just to name a few.

If they can come to some kind of an agreement, I don't blame the governments either. The governments are just coming out of sort of the dark ages. They have an opportunity now and they want to make sure that the deals that they make with foreign investments are right. Even the Canadian government does that. As you saw, the Liberals are now saying that we should have a moratorium against foreign takeovers. I hope it doesn't happen because we are part of the free-enterprise world.

Recently, you were rated as one of the best money managers by *Equity* magazine.

Yeah, they came in and they wanted to do an interview. Then they wanted to do a little more regular stuff. So I talked to them about how I view, basically, the natural resource sector. Some of the stuff that I'm just talking about here, I talked about in that article.

Is there anything else you wanted to get into?

The most interesting thing, in my opinion, is this whole globalization. This doesn't happen very frequently what we are going through. You have such a large chunk of the population that now have the opportunity to improve their standard of living. It's a very rare phenomenon, especially that there are so many people participating in it. It's actually beginning to work if you look at what's happening in China and other parts of the world. It's trickling down to, the rural areas and so on.

This was something that people talked about in the early '90s. You had the Asian Tigers and India and China, and it didn't work out at the time as well as it could've. Why was that and how's it different now?

Yeah, that's a good question. I guess the Asian Tiger was first. I don't think China and India were part of it, so you were looking at a much smaller scale. You had the Malaysia Tiger, and you did have Korea, which was going through an industrialization stage. In fact, Korea worked out very well. They are now a very advanced economy. The others were more export-related. I don't think they had a set of policies which were based on sound foundations. They had huge current account deficits and so on. They were very vulnerable on the currency side and their focus was more export-driven. Now, when we're talking about three billion people, the shift can be greater. That's why it's more interesting. China's got now currency reserves of 1.3 trillion U.S. dollars. When we had the collapse, they had no reserve. They had deficits, and so did India. So it has been a huge reversal.

Here's one thing I find a little confusing. You have this huge cost inflation that seems to be happening with the oil sands and with the gold companies. They are not profitable even though the price is higher. But you don't see the inflation in the CPI numbers. Is this because of the cheap imports coming in?

Yeah, I think....

That can't go on forever.

Cheap imports—well, it can go on for a long, long time, but it's not just imports. You're seeing enormous productivity improvements, even in the developed economies. I mean, Europe was growing at a pretty fast pace with low inflation, even with high commodity prices. Technology is a big part of it.

If we go back to stocks, I'll bring up Cisco again. It's a great company. They've doubled their earnings and the stock is still down 70 percent from the high. So is that something that you always look at, the price of the company compared to the growth rate?

Well you always have to. You mentioned Cisco, I guess, because it became part of the NASDAQ bubble.

Yeah, I just mentioned it because it's still a good company.

Well, NASDAQ is probably going to take another ten years before it gets to the level that we saw in 2001, because it got so inflated. That typically happens when you go through a bubble. So the question is, are we going to go through another bubble in other areas? Yes and no. We probably went through it in the housing sector. We had four years of a huge boom, and now it's correcting itself. It will come out of the woods, though, very similar to what happened in the U.K. If interest rates go to 10 percent, then it's very different.

So you don't see stagflation over the next few years.

I think it's more the central banks will have to manage growth.

What's China going to do with their $1.3 trillion in reserves?

They say they're going to buy equities. So it's a good thing.

Right. How about increasing their gold reserves?

I guess they could do that. It looks like strategically they want to buy oil sands. They want to buy commodities and so on. That's where the focus seems to be.

There's a parallel universe here. On one basis, the Chinese are our friends and we're trading with them. The other thing is that they're building up their military and we're kind of afraid of that. It's funny because it seems that each area is not paying attention to the other one. If China owns the oil sands, and China owns more resources, is that going to be okay for the world economy or do you think the Chinese are still communists politically?

They are adversaries. Why should America be the only country that has a right to arm itself? Now, if you were the Chinese, you would say, "Why can't we spend money on arms?" It can be destabilizing, I suppose, because you have the issue of Taiwan and so on. I would be very surprised if Americans think they're going to have a war over Taiwan with the Chinese.

Forgetting about peak oil, it seems like oil prices are going to be high for some period of time because there's just not any discoveries compared to the demand. Is that something you see?

The Chinese are going to have 100 million cars, right? They have about 20 million now, in a very short period. They're all going to run on petrol. It's not going to run on air, wind, or anything else.

Ethanol or solar?
I don't think the supply is catching up with the demand for oil.

People talk about replacing oil, but that's going to take twenty, twenty-five years?
On the market, we saw that solar became a popular thing in the '80s. None of the companies made any money and a lot of them disappeared. I'm not saying that it's a bad thing. Now the oil price is high enough that you can justify it again. But making money in an area which is subsidized by the government usually is a disaster.

Do you see the uranium prices still continuing to go up in the long run?
Well, if you talk to guys like John Borshoff—the guy from Paladin, who I have a lot of respect for—he thinks it's going to go to $250 easily. He said, "You have no idea on the supply and demand. In fact, some of the projections you see on the supply side are so very far-fetched." He thinks there's going to be more huge disappointments. The utilities are more interested in security of supply. They'll tell you it's only 2 percent of their cost the last time I saw. It's not going to make a huge difference, not at all. That's why you have to be bullish on uranium, you know?

Thanks for your time.
My pleasure.

Eric Sprott
Hitting Home Runs

"You want a stock to act good, early. You want confirmation that you're not the only guy in there, that you're seeing value and the stock's starting to sprint the minute you get going. The other guys see you coming and say, 'Man, I've been sitting here in the weeds and some other guy's buying it. I got to get in there.'"

Eric Sprott is at the top of the heap among money managers in Canada. Few, if any, managers have put up the numbers that Sprott has over the past quarter of a century. The Sprott Managed Accounts have an annualized return since 1982 of almost 25 percent a year. The TSE over this time frame averaged about 10 percent per year. Now hold on to your hat, because $100,000 invested in the Sprott Managed Accounts in 1982 would be worth about $40 million today! Over this time frame, a $100,000 investment in the TSE in would be worth about $1 million. Can you imagine having invested at the beginning? Well, according to Eric, there are investors that have been invested with him for fifteen, twenty years or more. "Eric won't look at a stock unless it is a possible multi-bagger," said one of the senior portfolio managers at Sprott.

In October of 2005, I attended and spoke at a hedge fund conference in Niagara Falls, Ontario. On the way back through Toronto, I stopped into Sprott Asset Management (SAM) on Bay Street and took a tour of the office, courtesy of Ida Khajadourian. "Wide open spaces" are the operative words when you get a first glimpse of the meeting reception area. Decorating the area are beautiful Inuit stone carvings that must be worth a mint. Smartly polished, and very well displayed, they make the office more than just a reception area. Each room is garnished with a different art theme. One room might be the Group of Seven, and other rooms would be other famous artists. I think it is important to explain the office and work environment, as this tells a lot about who the person is and how they think. A very large open boardroom stands out as soon as you walk into the reception, with its panoramic views. This is where the firm's 8:15 a.m. legendary strategy meeting happens every morning. That's right. This is where some of the best and brightest money people in the country gather every morning to bounce ideas off each other. I have often written that not only is Eric a fantastic stock picker, but he also picks people to work with him like no other, including Allan Jacobs, another Stock Market Superstar.

In one corner is a very neat and modern-looking space, Eric Sprott's office. However, he spends little time there. The majority of the time, he spends his days parked at the end of the trading desk. This keeps him in the action, allowing him to do what he does best: pick stocks. This is not a guy who has "progressed" from the day-to-day grind that has made the firm so successful. Admittedly, he is far more interested in picking stocks than "running" the business. Does he need the money? Of course not, he has hundreds of millions of dollars, but stock picking is still his passion. I lusted over the modern exercise room that is available for the seventy-five employees of the firm, and it was good to see that the firm is progressive in the whole "healthy body, healthy mind" thing.

A chartered accountant by profession, having graduated from Carleton University in Ottawa, his credentials are different than most other successful money managers. The accounting background, he says, has been indispensable in helping him to be a good stock picker, relating to the reading and understanding of the financial statements. Although he is known for his big 'macro' calls, like a housing collapse, or the peak-oil theory, or the decline of the U.S. dollar, he says he was primarily a stock picker, and really didn't worry about the big picture in the beginning. As his style evolved, he could see that if he could get certain themes correct, it would enhance his stock picking abilities.

From the morning strategy session in which the employees participate, to the on-site fitness centre, to the fantastic performance, there is something that makes this firm different and a bit mysterious. I wanted to see what it was.

Did he ever question his abilities during poor times, and what happened in October 1987, when there was no bid for many of his stocks? On October 20, 1987, he turned to Anne Spork, who had been part of the business from the beginning, and said "We could be done." The bids came back, however, and he ended up 20 percent for the year.

The firm was still relatively small in 2000, when they managed about $200 million. Then the bear market hit, the hedge fund was started, and Sprott had the best track record of any hedge fund in the world over the next few years. Assets under management skyrocketed, and J.F. Tardif was hired as a portfolio manager. In his own right, he has blown most other hedge managers out of the water with his risk-adjusted returns. Firm assets grew in the next five years to well over $6 billion, causing a few changes to the strategy.

My first of many interviews took place in a large ballroom at the Four Seasons in Vancouver, just before Eric Sprott talked to about 150 financial advisors about his outlook. We sat at a table as they started to prepare the bar for the afternoon activities. With lots of background noise, we decided to move to a calmer location within the ballroom, with our glasses of water. He was a great storyteller, using lots of colourful language, like "getting his head kicked in," from time to time with his stock positions during different times in his career. When I asked him what the secret to his success was, quite simply he said, "I see things before others do, and I simply connect the dots." Over the next years, I became well acquainted with almost all of "What bugs Eric the most?" Having his flagship Sprott Canadian Equity Fund penalized by rating agencies because it is "volatile," even though it has averaged 28 percent per year over the last ten years. That sounds ludicrous to me also, and Eric set out to prove it. Over the ten years, he looked at rolling twelve months' returns of the fund to see how many twelve-month periods the fund unitholders would have been down. Lo and behold, as of early 2008, and for 160 rolling periods, the fund only had twelve down month periods, while the TSX index had thirty-three. I see why he is upset.

One of the best reads is to review Eric's monthly *Markets at a Glance* reports at www.sprott.com. They are among the most insightful pieces I have seen, including March 9, 2000, on the impending tech bust, or the uranium article in 2004, or the peak oil article in 2004 when oil was $35 per barrel. The list goes on. What is his most important theme for the next few years? Well, you just have to read the interview.

Bob:

On a personal note—I think this is an important part of it—what was your family background? Was your father in the business, or your mother, or any family member?

Eric:

No. My mother certainly had nothing to do with the business. My dad was with the tax department. He's from Toronto, and was a B.Comm., but he was interested in stocks, and he invested in stocks, probably when I was just becoming a teenager. So I was interested in that. So I got some, certainly some sense from my dad, and when I went in the business, we would have spoken a lot about investing. So, yes, I would say that the involvement of my dad was quite significant.

You have a CA, right?
Yes.

Did you plan on being an accountant?
Well, when I graduated from university, I thought there's two places I might want to go, and one is to be in the financial business, in the investment business. The other might be the real estate brokerage business, something like that. I thought a CA was probably the ticket into the financial business, so that's why I took the CA.

Did it help you at all in the business, the CA?
Oh, yeah, immensely.

Is that right?
Immensely. I think feeling comfortable with a financial statement is really important. You know, to think that you can actually delve through a few things—see if maybe something doesn't quite come together—that's important because lots of people, they can look at financials, but they really don't sort of read between the lines. A lot of times, you need to look at all three statements to see a problem, if there's a problem. So, no, I thought it was invaluable.

I guess the next step was you went to be an institutional broker, is that right?

Well, I went into research at Merrill Lynch. The reason I got the job was that a friend of mine was in the department and I had already shown a big interest in stocks. I was buying and selling stocks, and investing in those days. I would have been twenty-four, twenty-five, something like that, and the research department at Merrill Lynch wanted a computer programmer to work in their research department. I had worked for summers with IBM, the IBM data centre in Ottawa as a programmer. So it was a perfect combination for me to go in and be this computer programmer. It was supposed to be 90 percent of my job, and 10 percent was research, and it quickly became 90 percent research and 10 percent computer programming. Most of the data back in those days was all "garbage in, garbage out," so you couldn't come up with anything anyway.

Do you remember the first stock you ever invested in yourself? Not managing other people's money, but yourself?

Well, I remember the first stock I bought when I was eighteen years old. It was called Canadian Keeley. I think it traded at $0.15 or something. It was a ridiculous investment.

Did you lose all your money?

No, I don't think we lost all our money, but I'm sure we didn't make money.

So then you went from the sell side to the buy side.

Well, I went from research at Merrill Lynch to becoming a salesperson with what was called then Royal Securities, which Merrill had bought. I spent a year and a half in institutional sales, then I went to Loewen Ondaatje back in 1970. I spent roughly ten years there, and then started Sprott Securities in 1981. So I was institutional sales about a year and a half after I was in the business. For a year and a half, I was in research.

Now, an associate of yours said when you started Sprott Securities, you had $50,000. Somebody gave you $50,000 and then a lawyer and an accountant gave you money. How did that all work out?

No, I think what she might have been referring to is when I started off as an investor, I borrowed $50,000 from an individual, and used that as sort of my grub stake to get into the investment business.

When I started Sprott Securities, I would have had way more than that. I might have had a half a million of value at the time, so, yeah, I wasn't totally on a shoestring.

Your office, when I went in there, was beautiful. Tell us a little bit about the Native sculptures and art.

Yes. First of all, I'm colour blind and I have no artistic concept whatsoever. [Laughs] So when I started buying, I said, "You know, this Inuit art is kind of interesting." It's more shapes and a little bit of colour. I couldn't tell you the colour, but a lot of it was just shapes and a historical representation of our Native people. I thought, that kind of works with a Canadian brokerage company, so we'll collect that Inuit art. I used to have a thing where every time we did an underwriting, I would buy a piece of Inuit carving until we got to 1993, when we were involved in about fifty underwritings. It became overwhelming, so I stopped doing that.

Do you have a specific room for artists different from the Group of Seven?

Well, we do now—one room that has just Norval Morrisscau—so we have a room, the main boardroom, that's dedicated to Alex Colville. We have one room that's at Sprott Asset Management we call the Canadiana room, and it's Group of Seven and things like that. We try to make the rooms a little thematic. We have the chiefs room where we have pictures of Native chiefs from about the mid-1800s by a Canadian artist.

I found this interesting. You have your desk right with the traders.

When I sit on the trading desk, yes I do. I probably spend most of my day there.

Why? So you don't feel isolated in your office?

Well, most of the intense work that I do is probably not done in the office. I have lots of meetings in the office, so I'm not on the desk all day long, but you sort of get a sense of things that are going on if you're out on a trading desk and watching the market and so on. I'm not much of an administrator, so I don't have meetings as to where the business is going or great plans or anything like that. I like to spend time in front of the market.

Your family—how old are your kids?

My daughters are 30 and 33.

Right, so you found time for family and the business? [Laughs]

It seems that I did, although they would probably say I didn't spend as much time as I should, and they're probably right. [Laughs]

You went to Carleton University, right?

Yeah.

So why did you start Sprott Securities in the first place? Did you see a need there in the industry?

Well, I think the reason I started Sprott Securities is that I sort of lost my home at Loewen Ondaatje. You know, I wanted them to go a little more aggressive in the underwriting business at the time, and they didn't seem inclined to do it, and I guess we decided we had to part ways to some extent. I thought I could do it on my own.

It was just you and Anne Spork, I guess, at the beginning, right?

Myself and Anne and fellow named Lorne Graham who started it off, yeah.

What happened on Black Monday in October of '87?

On October 20th, which was the Tuesday, Toronto figured out that we had a crash the day before. It was Tuesday that Toronto just got hit, like there was no bid, and I'd invited Anne into my room and we were looking at the screen, and at 10:30 in the morning, I said, "Geez, if these quotes stay the way they are, we're broke." [Laughs] Now that was a very temporary moment in time, right, because there was no bid on hardly anything, so it's like a $15 stock was probably $3 bid or something. By the end of the day, it was probably $11 bid.

[Laughs] In 2000, you managed about $200 million. Has it been a little difficult to manage that growth?

Well, not so far. It hasn't been so far, you know. We're always a little concerned that on our long side, we have a lot of money to run, and we'll have to see in time whether that affects us. I've always said if it does affect us, we'll have to do something about it. I still think that you can thematically pick things that should generate an above average return. We've certainly done it for the last many, many years in our equity fund. But even our hedge funds—they're doing okay, you know, they're beating the index.

It has, yes. So it's interesting how it works with the retail crowd. Do you notice that when your performance lags, you don't get any money, and when your performance is great, it just floods in?

Yeah, no question. In fact, you might even say if your performance lags, it flows out.

I would say that one of the things that probably disappoints me the most is the unwillingness of people to stay with you when you've done well but you don't theoretically do well for a short time period. But a short time period is not a very good measuring stick. Really, the longer term is a better measuring stick.

It is, and people take long-term investments and look at them month to month, and it's really unfortunate.

We have a sheet that we sometimes flash around that shows our performance from 1982, and I think it says, you know, if you started with 100 grand, it'd be worth some incredible number I don't even want to tell....

It would be worth $40 million.

But if I just had people stick around. I guess I've had some people stick around.

That was a question. Do you have any clients that have stuck with you for a long time?

Oh sure, we have clients that have been there for fifteen and twenty years.

Really?

Yeah, and they've all done incredibly well. Even they get worried when you don't do well for awhile. Oh my God, somebody who started off with 50 grand has $3 million, and they lose $300,000 in a three-month period and they're just freaking out. You know how it is.

Well, he used to be smart but he got stupid this month, right? He'll be smart again next month. [Laughs]

Oh, exactly. I've had that asked to me: "Are you losing it?"

That's funny. You brought on J.F. Tardif in 2000, right? Why?

Was it 2000?

Or 2001, right around there. For more depth, or he had some special skills that you saw?

Well, no, he had great skills. He's an idea hunter. He's looking for things, and I always think all of our research people are kind of hunters and gatherers. Every day there's new things going on and you notice something that's changing that would make us go here, go there, and I would say that Jean Francois is very good at that. He likes looking at news releases and interim reports and things like that, so he'll pick up on things that are evolving, which is what we have to do in our business.

Even John Templeton said, "If you're doing it the same way you were doing it twenty years ago, you won't be doing it right anymore."

Well the way to look at it, it always changes, right? It's different all the time; it really is. I mean, there was a time, in the '70s, when we all looked at money supply. Now, I mean, people would freak out if they looked at the money supply.

You have a meeting every morning at 8:15. Is that a strategy session?

It's a hash-out session. It's basically saying to anyone in the room, "What do you have that's different today that would be meaningful to the way that we should look at things?" Had we had a meeting this morning, I'm sure somebody would have discussed auto sales, retail sales, what happened in the energy markets, uranium, evolutionary things, or things that would thematically confirm where we are. Maybe things that are going on in the trading environment. You just never know what issue's going to come up, right?

I like the exercise room for your staff. Did you came up with that idea?

Well, we had people that thought it was a good idea. I usually use it every week I'm there.

Healthier body, healthier mind, right? Do some of your employees use it all the time?

Yeah.

Ida gave me the tour of the office.

Yeah, she's more of a workout freak than I am.

Now about the investment strategy. I think you said before you consider yourself to be a value investor.

I even use the terms now that I'm kind of a chicken investor, like we want to buy something that we think is really cheap. So if somebody comes to us and says, you know, a stock's at twenty times earnings and grows at 20 percent, we don't have much interest in that. I mean, what we'd really prefer to find is where you can literally buy a stock at one times two-year-out earnings, except people don't know what earnings are going to be two years out. You know, this could be really cheap because we see what's happening here and when it all comes together, everyone's going to realize how cheap it is. I can give you an example. Hurricane Hydrocarbons, when we bought it at $6, I thought, "They'll make six bucks two years from now. Man, I can buy this thing here." We bought Ceramic Protection at a $1.60. They're gonna earn a buck sixty next year. So just think how cheap it was at the time. You weren't 100 percent certain but you were certain enough that you thought your risk reward was incredibly compelling. If you were wrong, yeah, fine maybe it goes down 20 percent 'cause it's so cheap anyway, but if you're right, it can go up by a 1,000 percent or 2,000 percent. That's what we like to do—that's our perfect investment vehicle. You don't always get those.

That kind of leads into some other areas. Do you consider yourself a big-picture guy first and then a stock picker second? Most big-picture guys are horrible stock pickers. If I'm right, that's what's made you pretty successful, as you've got them both right over the past.

Well, I started off as a stock picker and I said to myself, "I don't even look at the market." Really, I'd never looked at the market, and I said, "If I can buy cheap enough stocks, I'll do okay." It seemed to work. It's only because my role evolved at Sprott Securities, I had to sort of have some view on the market. Then I became a student of the market. Then you realize that certain thematic things carry on for a long time. So I decided I would focus in on that and see what some of the themes were and try to work the names into the themes. Even when you have the themes, the stock selection is by far the most important thing. It's everything.

I calculated the correlation of the Sprott Managed Accounts yearly correlation to the TSX and it was about 0.25, which I found fantastic.

I don't know, what's the correlation supposed to be? [Laughs]

Well, the average fund is 1, right?

Yeah, I suppose. Yeah.

You have no economists to look at the big picture? It's a common sense sort of approach I think that you have, right?

Well, we are the economists. I don't think you need an economist to know what the hell's going on in the economy. I don't think there's any magic formula for economists, okay? Look at how modest the range of their expectations is. If GDP's going to be 3, the low guy's at 2 and the high guy's at 4. Well, not that 3, 2, or 4 makes any difference to your performance, really. So we don't have an economist, no. Well, guys probably like having economists because they can pitch them well, right, for their organizations. You know, "We got our own economist." It doesn't do anything for me.

In your managed accounts, it's long-only pretty much, right?

Yeah, it was only long-only.

Did you ever go to cash at all?

Oh God, yeah. Well I don't know what our max cash was. That's a damn good question. I certainly know it's been up to 35 on occasion and not that long ago. I don't know that it's ever been bigger than that. We'll go pretty deep in cash if we're concerned about things.

This is probably a question that takes three hours to answer, but how did you develop your big-picture philosophy? Where do you start from when you're looking at a particular theme?

You've got to read things, right? We read so many reports from various experts, whether it's Stephen Roach at Morgan Stanley or Don Coxe at BMO Nesbitt. We would read twenty different guys in a week that are all having a view on the economy. We'll just sort of select what we want. You read all the experts, you look at all the data yourself, in fact, you really rely on your own use of the data. You know, we can analyze oil and gas demand as well as anybody can; it's just numbers that somebody puts out. We can look at government cash flows, because the numbers are available. We can assess the store sales, and there's hardly anything you can't deal with.

I think it's having the practical approach to analyzing numbers too, and that's why economists don't necessarily do that well because it's a very theoretical approach. That's what people say about the Bank of Canada; it's very theoretical and not that practical.

We're looking differently than anyone else. We're looking for the unusual.

You've primarily invested in small to mid caps. Was there a reason for that, or is it just more inefficiencies in that space?

Well, I think there's market inefficiencies in small companies. You can find a company that just looks so incredibly inexpensive and it's a wonderful story, and nobody's there because it's off most people's radar screens. We've concentrated on that in Canada, and now as we get bigger, we have to migrate into the world markets to find small cap ideas that we can sink our teeth into.

Right, it's good that they got rid of the foreign content limits?

Oh, it's beautiful. We were just about to start a foreign fund.

Do you see the industry go towards shorting in mutual funds?

I like the idea of being short. I like the idea of hedge funds today. I probably would have spewed some bad words about short funds five years ago, but I think, if you go into a bear market, how do you cover yourself? You gotta short.

Has most of your performance in the past been from resource stocks, or has it been pretty mixed?

It's all over the place. I mean, there's no doubt that in resource plays, resource stocks, you can make a big score if something's happening in the commodity or the company. There's times when we had lumber plays and pulp plays and ethylene plays and molybdenum plays and things like that. If you can sort of see the play coming and you're early in uranium, coal, or whatever, you can get pretty good gains.

That's a good point. Commodity stocks versus the underlying commodity. At different times, one will outperform the other. I presume that's

why you have some gold bullion in your portfolios and silver bullion and....

Well, we have the bullion more for defense than anything else. Ultimately, I'm not a great believer in paper. I just don't believe in paper. You know, here's poor old Jimmy Rogers, who believes in commodities, but he had his paper somewhere [laughs] and now he's got nothing.

Exactly.

It's a killer, but that's what happens, right? Everyone believes in the paper, but, my God, the paper can just go poof so fast.

Once you buy a stock at the right price, how long do you usually hold it? What's your turnover?

I don't know. We don't have big turnover. It takes a while for a good idea to come to fruition. What would I imagine our average hold? I'm sure it's like two years. It's at least two years because it takes a while for something to prove that whatever you assumed actually happens.

When you are a value guy, that's the nature of it. Now, the most important thing I think is the selling. A lot of people say the buy decision is easy, but when do you sell it off?

It's tough to sell.

Maybe give us an example of Taser.

Oh, yeah, it was a good sale too. Well, you know, it had gone up so much that we were selling it all the way up, but we still had a huge piece of Taser. Then a quarter came out, I don't even remember which quarter it was, and we thought, "This quarter's not as good as we thought it should be, so we're going to take our eggs out.' But it's easy to take your eggs out when you're up as much as we were up, right? I'll give you another example of a stock I sold a couple years ago. I sold Fording Coal in the $50s because I was a little worried about the metallurgical coal price versus the thermal coal price, and I read their quarter and it said, "Well, our fourth quarter shipments will be this, providing there are no delays from our Chinese customers." I went, "Hmm, why are they putting that in there?" I could smell something, so, sure enough, I sold it. Six weeks later, "We've had delays from our Chinese customers." So, you know, you have to sense some deterioration in the fundamentals that something's happening.

Yeah, I was talking to Ahmet Okumus at a conference. Somehow your name came up. "Sprott." Yeah, he said, "I know him. He owned 13 percent of Taser, didn't he?"

Yeah, right.

Somehow you popped up on his radar screen. Now just as another example, a stock like Centurion Energy—when did you originally buy it?

Centurion—oh Centurion—we bought Centurion around two bucks. I forget the number; it could've been a buck eighty or something.

Ran up to $20 and then pulled way back.

I think that happens when they run that fast. We saw that in the gold stocks. Stocks can get out of sync for a while and scare some people off. So the stocks that have gone up a lot can come under a lot of pressure before the boldness comes back.

Momentum guys jump in and jump out.

Or the fundamentals really show themselves, right.

Does money, when it comes into a sector, usually go into the big caps first?

Yeah. That would be typical. There's more big money chasing big things than there is little money chasing little things.

If a U.S. manager is going to look at Canada, they're going to invest in EnCana before they invest in something else.

Oh, yeah, they're going to buy all the bigs up here. For sure. So you know, when those oils almost went parabolic, it's all that U.S. money coming in here. If it stays away for a while, then we get a little time to get our breath and separate the men from the boys. You have to have that thing happen where you actually get to compare—people not just madly buying something. It's a time process.

Jim Cramer likes EnCana.

Yeah. Good!

Have you used any technical analysis at all?

I shouldn't say no. I mean, we read certain technical analysts. To what extent do we rely on them? I mean, there's a few good guys, but even the good guys have lots of bad calls.

There's no rich technical analysts, as the saying goes?

Yeah. So it's really tough to buy into it, because it's so uncertain when they come to their conclusion.

Do you use technicals for market calls?

It could be for the market, it could be for an individual stock, it could be for a group of stocks, but I mean, when I see how many guys have been whipsawed in the market this year, "It's just breaking out," then it falls apart. Then it's breaking down. Then it goes back up again. Oh my God. You know, life shouldn't be so simple as just marking something on a chart and saying it's going to go higher.

Right. Everybody would be a billionaire.

Exactly.

If you buy a stock, own it for a couple of months, and then you say, "I don't think this was a great idea," and it goes down, do you average down?

No.

Many successful people cut their losses quick.

A good idea goes up early. The best ideas go up immediately. You keep buying them as they're going up. Yeah, they're the best stocks. When you start buying a stock and it starts pumping up, you know you're onto something, because there's more than you buying it, right?

Do you know what your biggest win was on an individual stock?

Well, in dollars, it probably was Taser, but we've had lots of big ones. We made huge amounts of money on a stock called Bowflex, which became Nautilus. It was a huge winner. God, the stock went from, like, a buck to a hundred. We've had lots of multi-thousand percent winners—many. I'm not going to say one versus the other that was our biggest. I mean, Hurricane Hydrocarbons would have been big for us, to go from $6 to $40, and we had a big piece of it.

How about your biggest regret?

Ooh, I made lots of mistakes. The biggest mistake I made was selling Precision Drilling in probably something like 1994. I bought it at $6 and I sold it at $18. It probably went to $1,000, and I had a lot of it.

You've been doing it a long time, and there's lots of mistakes you made. Anything you've learned from those mistakes along the way?

Yeah, you learn to stay long a little longer. You don't rush to the exits quickly. You learn to try to be calmer about things.

Things always go up further than you think and down further than you think too.

Oh, that's the most amazing thing. That's why selling is tough. I mean, if I had to define selling, it really is like a greater fool thing. When's the last idiot in here? How do you figure what an idiot's going to do?

So just a little bit on your performance. It's averaged around 25 percent a year since 1982. You had some great years in the early to mid-'80s. Did you have a theme at that time or can you remember that far back?

Oh, I had different themes at different times. You know, sometimes we were in lumber stocks. I can remember once being in what I called "poly and moly": polyurethane and molybdenum. We would have made a lot of money in NOVA Chemicals and Dupont and Highmont Mining and weird things like that. We had other great plays, and one of our great plays was Pine Point Mines. We bought it after they announced they were closing the mine. We bought it at $8 and sold it at $50, to Cominco.

The amazing thing is '82 to 2000 was basically a pretty bad time for commodities, but you found a lot of things to invest in. In 1990, obviously, we had a recession that year and it was a bad year for you.

We were down in 1990?

Down 10 percent.

I don't remember 1990: I don't remember what we did in 1990. I just don't remember what we did. We buy lots of earnings stocks and we suffer with the market when the market suffers. I mean our cruelest time was....

Nineteen ninety-eight.

Nineteen ninety-eight, yeah, when Long Term Capital was happening. No one would buy small caps. I remember that very well.

You went through the '87 crash, but you ended up 20 percent in '87?

Well, we stayed the course. We'd probably done well in the beginning of the year. I would imagine we probably did well, then we got hammered, and then we just stayed the course and it came back.

I think it's interesting to go through your whole history and see how the philosophies change. The early '90s was a big resource time again, '92, '93—

You know, probably the thing that changed the most is—and there were times when it was really tough in the market. From '68 to '82 you can hardly scratch two nickels together, right, in terms of making money because there were no multiples on anything. I'm trying to think of when we bought Midland Walwyn stock. I think we bought that in 1990. I would say our primary theme used to be just earnings. Now, when you move into resources, you have to look at other things. You don't get to buy at cheap earnings today. You have to anticipate earnings because it's easy for every computer to figure out what good earnings are, so you have to be a little ahead of the game.

I'm a pilot, and what they call that is being ahead of the power curve. Then you went through '96 up 60 percent, obviously some good times there. Did you ever have Bre-X in the portfolio?

No.

You never owned it?

Made a lot of money on it though.

Okay, because of the other....

No, I made a lot of money on it, but I never owned it; I shorted it.

Ah, all right. [Laughs] Really?

I shorted it. I never had any interest in it, because I hate anything that everyone loves. It's just, you know, you're not getting a good shake I don't think. Then after the guy's out of the helicopter, after the first report kind of said, "There's a problem here," the stock got down to 2 bucks or something and one day it roared up to five. Then I started reading about it, because I was fascinated about what the hell had happened here. I read some report saying, look, all these grains are rounded. You don't get rounded grains—those are alluvials. So this core has been salted, and this is before the results came out. They popped up to five bucks one day, I said, "Fine, short 100,000." I did at five, and then literally three months later there's nothing there. I bought it at $0.06 that day, then Monday it opened up.

Wayne Deans said he went to Busang with Robert Friedland, and he said they thought they were going to be eaten by cannibals and wild animals. I think at the time he said, "This would be a great place to actually have a scam because nobody's going to come here; you've got to fear for your life to get here." [Laughs]
You know one of the things I find fascinating about Bre-X retrospectively? All the mining analysts actually went there. Well, what's this about going to see the ore body? I don't think it works, okay? That I don't think.

Okay, so we get to '98, and I think the TSE was down 20, in August of that year. Did you start to question what you were doing?

Well, you always question what you're doing, but I think we probably had a portfolio of what would have been pretty cheap stocks, probably on an earnings basis. We knew we were going to have to ride this sucker out. We're not going to sell these things. I don't remember the specifics, but you know they all probably went from ten times earnings to seven times earnings, and we weren't about to cave in. So we just held on and it ended, luckily.

Did you lose any clients at that time, or did people get upset?
Probably. Yeah, they can't deal with it, right?

They can't. It's unfortunate because the average fund in the U.S. did 11 percent for the last twenty years and the average investor did 3.3 percent with those funds.
Really?

Yeah, those are the numbers in U.S. equity funds. It's unfortunate because I talk to people all the time and say, "Who cares whether they charged zero management fee or 5 percent, investors weren't making any money anyway." [Laughs]

[Laughs] That's right, yeah.

I think the most important factor is behavioural finance from an investor perspective.

It's shocking. I didn't even know that data point, but that's shocking. It's awful in a way. Yeah, emotions are tough to control. People are their own worst enemies.

In '98, the market fell by 20 percent, and like you said, cheap stocks got cheaper. That's what happened in 2002 also. Your performance was great, but a lot of value managers like Cundill had this big drop too because everything just got cheaper. Even if it was 30 percent below book value, it went 50 percent below book value.

Well, we weren't that bad in '02. There's one reason we handled '02, and that was because we were bears then, right, and we bought things that theoretically should do well in a bear market. The gold just bailed us out.

Let's talk about 2000 to 2005, because you did fantastically well in the Sprott Managed accounts, being long-only and you also did fantastically well in the hedge fund. With the hedge, you can see why, because of all the shorts. On March 9th, 2000, you wrote your _Markets at a Glance,_ titled "Excessive Speculation." The NASDAQ peaked on March 10th, and your last sentence says, "You know, this isn't going to be years; this is going to be a few weeks before the NASDAQ starts to crumble," and it happened the next day. In April '99, in the Sprott Canadian Equity, you were up 26 percent in one month. I'm sure you don't know why, but that was half the year's returns right there, and then in February of 2000, you were up 22 percent. Were you in tech stocks at the time, because in February 2000, the NASDAQ went up 20 percent?

Yeah. No, we wouldn't have been in tech stocks. Oh, I know what we would have been in. We could have been in things like, oh God, it was a fuel cell company, Global Thermoelectric. That's one that we owned. We bought it at a buck on an earnings play.

C.M. Oliver did that at a buck. I worked for them at the time.

Bought at a buck, it was an earnings play, and it became this huge high-tech thing that went to $50 or $60 and we had a lot of it, so we would have done well there. We would have had other names that would have been carried up by the market, because they became darlings or some damn thing. Actually, we probably would have been playing in some of that stuff, we probably were. I don't recall.

We talked about your biggest failure, because I think that's important.

Which was the biggest failure again?

I forget. Anyway, it's on the tape. [Laughs]

It's funny because I had an interview with somebody who said, "Well you talk about all these winners; did you have any losers?" I said, "I got all sorts of losers!" "Well, tell me one of them." "Aaaah, I can't think of it right now." [Laughs]

That's a good point. A lot of money managers say if they buy ten stocks, it's three of them that give them all their performance. Three of them do horribly, and they cut their losses, and four are okay. Does that make sense?

Yeah, for sure. You know, I like the Peter Lynch thesis that you get these multi-baggers. You must get multi-baggers. Like him, we have lots of stocks, and then when something starts working because you're in it, you go deeper, and then it just keeps getting better and better and better.

Now that's a good point. Are there any books that you've really liked in the past that you require your staff to read?

I like them to read the Peter Lynch books, *One Up on Wall Street* or *Beating the Street*. I like those. I like them to read a book called *Stock Market Logic,* which was by, I think, Norman Fosback. It discusses all sorts of ways of looking at stocks and which ones work and which ones don't work. The ultimate conclusion is that earnings works, and earnings growth works. That's what works, I can guarantee you.

Let's talk about the hedge fund. Why did you start the hedge fund in 2001? What was the need?

We'd already thought about it because we saw the bear market arriving, and even when we decided we should do it, it took a while to get the paperwork done and all that. We probably made the decision to do it in, let's say, April or May of 2000, but we hadn't started a hedge fund before and had to get the OSC approval and all that stuff. It took a little while to get it going. We did it because we thought we were in a bear market, so we'd have a little protection on the down side.

Had you had experience shorting stocks?

I had experience shorting stocks, yes I did, but not running a hedge fund. When I ran Sprott Securities, we did short stocks and I've shorted stocks my whole career on occasion.

It's so important because you see a lot of money managers that start a hedge fund and the first two years are difficult, because shorting stocks is a very different skill set.

It's a tough thing, it's brutal in a bull market. I mean the worst stocks go up the most. So you could be a great analyst, and you're going to get your clock cleaned if you go to analytic shorts.

That's a good point, I think. Do you short now based upon valuation of stocks or short based upon deteriorating fundamentals, or both? Shorting strictly on valuation can kill you sometimes.

Well, I would almost say that we use a short side as a backstop to our long side. So we should short big marketable stocks and we look upon thematic areas that we think will be weak, like North American automotive stocks or financial stocks like Fannie and Freddie. They're big. Those are all big shorts that we have had. You can sort of see these problems evolving. We're shorting lots of financials, and we've shorted home builders in the past. It's more of a market proxy that you're going to try to create your action on the long side, but you want to save yourself on the short side. If the market breaks 20 percent, I think we'd make it. [Knocking sound] Trying to find some wood here. It's a damn plastic table [laughs], and that's horrible toast.

There was a hedge conference a few years ago that I attended. You know, at these hedge fund conferences, they love to talk about draw down and correlation and sharp ratios. Then you got up and you said, "You know, I don't know what any of that stuff is. All I know is I make money for people." Maybe comment a little bit about that, because I think there's too much of that in the hedge fund industry. You have to have some volatility to make some money.

Well, the funny part is, guys used to say we had too much volatility, and I said, "Well, how can we not have volatility when we're up that much every year?" You have to have volatility, so that's a bad thing? I've never fallen into the camp that use statistics as my selling mechanism. I mean, I am a great believer about having negative beta, which I think is very important with the environment we have.

At the hedge fund conference, I talked on the original Alfred Jones model. Somebody asked me at the end of it, as they always do, "What's a good hedge fund?" I said, "Well, a hedge fund should lower your overall portfolio volatility on the downside." I said, "If you go by that definition, then Sprott has the best hedge fund for your existing portfolio because it has a negative beta." People don't understand that. They look at it in isolation and say, "Well, it's too volatile." I say, "Well, look at it in comparison with the rest of the portfolio and look at your bottom line volatility."

Yeah. I'm a huge believer in the hedge fund. I've never publicly recommended people buy our equity fund because it's just relatively risky.

Now, 2001 and 2002—let's start with that. You were up 130 percent in those two years combined. You were presumably long gold and energy and short tech.

Not that much energy in '01 and '02. We would have been long PetroKazakhstan or Hurricane Hydrocarbons then, but we weren't long that many oil stocks. It was mostly gold stocks and special situations and, you know, maybe it was Bowflex. It wouldn't have been Taser yet. I don't know what special situations we had then. We always seem to come up with some damn thing that does well.

Well you said a while ago, it always surprises you at the end of the year when you are up so much.

It's funny. I used to say to people, "When we get the results for the end of the year and we look at the top ten performers on the markets, I like to think we've had two of them." Typically, we did. I don't know where we'd get them from. You know, you find your way in there somehow, to something that's going up.

Were you short mainly tech at that time?

Yes, for sure. We were short a lot of NASDAQ at the top.

It must have driven you a bit crazy because a lot of people tried to short tech and, you know, Yahoo! would bounce 25 percent. They kept getting stopped out. Do you have stop losses on the shorts?

We don't, no.

That's probably why. A lot of these people that did the stop losses would get stopped out, do it again, then stopped again. They didn't make any money because they kept getting stopped out on the way down.

Yeah. Well, we would have had shorts going into the exact peak on March 9, 2000. After it peaked is probably when we stepped it up a little, when you knew it was kind of going your way. The market was breaking down.

The fundamentals were breaking with the tech stocks.

Oh, everything was falling apart, right? I mean, you get data points that said, look, this is not going to hold together here.

You've been around long enough to remember '73, '74. Warren Buffett gave all the money back to investors in '69 because he said he couldn't find value but the market carried forward for another couple of years—the Nifty Fifty stocks, right?

Yeah.

Then, '73, '74 was the big drop. It was an exact duplicate of that this time. The market basically peaked in the U.S. in '98, and then the tech stocks were the only things that went up in '99. Then we had our 2001, 2002. When you look at 1966 to 1982, the market did absolutely nothing.

Do you think we're maybe in a long-term bear?

That's what we think. We think we'll have a long-term secular bear market here. That's what I would guess.

Jim Rogers says in his book that commodity bull markets and stock market bear markets completely overlap each other. In other words, they are highly negatively correlated.

Mm-hmm. Well, one probably causes the other.

It makes sense. He goes back to '33—to '53—when there was a commodity bull market. Even though they were in the Great Depression, commodity prices still went up. Then from '53 to '66, there was a good stock market, and commodities didn't do well. In '66 to '82 there was a commodity bull market again, and gold went to $850, etc. Stocks did poorly. From '82 to 2000, was stocks, and 2000 to 2015 is commodities?

I didn't actually realize that in the Depression that commodities went up. They must have at the bottom of the Depression or something. I would not have thought that.

Exactly. It's something that he brought up. It was just the supply/demand imbalance was so huge because undercapitalization for twenty years. The same as what we have had now.

Yeah.

I mean, Kellogg's isn't going to make any money if they have to buy grain, and if grain prices have gone up by ten times, they can't pass that completely on to the consumer.

I guess there were real shortages of everything, and then the commodities went up just 'cause there's shortages. I mean, it just kills everybody, right? 'Cause the wages can't keep up.

Now, this is interesting. I remember the conference call in 2003 when your hedge fund was having its problems. I think at that time you were adding to your shorts because the market was going up.

'03, okay. We ultimately had to decide to cut the shorts. We had to. There was no use, so we cut them drastically.

Don't fight the trend. [Laughs]

We said to ourselves, "Okay, we hate the idea, but we've got to go find some stocks." And we found them. Like, geez, I was shocked when we put our minds to think, "Okay, we're going to buy something just 'cause we've got to buy something." We turned it on pretty fast after that.

Do you try to have the hedge fund balanced between the longs and shorts?

Pretty well, unless I really sort of get torqued out of one side or the other. If I really thought we're in it on the down side, I'd probably try to cut the longs. We try to buy negative beta longs too, so I don't go into a market decline with the same worry that most people would.

Hopefully it works.

Do you ever do any pairs trading at all?

No. It eats up too much money.

So your philosophy is mainly: We'll take an industry that we like, or a theme that we like, and we'll go long. Then we will take shorts in themes that we don't like. Then we will pick fundamentally the best stocks according to our themes?

You mentioned real estate. We shorted housing, not real estate. I've never owned a real estate stock or been short a real estate stock, 'cause I just don't understand it. How do you know what the company's worth? I mean it's worth its buildings right? What do I know about the buildings?

Are there any rules that you have in your mind that you never break?

No. [Laughs] I don't have any rules that I don't break, but certain things are important. I mean, you want a stock to act good, early. You want confirmation that you're not the only guy in there, that you're seeing value and the stock's starting to sprint the minute you get going. The other guys see you coming and say, "Man, I've been sitting here in the weeds and some other guy's buying it and I got to get in there." Then you got to get in front of him and he's got to get in front of you and, you know, that's how I like to see that. In the commodities side, I like to see a commodity move by in excess of 20 percent, then you know something's changed. You kind of know something's happening here. So when oil went really from $11 to $13 the first time, I said to our guys at Sprott Securities, "Don't stop this price. Do not even think of a price, 'cause you'd be making a mistake." Obviously, things change for something to go up 20 percent. Look at any commodity that's been up 20 percent; it turned around and went up 100 percent. Almost any stock that went up 20 percent went up 100 percent.

This is maybe a difficult question, but is there anything that you figure you could've done a lot better in the past?

Well, I don't think I'm a great businessman. I'm not great at running the business. I hardly even spend any time thinking about the business. I think about owning stock and trying to make money for clients, and if we make money for clients, we'll do well.

Why did you get rid of Sprott Securities?

Well, because Sprott Asset Management was becoming a big business within Sprott Securities. It was really where my interest lay—finding ideas, investing, and making money. That's what I always did, even at Sprott Securities, except then you became the underwriter. So, it was an easy extension.

What was your idea with the uranium participation units? I think Sprott Securities underwrote them?

We knew that the uranium price would go up—uranium had to go up. I said, "Geez, you know, you guys might think about starting a Uranium Participation Corp." [Laughs] We said we'd participate in it.

Talk a little bit about peak oil, Matt Simmons, and the whole idea. In Saudi Arabia, we haven't had an independent audit in twenty-five or thirty years. Are we under the impression that if Saudi Arabia has peaked then oil has peaked?

There is a big peak, lookout! [Laughs] I think peak oil is a numbers game. It's just numbers and it's a depletion rate. How do you stop—how do you arrest depletion? Man, it's almost defined how much oil is in the world. Good geophysicists—or whatever the hell they're called, petrophysicists or something—know there should be something like three trillion barrels of oil in the world and once you've consumed a trillion and a half, you're on the down side. That's how they predicted the peak in the U.S. lower forty-eight states. They figured half the oil's gone, based on everything we know and where it should be. Oil's easier than gas because below a certain level, you don't get oil. Oil can only go down to like 17,000 feet or so and that's it for oil.

The naysayers would say, "Yeah but, you know, when oil prices go up a lot, then demand is going to go down." It's going to be a self-correcting mechanism.

Well, all we know is that the oil consumption has been inelastic. I think consumption's gone down one year in the last, I can say, forty. It went down in 1990, half of one percent or something. We were in a recession, and it only went down half of one percent.

Talking about gold, gold is supposed to be the defensive. Why do you own so much gold?

Well, obviously I think it's defensive, and I think it's rigged. We know that central banks continue to sell gold and they always announce it ahead of time and they're always in your face on it. It sounds like the dumbest thing of all time. Why would you tell everybody you're selling? Why don't you just sell on the QT? 'Cause they want the price of gold to be down. We know that.

Why would they want....

Because they want it to be down so that people buy into paper currencies. People buy into no fear in the financial markets, so people buy into low inflation. If gold popped up fifty bucks in one day, what the hell would everyone be thinking the next day? You know what they'd be thinking, "Oh, something's wrong!" So they're not going to let it go up fifty bucks, even though it should be a very emotional commodity. They don't let it act emotionally. It is probably the most modest volatility on the upside of anything you can imagine, including bonds and wheat and you name it. Everything would be more volatile than gold. Statistically, you can almost prove it's rigged.

How about the gold-to-oil ratio, have you ever looked at that?

John Embry looks at it a lot, and I've seen lots of studies on it. It's not something that I put a lot of emphasis on. I don't know that there's some logical linkage between the two. I mean, both are signs of inflation, I guess. But do I really think that because we have peak oil the price of gold should go up? No, I don't think that.

You know, all money managers that you talk to, most of whom are mediocre, all say the same thing, "I look for undervalued stocks that have been a good balance sheet, etc." Everybody says the same thing, but there are some people, probably 10 percent, who do a good job and the rest don't. How do you think you're different from the rest of them?

Yeah, I think we take measured risks. We know we take risky situations, but we have to measure it out. We have an idea of what the reward is, and therefore you're prepared to take the risk. Most people don't want to venture away from something that's not the norm. Not only are we prepared to venture away, we'll take a good position and we'll buy 10 percent of a company that no one's heard of. When they figure it out, it will trade and it won't be a problem. We had over 10 percent of Taser early on.

Somebody asked you about that once on a conference call, about owning a large piece of a company and then having it not trade that much. I think you came up with an answer that when you want to sell it, basically down the road, that liquidity always....

If it works, you never have a problem. You have a huge problem if it doesn't work.

Then you just sit on it as long the fundamentals are good....

No, if it's not working, it's not working. [Laughs] You know, you've got to deal with it, right? So you're going to lose money on it for sure. It's like the guys in private equity. They will buy ten things and eight don't work, but the two that work go big time for them, right? It's a little that way with us. How many thousand percenters do you need to offset a bunch of losers? We're not likely to lose 100 percent on something.

Do you think that in the next ten years a money manager can do a lot better job if he knows how to short, rather than just being long only?

I would think so, yeah. Yeah, that is the market environment we're looking at, sure. I mentioned that I don't like analytic shorts anymore—I like market shorts. Just stick with the market 'cause these damn analytic shorts can kill you. When it's starting to break down, yeah, analytic shorts are great. But if you're sort of waiting around, you don't want to be short Nortel. You've analyzed, it's not working, and meanwhile the damn stock goes from $0.70 to $3. You're getting your head kicked in. You want to wait for it to roll and then go, but it was a lot easier short at 128, I gotta tell you.

The nice thing about going long is if you're wrong, it goes away. If you're short, it doubles in size and gets bigger. [Laughs]

Oh no, that's the big risk! Yeah, I've had stocks that have gone against me, like, you know, probably many hundreds of percent.

Social Security and Medicare are something that not a lot of people know about. You've talked about $25 trillion, or $20 trillion deficit?

Yeah, Medicare has something like a $23 trillion deficit. Something like 23, and there's like $12 trillion in Social Security. Look at the U.S. medical system. Jesus, first of all, more and more people every day don't have coverage, and you don't want to get sick down there. I mean everybody gets sick some day.

In 1999, I remember I was taking cabs, and the cab drivers would all say, "Oh, you're an investment advisor. I put this money into this stock." I thought of the story at the time—it was either Joe Kennedy or J.P. Morgan, one of the two, that got their shoes shined in 1929....

It was Joe Kennedy.

The shoeshine boy said, "I'm making all this money," and right away, Joe Kennedy sold his stocks.

Yeah, yeah right.

I thought, "Wait a second. The cab drivers are all making money in stocks; this must be the speculative blowoff."

We'll look anywhere. I mean, the reason we go to some of these obtuse countries—non–North American, I would call them—is because we're looking for a specific commodity. Australia is huge in coal. We're looking for uranium—well, Paladin Resources is in Namibia, so we buy in South Africa. It's the commodity that takes us there.

What is your history over the past twenty-five years in political risk with investing in foreign stocks?

Not bad.

Venezuela?

No, it's been fine. Well, I'm not in Venezuela, but I don't think there's many times that we've suffered from that. I mean, for example, when we owned PetroKazakhstan there were many times that the stock would break five bucks because of some issue in Kazakhstan, but, ultimately, we did quite well.

Can you comment on how fund-rating services rate your funds?

I know we get criticized for being volatile. I always think, how the hell can we not be volatile if we produce 28 percent a year return, which really means post-your-fees as much as 35 percent. That means on the stocks you're invested in, you've got to make 38 percent because you've got a lot of cash. If you're making 38, you have lots of stocks that are up hundreds of percent.

Right.

Stocks that are up hundreds in a year are volatile. I know when I had that Morningstar guy in here, I said, "I want to see your format. I haven't seen it yet. I don't know whether our people have it." Their biggest emphasis was on downside volatility. Well, you look at our equity fund, or some of our hedge funds, and they were up 14 percent last month. Well, you know what? They're down this month. If you have a 15 percent month, you're more likely to be down the next month because to get 15, you had something that's really gone crazy.

But I like volatility. It's upside deviation. They don't get that. We did a little bit of work here. I said, "I'm getting so tired of this volatility question; let's do this. Let's look at a twelve-month period and we'll do all the twelve-month periods since the fund started. Let's see how many months any one of our unitholders could look year-over-year and say they're down." There were thirteen months we were down in 120 or 190 periods. The closest guy to us was something like he was fourteen or fifteen months down. The TSX was down thirty-three of those months. I said, "Well, you know, isn't that what our clients really want? He wants us to be up and not have to get all jittery."

People talk about the extreme volatility. When you look at the Sprott Managed Account since 1982, there's only been five down years. I mean, '98 was a problem and the rest of the years—minus five, minus six—very minor.

It happens. Last week, we got our head kicked in.

I saw the financials rally and golds collapse.

[Eric was long gold and short financials at the time.]

You get your head kicked in. A week later, you're right back. What are we supposed to do, trade that? You can't have a mega-theory and trade it in a week.

You've been in the business a long time. We haven't seen this sort of market volatility for a long time, have we?

Let's look at our Canadian equity fund last year as an example. We were up 17 at one point, down to zero, up 17 again, down to zero, up 17. We ended up on the year whatever the hell it was, 13 or 14. When I give speeches, I say, "Well, what do you think we did in each of those time periods? We did nothing." So who was right, the market or us? What are we supposed to do? The market has a hissy fit about gold or oil or whatever, and it goes down. At the end of the year, you end up being up. What are you supposed to do? You can't trade the thing.

If some guy wants to knock oil down to $85 for a month, they knock it down. And the oil stocks tank. We don't take a short-term view. We're taking a long-term view of where the price should be, and you hang in there. I don't think risk is a thing you can determine at a minute in time. I think it's something that only on a two-year look-back can you understand what risk was. I use the examples of us buying gold stocks in 2000, which looked like the most idiotic thing you could ever do. Two years later, those stocks were up 300 percent and 400 percent. The price of gold's gone up and everything's changed. In 2003, the price of uranium had already doubled to 14 before we even got started. You're buying all these crappy little uranium companies. Two years later, they're up 300 percent to 500 percent. The price of uranium's at $100. You look back and say, "Well, was it risky?"

People say you have a lot of risk because half the fund is in gold. Like you said, at $250 an ounce, was gold risky or were technology stocks risky?

Well, they wouldn't have been considered risky at the time, right? Are bank stocks risky? I say they are. The powers that be say they aren't. The powers that be don't know what they're doing, okay? They're not investors, unfortunately. They don't have to put their money on the line.

One thing that you have mentioned to me before is that you tend to identify trends and things early, before others, and you stick with your themes and don't trade a lot. I wasn't surprised by the real estate crisis or subprime or credit crunch, but everybody else in the world was. You had been writing about it for two years already!

Yeah. They just don't see it.

How did these brokerage firms get themselves in difficulty like that when you were writing about it two or three years ago? That's happened over and over and over again. On March 9, 2000, your piece on technology came out, in which you were shouting in your article about the market collapsing imminently. The peak for the NASDAQ was the next day.

You know what's funny? I don't pretend that I'm a prognosticator. I just know how to see the dots and connect them. For example, today in our morning meeting, I talked about California house prices being down 29 percent! This is public information. I said, "Guys, what the hell is going to happen here? We haven't begun to experience a recession/depression yet. It's going down so fast, people hardly even know it yet. It's just a data point that's there. You just connect the points and say, "Well, it's going to be a problem." You could be a little forward-thinking about it. A trend, once in motion, is hard to stop. Who's to say that with house prices, we won't be sitting here in six months and they'll be down 40 percent in California?

I think Goldman Sachs said a 30 percent to 40 percent decline from the top for the California real estate prices was their outlook.

Then what's to spill out of all of that, you know?

Everybody you talk to says, "Well, that was just obvious that the real estate was going to go down." It was the same after the tech crisis: "Well, that was just obvious that that was going to happen." Great 20/20 hindsight!

It's funny. I remember reading some significant articles that people miss sometimes. One of them was on the real estate appraisals. I think it was written in 2003 in the *Wall Street Journal*. It basically said, "Appraisals are all a fraud because all the lenders are making the guys raise the appraisals." Now, you don't have to read too much farther to know where you're all heading.

I remember I read something in *Bloomberg* magazine two or three years ago that talked about rating agencies, and it talked about the fees that they received to rate the asset-backed paper versus regular bonds. It was triple or quadruple, or whatever the case was.

While we're talking about it, I attended a lunch with Alan Greenspan. He was in Vancouver a while ago. He said, "We were completely blown away by the subprime. We had no idea that the problem was as big as it was."

Wow! Wow! They're so cocoonish. I can't believe that he couldn't know. I can't believe it.

Obviously you have been bullish on gold for a long time. You put half your fund in bullion and also the gold and silver stocks. The bullion outperforms the stocks sometimes, like last year.

Yeah, it was surprising.

The stocks outperform sometimes. Do you just say, "Well, let's put it half and half and we'll see which one does better," and have exposure to both?

I don't even know if it is exactly half and half. It might be close to that. There are a whole bunch of theories that you're working with all the time. One of them is the total debasement of currencies, which you almost see happening here. I mean, we're almost in it. If there's a total debasement of currencies, not much survives. I keep thinking, "Man, you've got to have some gold for survival." Like everything else might just disappear and it's just a piece of paper, but the gold won't. Sometimes I think to myself, "That 25 percent that we have in gold in our equity fund might carry us all the away through." At least you're going to relatively be better off.

It's your insurance.

Whether or not you have positive performance, I don't know. But you're going to have relatively positive performance.

This is just common sense, but Ross Healy described it in an interesting way a couple of weeks ago to me. He said, "If the company's insolvent, what do investors do? They sell their stock and their stock goes down." He said, "If the country is insolvent, you're in trouble. You sell the country's stock, but there is no stock, so you sell the currency, instead

the currency goes down. Currency is just the stock of the country." I
thought that was just an interesting way of saying it.

I mean, I really do worry. I think the U.S. is bankrupt, quite frankly. I don't
even think those guys have any sense of what they're doing. They think they're
printing money and that it's worth something?

**When I chatted with you previously, you didn't have a lot of base
metal exposure because of a pending U.S. recession. I think you changed
that around and decided to go into base metals.**

Yeah. I was always a little worried about the recession because it had to
happen, but it was delayed. In the meantime, the growth in China just became
more and more significant because it's the law of numbers, right? The numbers get so much bigger all the time. Where they were in 2000 versus where
they are in 2008, and what a 10 percent increase in copper production in China
does this year versus 2000, is stunning. I think the reason we might have gone
there is the prices of the commodities stayed up. They didn't come off. The
stocks were always kind of herky-jerky. With the price where it was of, let's
say, copper or moly or something, you could say, "Man, that stock's really
damn cheap here. I think I'm willing to take that risk that even if I'm wrong
about the recession, the stocks are so inexpensive, I don't mind going there. I'll
take that risk."

Quadra Mining was one of the first ones we bought, when it was at six. I
thought, "I think this company could make six in dollar per share a few years."
I haven't seen an estimate like that yet, but they're getting up there. I think
there are estimates of $4 today and when they bring on the new mine in '08 and
maybe in '09 or '10 we'll see a $6 number. I mean, the stock was at six, I can
kind of see it all coming together to earn six. Let's buy. Let's risk it. We've got
to take that risk.

Same thing with coal. I was looking at the coal stocks just a few months
ago. We are already in coal and the price of coal was going nuts. I said, "Guys,
this Grande Cache company—they've got cash flow of two bucks and the
stock's at a buck. Shouldn't we be doing something?" I did. The stock's gone
from a $1 to almost $5 now.

That much?

In three months. So there's certain times the reward is so overwhelming
that you have to go there. For example, I discussed a stock called New Millen-

nium today. It has iron ore properties in Quebec. Some company in India is in print saying they're going to submit a bid to the company in mid-April. It's in print—a big iron-ore company. I went, "Oh, mid-April. That's three weeks from now." The stock's at $1.40. Some guy who I respect at Raymond James says, "With today's iron ore prices, the NAV is $58." I said, "Guys, at $1.40, and a bid coming, we've got to forget the recession and all that. I've just got to."

You mentioned that you said, "We decided in 2003 that if we're going to be bearish and it gets put off for a while, we better figure out a way to make some money."
Right, you've got to find ways. Yeah, like Timminco. They're sort of a techy stock, and a little bit of an energy play. You've got to go out and find things to do even though they're not totally thematic. You have to leave room for being a little wrong.

There's a guy in New York—Nandu Narayanan is his name, and I know him well—he runs the CI Trident Fund. You probably never talked to him.
You wrote about him, didn't you?

I did, yeah. He says exactly what you say. He is exactly the same.
Really?

There's hardly anybody like that. I actually sent him some of your notes. He used to work at Tiger Management for Julian Robertson, and his sister's the CEO of Pepsi Worldwide.
Really? Wow.

Yeah, so it's a pretty bright family. It's funny. He did it a little bit different way. He wrote a couple forward contracts last year against MBIA and Ambac, with Goldman Sachs as his counterparty. He says the counterparties are going to blow up. He also did a smaller one with Bear Stearns, and then he told me a few months ago, "I got Goldman Sachs to insure Bear Stearns' contract because I'm not too sure about Bear Stearns."
Really?

It's really, really interesting that your two philosophies couldn't be more identical.

I think the broker call is the easiest call in the world There's no M&A. There's no IPOs. There's no packaging.

They're levered 30 to 1.

Ah, it's brutal.

You mentioned on the conference call a couple Canadian banks were levered 30 to 1. CIBC came in yesterday with $25 billion in derivatives exposure.

Stuff you didn't even know was there.

Two thousand and eight you said was the year of the counterparty failures, right? I think you said that a while ago and it's starting to happen, right?

I might have said that. That sounds like something I would say, yes. We've really not heard much about derivatives yet, right? There are $500 trillion of derivatives? I don't even know where they come from or who has them. I just see everything fluctuates 1 percent a day no matter what it is. You've got $500 trillion of notional value moving $5 trillion a day.

I know you don't talk about the short positions a lot, but Bear Stearns you probably were short?

We were short that, yeah, but we're short everything. We're short all major U.S. financials pretty well.

Are you short Washington Mutual?

Oh, yeah. Oh, yeah. That was a favourite. Well, speaking of favourites, did you see my favourite analyst today is a lady named Meredith Whitney? She's the bank analyst that works at Oppenheimer who said Citigroup needed to cut their dividend six months ago. She's the one who started the whole thing. I love her. She was being interviewed a while ago on CNBC. The commentator said, "Well, what about your favourite financial stocks?", because she's trashing everything. She goes, "Of all my favourite financial stocks, I don't like any of them."

Well, you don't get many analysts that speak out like that.

Oh, so incredible! It was so ballsy. I loved it. She's a good analyst, that one.

The thing you still hear from most Canadians when you talk about Canadian bank stocks is they say, "Oh, no, no, I'm not going to sell my bank stocks. I feel safe with my banks. I feel safe." I guess as long as you continue to hear that, there is a lot more downside risk. You want to hear people say, "I'm never going to invest in a bank ever again," and then you've probably hit the bottom in the banks. Canadians love the Canadian banks. They look at the last twenty years and just say, "I feel safe."

I don't think people realize the extent of the reveres leverage, right? It's just so incredible. I just think that over a twenty- or thirty- or sixty-year period, the banks have been allowed to get more and more and more leveraged—more creatively leveraged. People have no idea of how little it would take to absolutely wipe out the capital, if it hasn't already been wiped out.

At 30-to-1 leverage, it only takes a 3-percent drop to wipe you out.

Yeah. Well, what hasn't moved down by 3 percent? LBO, CDSs, CDOs, subprime, commercial real estate, residential real estate, auto loans, credit card loans, munis, auction rate securities, you name it.

But if that happens, they just change the computer models to revalue it.

Well, they did change the computer models. You saw that. Did you read the article that described where the models said with 100 percent certainty the whole system's going to fall apart? What's the guys name, Taleb? Do you read his books? Did you read *The Black Swan*?

Yes, yes.

What's the other one? Oh, God, I wish I could remember that. He's written two very, very good books, and the latest one was *Black Swan*. Everyone thinks there aren't many black swans. Well, there are black swans. They might call Bear Stearns a black swan now, who knows? Maybe they'll be calling Lehman a black swan or some other thing.

Now, the people out there say supply always catches up with demand, obviously, to bring commodity prices down. I think other than the demand increases, we've had a lot of supply disruptions out there.

It's huge. Huge. I think we're in a period of logistical problems around the world. I heard of one recently. They're building all these ships, and there's no captains.

Really?
No people to operate the ships.

The mining industry has been a problem for years. There's also no mining engineers coming out of school.

Well, we've got more power problems, we've got water problems, we've got environmental problems, we've got natural gas problems. Ah, there's always something coming along.

That's a good point because you're always looking for the next theme. I know you don't write a tremendous amount of big research reports, but you wrote one a year and a half ago on global warming—a big seventy-page deal. Was that your next idea far as themes?
Well, I think the biggest theme is peak oil. That's what I believe. Well, the fact that the price of oil is well over $100, like, duh, do you get it yet?

Well, exactly, you're in a recession and it's at all-time highs, yes.
Right.

They say, "Oh, but they found nine billion barrels off of Brazil or something, 27,000 feet down through 6,000 feet of rock and another 5,000 feet of salt." How much is that going to cost?
People don't get it—even nine billion—we use a billion every twelve days. So big deal? You've got three months taken care of. What are you going to do for the next nine months this year in terms of finding the other twenty-seven billion you have to find? We don't make many major discoveries anymore.

You've got political risk now, anywhere and everywhere. Kazakhstan's got the huge field there, but....
And development risk.

Yeah. If I was Exxon spending $25 billion, I would be a little wary in Kazakhstan.

Yeah. You find all sorts of development risk everywhere.

Interesting. The biggest endowment fund in the U.S. is Harvard or Yale, right?

Mm-hmm.

The second biggest is the University of Texas. The University of Texas was very, very poor early on. The government gave them this vast land deposit in West Texas.

Hey, I didn't know that.

Then oil was discovered and the royalties are still coming in.

That's beautiful. That's a good way of doing it.

Now, let's go back to 2001 and 2002. There was actually a few people out there that called the technology thing and went short, but they weren't up 130 percent like you were in 2001 and 2002 because they kept getting stopped out, because of their stop buys. Yahoo! would go up 20 percent and they'd say, "Okay, now we have to cut our losses and cover."

Yeah. You know what's funny? I'm shocked when I think of what we do on our short side because I've been short Citigroup for seven years, and Fannie Mae and General Motors and all these stocks for a long, long, long, long time. It is the same with housing stocks. These shorts have rallies. For example, the housing stocks went up 60 percent in 2006. I was short them the whole way. I kind of think to myself, "Well, how can you hang in there?" It's because the longs are protecting you. As long as your longs are keeping your head above water for the fund, you don't worry about one specific short if the reason that you're short has not changed. So you know, we see that rally in the financials last week when they all went up 15 percent and we just hang in there because we believe we are right, and then everything will come back into balance again.

That was short covering. It's got to be, when it jumps 15 percent like that; it's got to be a little short covering.

So many guys have got their fingers on the trigger, right? I can't believe the number of people that are trading on margins and leverage and, oh, boy, it makes them do stupid things.

I know you got out of Delta Petroleum, but Kirk Kerkorian bought one-third of the company for $650 million.
Yeah, we still own some Delta. I'm quite sure we've got 1 percent or 2 percent in Delta. The reason I got out of Delta is most of the things they did or were promised to us didn't happen. I just can't take it anymore. It wasn't that bad a play. We started buying it at $6 and it's at $24, but I got tired of each play not kind of coming together like I wanted it to. I like a little more certainty when I'm investing. The big play, of course, the Columbia River Basin, so far has been a dud, not that anybody's ever announced any results yet, which is funny.

That's very strange because EnCana's done two or three or four wells, or whatever the case is, but they aren't giving any results. Then they sold off some of their properties for pennies. That was something's weird about that, right?
Yeah. It might still come together because they've got this new technology in the shale business called Packer Plus, which is what they're using in Northeastern B.C. It might make a lot of things economic that weren't before economic. We'll see.

When Peter Hodgson came to Sprott, he told me, "You know, Bob, I thought I was doing well if there was a 50 percent upside in a stock." He says, "I talked to Eric and he says he won't buy a stock unless it's a possible four-bagger." He says, "I had to kind of ramp up my expectations for the big ones."
If you want to produce 28 percent a year return, you've got to be shooting for 100. You've got to be.

Right, right. I'll just take a couple more minutes because I know the market's opening. Actually, it opened a couple minutes ago. When this whole credit debacle happened, you shorted homebuilders first? What was the sequence there?
No, we have been short the financials for a long time, and probably the financials first coming off the 2000 top. Knowing that you're probably going into a Kondratieff-type winter. But it kept getting pushed off, right, by the Fed taking rates down to one or zero. Here we're doing the same thing again. They

keep delaying the real fallout and what should happen. So we would've been short the financials first and things like brokers for sure because coming off the peak in NASDAQ, the brokers had to suffer. It's just they created this other boom when they found new ways to make money and everybody recovered. We don't really make a lot of changes in our thematic portfolios. We just find things that come along that look like, "Gee, maybe we could short those, maybe the mono lines last year." You realize, "Holy crap, these guys have problems here," and you look at the balance sheet again.

Right.

I put a big short position on E*TRADE because I'm looking at them and going, "My God, they must be broke. Look at the assets they've got." I don't care if they've got a good trading business. The guy went and put all his money into subprime crap and the packaged papers and stuff like that. It's an incredible amount of money. So I don't know how he's going to make it. There are a lot of things like that that come along. Real estate I think is going to be under a lot of pressure here—commercial real estate. You can see it happening already.

All right. Well I think that's great. I'll let you get back to your desk.
Thanks, Bob.

Irwin Michael
The Art of Opportunistic Value

**"Either you want to eat well, or you want to sleep well.
If you want to eat well, you have to take on some risk."**

I used to read about Irwin Michael a decade or so ago and wonder who this guy was and how he put up the numbers he did. The name ABC Funds is not something you easily forget, and neither is the performance. Value investing with a twist is how I describe Irwin's style and the flexibility has generally kept him in the game even when value investing struggles.

Coming up to a nineteen-year track record, the results have been nothing short of spectacular, with a 16 percent annualized return compared to the TSX Total return index of around 10 percent. The longer the time frame, the greater the effect of compound growth. To put this into numbers, $100,000 invested with ABC on the inception date of March 20, 1989, would be worth over $1.6 million dollars at the end of 2007, whereas the same amount in the TSX would be worth about $600,000. This is almost three times the performance of the TSX in dollar terms! Believe it or not, I still hear the academics and pundits out there say that it is impossible to beat the markets. Nonsense.

I'll say that Irwin Michael is one of the only Stock Market Superstars profiled in this book that fits the mold. His thinking is strictly non-traditional, but his education isn't. You can't get much better than an undergrad degree from

McGill University and an MBA from Wharton at the University of Pennsylvania. Wharton just happens to be one of the most prestigious and top-rated business schools in the U.S. One of the hallmarks of value investing is that the margin of safety that a true value manager craves when they buy a stock acts as a cushion to the portfolio. Buying "out of favour" stocks is tough because it inherently makes you feel uncomfortable. This is probably why Irwin mentioned during the interview that if he were to take one more course to cap his career off, it would be a course in child psychology. This means that temporary losses of capital surely can present themselves from time to time, but permanent losses of capital are generally avoided. This was evident in the flagship fund, ABC Fundamental-Value Fund, stewarded by Irwin. It returned 26 percent in 2001 and 7.6 percent in 2002, remarkable when many other funds were going down 25 percent. Value investing generally gives "an easier ride," I like to say. Losses kill because you have to make up for all the lost ground, and that takes time. One of the great attributes of Irwin's style has been the ability to be consistent, and generally avoid the big declines. The fund has only had three down years in its eighteen calendar-year history. You can't forecast future gains, but I will tell you something: 2007 was one of those down years, and the other two times Irwin has lost money over a calendar year, the fund has roared back with some pretty remarkable returns over the ensuing few years. It is just the nature of the style.

Go back to 1999 and early 2000. Investors were calling Irwin and ridiculing him for not being in tech stocks. One guy even threatened to sue him. Tech stocks, the New Economy, and the Internet were all the rage. Stocks were not valued on earnings, but price/sales. I remember the time, and so does Irwin. With no tech stocks, how can you forget getting screamed at by greedy investors who are comparing you to the latest tech fund?

During the course of the interview, I asked what I thought was a question I would definitely know the answer to: "Do you use technical analysis?" Of course I knew that generally this is not what value investors do, but, then again, many value investors have the chronic problem of buying too early. To my surprise, Irwin said, "Of course I use technical analysis. I'll look at the technicals to determine entry or exit points once I have identified a stock to purchase or sell." That's one of the things that makes the style intriguing and helps Irwin stand out from the norm of even the best value managers.

The interview took place in the boardroom of ABC's downtown Toronto offices. While being a wide open space, similar to a bullpen, except for Irwin's office and the boardroom, it was one of the most professional offices I was in during the course of my interviews. I think I was the only guy in the office without a suit and tie. Irwin said this was done by design, as dealing directly with the public, he thought a professional office setting was mandatory. I respect that, and next time I go to his office, I'll wear a tie!

Another interesting quality of the office was a backroom that was used for investor learning sessions. Investors could include current clients or prospective clients, and this made the firm very unusual. Those of us in the know are aware of the fact that it is not the markets or funds that don't perform, it is how people react to the volatility in the markets that can destroy investor returns. I could see how these investor learning sessions could help allay investor fears and increase the end return to the investor. As an aside, ABC Funds gets top marks for its website, www.abcfunds.com. I have never seen so much transparency in a website, and so much useful information. From the reasoning behind the purchase or sale of each stock in the portfolio (with updates) to the value investing philosophy, the website generates some serious confidence in how money is run at this firm.

Bob:

You went to McGill, and then you received your MBA from Wharton. Did that help to shape your philosophy?

Irwin:

I think it was a great experience. When I went to McGill for my undergrad, the professors were good, but when I went to Wharton, the professors who taught me were the ones who wrote the book. In fact, I was fortunate enough to have in my last semester, Harry Markowitz, the father of portfolio theory. He was a visiting professor. He came down from, I guess, New York every Friday. So, it was a great opportunity to meet the man. He was very humble. I had a chance also to be taught by Marshall Blume of the famous dart throwing experiment. I was interested in the stock market before I went down to Wharton, but once I got there, it was just in the air; you breathe it. So, it was a great opportunity and I met a lot of people. There were only three Canadians when I went down there, in the entering class of five hundred. It was just a wonderful, wonderful opportunity.

That's fantastic to be taught by Markowitz. Now, obviously, with value investing, you're not necessarily believing in the efficient market.

Quite frankly, the market is imperfect. We find a lot of anomalies, particularly in the small- to mid-cap area, with something like 45 percent of public U.S. companies having no analytical following. It presents a lot of opportunities, so we want to take advantage of them.

Did you invest in stocks when you went to McGill and Wharton?

I didn't have very much money. I know that my late father invested in stocks. In fact, my great grandfather came from Johannesburg and he played the stock market extensively, but got blown away in 1929. So, I have that in the back of my mind. I have to be careful. But having said that, I didn't have any money when I was in high school and I was just struggling to put myself through university. Once I graduated, I bought the stock market, although my first job was not in stocks. It was in the bond market.

Right. I want to talk about that. Do you remember the first stock you ever bought for yourself?

Yes. I bought it and I should have held it today, because the first stock I bought was Toromont, which is still around today. I first bought the stock in 1972.

Now, you started in fixed income. In fixed income, you have to be more of a big-picture person, rather than a bottom-up person?

Yeah, well, the interesting thing is that I was trained for the stock market. When I was living in Philadelphia, wanting to come back to Canada, I wrote a lot of letters in between my first and second year of my MBA class. I only had around five positive replies out of maybe a couple of hundred. One of them was from Jordie Hodgson of Hodgson Roberton Laing. He said they had never hired a summer student before, but, "Come on in." So, I went to Montreal where I grew up. I met with him, and they offered me a summer position. They said to me, after that summer, that when I graduated, if I wished, I could have a position as well.

Well, I completed my final year at Wharton, was interviewed by a lot of firms, but to make a very long story short, they offered me a job to work with them. They were reputed to be the first investment counsel in Canada. It started in 19—I think—28. So, I contracted to work for them, but I didn't work right away. I decided to go to Europe with a knapsack and a sleeping bag.

When I came back, ready to start as an equity analyst, the bond trader had left the week before I joined them. You know how it is in this business? Last going in gets the job. The problem was I never knew anything about bonds. I always thought of bonds as Canada Savings Bonds. You buy them, and you tuck them away. To their credit, they had trust in me. They gave me a couple of hundred million to manage. Fortunately, I've got a fairly quick learning curve. I was just doing all sorts of spread trading, etc. The beauty of that really serendipitous event by not being a stock analyst, but becoming a bond trader, was that bond trading is a terrific discipline to have. First, you're forced to look very macro. When I'd wake up in the morning, I would check to see what T-bills were doing and what Europe was doing. More importantly, it taught me how to think very quickly on my feet, because bond trading is an over-the-counter market. The moment you drop the receiver down on the phone, the trade is dead.

Now, I got eaten up a little bit at the beginning. You know, it's sink or swim. Fortunately, you learn from your mistakes. It sharpened my mind, and it taught me how to speak. It taught me how to think very, very quickly, such that when I was courting my wife a number of years later, she couldn't believe how fast I talked, and how abrupt I could be. It is simply because you take maybe a hundred calls a day on the phone just on bond trading. She said, "You're the rudest person I've ever met." I said, "Look, that's part of our business. We're doing it short, and right to the point."

It's interesting because Wayne Deans started with the Bank of Canada....
He used to cover me, by the way.

Did he? Is that right?
Yeah, I used to speak with him, and we'd have lunch. He was in Montreal as I was.

Now, from then to ABC, why did you start the company here? Why did you call it ABC?
Well, first of all, I worked at Hodgson Roberton Laing and I did that for a little over two years. I became bored, and I was covered by Morgan Stanley. They approached me. The fact that I was Canadian, American educated, and fluently bilingual, they gave me an offer I could not refuse to move to New York, and, eventually, to go back to the Canadian office. Now, I had to change my hat from buy side to sell side, and it was a terrific experience. I got to work in New York, I remember, on the bond desk. David Mezzacappa, Louis Mendez—these were legends in the business. More importantly, I worked on the same trading desk as John Mack; they call him Mack the Knife. It was a great experience. Morgan Stanley was a great learning ground. They took me right through the company. I worked in virtually every area, from the syndicate desk, to sitting in on research meetings, you name it. I even was taken down to the floor of the Exchange in New York. In retrospect, perhaps, I should have paid them. Then they sent me back to the Canadian office.

At the time, the Parti Quebecois had won the Quebec election. Things were very, very tough in Quebec. All of our accounts were leaving, including Sun Life and a lot of the other insurance companies; a lot of my accounts. To make a long story short, one of my accounts that was in the process of leaving was Beutel Goodman. They wanted to meet with me. They made me an offer I could not refuse to move to Toronto. I moved to Toronto, became a partner, a junior partner with Beutel Goodman.

I was born, unfortunately, ten, fifteen years too late. They were all older than me—Seymour Schulich, Ned Goodman, Austin Beutel—but it was a great experience there. They were all very bright. They basically gave me that entrepreneurial spark. Now, keep in mind that I'm a fourth generation entrepreneur. My late father was, my grandfather, and my great-grandfather. They gave me the kick I needed, such that when I resigned from Beutel Goodman, approximately four years after I joined them, I was Vice-President of Fixed Income.

I was managing, at the time, about three quarters of a billion dollars of money market bonds with another person. When I left them, it freed me to do a lot of other things. For one, I did not have a job on the other side. I wanted to refocus on getting back into the stock market. So, for the next several years, it was the re-education of Irwin Michael. I joined the Annex Club, went to a lot of luncheon meetings, went to dog and pony shows, even became a Vice-President of the Toronto Futures Exchange. I call that my union card on Bay Street. I did everything, until I was ready to officially manage money. Now, although I left Beutel Goodman in 1982, I sold out my interest in 1985. So, even if I wanted a job in those three years, it was very difficult because there was a conflict of interest. No one wanted to hire me because I was still a principal. But once I sold out of Beutel in 1985, I started I.A. Michael, and started to manage money unofficially. Then I incorporated I.A. Michael Investment Counsel in late '85, about six months after I sold out of Beutel Goodman. I started off initially with individual accounts, and did a lot of research. To make a very long story short again, I started my first ABC fund in February of 1988, the balanced fund, called the Fully Managed Fund. What I wanted to do, in doing all my research, was cater to a high-net-worth clientele. So, my minimum was $150,000 and I put in the first bit of money. My father had passed away about six months before, so I convinced my widowed mother I'd look after the money, given that I was looking after it anyways. Then I developed a track record. A year later, I started the ABC Fundamental-Value Fund, which is, basically, our showcase fund at this point. It's now $750 million. Am I talking too much?

No, continue.

Then in 1996, I made a conscious decision. At the time, Canadian foreign content restriction was at 10 percent, and I felt, at some point, they were going to increase that. So I wanted to develop an expertise. I started the ABC American-Value Fund. Everyone said to me, "You don't have an expertise." I said, "Look, I'm American educated. I can bone up pretty quickly." Anyway, we started that fund. I put in the first few dollars as well, and here it is a decade and a bit later. We've got first quartile performance, and, because of that, we started two new funds. They are closed-end funds because I had a near-death experience with three pension funds that went into my Fundamental-Value Fund. They cashed out right at the bottom of the value market. I always want a little bit of ballast for our three open-ended funds. So, I have now two closed-end funds, ABC North American Deep-Value Fund, which strictly buys North American deep-value stocks, and, lastly, the ABC Dirt-Cheap Stock Fund, which is a go-anywhere fund. I can buy any dirt-cheap stock in the world. I remain the single largest unitholder of my funds. So, the funds have been good to me, particularly when you look at my Fundamental-Value Fund, which is showing a compound rate of return of about 16 percent for fifteen years. Boy, it doesn't take very much for money to grow.

I might be wrong here, but I describe your style as opportunistic value. Does that make sense?

Well, I'll give you as many adjectives as I can. It's opportunistic, deep-value, contrarian, patient, proactive, disciplined, focused, with a sense of urgency. Want more?

No. No, that's descriptive. How much quantitative versus qualitative analysis when you're going to buy stock? I think you described yourself as 80 percent value, 20 percent growth. Is that right?

We're primarily deep-value, but you want to be careful you're not buying a value trap. So, we're constantly looking for stocks, which are maybe beaten up companies that have potential to grow.

A lot of other value managers, whether it's Cundill, or Templeton, or Brandes, or Puccetti, have few resource stocks in their portfolio. It doesn't fit in with their discipline, whereas I know you had Lionore Mining and lots of different resource companies.

Yeah. I mean we have HudBay Mining. We made a lot of money on FNX Mining.

Do you still own FNX?

No, we sold it a while ago; took our profit. We bought it around $4.75; I sold it all around $12. Thank you very much. Then we took all that money, and we found HudBay Mining. It was at $2.75, and we ended up cleaning out five institutions. We thought it was dirt cheap. We met with Peter Jones, the manager, and I loved him because he was wearing a short-sleeved shirt with a plastic pad for his pen. His hands were maybe a little grimy. It was beautiful. We believed in him, his management, and also the fact that we thought they had a great business plan and great business models.

That company had a bit of a bad reputation previously. It had some earlier management problems, but that all changed. The market didn't factor that in, right?
Yeah, you know, when we met Peter, we were just blown away.

How much quantitative and how much qualitative research do you use?
We're very eclectic here; we're stock pickers. We're NAV buyers. So, whether it's a widget company, or whether it's a resource company, we break down the company into many pieces and put it back together to see what it's worth relative to where it's trading. So, there was no real difference between, say, maybe a HudBay Mining and a Canam Group. They both had good management, and we thought they were both trading at a significant discount to what they were worth. So, we were the lead order when Canam did that financing at $5.75.

Are there different parameters you look at with resource companies?
No, we use the same principles. I mean I look at a mining company much the same way I'd look at any other industrial. We look at book value, breakup, net asset value, cash flow, quality of management, and hidden assets. The fact is that I didn't feel like buying Inco, but we felt that relative to Inco, we should be buying HudBay Mining and, previous to that, FNX Mining. We did the same thing with EuroZinc.

Tell me about EuroZinc.
We bought it at $0.60. No one liked it. In fact, it even went below our cost, and we couldn't understand it. So, we bought a little more but, ultimately, we scaled up. We had over 20 million shares, and I guess we sold it all the way up.

Are companies going private more in the U.S. with Sarbanes-Oxley?

Well, we believe that Sarbanes-Oxley, particularly Section 404, is perhaps one of the greatest catalysts for companies to go private because it's so costly. Actually, it's not so much that it's such an onerous law, but we believe a lot of foreigners have not bought the U.S. market, or even listed on the American exchanges, because they're worried about Sarbanes-Oxley. They worry about all the filing and the incremental costs that go along with it. That's why we love the U.S. market and, in particular, the small microcap area. We've had numerous small and microcap U.S. companies that have gone private.

Sometimes your personality is reflected in your investment style. Value managers tend to be frugal, and growth managers are more risk takers in their personal lives.

You're asking me? You have to learn to write on both sides of a piece of paper. What I will say is that when you become an entrepreneur—and I've had to teach all my guys that work with me—it's not a question of about being cheap. I spend a lot of money on the latest technology. Yes, I'm in a B building. I don't feel I have to have a lot of marble and granite. I can have it at home, but I drive an eight-year-old car, and my wife drives a brand new one. So, I mean everyone has their style. I guess the bottom line is you have to believe in your philosophy. I believe in conserving, you know, not to throw things out. More importantly, one man's poison is another man's meat. Quite often, we'll find stocks that are just so beaten up that they look cheap. It's part of our mystique with clients. They like to come into our office. I mean it's very presentable, but there's no marble. Because I'm the single largest unitholder of my own funds, the buck stops here.

Sure.

One of my all-time heroes is Harry Truman. We're the same way, so we run a tight ship. Because we've watched our bottom line, whether it be in picking stocks, or in the office, we've never had to cut salaries. We've always paid our bills on time. It's part of my philosophy. I watched my late father, who was a retail grocer. He quit high school at 16 to join the Canadian army in 1939. When he left the army in '45, he came back at 22, and had no education. I watched him run a retail grocery store. As I wrote in the January ABC perspective a couple years ago, I learned a lot from the way my father ran his business. I used to work on a truck, and there are a lot of similarities between running maybe a corner grocery store and properly running an investment management company. You have to watch your bottom line and you have to be very sensitive to not only employees but to the people whose money you look after.

Well, that's very interesting because it's a different skill set—picking stocks and running your own business properly. Do you think what you look for when picking stocks has an influence on the way you run your business here?

We have a very open mind. A few years ago, we bought a number of hotels. People look at them on a revenue-per-room basis, RevPAR. We don't. We look at it on net asset value basis. When I looked at the replacement cost of the Royal York Hotel, you can't find that property anywhere. So, Legacy Hotel REIT was one of our big stocks—the same thing with Royal Host. We take a different perspective on things, and we'll go quite often where other people aren't. The other thing I'll say is that cheap stocks tend to lie in cheap industries. We don't have any banks in our portfolio. The last one I had was Laurentian, and I sold it. I don't feel I have to have all the banks. If I find five mining companies, or if I find five hotel common shares that look really cheap, I'll buy them all.

Just a little bit more about the firm. It's very professional. I've gone into some companies and people were wearing jeans.

No, there are no casual Fridays here. We all have to wear a suit and a tie, and that goes for me. It's me but, more importantly, it's respect for our clients who come in. All of my competitors, they can wear whatever they want. Here, when our clients come in, I expect my guys to be well groomed with a suit and tie. The bottom line is respect for the client when he comes in; he's a king. As long as he or she comes in, as long as they don't make a pest of themselves, we'll answer their phone calls anytime. We'll give them personal gilt-edged service. Being properly attired is part of that. It's very old school.

Has your style evolved over time? You probably manage money a little bit differently than you did fifteen years ago.

Yeah, naturally it has. I wrote a piece on the back page of my ABC perspective. I entitled it "Portfolio Management: Like Aging Fine Wine." The analogy I gave is you take a hockey player, baseball player, tennis player, or even a football player. They peak between their late 20s and early 30s, and they're gone. At that age, a portfolio manager is still a rookie. A portfolio manager gets better over time. You learn from your mistakes, hundreds of mistakes that you make, and hundreds of wins. You develop, and you probably peak, or you level off, in performance and style, in your late 40s or early to mid-50s.

But you have to be adaptive along the way?

Absolutely. Absolutely. You've got to be a free thinker. You've got to be very pliable. No one's ever too old to learn.

We were in a commodity bear market for a lot of years with some little cyclical bulls in there. Where did you find value in the early '90s, the late '90s, this decade?

Yeah, when high-tech was running like crazy in the late '90s, we refused to go there. We looked at Nortel on the way up right to where it peaked at $124.50. It had a book value of $11, half of which was goodwill. Goodwill is air, as far as I'm concerned. So, I wouldn't touch it. Maybe it was good around $1. We don't buy stocks that trade at a hundred times earnings. I lost a lot of clients because of that, but I refused to buy it. Instead, I bought stocks like Canada Bread, which had gone from $40 down to $10. I bought it at $10, and no sooner did I buy it, it was trading at $8.75. So I looked like an idiot to my clients. They were very upset, but that was one of our big winners, because it didn't collapse.

We had a number of other stocks like that that held up very well, so we did rather well on the bounce, when the baton was handed from the high-tech to the value players. Basically, we just stuck to our deep-value style, picking stocks in Canada and the U.S. We've also had a lot of takeovers. A few years ago we were buying a lot of resource stocks, oil and gas. I think two of our biggest winners, in the last several years, have been Nexen and Talisman. The only reason why I bought them both, they were both so cheap I couldn't make up my mind. So I bought them both.

We were very heavy in the forestry side. We owned Riverside Forest Products. We bought at around $8.75, $9.00, and we were taken out, or we sold, in the early $30s. We're very pliable, very pliable. That's part of our success, being pliable, disciplined, and focused. We have a very low coefficient of correlation or affinity to the TSX index. When we started our ABC Dirt-Cheap Stock Fund, an associate said to me, "There's no doubt in my mind that if you name a fund the ABC Dirt-Cheap Stock Fund, there's no chance of style drift." That's the beauty, and, really, that is our style. We try not to style drift. So, when I look at a lot of the stocks in the TSE index, quite frankly, they're not cheap. So, we owned no banks, and no Bombardier. When you go right through the piece, no utilities, and yet, we owned 9.9 percent of Andres Wine at one point. We owned Arbor Memorial Services. No one covered those stocks, so we have a lot of names which are very, very different.

Do you think when stocks are heavily covered by analysts that the opportunity set for making a good amount of money is gone already?

Well, it's funny. The analogy I often give is, you know, roll back about eight years. You had thirty analysts maybe following Nortel. What was the marginal utility of the thirty-first analyst who's going to follow Nortel? Yet, you'll get a company like Morguard Corporation, which controls Morguard REIT. No one followed them. We bought it very cheaply. There's only one analyst, from Dominion Securities, who covered it. We bought it at $20 and it probably had an NAV of between $45 and $50, yet no one followed it. So, you get a lot of stocks like that, and it's kind of neat.

Maybe you can't speak for other managers, but why do most fund managers hesitate to stray from the index?

I'm not going to speak for other people, but my sense is there are a lot of index huggers out there. We never have been because I think we're not a core manager. If you're a core manager, you want to stay close to the index to protect yourself, but from our point of view, we're specialty managers. We're a great complement to a core manager. It's the old saying, "Either you want to eat well or sleep well." If you want to eat well, you have to take a little bit of risk. I don't mind taking a little bit of risk, particularly if it's calculated and defined. I've got good analysts who work with me. We review stocks and we'll calculate whether it's worth taking that plunge.

Now, value managers have said in the past they tend to be early in on a stock, and early out, meaning they buy too early and they generally sell too early.

Early in, early out, yeah.

Do you accept that, and say it's fine?

You know what? I buy it because it looks cheap, and I sell it because it looks expensive on a value basis. You're constantly handing the baton over to someone else who takes a different view, and that is they say, "Hey, man, this thing has momentum." They don't mind paying two and a half times book, but I do. By then, there's always another bus to catch, and particularly in the U.S. market, where we find a significant number of dirt-cheap stocks. I wish I had more money to manage.

I think I know the answer to this, but just to cover it: You wouldn't use technical analysis ever, would you?

We do.

Oh, you do? That is a surprise.

Yeah. We do the fundamental analysis, but then, at the same time, before we put in any orders, we like to look at the technicals.

I think that's real important for executing a buy and sell.

Absolutely. Absolutely. We look at the charts.

What is your selling discipline?

It's a very tough discipline, and over twenty years ago, I wrote an article for the *Financial Post*. It was entitled "Buying is easy; selling is hard." I use this analogy all the time. You buy into a company, you become friendly with the president, and you go out for dinner. You even have their kids over to your pool, and you have to differentiate between liking the company and management and liking the stock price. The bottom line is that the stock price goes up—you still like the president, you still like his company, but it's no longer cheap. The stock has doubled. It's trading at say a P/E of 25, and you decide your selling discipline goes in here. If you sell it the next time he calls you to go for a round of golf, you feel like you're Benedict Arnold. You know what I mean?

Right.

But the fact is you have to differentiate it. I'm hard and cruel when it comes to my stocks. When it comes to my wife and kids, I'm soft. Maybe that's how it should be.

Considering that you find dirt-cheap stocks, I'm sure you find usually expensive stocks like Nortel and things like that. Have you ever wanted to short stocks in the portfolio?

No. I've shorted once in my life personally. I made 50 percent on my money, but it wasn't worth it because I was calling the broker every ten minutes. The bottom line is when you short a stock, you have unlimited liability. I think you have to have a certain mentality to go long or to go short. I have a long mentality, a long investor mentality. Quite frankly, I want to sleep well at night. I don't mind buying 9.9 percent of Andres Wine, or buying Kansas City Life in the States, or American National Insurance, but I want to be long only. I bought these companies because I thought they were cheap.

Right. It isn't a very good risk/reward trade when you have unlimited losses and limited gains. In a short, you have a 100 percent maximum gain.

Exactly.

On a different note, you have quite a website. I don't think there's anybody that I've ever seen that's more transparent than you. Obviously, people can take ideas off the site. Do you ever wonder if people are latching onto your ideas?

Yeah, I mean it's a free world. We decided to do that, and we have two websites, abcfunds.com and valueinvestigator.com. We didn't have to have the second site, but I decided right at the bottom of the value market in late 1999, early 2000, that we needed a vehicle to expound what we're doing. More importantly, it is to explain the philosophy to our clients. I must admit that I'd say two-thirds of our clients do not reside in the Greater Toronto Area. Our clients are all around the world, Canadians that have moved out. We've got clients in Malta, in the Channel Islands, in the U.K., in the United States. I've got a Canadian client who lives in Prague, Czech Republic, and he said the only way he can keep in touch is through our website. He gets everything. We only do an analysis of the company to put on our website when we have our full position. It's my duty to make sure the world knows. After we've sold something, as you know, and it's on our website, we will explain that we sold it. It'll stay on our website for three months. We try and be intellectually honest. Yeah, people can steal from us, and that's fine. More importantly, we've picked up a lot of clients thanks to our website. I had people buy a few stocks that I had, and then they e-mailed me, or they called me, and they said, "Do you still own this?" I said, "No." I mean they're not even clients of mine. I said, "No, we sold that three months ago."

Because of your fixed income background, maybe just talk about the Fully-Managed Fund for a bit. If we look at the bonds that you have in there, a lot could be corporate, or high-yields.

Yeah, it can be anything. The reason why we don't have any government bonds is that we found them all to be expensive. Whatever we did buy, whether it was a Nexen Bond 6.85 percent, or the Nova Chemicals, they were relatively cheap compared to Canadians. So, I still have that trading mentality of spread trading that I'd picked up when I was managing money at Hodgson Roberton Laing. I use the same concept for stocks. In other words, I'll look at a spread between a small cap and a large cap in terms of P/E multiples, discount to book, price earnings ratios, etc. That's important to me.

If you own a common stock, will you own the bond sometimes also?

Yeah, we've done it. I mean we have that in a few cases. We owned Aecon Group convertible debentures, and I also owned the stock in one of my other funds. We thought for a balanced fund it was appropriate to buy a convertible debenture.

I think that's so important, because you're adding a lot of value on the bonds. Ninety percent of balanced funds invest in five-, ten- or twenty-year government bonds, and then some stocks. It's not worth it. There's really not the value that you can provide when half of your bond return is being taken away by the management cost.

Mm-hmm.

You're adding value in the bonds, and most people don't do that. You managed the Dynamic Income Fund at Beutel Goodman?

Yes, at Beutel.

If you can't find value in stocks to fit your criteria, will you build up the cash position in the portfolio, or do you just say, "I'll just make my positions bigger"?

If I can't find any stocks to be bought, I'll build cash. If we're finding a lot of stocks to be bought, it tells me the market is cheap. If I can't find things to be bought, the market's expensive. Again, we're stock pickers—we're not market timers—and we're always looking. It's funny. We will probably always find cheap stocks out there, no matter how bad the market is, just because we're always sleuthing about. For instance, we owned at one time just under 5 percent of a company called S&K Famous Brands, a haberdashery chain out of Richmond, Virginia. They paid us a $6 special dividend. That's terrific. No one followed it and it shouldn't even have been a public company. We owned a company called Foodarama Grocery Stores out of New Jersey. They had less than a million shares total. I put that in my North American Deep-Value Fund. We bought at $37; and it went to $32. I was white-knuckled but then we get taken out, in the late $50s, low $60s.

Has there ever been a time when you questioned your style? You know, when people were ragging on you and taking money out?

You know, it's funny. Back in 1999, early 2000, when Nortel, 360 Networks, Red Hat, were all running like crazy, we had a lot of clients yelling and screaming at me literally. One client, he said I was yesterday's man because I refused to buy high technology. "That's the way it's going. We're going into a new decade." It's the same sort of thing I believe Warren Buffett went through. It's funny, one client was so irate he said he was thinking of suing me and exposing me to the media. I said, "For what? For doing my job?" I said, "I refuse to buy Nortel." I said, "You know darn well what we sold our services for. We're deep-value managers." He was very upset, and I was delighted when he left because he was calling fairly regularly. After a while, I couldn't take his phone calls. But the bottom line was we stuck to our style. We didn't play for the crowd, so to speak. Whatever we did, I would do exactly again. Was it easy? No. We had to be very focused.

I remember my wife said to me, when times were really tough, "No matter what you do, you wear it on your sleeve, and you come home with it." She said, "You know, maybe it's time to hang up your cleats." I said, "On the contrary." I decided to rebuild. I started the Value Investigator website. I bulked up, hired some new people to work with me, to again focus on deep value. I don't regret it to this day.

That was the point of maximum pessimism, right, which is when John Templeton says you should buy. There was an article a while ago that

somebody from PH&N wrote. He said, "If you feel very, very uncomfortable with your portfolio, you've probably got a great portfolio. If you feel very comfortable with the herd," then he says, "you probably should change your portfolio around." Does that make sense from your viewpoint? Did you feel comfortable with being uncomfortable?

I'll say this: If I have to take one more course to be the capstone of my career, after the B.Comm. McGill, Wharton MBA and CFA, it'd be a course in child psychology. It's one thing to do your deep analysis for stocks, but it's another thing to know the game of psychology. I guess the point I'm trying to get at is that when you start feeling that queasiness in your stomach, when you want to puke, vomit, or, in the vernacular, if you're ready to barf, it probably tells you you're close to the bottom. The human mind can only take so much, and then you throw in the towel.

I've been an investment advisor and portfolio manager for fifteen years, and I have that sense now. I remember numerous occasions when the market was crashing seven days in a row and I thought, "Okay, this is climaxing. This is getting to the end." Sure enough, the market moves up. You just get that feel.

I'm one of the very few that was actually trained for the business. I mean, the opportunity of a lifetime was to study under Harry Markowitz. Actually, the course was more matrix algebra than anything else. Having said that, the psychology that I took suits the stock market because the stock market is a bunch of greedy people trying to make money.

That's what I found. A lot of academics don't factor in human emotion. Long-Term Capital Management had two Nobel Laureates, super-smart people, but they didn't factor in any emotions in the market.
Yeah.

Why do computer-modelled hundred-year events happen every six years?
Funny, you bring up another factor. When I was going to the Wharton School, I worked for two years as a waiter in a fraternity house. I worked for two black men. I remember Sparky McIvor, who was the cook, said to me one day, "So, what are you learning? What are you learning at this Wharton School?" It was right on campus. He'd been there for years, and was probably

in his early 60s by then. I said, "Well, they teach me how to analyze companies and find out what is cheap, and then I buy them." This is a man from the ghettoes. He said, "Okay. So, tell me more." I said, "Well, we analyze them. I decide if I'm going to buy something, and I buy stock." He said, "Well, what does that mean?" I said, "Well, I buy stock, and I write a cheque, hard money. I write a cheque, and I give it to the broker." He says, "Well, what do you get back?" I said, "A certificate." He says, "Well, what's that?" I said, "A piece of paper." I heard the deepest baritone belly laugh. He turned to his sidekick, Gene Ross, who's a part-time Baptist minister, and said, "Gene, you hear that? This crazy guy, he's giving real hard-earned money to get a piece of paper."

You know, when you think about it, Sparky wasn't too far wrong, particularly after all the shenanigans that went on in the marketplace. This business is built upon one word; it's *trust*. You're a president of a company. You come in here. You could be selling me a bill of goods. I have to trust you. I've been burned before and everyone's been burned before by guys who lie or tell tall tales or whatever. When you really think of it, that's what we're doing. We're just buying pieces of paper with the view that, hopefully, this piece of paper is going to be worth a lot more. That's why I have on the wall that Bre-X certificate that cost me $7. A hundred shares cost me $7. At the peak it was worth $2,800. That's so I don't forget what Sparky taught me.

Do you meet with most clients?

We've got two thousand clients. They're all around the world, but we talk to them on the phone. I've got a 1-800 line. They can call in anytime. We'll tell them whether we think it's appropriate for them. We don't want all of everyone's money. Now, I break the rules because I have all my money in this. I trust my management, but I don't trust other people.

When I first got into the business, the only thing I worried about was: How am I going to attract clients that believe in my philosophy? It worked out over time, and I think that was because the clients who didn't believe in the philosophy left and ones that did stayed. Is that what you found?

Well, look, they do or they don't. You're always going to be losing clients for whatever reason. You know, they're providing a mortgage for their kid's house, or they may need an operation, whatever. So, that's part of the game. But, I mean, there's a metamorphosis of clients. You know, at the beginning, when I needed money to start off my funds, I got certain clientele. They might have left me three or four years later. As one of my mentors said to me, "They provided you with a purpose. They came in when you were a little higher risk, when you were starting out. Now you have new clients who come in who see a different you." You're constantly restocking clientele, as you are with stocks, but, more importantly, we develop a certain following, a certain comfort level, and you will attract different clients as you go along.

Obviously, when you're buying stocks, you are buying businesses based upon a price on the market. Prices go down significantly from your purchase price. Do you reassess what you've done? Have you ever just said, "Okay, I'm wrong," and cut losses?

I've done that. I've done that.

Average down?

Yeah, we'll average down if we think it's good. We bought a lot of companies where we took an initial position expecting it to go down, because you can't buy everything right at the bottom. As long as you get the major trend, we like to buy on the way down as opposed to on the way up. On the way down, I have no competition. We just keep on buying, buying, buying, and then eventually it'll work. Particularly now that we're so large, you can't buy it all in one fell swoop.

I've read through almost all of your information from the past. Something you mentioned, which I thought was interesting, is that we're losing our companies here in Canada. I guess that must be because of M&As. Is that going to continue to increase?

Yes. Well, particularly if you lose stock like Inco. You know, to my knowledge, a company out of Arizona, Phelps, isn't exactly a Canadian company, so, again, that was one of the reasons why I'd started the American Fund in 1996. That's why I've started my two new funds, more particularly my Dirt-Cheap Stock Fund, which gives me the ability to go around the world.

You find more value in the U.S. than in Canada?

Well, in insurance companies, we definitely found that. I mean Manulife, Sun Life, and Great West did very well, but we didn't buy them trading at two and a half times book. I was prepared to own American National Insurance out of Galveston, Texas; Presidential Life out of New York; or Phoenix Companies out of Connecticut that were all trading at book or below.

It's the same with the banks?

I have used insurance companies as my surrogate for banks. You're going to have banks that become insurance companies as well, and vice versa.

Is there a stock that stands out in your mind that was your biggest win over the last seventeen or eighteen years?

Well, one stock in particular. We bought Electrohome, and it was a manufacturing company that owned a couple of television stations. It never did anything. I must admit I was getting a little impatient, then it sold its television stations to CTV and I ended up having Baton stock. Then Baton was bought out by Bell Canada. So, here we had a stock that I think we made ten times on just because the value was there.

Is it hard to maintain that type of patience?

Yeah, you've got to be patient. I mean you make the best decision given certain information at the particular time, right? It's a judgment call.

That gets to the Dirt-Cheap Fund you talked about. That's the same philosophy?

It's global, but, more importantly, it's more aggressive. I think the risk to reward, in the long run, will be quite favourable for the holders. That's why I bought into it in a good size as well.

We also have an interesting relationship with Canada Life. To make a long story short, we were the first non-Canada Life investment product to go in their Universal Life menu. I bought the first policy, all invested in my Fundamental-Value Fund. So, it's kind of neat to get good sticky money that comes in from a life company. So, the bottom line is you're always going to have shifting between funds. For the life of me, I don't question people's libido as to why they're doing this, or doing that, as long as it makes sense. They're all over twenty-one. If they want to sell one fund and buy the other, I mean, what am I going to do?

During the last commodity cycle 1966 to 1982, the U.S. stock market was flat, 1,000 to 1,000. That's what it ended at. We have another commodity cycle going on and the U.S. market has been relatively flat in the last seven years. Can you make good money in a flat market?

I think so, and that is explained by the fact that the market is imperfect.

From a big-picture perspective, do you think we're in a secular bull commodity cycle?

For the moment. You know, all things…trees don't grow to the sky. All things must pass. So, the bottom line is for the moment, things look good. I mean you can't always depend upon China and India to drive the world economies. Eventually, the economies are going to slow down. Hopefully, we'll be wise enough to remember to get off the bus and move into something else.

You hear people talking about commodity bubbles and comparing it to tech. But you still found lots of value?

Yeah, when I fall asleep at night, I tend to fall asleep listening to the radio. We brought a radio company outside of Canada.

Boring businesses?

Very boring. It's cash flow.

The old Buffett thing?

The Irwin Michael thing. I mean I don't look at Buffett. I look at ourselves, and we're able to buy it. I mean we're probably doing what Buffett did twenty or thirty years ago. I mean for him to buy something, he's got to go big into a company to buy a multi-billion dollar position. The beauty of us is that we can take a $25, $30, or $40 million position in something. That's a full position. I'll put it right across the board in all of my funds. So, it's kind of neat. You don't want to be too big. You should still have the flexibility to do interesting things in the stock market.

I think Buffett put in his annual report, "If anybody knows of any really undervalued companies out there, just please let me know. But I have to put in at least $5 billion into the company." He said, "If anybody knows of any, give me a call because I'm always looking."

Well, we found one and I'm buying it right now. We found a number of those in the United States.

Things tend to go in cycles. Sometimes large caps are more undervalued than small caps.

Yeah.

So, you'll go into large caps. You've done that in the past?

Yeah. We're like a chameleon—we'll move around a lot. We're not predisposed to any one sector, any one industry, any type of stock in terms of size. In fact, we are all cap deep-valued. While we find the most imperfections in small and microcap, ideally, I'd love to buy a large cap. It's less stressful because I can buy all I want, and sell it in one fell swoop.

Well, I always use the analogy about how cockroaches survived and dinosaurs didn't. Cockroaches were adaptable to whatever the climate change was at that time.

You have a very concentrated portfolio and think a lot of very successful people do. You don't use the spray and pray approach like some managers will do. How important, do you think, is that?

Well, the bottom line is when I went to the Wharton School, they did a study. They said that it was eleven or twelve stocks that gave you maximum utility in a portfolio. I couldn't sleep if I had had eleven stocks, but I think if you can put in thirty or forty stocks in a portfolio, and if you call that concentrated, I can live with that. That's what we have, basically, in our ABC Fundamental-Value Fund. It's a three quarters of a billion dollar portfolio. You don't want to overly diversify for several reasons. One is you'll never be able to follow all the stocks as an analyst. More importantly, I remember reading a *Wall Street Journal* article about ten or fifteen years ago, and it related to the fact that successful managers who did really well had their top ten holdings equal to at least 40 percent. In other words, let your winners run, and don't constantly sell them off to get back on track. So, we tend to let our winners run unless we feel uncomfortable. I like to sleep well.

That's important because human emotion makes you sell your winners and hold onto your losers till they get back to the price you paid.

Absolutely.

Then you see people with a portfolio of losers.

Oh, exactly. That's human nature, as you say. It's funny, when we had a run on our fund back in 2000 and three pension funds decided to leave us, I had to raise $100 million out of a $330 million portfolio within two weeks. What I did was I kept my good stocks, and sold all my junk. I wouldn't call them junk, but they were my weaker stocks. In consequence, it made my performance very good the next year because the good stocks became a greater proportion of the portfolio. And I let them run.

You used to be a VP of the Toronto Futures Exchange, is that right?
Correct. Yeah.

That's a different mindset?
No, I did that because I was still unofficially a partner at Beutel Goodman before I sold out in 1985. More importantly, at Beutel, I used to work at Yonge and Eglinton. I never even knew downtown. I figured, "What the heck? Let me buy a seat on the Exchange," which was $6,500. Then I decided to run for Vice-President of the Exchange. When they had the election a couple of weeks later, I lost by maybe one or two votes. They were so impressed with my speech, they said, "Hey, why don't you help us?" I said, "What do you mean?" "Well, we'll make you Vice-President. We'll pay you real money." They were foolish because if they had let me be Vice-President of the Exchange, I would have done it for nothing.

Let's take a look at the outliers of your return: 1993 was a big year; you were up very, very big.
One hundred twenty-one percent. That was my Tiger Woods year. You know, you're hitting holes-in-one everywhere. Even my mistakes made me money. My biggest winner that year? Well, I started off with cutting a deal with Goodyear, but that was small. My biggest winner was Global Stone. That was an aggregates company that did extremely well. I bought it at $3. You got one share and half of warrant. The first trade, when it started to trade, was down at $2.75. So, I was already offside 10 percent.

I went back to the drawing board. I said, "Now, this thing is cheap, and the market doesn't know how to value this," so I bought more. I won't say I doubled up, but it was close. Within six months, the stock was at around $4.50, $5. The warrants, which I basically got for nothing, I sold at I think at $3. Then I kept on rolling into other things that did very well for us.

A home-run year in lots of things. On the other side, the other outliers—1998?
That was a bad year for me because my small caps, after the Asian flu, didn't come back in time. They did come back, but it was in the next year

1999, so I had to suffer through it. One of my mistakes in my good year, in 1993, was that I stayed a little too long with my small caps. Small caps made me a lot of money in 1993. In retrospect, I should have sold them a little more aggressively in the fall to early winter of 1994. The market was down, but I still would have made a lot more money. You've got to sell when the demand is there, particularly with small caps. You can always get out of Bell Canada.

Sure, but the liquidity dried up in small caps
Exactly, very much so.

You had positive years in both 2001 and 2002. Hardly any managers in the country were able to do that. Is that just a function of the style?
No, whatever I did back in 1999 to 2000….

It came to fruition.
It came to fruition. I was patient enough, to my credit, and to my clients' credit. Those who trusted our instincts, benefited,

You saw a lot of value in oils at that time. What was it, $10 or $11 a barrel?
Yeah, a little bit in oils, but we had a lot of stocks like Canada Bread. We were buying a lot of things that people didn't want to touch. I mean, one of our big winners over the last several years has been E-L Financial, Hal Jackman's company. We bought it at $240. It paid us a $24 dividend. You've got to hand it to Hal, and his son, Duncan. They've done a great job of running this company, which, in effect, is almost like a private corporation.

Have you ever hedged your currency exposure?
I did it up until the Canadian dollar was at $0.80. It was too stressful, too costly, and I decided no. That's hurt me, particularly my American fund. My two Canadian funds have about 25 to 28 percent U.S. content. Do you play chess?

I do.
I'm willing to give up a rook to steal a queen. So I'm willing to lose 5 or 6 percent or 7 percent on currency to make 40, 50, 60 percent on a cheap U.S. stock. And that's what's happened.

Right. At the beginning, was it just you running money.

Yeah. I started off just by myself.

As far as managing the business, is that a tough decision to know when to get bigger?

Well, when I left Beutel Goodman, I called up a good friend, Ann Marshall, of James P. Marshall, to let her know I was leaving Beutel. She was a pension consultant. She says, "Well, what are you going to do?" I said, "Well, I'd like to put out my own shingle, and start to build up an investment counselling firm." She said, "Look, I have a spare office if you'd like to come in until you get your head together and do it." I was there from '82 till '90, for eight years. She was kind enough, and she was very helpful to me as a sounding board, and was a very disciplined constructive criticizer.

How is it structured with the analysts? Do they have specific industries they look at, or do they just come up with random ideas?

One fellow handles all the income trusts—one fellow all Canadian stocks. Another fellow does the U.S., but there's inter-lapping. When we go into a meeting, I'll take two analysts with me because I like to have a sounding board, someone with a different take.

But you make the decisions?

With them. Ultimately, someone has to tip it, but the bottom line is I respect their judgment very much.

You know, when you talk to a lot of value investors, a lot of them say the same thing. Some are a lot more successful than others. If there was something that could differentiate you from other value investors, the kind of the secret to your success, what would it be?

Well, I spend a lot of time doing this. I wake up early in the morning to philosophize, and to see where I've gone wrong, and where I'm doing things right. I'm blessed to have a wife who's been very supportive, and four kids who probably have given up some of our family time so that we can do this. You know, my oldest son, who is 16, says to me, "Dad, just continue to do what you're doing. I'd like to join you. I like what you people do in the firm." So, we'll see. Right now, I regard it as fun. I enjoy it. I've been able to contain my stress. Yeah, I mean you can have a tough day at the office, but, on balance, I love the excitement. You know, it's not one discipline. One day you're using your mathematics. Another day, it's microanalysis. One day, micro accounting, and then your macroeconomics, and then you use everything. You use your history, your sense of reading people and their body language. This takes time.

I guess you're dealing with higher net worth people, but they are retail investors.

Mm-hmm.

Obviously, emotions wear on them. Behavioral finance I think is really important. This distinguishes the good investor from a bad one. Is that why you have so much educational material on your website?

I liken our two websites to the *New York Times*—the *Sunday Times*—we archive everything. We want people to really know what we're all about before they give us money. By knowing us, we're able to retain clients longer. So they don't just write us a "Dear John" letter at the drop of a hat just because the market's off 5 percent. In addition to that, we run investment meetings in the back, and I'll show you after. We do it sometimes once to twice a month, and we do conferences.

Are there any rules that you have that you just never break?

Not really. I mean a lot of it's just plain common sense. If I make a mistake, I fess up to it. You try not to believe your own BS. In other words, no one's invincible. We do make mistakes. That's why they put erasers at the end of pencils.

I've forgotten whether I've asked you what your biggest mistake was.

I probably have some, but you know what? I don't want to remember. It's common sense. We manage money for a lot of new Canadians—Asian, East Asian. I'm very proud of that. Their language is poor, but they trust us. That excites me. We manage money for a lot of unilingual French Canadians, and we do our best. We're trying to do whatever we can, and we're still a small company. Having said that, we try to offer you the best bang for your buck. I can't leave here because I'm the largest client. My whole RSP is in the funds, and so is my wife's, and as I told my four kids, they better be good because Daddy manages their RESP and it's all in the Fundamental-Value Fund. I jokingly said to one of my sons, "You better be good to me." My son facetiously said, "Like why should I?" I said, "Because it'll be the difference between going to a small junior college and maybe the Harvard Business School."

Is it $150,000 minimum for RSPs also?

Yes, for everything, but you can make up your $150,000 by virtue of having part in your RSP and part in your non-registered money.

Have you thought about what your max capacity is, the maximum amount of money you could manage?

We could probably go up to $2 billion without adding any people just because I've hired a couple of new people. We're integrating them gradually, and we have the ability to take on more money.

Did you have any books that you've read that you think are great books for people to read? I see *Security Analysis* on the shelf. That's a rough one for people to read through, but anything that you found most valuable?

I read a lot. In fact, I was asked a question today. I was reading a book about exploits of World War II, allied soldiers and fifty different things. It is a book that has nothing to do with investments, but what struck me is that it shows ingenuity and simplicity. We have a problem. How do we attain the objective we want? That's the same thing in a stock market. How do I invest this money properly?

So things outside the investment community relate?

There are a lot of things. I mean I like reading psychology books. Yeah, I read the odd financial book. I read newspapers—three, four, five newspapers a day. I mean I can spend a whole day just googling at home. But I don't have the time.

In the past, any sorts of events that kind of shaped your investment philosophy, where you said, "Wow, this is the direction I should go in"?

No, I mean, as one of my good friends once said to me years ago, "Interesting style Irwin Michael has. He'll buy a stock. He'll then take like two years of grief from clients owning it. Then the next day, there's a big takeover and he makes all this money." That's it. Exactly.

Peter Puccetti said that. He said he has a good friend that jokes with him. He says, "Peter, I just wait till you buy a stock, then wait a couple of years, and then I'll buy it."

That's it. Yeah. That's what happens.

The technical analysis, would you just comment again on that? Moving averages? You look at RSI?

Yeah, we can look at that.

That's a differentiating factor right there. I think that's good because of all the people I've talked to, only the growth managers will look at it. The value managers will say, "You know, I don't pay any attention to that."

It behooves me to do that. I mean, before you buy a stock, you should always check the technicals. I like to find out the lay of the land and how much volume has gone through, and anything like that. I want to cover all the bases. When I don't, that's when I make a mistake.

What do the technicals tell you? Basically the perception of that stock in the market?

Well, I like to look at uptrends, downtrends, and that sort of thing, and there're a couple of guys I talk to. I'll just say, "What do you think of this stock technically?" If there are bullish patterns that confirm my fundamental analysis, I'd buy it.

I think that's most of it. Thanks.

Good. Okay.

ABC Funds' Value Investing
10 Commandments

Low Price-to-Earnings Multiples

We search out stocks trading at under ten times price-to-earnings multiples, which reduces the risk of overpaying for a security.

Low Cash Flow Multiples

We look for companies trading at under five times price to cash flow. This also reduces the risk of overpaying and uncovers many "dirt cheap" equities.

Discount to Book/Net Asset Value

We like to buy stocks trading at a discount to book/net asset value. In many cases, this not only uncovers significantly undervalued stocks but also prime takeover candidates.

Hidden Assets

Some examples of hidden assets that can be uncovered after a thorough analysis are tax-loss carry forwards, overfunded pension funds, real estate, potential spinoffs, IPOs, and favourable litigation.

Management

Two types of management could be key in the search for a turnaround candidate: a) solid, proactive management, and b) poor management, which leaves the company ripe for a proactive acquisition or merger.

Products/Services in Tune with 2000 and Beyond

This includes expandable growing markets with good margins. We tend to avoid companies with outdated shrinking products.

Value Catalyst

In order to push up the value of a stock, we look for a significant value creator. Some examples of possible value creators are fresh management with new directions, an important sale or purchase of a meaningful asset, an unsolicited takeover bid, or disgruntled and impatient proactive shareholders who may put pressure on management to make changes or sell.

Discounted Valuations Compared to Its Peers

Comparative valuation measures such as price to earnings and cash flow could indicate a take-over by relatively expensive Canadian or foreign competitors looking to expand market presence.

Contrary Opinion and Underfollowed by Investment Analysts

With little investor exposure, undervalued stocks are "pregnant with possibilities," providing very little buying competition when attempting to accumulate them. Generally, an undervalued and underfollowed security will offer terrific capital gains opportunities.

Discipline

Stay on track and adhere to strict value discipline of low P/Es, strong cash flows, and price targets. Do not get sucked into buying the flavour of the day! Combine patience and persistence to attain superior performance. Patience! Patience! Patience!

Frank Mersch
Non-Linear Thinking
Can Make You Rich

**"Where the greatest amount of capital spending is,
that is where you want to position your thematic portfolios."**

It is difficult to quantify exactly Frank Mersch's track record over the years, but I think we can safely say that his returns have averaged close to 20 percent per year over the last twenty years. Not bad for a philosophy major whose thesis was "to prove that there are angels in the world." There is nothing like a little non-linear thinking to help Frank think outside the box and be ahead of others. That sort of return gives an investor six times their money in ten years, helping one to accumulate a sizeable fortune in short order.

I had been to Front Street Capital's offices before, but on the morning I interviewed Frank Mersch, I was once again impressed. The building on Front Street is older with a historic air about it. It is definitely refreshing after the concrete jungle of the skyscrapers of downtown Toronto, even though Front Street is only a few blocks from the downtown core. When you walk into the building and see the setup, you get the definite impression that the inhabitants of this money management operation are decidedly unique and non-traditional. It's funny, but you can tell a lot about the operation and the principles that guide the money managers by the type of corporate offices they reside in.

Coming off the elevator at the fourth floor, the reception is right there, and if you look to the right, the operation opens up in front of you. There is nothing ostentatious about the office—no marble, fancy pictures, wood panelling, or famous sculptures, or none that I saw at least. Up a small flight of stairs, and just a stone's throw from the reception area, is the core of the operation, a large desk out in the open, housing all of the portfolio managers. Facing the reception is where Frank Mersch and Normand Lamarche sit, side by side, at their computer terminals.

These two esteemed money managers, who worked with each other at Altamira, both built their separate firms before once again deciding to get back together to form Front Street Capital. Frank's firm was called Casurina and was a primarily a long/short hedge firm, although in the earlier days, other strategies such as arbitrage were used. "Arb" type trades helped him to make a killing in 2000, being up 75 percent for the year. Capitalizing on his strengths, the firm has been able to grow fairly rapidly. Though according to Front Street's management, the idea is not to manage huge sums of money. This will only deter from performance.

Gary Selke runs the firm, and this allows Frank to spend all his time managing money. Frank told me that this has been one of the keys to the success of the firm, as a problem with some boutique shops is that the money manager tries to run the business as well. Since running a business and managing money require different skills, separation of the two jobs is definitely a good idea. Since the lion's share of fee-based income that comes to the firm is in the form of performance fees, it is important to keep the performance up. In any case, being out of the spotlight on Front Street and being a boutique firm are light years away from the famous Altamira presentations, where a thousand people at a time would come out to worship everything Frank Mersch said.

I interviewed Frank in the company boardroom, just steps from the trading desk and just about everything else in the firm. I definitely liked the small homey office and, again, I got the distinct impression this was not a huge corporate leviathan. I didn't realize it before the scheduled interview, but Frank was on vacation for a few days and actually came into the office just to do the interview with me. Other than being appreciative, I also got a sense that he was more relaxed than he would otherwise have been. He was humble and actually quite soft spoken, which I didn't necessarily expect.

We spent two hours, which took us well past the opening of the market, even though we started at 8:00 a.m. During a normal business day, my research told me that it would have been difficult to have such a relaxed discussion with Frank during market hours, and he mentioned during the interview that even though he and Norm sit side by side, they barely say two sentences to each other during market hours.

From the whys and wherefores of his degree in philosophy and history to his older Ford F-150 and to his hockey-coaching abilities, we covered it all. It's not like Frank needs to keep managing money, with way over $100 million of his own money invested in the funds. That's what makes it even more interesting to see what makes Frank tick, and why he does what he does. Is it ego, a love of the business, or simply just not trusting others to manage his money? These types of questions are the qualitative ones that really tell you about someone and the reason for their success.

Bob:

I always found it interesting that your undergrad degree was in philosophy. Did that help shape your investing process at all?

Frank:

I think so. It was both history and philosophy, actually. History does repeat itself. History as it relates to markets and as it relates to general themes and strategies is important. History does come back and repeat itself constantly. It has different pressure points and different pinch points, but at the end of the day, especially in Canada because of the cyclical nature of it, history and seasonality and all these things affect the markets. Philosophy-wise, it's not simply linear thinking; it's multi-dimensional thinking and challenging the norm. My thesis was an argument for the existence of angels. I had to argue that angels existed. It's academic if they do or they don't. It's the argument that you put forth and the logic that you use to make a case that angels exist. It was a primary thesis of Thomas Aquinas from the Jesuits. So to compare my thesis to his was an interesting exercise. Obviously, his arguments and his logic were much more refined and stronger than mine were, but, nevertheless, it was an interesting piece of work.

I was told that if you weren't going to be a money manager, you would have been a great philosophy professor. [Laughs] You are a deep thinker. I think that's obviously half of it in the market. Everybody looks at the same balance sheets.

Yeah. I think every great manager has to think kind of out of the box, and the ones that have some semblance of duration and history and longevity in the business have a certain style and a certain premise that they operate from. But they do always deviate from that. So it isn't simply an exercise in linear thinking. It's something that is multi-dimensional.

Have you always been interested in the market, when you went to university, or when you were a kid?

I had no idea that the market existed. I grew up in Scarborough. My father's a mechanic. My mother was a housewife and caregiver. My parents immigrated in 1954 from Germany and my dad worked for Volkswagen of Canada all his life. Surprisingly, he wasn't a risk-taker, and that's one thing that I saw. He had the ability to open up a number of dealerships in this country and he never took the risk. He stayed with the company. It's interesting of my other two brothers: one's a risk-taker and the other one isn't—he works for Volkswagen of America. My dad opened up much of Ontario. He was the third employee for Volkswagen Canada, and he opened up all the service side for Volkswagen of Canada throughout the country and many of the dealerships, and not speaking a word of English.

How did you get into the industry, then?

My father was a mechanic in the transportation business; my grandfather was an engineer, a train engineer; my great-grandfather was a train engineer. Everybody was in transportation, so I had taken a pilot's license. I had my commercial pilot's license, and my intent was to get in the Air Canada program.

You too? I have 300 hours. I got my license at 17 and was going for my commercial.

Yeah, I was the same way. I got into the Air Canada program. At a very young age, I started to wear glasses and they basically said, "You can fly cargo for us and spend the rest of your life in the Northwest Territories, or think about another career." That's what I did. After getting my pilot's license I completed university.

I went away to Europe for a year, and when I came back, there weren't a lot of job openings for a philosophy and history major. What are the options? Sell insurance. I didn't really want to sell insurance, so I went into Crown Trust. They had two job openings—one in the transfer department and the other one in a thing called the investment department. I didn't really like the guy who was the head of the transfer department at Crown Trust, and the guy in the investment department seemed cool. He seemed like an interesting guy, and I said, "Well, sure, I'll take that."

For the first nine months, my job was to put CUSIP numbers on securities because CUSIP was just introduced. Then after nine months, I started doing demand deposits and cash management—money market things. Any time there was an auction of Canada bonds, I'd sit on the desk with the money managers trying to collect Canada bonds from all the different dealers, so we'd make phone calls and get our fills.

From money market, I did some stock trading for about a year. While doing that, I took all the courses. You know, the Canadian Securities Courses and the like. I started doing my own analysis and stuff and presented it to them, and they said, "Well, you know, you can be analyst now," so I was a mining analyst at the tail end of the last mining cycle, which was interesting.

I think the first year that I was an analyst, Falconbridge lost $18 a share, and the following year it made $18 a share, so volatility in commodities I learned at a very early age. Actually, Falconbridge went from $18 a share to $180 while I was a mining analyst. You had Noranda, and you had the evolution of the gold camps in Northern Ontario, like Lac Minerals and Hollinger Mines. You had all those really classic gold mines that are now the Goldcorp camp.

So I did that, and then I went a year to National Life as an analyst/junior portfolio manager. I did that for a year but didn't particularly like the person I worked for. I didn't find the experience great. I went back to Crown Trust and furthered my career as an analyst and an assistant portfolio manager, which really means you don't do anything. You basically go to all the luncheons, and you do your analytical work. Then I went to Morgan Trust, and they kind of hoodwinked me and said, "Come in here and you can manage $300 million," and I got in there and there was no money. The money was managed by Laketon at the time, so I said, "What did you hire me for? I don't have anything to do." So I convinced them that we should have a contest, and the guy with the best returns over a year would subsequently bring the money back in-house. I did okay in that year and the money came back in-house. Then in the desire to run more and more money, we set up mutual funds. We went to Europe and we got money that way.

From Morgan Trust, I went to Guardian Capital. I originally went to Ruggles Crysdale under Bob Ruggles, who was very good friends with Seymour Schulich at the time. So I had my introduction to Seymour. Then Ruggles and Guardian merged, and I became president of special investments—all private investments and all the offbeat type of investments for about a year or year and a half.

Then, I don't know why I did it—I have no idea why I did it—but I left Guardian. I had a pretty good job. I was, you know, there before Bob Krembil. It was very interesting because Norman Short was there. There was a handful of money managers in those days that stepped out of the norm. Norman Short was bright, extremely bright, but a very hard taskmaster. Kiki Delaney was there. So it was a great incubator for different ideas and different thoughts. Through Norman Short at that point in time I met Peter Monk and Joe Rotman and that whole milieu of people, and also Gerry Schwartz, who had just came back from New York. So you had all these aggressive young guys building companies and the like.

I remember the genesis of Barrick, when Joe Rotman sold the gold assets in Nevada out of his oil company. You know, it was hot, hot ground. It was geothermal ground. Until Bob Smith came along, nobody could touch that gold because you couldn't mine it and he was able to vent the heat out of Nevada and develop the American Barrick model and everything.

Then, of course, we had Gerry Schwartz, who is in mergers and acquisitions and leveraged buyouts and the like. So you had that big Jewish contingent who were fighting and clawing their way in an establishment.

I came in at Crown Trust. That was the establishment. They were there, and you couldn't crack it. It wasn't until I got into Altamira that finally all that establishment started to break down. So while I was at Guardian, you could already see a shift away from the Sun Lifes and the evolution of mutual funds. In those days, you know, Mackenzie had just started. So the training ground for most of the analysts and most of the portfolio managers came out of life insurance. It was an incubator. It was a training ground. It was a place where people learned the business.

It's interesting you say that because I've noticed that from Robert Krembil and others. They all started at the life insurance companies.

Well, that's just the way it was. It was also the trust side because the country was an old boys' network. It was the Toronto Club. It was the National Club. You couldn't break in, especially a boy from Scarborough. There was no chance in hell. But you had the evolution of these guys. Krembil had started, and then Austin Beutel and Shulich were at Beutel Goodman. You had the guys at Mackenzie. You had the AGF evolution. Then you had Martin Seagerman, who was at that time one of the top managers in the country. I just watched them, and I looked at how they invested. They didn't invest conventionally. They took risks. They looked at different things, and it was a great observation and training ground.

Wayne Deans said he worked for the Bank of Canada, and he was told that he would be very, very successful if he was making in thousands of dollars what his age was. So he said, "I was 35 years old and I said, 'At 60, I'll be making sixty grand. There's got to be something better than this.'" [Laughs]

Yeah, that's true. My first job I think I was making $9,000 a year. It wasn't until I went to Morgan Trust, where I was finally making $90,000 or

$80,000 a year or $70,000. Then I went to Altamira, there was nothing. Just absolutely nothing. Again, I met Ron Meade and he says, "Well, we've got to build a counselling firm." He was a fixed-income guy. He said, "Well, we've got a little equity money. We need an equity manager, and I want balanced funds. Would you come over?" I said, sure.

You got equity in the company, right?

He promised me equity. Then after I got in there, I had to mortgage my house to get a piece of equity to buy in until I paid it down. It was a very nominal amount. But, you know, I joined Altamira because he said, "This is the place where you can make a million dollars." To me, a million dollars was a horrendous amount of money. So I said sure. He said, "I'll make you a millionaire. I have made lots of people millionaires." The old Altamira was a venture capital group with the venture capital side under Baker. There was Lowenstein and Ron Meade and Baker. They were the three guys who were one of the founders of VCs in Canada. They were the guys behind Altamira, the subsequent sale of Altamira, and all the problems that evolved from there. But Altamira was a great training ground. We built that from nothing to $17 billion over thirteen years.

You had quite a team there. Will Sutherland, Barry Allan was there, and Norm Lamarche. Dave Taylor also.

Yeah. No, we bred success because it was a very open shop and we let people run money. People, you know, go their own way and made their own mistakes and we had an extraordinary number of really bright people. We had Ainsworth, and after I left, he became money manager of the year for two years running during that tech bubble. Then we had Ian Joseph, and Sue Coleman.

Sue. Right. She had a couple kids.

Sue was a very bright small cap manager, and then Norm. He was working for the Bank of Canada before Altamira.

I used to see you back in the Altamira days in '93. Do you ever miss the thousand-people crowds coming out to watch you? Remember the financial forums, and they'd gather around you, hundreds of people?

No, I don't miss that at all. I don't miss getting on airplanes and people wanting to talk to me. It was very flattering at the time. You get a fat head after a while. But with that came all the attention and everything else—the subsequent issues that I had with the regulators that came with that.

Was the Altamira ownership fight kind of a distraction there for a while?

Yeah, it was a distraction. We were tired, and Will and myself and the senior guys were tired. We wanted to sell, and we wanted to sell earlier. I think it was a year too late. Probably a year earlier, we would have sold to TD or one of the major banks and I'd probably be working at a bank right now. Well, I probably wouldn't be, but my investing period would be done and I'd be doing something else. It was a distraction in the sense that we had a plan.

We basically said we're going to build this thing and we're going to sell it, because we had venture capitalists and shareholders. Early on, we decided we needed a distribution partner, and that was Manulife. So we set the whole plan up. We also designated how many clients we needed to make ourselves look appropriate to a buyer. It worked to perfection. Unfortunately, for about four years in doing that, I just spent every minute of my life either marketing, selling, or managing portfolios, and you just burn out. I logged a ton of air time and really didn't have much of a life at the end of it.

Manulife bought about 20 percent of Canaccord at two bucks or something in 2002. They say that's one of the best investments they've made.

Yeah, it's probably been a great investment, just like Altamira.

They ended up taking out $450, $460 million out in that investment, and they really didn't give up anything. Their ownership was a result of them vending in [ManuVest]. It had a billion dollars of assets and poor performance, and for that billion dollars of assets, they ended up owning a good third of Altamira. But we needed it at the time. We needed bulk to get on SEI, the consultants list, to sell pension funds. We ran pension money and development money for some of the biggest universities and corporations in the country. But you lose sight of all that. You just work and work and work and work.

When you look from the outside, you see it from the start to the end, but when you're doing it, you don't see....

Yeah, you just sort of get on a plane and you come home Saturday morning and then you get back on a plane on Sunday. You know, what did we have? The whole process of selling to pension funds was a long and tedious process. So it was an interesting period of time. Money flooded in both on the mutual fund side and the pension side.

You once said at Altamira that the Canadian market worked only once every three or four years. Was that because we were in a commodity bear market in the '90s?

Yeah. You know, the only reason the commodity cycle worked for us was we identified the sea change within the oil and gas area. It wasn't that the commodity was really great because it was very cyclical. It was that many of the majors were leaving the country and looking at places like Nigeria and Venezuela and stuff like that. All the hot spots. They were selling assets, and it was not that difficult because they were selling assets at $5 a barrel, production-wise. Their netbacks were five to six bucks. The more money we gave these guys, the more money they made on a cash flow basis, because the netbacks were there and the properties were there, and there was new technology in place like 2D and subsequently 3D seismic and horizontal drilling. Horizontal drilling allowed a greater amount of the bore head to be exposed to it and therefore you could drill it faster and your depletions were higher. That was the basis of our performance for the longest period of time.

Everybody associated us as a resource house, but we were also very successful in other areas. We were quite involved in a lot of takeovers in multiple sectors. We were one of the largest shareholders of Labatt's. We sold a portion of our stock to Gerry Schwartz and then we bought it back. Then we sold another portion to Stuart Belkin and then we sold a portion to Jimmy Pattison, and we tried to get everybody fighting about it. Labatt's is really one of the last old boys' companies, right? They are out of London, Ontario.

You had Canada Trust, and these guys were really arrogant. And they didn't respect the fact that we owned that much stock. We were the largest shareholder of Lac Minerals, and that ended up in Barrick. We were the largest shareholder of Arequipa and that ended up in Barrick. We were involved in a lot of the packaging companies that the Belkins had. But, conversely, we were also one of the earliest and largest shareholders of RIM before it went public. In fact, the last mezzanine financing that RIM did, we wanted to buy it all. Then when RIM was public, they were wanting to buy a division. We advised against it, which was fortunate because it was a set-top box business that subsequently went to zero. RIM just stayed with their knitting. So we were involved in those areas of the marketplace, not just simply resource.

Because the Canadian market's more cyclical than maybe some other markets, is it necessary to trade more in Canada? I mean, can you be a great buy-and-hold investor?

Well, by nature in cyclicals, you can't be buy-and-hold. Certainly, we have a supercycle right now. I wish I had done more buy-and-hold. When I think back at what Altamira owned in those days, you could own more than 10 percent without filing. At one point, we owned 35, 38 percent of CNQ at $0.10 a share—$0.10 a share! All the major oil and gas companies today were penny stocks when we were there, and we owned, like, 20, 25 percent of Bow Valley, which became Talisman. We put over $7 billion into Western Canada while I was at Altamira, including Precision Drilling. There were five or six drilling companies. Everybody was worried we were going to put them together, and we didn't want to put them together because we didn't want drilling costs to go up because we had 90 percent of our portfolio in oil and gas assets, not in drilling assets. So we had huge positions in things like Ensign and Precision and all those things in the early days. We were aggressive, you know. We were extremely aggressive in the way we accumulated stuff. We just got, in some respects, too big—then the distraction of selling the business.

That was the next question. Obviously, the bigger you get, the harder it is to manage money. So why did you start up Casurina originally and the hedge structure, the long/short model?

Well, I knew that the last three or four years at Altamira, the Americans started coming into our market. The Canadian market had waves of foreign investing. You had the Europeans come in; you know, the heyday of the oil market. But they sort of came in and left. Just like the brokerage firms did. Merrill Lynch comes in, Merrill Lynch goes out. Goldman comes in, they go out.

Come in at the top, leave at the bottom.

Yeah, but you never really saw the consistency. And then all of a sudden, the last four or five years, six years, at Altamira, we saw Fidelity come in first from their U.S. side, and then they started selling funds in Canada. We saw Wellington come in and make big investments in the group. So all of a sudden, we saw more long-term investors in the marketplace. But the other group that

came in, which I always found intriguing, was the people like Julian Robertson, from Tiger Management and Soros. Before they became macro-managers,
they were long-short stock pickers, activists, and all these things. I saw them
buy into mid-tier to small cap stocks in many of the names that I had. I watched
the way they operated, and I got more and more intrigued by it. Then I kept
reading about Julian Robertson and Soros, and Julian Robertson made the mistake in the sense that he was a very good stock picker. This group were great
stock pickers. But then they wanted to be like Soros and they wanted to do the
big macro calls, and then they started diversifying all over the place.

Because they got too big, maybe they had to start doing that.
Yeah, they got too big. Then the smarter older managers were doing things
different like Seymour Schulich: leaving the money management business and
going to the royalty side. So you saw a change in investment style. I saw these
guys coming in, the hedge funds from the United States, in their activists roles,
and then I started to participate in a lot of the deals that they were doing. I was
intrigued by how they ran money. Then the fact that they were shorting and
hedging stuff off, and I thought that was interesting.

Actually, the last two years of Altamira, I was pushing to set up a hedge
fund group within Altamira. I wanted to head it, and they said, "No, no, no. You
run our flagship funds. You can't do that." I said, "Look, I'm tired. I want a
change. I don't want to run all this money. I want to get stimulated again."
They said, "No, no, no. The company's up for sale. We can't afford you to
leave or anything like that." So it never happened, but after I left Altamira, I
went back and said, "Look, this is what I want to do. I don't know how to
hedge off stuff. I don't know how to do it." So then I got Parm and Brian in
initially, and we started from that small base.

It wasn't easy because of the regulatory issues. All the people knew my history, my numbers, and everything else. We only raised about $35, $40 million
our first year, which was good. I think the first year or second year, we had just
huge numbers—absolutely killer numbers at the tail end of the tech market.

Ninety-nine?
Ninety-nine, 2000, 2001. We leveraged the hell out of it and stuff. We
stumbled in '01, '02, and then I realized that, I didn't necessarily want that
style. So then I went more conventional long/short. I also saw another commodity cycle developing, and Norm had been on his own with Tuscarora for

a while. They were doing flow-throughs and they were managing money for CIBC. There was a business there, but they were really working for other people. I said, "Norm, there's another energy cycle coming. It could be a big cycle. Why don't we just hook up again?" So we did, and it was good because we brought a businessman in to manage the business. Norm and I simply run the money. Gary Selke is the businessman in this equation, and I had kind of that at Altamira. I had good systems people, good accounting people, good business people, and I ran the money. I wanted the same kind of configuration. Norm is an extraordinarily great resource manager, probably the best I've ever seen. I've seen a lot of them. I felt that with this cycle coming, it was time to go after this area. Basically, the thesis that I always have in money management is to chase capital spending. Where the greatest amount of capital spending is, that is where you want to position your thematic portfolios. We saw, basically, energy consumption on the rise. We saw the evolution of China fairly early. We also recognized the size of the resource in Western Canada, that being the tar sands, the oil sands. We went to Europe several years ago and started talking about Canada having a resource base similar to Saudi Arabia. Everybody thought we were smoking dope, you know. Because we saw Chinese consumption really start to rise, we thought, "Well, you know, you've got China and you've got India." Then they became big thematic things. Developing countries like Korea use an enormous amount of energy and build a lot of infrastructure.

How do you describe your process and how did that evolve? Does it start with the macro and then try to get in early on a particular theme?

Yeah. You know, you want to focus where the capital spending is. It always comes down to a basic thing: What is the thing that's driving it? If you look at the last cycle, it was the Internet. Cool. You know, the Internet was a great science project. But until they move that science project from household to household and business to business, it was just a science project. When I first started in this business, there was no fax machine. The fax machine was unbelievable. I remember getting the first fax machine and everybody was excited and everybody started to fax. It was good for coated paper, but the fax machine was just minor compared to what the Internet became. So you had this Internet, and what you needed was pipe. You needed pipeline, and you needed distribution. All of that spending and everything else created that Internet bubble. So you had that framework and there was an enormous amount of capital spending like laying of fibre and Global Crossing and all those things. Then, like everything else, it matures, and then you have the winners and losers. Now the Internet is really not a supersized fax machine, but it's distribution. This cycle is the pent-up Chinese demand, but not just China. It's like the globalization. The beginnings of it started with Clinton when he opened the world, and more free trade. These are very subtle things, but as much as everybody looks back and says he's famous for his cigar thing and everything else, in reality, the Cold War disappeared. The walls came down. The world became global. Free trade came into the picture. Barriers of trade disappeared. That was the evolution of China, but it is much more now with China. We have a cycle that's based on this economy that's gone from nothing to the fourth largest economy in the world but they also use enormous amounts of energy. That was the thesis of why Norm and I came back, a big capital-spending cycle. The cycle typically lasts five or six years commodity-wise, then in between year four to seven is infrastructure build. We're beginning the infrastructure build. Thirty-three nuclear reactors and refining pipeline and all this stuff is coming. The Mackenzie-Delta pipeline hasn't been done. The Alaska pipeline hasn't been done. So we've still got that coming. Then the tail end of that cycle is the rate-based cycle. It's distribution, similar to the Internet. It becomes a rate-based type of structure.

The whole commodity cycle seemed to last, if you look back in history, fifteen, sixteen years. Is that because it takes that long to get the lead out of the ground once you find it?

Well, in the case of mining, by the time you find something, it's eight years before you get any cash flow. I've always favored the oil business because it's a lot easier. For a money manager, the oil business is a lot better than the mining business because you get instant cash from it. You drill something, and as long as you've got pipe near you or very close to you, you can get cash flow within sixty, ninety days. With the mining business, the worst thing that can ever happen to you is you find something.

A lot of infrastructure?

A lot of infrastructure and a lot of spending. Grades vary and size varies. Everybody's always going around shaking their heads. But even within that broad theme, there are other themes that evolve. The whole wireless theme is part of the evolution of developing countries. The evolution of GPS and everybody having GPS and now knowing where every sex offender is in the country. Everybody blogs onto that simple thing called Google Earth and that has now created a whole industry around it. The higher cost of energy is going to cause the automotive industry to change.

Eric Sprott said, "I originally said I was a stock picker and I was a good stock picker." He says, "Things evolve. I figured if I could get maybe the big picture right, then I could enhance my returns a lot."
It allows you to run more money.

Has your process evolved over time?
Yeah. I'm, again, in many respects, a pretty good stock picker. My problem is that I lose patience. Two, three years and I move on and I don't like to buy and hold forever. I love finding gems. I love finding great companies that are at early stages. I've always been able to identify companies earlier and have always had them in the portfolio. I just don't own them long enough.

CNQ at $0.10?
Oh, yeah.

I remember in the early days of Altamira, I had this huge—4, 5 percent of my portfolio—in Newbridge. I bought it at nine bucks and the stock went to six. Then Terry Matthews filed, and I thought, "Oh my God, I've just blown up the firm. Our performance is gone. The stock's going to three bucks." He filed, but he didn't sell the stock. Within six months the stock was at $18. Within a year it was at $26, and I thought, "That's a pretty good return." Within two years, it was at $130. My mother always reminds me; she says, "You know, if you would have held that stock, you wouldn't worry so much." As I get older, I'm beginning to hold them longer.

In the long run and in the short run, do you average down on positions or do you cut your losses quickly to get out?
It varies. It varies. It varies. Like Ipsco, I bought it for the right reasons and the stock went from $20, $18 to $12. I sold it, and within a year it was at $60. So that was a case in point. In this cycle, now it's a $100 stock.

Well, I think that's a good point. I mean, the best poker players in the

world lose seven hands out of ten, but the three that they've got as great hands, they go all in and they make all their money. They cut their losses quickly on the seven out of ten.

Yeah, I do too. I have a lot of names. I take a shotgun approach and see how they evolve. Prune them as you go along. Focus your attention. Even as time goes on you learn different things. What I'm now trying to focus on is companies that create standards for their industry. When I'm talking non-commodity, I want companies that create the standard. So RIM would be a standard bearer in mobile, e-mailing, and the like. Certicom to me is a standard company. Descartes is the largest logistical company. I didn't own Descartes until about two years ago until they went back to their knitting. All of sudden, they had six solid quarters in a row and the management is the original management, the guys that built the business and honed the idea of logistics standards. They only own 8 percent or 9 percent of the market, but they are the largest in that area.

So we're constantly looking for Canadian companies, and there's very few of them that become standard-bearers for their industry. Those are the ones you want to hold. As I get older, I realize those are the things you might want to put in your back pocket and give it to your kids and say, "Don't sell it for twenty years." But, at the end of the day, you've got to be careful because managements deviate. It's like if RIM had gone the business on the set-top side, that company would be gone. The evolution of what RIM is today is nothing what it was when we first invested in them. So these companies change.

It's funny, because I started to worry when Magna bought amusement parks in Austria. I thought, "I don't know, is that the core business or what?"

Yeah, but the thing was that those were like diversions for him. Frank Stronach isn't a businessman. What he is good at is collecting a whole bunch of people like my father, immigrants, and tool-and-die makers—great guys that liked to run the businesses but didn't have a vision on the bigger risk side. He collected all these guys and he said, "I will lead you." They said, "Great. You take care of us." In many respects, that's what I'm doing here. I've got Gary and he'll lead me, and then I'll just do my job.

Half of hedge firms that fail, fail because of the operational side.

They've got a great money manager but the business fails.

Yeah. I personally think there's a lot of better money managers out there than me. But what I've learned is how to build a business. What I know is that there are very few people that can also be good businessmen and be good money managers. You know, Eric Sprott could fit that bill in some respects. Eric's a good businessman because of his years of building a brokerage operation, and now this. But Eric is an extraordinary money manager. He's a great stock picker.

I asked Eric, "What's your one regret or what you could have done better?" Eric looked and he said, "I think I should have run my business a bit better. I think I could have done a better job of that."

Eric could run a better business. There's no doubt about that. But then, Eric wants it all. He's not going to give up interest, and therefore it becomes difficult. Whereas me, when I merged with Norm and Gary, it's one-third, one-third, one-third. I wasn't here to own 100 percent of this firm, and my interest isn't to own 100 percent. I don't want to be a billionaire or anything like that. I just want a job, and I want somebody to take care of the business side of it. I'm quite willing to give that person equal share so I don't have to deal with personnel and people. You know, Norm and I are in many respects the same way. We don't like people.

Norm said a lot of times he just reads annual reports.

Norm and I sit together, and we might say, on a good day, two sentences to each other. That's on a good day.

There was a study done recently. They gave some investing problems to normal people. Then they gave them to sociopaths in prison. The sociopaths won because they didn't have any emotional attachment to anything. So how do you fight that emotional part of investing? Like you said, you become impatient sometimes.

I learned it the hard way. It's terrible to make investments for personal reasons. My dad died of esophageal cancer, and I owned QLT believing and believing and believing that they would solve this. That stock just never went anywhere and, actually, after I sold it, it finally went up. I owned it for four or five years. The progress was great. The company was good, but I bought it because I thought this is going to cure esophageal cancer.

When did you own that? What years? I just ask because a girlfriend's father was CEO of QLT just for a couple years in the early to mid-'90s.
Miller?

Randal Chase is his name.
Well, this was Julia....

Julia Levy. Yeah.
I remember you bring up all these things from the past. In 1993, I remember a story you told. There was an Altamira client that you called at the end of the year because at the beginning of year he owned the Altamira Equity Fund and at the end of the year, he owned the Altamira Equity Fund, and he owned every single fund that Altamira had during the course of the year. I think you calculated his return at 32 percent, and the Altamira Equity Fund obviously did 46 that year. You called him and said, "You know, if you had kind of been in the Altamira Equity Fund all year and not switched between all our funds, you would have done better."
He was trading the fund. I think the guy must have done 180 trades. I asked him, "Well, why did you do this?" Because I also took a personal affront when anybody redeemed it from me in those days. In the early days when I was at Altamira, if somebody redeemed, I would phone them. I'd say, "Why are you redeeming? Is there something I did wrong? You don't like me?" I think most money managers need a great big dose of paranoia to be good. Common sense and paranoia. In many cases, we're very insecure people. In one respect, we're not necessarily emotionally connected like everybody else.

People aren't emotionally wired to actually do well in investing at all.
We're very up and down. I've always said that money management gives you the biggest highs and the biggest lows. Anxiety attacks and failure are a constant thing in our business. It can eat you up. It can freeze you. I see great minds, Ph.D.s, that are the worst money managers in the world because they overanalyze. There's got to be a certain amount of stupidity, a certain lack of fear. There's a great amount of paranoia that's required, and the fact that you want to keep your job.

It's a lot of the same attributes as gambling. Not to equate gambling and investing, but it needs a lot of the same attributes as an expert poker

player. You've got to stick with your guns.

Yeah, and sometimes you just go out on a limb. Sometimes you're right and sometimes you're wrong. One of the guys that I admire is Rohit because he can change on a dime.

Rohit told me, "I don't know what the reason is." I interviewed him down in Tucson, Arizona, and he said, "I've done extraordinarily well at trading out of things a week or two or three or four before things go bad." He said, "I can't explain it. I've just done all right at that."

Well, he's had some blowups too. But one thing that Rohit does is he'll be down 17 percent or 18 percent—you know, he's older than I am. As I get older, I don't want that all the time, okay? He seems to embrace it. I'm not embracing volatility as much as I used to, because I don't need to. I don't need the volatility. As I get older, more slow and steady is good. I'm doing this more because I like what I do, but I don't need the inherent volatility that comes from big bets. I don't want to blow up.

What's your biggest mistake on the investment side that cost the most money?

I'll tell you, one year when I was at Altamira, I underperformed the index by 5 percent. The biggest mistake I made was not calling Bre-X that year. It's not because I didn't believe there was gold in there. It's only because I never thought they'd ever own the property. My brother worked in Indonesia and he worked in Asia, and he said, "Frank, they could have a mountain of gold. The Indonesian government's going to step in there and take it over." They subsequently did. People forget that. The Indonesians basically expropriated that whole thing. But by not having that in my portfolio, I underperformed the index by 5 percent. By not having, probably, Nortel in my portfolio, I severely underperformed. So that was a big mistake. Every year, I have one big blowup.

I don't have those 5 or 6 percent positions anymore that blow up, but I do always have a stinker. I always get suckered into something—a new concept, like, pay cards or something like that. Where I always make the mistake is saying, "Great concept, but there's something about management I don't trust." But the concept's so good that I override my underlying gut problem with management. That's where I always lose. I've had great ideas, and long term they've all worked out conceptually. But having it run by the wrong guy or wrong management group has always hurt me. Every so often I will step out of that rule and say the concept is so great that it will outweigh poor management. By the way, it never happens. It never ever happens.

It comes back to management. That was another question: How important is management?

Oh, unbelievably important. Unbelievably important. That's why I don't invest globally, because I have to be able to meet the management. I have to sit across the table. I have to occasionally be able to consult them. Norm's the same way. He's going to miss a lot of great oil and gas companies because he doesn't know their management. But then he'll also avoid some real stinkers. For me, the mistake I always make is believing the company or the concept is bigger than the people that run it.

How about your decision to sell? Buying, some people say, is easier than deciding when to sell.

Sometimes you look at the price and say, "I made enough money. Let somebody else make it." My problem is I always find something else and I have to kick something else out. My problem is I'm always early, too early sometimes. My biggest challenge is patience and letting things evolve, and then coming in. I love owning stocks at $0.10 or $0.20 and seeing them at $2, but it would be nicer to see them at $200.

What do you think were the biggest wins you've ever had? I think Norm said it was probably Profico.

I've had a lot of huge wins. I had Seven Seas in Colombia that I bought at $0.35 and it got to $60 U.S. I've had a lot of stocks where I've held stock that had gone up horrendous amounts, like Clearly Canadian from $0.50 to $40 U.S. and back to $0.30 while I was in the hold period. That's why I went into the hedge fund business, because I don't know how many special warrants or private placements I've owned that are hold stock. I see them go up horrendous amounts and I can never get out of them. We had RIM and we had Arequipa. We had Seven Seas. Just a horrendous number of big wins over the years. Big, big wins. Profico's been a big win for Norm. Most recently is HudBay. Look at that and it's cheaper today than it was a year ago. I still have the original warrants. Well, not any more because they were exercised. But the stock itself was a $0.90 issue with a warrant attached to it. Or $0.09 issue, sorry.

Dave Taylor told me about it a few years ago. We went for lunch and he said there's this great little company nobody knows about called Hud Bay Minerals at three bucks.

Yeah, Dave Taylor's a big value manager. Dave's a very bright guy, too.

Yeah. He started up his little hedge fund at Dynamic a couple of years ago. He was up 55 percent the first year. Just loves special situation little companies. You can do that when it's twenty million bucks or ten million bucks. It's interesting.

Yeah. I find that interesting, that whole Dynamic group. How you can run long money and be long/short? I don't know how conflicts of interest don't arise.

So China, obviously, is a central theme.

No, it's the world. It's really global free trade. It's not just China.

I hope I live long enough, because I think within the next twenty, twenty-five years the U.S. dollar will not be the reserve currency of the world. I really firmly believe that we're seeing the beginning of the end for the U.S. dollar.

Gold's going to the moon?

I don't believe that. I've never believed that gold is a hedge. I think the best hedge is a good currency, the right currency at the right time. Back in the '70s, when oil went through the roof and gold was strong but was being manipulated higher, the absolute best store of wealth was the Singaporean dollar and the Swiss franc. If you're going to see a destruction of the U.S. dollar, remember gold is valued in U.S. dollars. The French, the British, and now the Americans, the Romans, the Greeks, they all were the reserve currencies for a period of time. There are very, very strong parallels in history between the U.K. and the United States, as it relates to disposable income, debt per capita, colonialism, imperialism. All those things equate to the United States and the U.K. before it finally collapsed as the reserve currency.

What began the slide for the U.K. was its involvement in Iran and in Iraq. Most people don't realize that today's Iraq was formed by the British. They split it up. They split up much of the Middle East. That was the beginning of the end for them. The parallels to history are very, very strong right now between the U.S. and the U.K. It is in a declining phase as a reserve currency.

You're simply mortgaging your future. At some point, you're already hearing the noise about maybe we should take a basket approach to currencies. If I had to bet on a currency, it's probably going to be that the Chinese currency is the next reserve currency, barring any war.

They have hundreds of billions of U.S. dollars because that's what they get paid in when they sell their products. And I don't think they're too happy right now because they want to use those U.S. dollars to come and buy companies, and, obviously, they went to buy Unocal, which was nixed. I guess that's the point; they're going to say, "We're in a currency here that's devaluing. Why are we continuing to hold this currency?"

Because it's the biggest market right now while they're developing. Until they get per capita income up, they need the U.S. They hold the trump card with the U.S. dollars. They pull that trump card, the U.S. falters, their biggest export market disappears. They'll be the banker for the United States.

So they're not going to stab themselves, right?

No. The U.S. consumer is the biggest prize for a manufacturing country such as China, during its development phase. They've basically taken the blueprint from Japan, Korea, and Malaysia and using that simple blueprint and developing it. The one thing about China versus the Japanese, and it's very cultural, is that the Chinese are much more entrepreneurial than the Japanese have ever been historically. The other thing too is that Chinese women work as hard as the men, and they are not subservient to their men, whereas the Japanese woman is totally subservient. That's one lesson I learned a long time ago from my brother who worked overseas. I said, "Well, where should I put my money? Should I put it in Japan?" And he said, "Frank, if you ever get an opportunity, invest in China." I said, "Why?" And he said, "The women work, and they're smarter than the men. The families work." The women work and they're smarter and they're more devious, whereas a Japanese woman is totally subservient. So not only do you have this mass population in China of males, but you have this mass population of entrepreneurial women as well.

But when a theme becomes the consensus that everybody believes in, then the opportunity for gain is usually limited. Is this consensus now? Is everybody going to believe in this Chinese thing?

Yeah. I'm tired of it because everybody translates it to commodities. Great, that's fine. But, then, the biggest part of commodities is the lack of investment for fifteen years. It's not purely because of the Chinese and the Indians and stuff like that.

I look back at history, and during the Great Depression, obviously, stock markets did poorly, but commodities actually went up.
Commodities have a negative correlation to the stock market.

It seems like perfectly negative. It seems like fifteen-, or sixteen-year cycles. Now, once you start to bet on that, then it changes. But it's amazing how it works. Here we are, seven years into the commodity cycle and the U.S. market's done nothing while commodities are up.
In my opinion, there's only one country in the world that has an energy policy right now and that's China. To a lesser degree, India. But with China, we don't raise any stink about them building thirty-three nuclear reactors. We don't raise any stink that, militarily, they will have more firepower in ten years than we can even dream of. The biggest war is going to be between China and Russia at some point.

That's what I always find interesting is that it's like we're living in parallel universes. We are their biggest trading partner and we're trading with them, but militarily we're not sure of the Chinese and we don't want them to build up. We love to trade, but they're an enemy militarily. It's funny how it works like that.
Yeah, I heard Clinton speak, and it was interesting how he described the U.S.'s relationship with China. You're there, but we have to be really, really careful of you. You're going to be a power, but we have to tread gently with you. He's very aware that this is not a democracy. This is a military state—a socialist, military, managed economy. One that's got all the pressures coming up from underneath with the people and the proletariat, and you have to satisfy that while still maintaining a face to the rest of the world.

A dictatorship is actually far more efficient than a democracy. A benevolent dictatorship is the best. Singapore, right? But the problem is it's not benevolent for very long.
The thing is, in that kind of economy, if you want to build something, you just build it. You want a coal-fired plant? They're opening one coal-fired plant

every month. They've got enormous amounts of coal reserves, and that's what they're focused on. They've got an energy policy. They've got nuclear, they've got coal, they're trying to balance their foreign deficits by buying assets globally in the oil market to offset the cost of buying oil. I think there's maybe two, three years left in it, and then that economy will shift and become more consumer oriented. You've already got major brands like ChinaTel on the wireless side. It's just going to be a huge, huge economy at some point.

Do you think it's similar to Japan? Similar growth?

Yeah. But much more at the end of it, more consumer based. The Japanese don't consume. Chinese consume. They save, and they consume.

I think you bought into Ceramic Protection fairly early, didn't you? Just to give an idea of the process, what did you see there? Did you like the management?

Well, it was the whole 9/11 and Homeland Security stuff.

So it was the theme of the security situation?

Yeah. I did the CPC for $0.10; they sold it at $0.04 because the management wasn't executing the way I thought. Ceramic was a Murray Edwards company. Murray has had great success in the oil patch.

What do you think, going forward, of the mutual fund industry versus the hedge fund industry?

I personally think that it's all a damn sham right now. There is no hedge fund right now in this country. The guys that are winning are doing what they've done as a long manager. I think Eric will short. I'm not sure that Rohit will ever short. The proof in the pudding is going to be over the next little while. Who will short? Who will neutralize?

I'm going for lunch with J.F. Tardif tomorrow. He works for Eric.

He's a very bright kid.

He is. Boy, he's traded in and out of this market a lot of times in the high beta stocks and made great money.

Well, he ran a small amount of money as well. It's all these guys running a small amount of money. It's going to be interesting. To be honest with you, we're all in the hedge fund business because the fees are very good. The guys that you're interviewing have always been good long managers that will take non-index risk into their portfolios. None of them are really hedge fund managers. I'm not even sure I am yet. I have been neutral twice—50 percent long, 50 percent short—zero market exposure twice in the last five years.

When were those times?

I think it was the summer of '04 and the summer of '02, because I just didn't know what to do. The longer I stay in this thing, the more I realize there's less and less fundamentals on the fringes of this market. There's no reality to this market because there's so much funny money now. About ten years ago, there was funny money, but that was the Hunts and stuff like this. Now you've got a thousand Hunt brothers. You've got a thousand idiots.

There is a lot of volatility in the market.

Yeah. You get these meltdowns, and the volatility is increasing because there's so many momentum traders.

Right. I guess volatility creates opportunities but makes life more difficult. Now, one thing with your hedge fund: You have a 6 percent hurdle rate, right?

Yeah. I think you should at least make T-bills, right? Before you charge anybody anything. It's a legacy. It's a little different than Ira Gluskin has his 15 percent legacy. In many respects, when Ira was doing his road show, I said, "Ira, why have you got a 15 percent hurdle release?" "Well, that's how it was when I first started. Interest rates were 18 and 19." I said, "Why do you still have it?" He said, "It's bad luck. As soon as you lift that, you know you're going to have a terrible year." I can understand that. See? There's your paranoia. We probably all don't change our underwear when we're on a good roll, you know. We're like hockey players with our stocks. Ira's the same way. He says, "If I change that, it'll be the kiss of death." Are you going to interview Ira?

I should. I don't have him on the list, but definitely the next book.

Ira is probably one of the best money managers that I've seen, as well as stock picker. Everything. Eric's very good. Ira's in the same league—Ira's in the same league as Eric, just not as well known. Ira identified the trust areas so much earlier than anybody else. Of all the guys that you've interviewing, none of us really play the trust market. Ira identified it early and then made a ton of money on it. Ira, because of his background as a real estate analyst, he looks at everything like real estate. Asset versus income. He identified the trust area so early. That's why he's $3.5, $4 billion in assets. But Ira's always been a great stock picker. So he's a guy I've always admired.

Can you comment about your new three prospectus funds? Did the OSC give you exemption, I guess, as far as how you can hedge?

That's just the biggest problem we're having. There's only so many exempt accounts and a lot of investment advisors just don't want to fill out forms. So we're all setting up these funds. I firmly believe that we need to keep retail investors—Canadian retail investors. One thing we've done poorly in the business is we have not captured enough attention. We have not built a brand yet at Front Street. We're a resource manager and we don't even have a Canadian resource fund.

You know, we manage money for non-residents. We do not have an energy fund for Canadian retail investors. We're supposed to be the pros at this. We've done some things very good in the business, like capturing closed-ends funds and stuff like that. But that's gone now. You can't get it. So our biggest challenge in the next three years is to remake ourselves and find new distribution. These three new funds are the beginning of a conventional approach to mutual funds.

How much more money can you manage?

Well, what we'd like to do is get rid of the CIBC money, which is $500 million. We've already gotten rid of three different funds. Our goal is really to be in that $3 billion level. It's a challenge. It's a constant discussion that we have internally. Do we want to grow, or do we want to stay where we are, or do we want to collapse and just run our own money?

That's why you started up Casurina originally. It was your Altamira Equity that you cashed out. I think you said you didn't trust anybody else to manage your money.

Yeah. We made a policy that none of the managers can own stocks personally, whereas Eric can, and he does. We don't. So all our money's tied up in the funds. I think if we can do this for another five years, we collectively, the partners and the employees, will probably have $250 to $300 million of our own money here. At that level, you might want to think about getting rid of all our clients and just running our own affairs. We're not there yet. At the top, it's weird. At the top of the markets, everybody can always handle more, and at the bottom of the markets....

Liquidity dries up.

Liquidity dries up and you've got too much, which shouldn't be. It's the perverse thing. You want to have more money at the bottom of the markets and less money at the top.

I bought Norm's Mining Opportunities Fund myself at ten bucks. It's up by three times in three years.

Yeah. I'm thinking of starting a tech fund—industrial tech fund—because I think we're getting close. Not yet, but within the next year, we'll set that fund up. There's a lot of neat little technology companies that help industry. One big theme I think that we're all going to be challenged with is water and technology around water.

Do you think that's one of your reasons for success is you tend to see themes early? That's when you make the most money.

Yeah. When I read the paper, I pick up really obscure things. One thing I saw last year that really shocked me was that Alberta sent their Minister of Infrastructure to Israel to learn how to manage water. I went, "Why?" You've got the Rockies, lots of snow, lots of rivers. You've got the Bow River. Why? Then I realized that the oil industry uses 30 percent of the watershed in Western Canada. For every one barrel of oil sand it's ten barrels of water for the steam injection. The oil industry doesn't pay for water. We—you and I—pay for water. We water our lawns, we shower, we pay for it. The oil industry does not pay for water. It's hard to play because it's owned federally, right? There's a whole bunch of companies out there that are doing purification.

Trojan Technologies.

Yeah, that's one. These things are all gone because GE's basically buying up all these things. You've got to think in terms of water maybe being a big cost factor in the oil industry at some point.

Well, there's huge cost. There's natural gas cost. Who was it? Connacher bought a gas company to supply them with gas for their oil sands project, right?

Now, analysts seem not to want to stray from consensus and analysts seems to be lemmings in a lot of respects. Do you pay attention a lot to what analysts say? Why don't they stray from consensus? Why don't they stand out from the crowd?

Less so now because of Sarbanes-Oxley.

I mean, I'm sure there's good ones out there, definitely. I guess if you stray from consensus and you're wrong, you get fired. If you stray from consensus and you're right, you get a $10,000 bonus or whatever. [Laughs] So the risk of being wrong is a lot greater than the risk of being right.

To find one good company a year is hard.

Can you beat the market over time just investing in large cap stocks?
Yeah. Actually, I think if you forget all the nonsense and everything else we do, if we all would have bought bank stocks fifteen years ago and held them, it would be the best-performing portfolio out there.

Actually, they're the biggest hedge funds anyway.
The one thing about my funds is that I will try to get less volatility going forward rather than more. I want more volatility with the market after we have a sizeable correction. I don't want to have the best results at the top of the market. I'd rather have the worst results at the top of the market. If the market's up 50 percent and I'm up 10, great.

You say 12 percent is what your target is over time, and I think being humble like that is great. When people start to say, "I'm the best money manager in Canada," that's when, you know, six months later, the fall happens.
Yeah. Yeah, I don't need it. I just don't need it anymore.

Well, I think the important thing is your own money's in it too.
It is my own money.

Well, it is, but, I mean, between Gary and Norm and you and all the other staff….

Most of it's mine.

That's the big deal, and you're not going to take huge risks, obviously, with your own money.

Yeah. Well, I just think that you can get overly greedy. To achieve 12 or 13 percent if that's your target. Hopefully, you'll do better than that over time, but that's my goal.

Do you have any role models that you've patterned yourself after over the years?

Well…Eric Sprott. I've always admired independent thinkers.

It's the only way you can be successful, right? If you're going to head along the consensus lines, you're going to….

I admire the fortitude of Rohit and his ability to change on a dime. I admire Eric's stock picking and his doomsday scenario.

And sticking with it.

I always find it interesting how the markets think. Like, everybody's going, "Well, inflation's coming. Better sell all your commodities." You know, the best hedge for inflation is commodities. Then everybody's saying, "Well, you've got to get out of the commodity market." I'm going, "No, no, no. You've got to stay in the commodity market because you want hard assets." I have all the commodities right now. The other area that's really in short supply is diamonds. Rough diamonds. I made a lot of money historically in the diamond market. Early on in Aber, we were big. Up until three years ago, we were the largest. We owned 10 percent of Kensingston. There's no rough diamonds and there's a severe shortage of rough diamonds. De Beers is shutting down two of the largest diamond mines in Africa, South Africa. Three of the five are unprofitable. There is a real shortage of diamonds coming. A real shortage. There aren't any new supplies.

And people aren't talking about that a lot, so there's probably a lot of opportunity there.

Unfortunately, you can't do a fund because diamonds are so subjective.

There's yellows, there's blue, there's stuff like that. It's not like yellowcake, where you simply go out and buy yellowcake. Diamonds aren't that way. We've investigated setting up a diamond fund, and it is impossible. You have to almost own a sorting house to set up a diamond fund. There are no diamonds. There are no diamonds anywhere and no rough diamonds. There is a severe, severe shortage of rough diamonds. If you've got a developing class in China and India, I don't know where you're going to get the diamonds from.

There's not really many uranium producers. There's Paladin. There's Cameco and there's a couple others, UEX and International Uranium.

Paladin and SXR are the two to come on stream and that's it. Of course, you have Cameco and the rest. But I don't know. So you've got uranium and you've got diamonds. To me, those are the two demand cycles that are not being properly reflected in the marketplace. Then there is water. I don't know how to play the water. I'm still trying to figure it out. I know it's going to be a cost pressure, and I know that it's going to be a very, very valuable asset. But I don't know how to own it.

Are there any books that you recommend?
Yeah, I read all those books that everybody reads.

Have you ever read *Reminiscences of a Stock Operator*?
Oh, yeah. I read all that stuff.

I thought that was interesting.
I read all that stuff. Now I'm reading all these China books.

Are there any rules that you never break? Or are you pretty flexible and adaptable?
The rule is management, management, management. [Laughs] Every stock that I've lost money on, I've misgauged management—every stock. It's very trite. There have been great managers in really lousy industries, and the stocks still do nothing. But you want to be in the right area with the right manager.

So you find the theme, find the right area, and pick the best stocks within that area.
I guess onto your personal life, you coach hockey for your daughter?
Yeah, I coach my daughter and also I coach my son.

Is it just a way to relax for you?

Yeah, it's a nice diversion. It's like running a portfolio. There are seventeen kids and they're all different. They all perform differently. They all have a rhythm, and the key is trying to bring them all together at the right time to get the performance you need. It's no different than the stock portfolio. They've done pretty well.

Yeah, they're okay? They're near the top?

Yeah. I was Coach of the Year, what, two years ago on Emily's side. For the boys, they were at the bottom and I brought them into second place. I'm not coaching girls' hockey this year. But my daughter, you know, all the girls have gone from house league and now they're at the second highest tier. I'm so proud of all of them. They've come along so far. But, you know, all the teams just never, never quite became "the best." So it's just like my portfolios.

[Laughs]

And maybe I shouldn't strive for the best, but you always try to.

Did you have a family in the Altamira days?

Yeah.

How did you manage that with traveling all the time?

It cost me. I've been married twice.

Yeah. Norm has a family too. This is so intensive. You would think that— like you said, it's a pressure cooker all the time, and to have a family....

That's the other reason that I'm doing this. I don't market as much, and I don't push as much. I don't go on TV because I want to spend more time with family. My kids are at an age where I need to spend time with them. My oldest son is going to be 18, so he'll be going to university. And my youngest daughter is in high school. So hockey takes up a lot of time.

Do the kids have any interest in what Dad does?

No. Well, a little bit because they see all the perks and everything else that comes with it. They also see the stress and everything else that goes with it.

It's tough to motivate the second generation.

My opinion is that after the regulator thing, I never forget that. I went to the cottage and my kids were young. They said, "Dad, Dad, You're on the front page of the paper." "Daddy, Daddy, why is the reporter in the backyard taking pictures of us?"

Yeah, it sticks in your mind, doesn't it?

Yeah. It happens. Even to this day, I have to explain it. With every new client, and every prospectus. It's in every prospectus. It's a blemish, and it's something that you can never live down. I question why I still do it, but I like it.

You have enough money that you could live for the rest of your life without any problems, so why do you still do it?

I don't spend a dime. I drive a 1997 Ford F-150 pickup truck. I was off for a year and I didn't know what to do. I set up a restaurant and hated that. I'm not a real estate guy. I don't believe in real estate. This is a great business because you can travel. You can go to China and do research. You can go to Africa and do research. This business challenges you. The weather changes and your portfolios change. There's a hurricane. There's a volcano. There's a virus. There's a new discovery. You know, it's like *Star Trek* the whole time. [Laughs]

Well, it allows you to be flexible and….

And it's the best for your ego and it's the worst for your ego.

Right. You're a winner. You're a loser.

You want to be the best at what you do, but then to be at the top, you have to embrace volatility. And, therefore, you have to have a really thick skin when you're down 17, 18, 19, 20 percent. You're sitting there going, "Oh my God, I've blown myself up. I'm done. I'll never work again. I'm an idiot."

I was talking to Rohit, and he had just been down 17 percent and he had just nerves of steel. He said, "Stick with it. It's fine." Then I thought, "Whew, that's tough, man."

Last year, he was down 17 percent and he stayed with the oil picture.

He was down in a week that much and I thought, "Wow, that's some serious volatility."

The metals are not like the oils. When they go no-bid, they don't go no-bid because the grades disappear. At least with oil, it doesn't really blow up. Then mining's tight. All of a sudden there's a war in the Congo, and you've got 20 percent of your portfolio in the DRC, okay? You've got your Lundin—you've got all these things, okay? You've got your Katanga and you've got your First Quantum. They're all in not very great places.

There's six countries in the world that supply much of the oil: Venezuela, Iran, Iraq, Russia, Nigeria, etc. Name one that's actually stable.

Well, to me, the most politically stable place—outside of the known areas like North America—right now is Colombia. In South America, Colombia is a little beacon of democracy and has the best royalty regime—is a very undiscovered oil basin. Ecuador's gone. Venezuela's gone. Chile and Peru aren't really oil sectors. Argentina is up and down and all over the place, and it really isn't a great oil basin. But Colombia, you know, comes in from Venezuela. It's a wonderful, wonderful oil basin that hasn't been fully exploited. That's where I'm looking. I've got two or three private companies that are Western Canadian oil guys that are in Colombia. I like Colombia.

Thanks, Frank, I appreciate it.

Peter Puccetti
Private Equity Approach with Public Stocks

"The attitude is all about knowing enough about that file or that industry or that company so that it becomes very obvious to you when you should strike, when you should go big."

Away from the downtown skyscrapers of Toronto and in an older heritage building on King Street West, sits the offices of Goodwood Capital. *Nondescript* and *low key* are the words that best describe the operation, and this makes sense at a deep value shop such as this. Trading turnover is low, and the theory is that if Chief Investment Officer Peter Pucetti can get just a handful of good ideas each year, and then take a big position, performance can be extraordinary. Well, so far, it has worked according to plan.

Since inception of the Goodwood Fund in 1996, the fund averaged about 19 percent until the end of 2007, whereas the total return of the Toronto Stock Exchange was about 10 percent. And they say the markets are efficient and you can't beat the index. Nothing could be further from the truth. This is in spite of two severe headwinds in the past few years. Number one is the rise of Canadian dollar versus the U.S. dollar. This hurts when your U.S. dollar exposure is not hedged. Second, most of the action on the Canadian market in the last few years has been focused in the resource sector. Peter has had little to no resource exposure because it has not fit into his investment mandate. Peter's performance is almost dead on his target of 20 percent net to investors over a five-year period.

Peter's is another story of an exceptional money manager not quite fitting into the traditional box. On the wall of his office are a couple dozen framed letters that act as a reminder that this firm is different. Interestingly, they are letters of refusal for employment. You see, when Peter wanted to enter the business years ago, he had a tough time finding employment. Nobody was hiring; he just didn't fit into the mold, or the people he applied to just didn't get him. Whatever the case, not getting a job at the traditional shops was probably a good thing for two reasons. First, at a traditional company, you are hardly ever given the flexibility to follow your instincts. In Peter's case, with a very concentrated portfolio, some positions become 10 percent of the equity, and once in a while they hit 15 percent. This would generally not be allowed at a traditional firm. Second, undoubtedly with the constraints that are put on most traditional money managers, performance becomes remarkably close to the index, thus mediocre. In Goodwood's case, Peter describes his performance as "lumpy" because when he buys big chunks of out-of-favour, disliked, beaten-up stocks, it takes them a while to come to fruition. It also can give a huge upside when the market starts to recognize the potential.

The interviews with Peter all have been casual and relaxed. It was tough to find a place to put my notes, as his desk is piled high with research and notes. As they say, a clean desk is indicative of a sick mind. During the interview, he paid close attention to the flashing stock quotes in front of him, and a couple times called a trader to see what was happening with a couple of his positions. I am a great believer in keeping things simple, and the best part was when Peter showed me the sheet of paper where he kept his new ideas for the portfolio. He pulled out a piece of torn notebook paper with a few names of companies scribbled on it. These were ideas that came to him from his analysts, his industry contacts, or were on his own.

These "keys" to the future of the portfolio, which were scribbled on a piece of paper, were a classic display of how being a great stock picker was far more "common sense" and insightful than going high tech or being too quantitative about the process. It made me think how I'd bet someone like Warren Buffett did the same thing. I just can't see Buffett having endless spreadsheets that dictate which stocks he will buy. In fact, Peter mentioned that he used to put these ideas in a computer, but got tired of it. When you only need a very few great ideas each year, you can certainly do it this way. I think it tells a lot about his style. A momentum manager with huge turnover would surely not be able to run things this way.

Peter was adamant that much of his performance was due to the team that Goodwood had assembled, including President and CEO Cam McDonald. Having a team with so many industry contacts keeps the flow of ideas coming and helps to reload the portfolio when past ideas come to fruition or portfolio companies get bought out. Shareholder activism has increased a lot in the last few years, and Goodwood has been at the forefront, having been involved in creating catalyst type events with Creo, Dofasco, the Great Atlantic & Pacific Tea Company, and, most recently, Cenveo and ATS Automation. This is why Goodwood most often performs the function of being a private equity manager in the public markets.

I interviewed Peter for a second time in early 2008, after value investing and catalyst investing had just gone through a really rough patch. Value managers all over the world had been beaten, but it is times like these that give portfolios like Goodwood's the best upside over the mid term. In fact, he mentioned that he had not seen the current names in his portfolio as undervalued since 2002. What happened in the years immediately following? Some pretty extraordinary performance. "Invest at the point of maximum pessimism" is what the famous investor John Templeton said, and nothing could describe Peter and Goodwood's philosophy better.

Bob:

The first thing I think I wanted to do is give us a bit of your educational experience. How did it build through the years, and how did you decide to be involved with stocks?

Peter:

I think I read about the market when I was a teenager at some point and got interested in investing. I had a relative in Chicago who was involved in the commodity business, but I didn't know anything about that, so that kind of fascinated me too. Somehow in a roundabout way, I ended up being interested in stocks and knew that I wanted to be in the investment business in some way, shape, or form pretty early on.

When you were going to university?

Yeah, like any kid, I moved around a lot, trying to figure out what I wanted to do exactly. Eventually, it became pretty clear. I did a B.A. in economics and did my Canadian Securities course while I was in university and got summer jobs at brokerage firms.

Right. So you were influenced a little bit by a family member who was in the commodities business?

He and I never really talked. He was my dad's uncle. He was quite old, and by the time I was of a mature enough age to really have a discussion with him, he had already retired. Just knowing that he was in the business and that he had done well, I think, sort of gave me further interest in the business. He was a commodities broker.

How about your dad? Was he involved at all?

No, not at all. He was an academic professor of philosophy. Very much an academic.

Did he talk about philosophy a lot with you?

He did.

It's interesting because Frank Mersch has a degree in philosophy. He said it helped him a lot, actually, being a money manager and a non-linear thinker.

The only thing I think it helped me with is we used to have a lot of our arguments at the dinner table. Not just my dad and I, but the whole family. You learn to argue a bit when your dad's a professor of philosophy.

Now, as you progressed through university, did you try and get a job on Bay Street right after university?

Well, I was in Halifax, so I did get a job in the summers working at what was then known as Scotia Bond, which subsequently was bought by Midland Walwyn. After I graduated with a B.A. in economics, I started at Scotia Bond. I had an acceptance to do an M.B.A. at Western but I deferred it. I ended up applying for work in Toronto to be an analyst because I wanted to be an analyst and learn more about the analytical side of the business. I knew I didn't want to be a retail broker. I had already made that decision. The Belzberg family was relocating First City Trust head office into Toronto from Vancouver, so I ended up getting a job as a junior analyst and working underneath a guy who, in turn, was under Brent Belzberg. Actually, Peter Munroe was the CFO of the company at the time. I think he went to Great-West Life or London Life or somewhere as a CFO.

What was their investing philosophy?

It was pretty varied. I kind of got thrown into the deep end, which was great. I got to help look after the preferred shares. I had a few sectors that I was supposed to follow. I think it was real estate paper, forest products, and something else. It also gave me a chance to do sort of special sits–type research. I distinctly remember one situation. We had about a billion dollars of capital at the trust company. I remember there was a point where my analytical light bulb really went on, and I said, "Oh, this is kind of cool when you can find a situation like this and nobody else really understands what's happening. Look at all the money you can make." And that was the spinoff of Inner City Products out of Inner City Gas. It was done with a convertible preferred as well as the common, and the terms of the conversion rate on the preferred were going to be a function of the future trading price. I think it was the thirty-day or sixty-day or ninety-day trading price of the stock. I figured it out before it actually started trading, and I was very, very proud of myself at the time because this was the first time I had ever looked at something like this. I figured out that, of course, people were going to buy the preferred and short the hell out of the common. Therefore, the common was going to drop precipitously. I think it originally was issued at nine bucks or ten bucks or something. I think it eventually bottomed at a buck and change. The preferred held steady because the conversion rate on the preferred just got better to offset the decline in the stock. So I was very proud that I figured this out in advance. We had owned the Inner City gas stock, so we ended up with both pieces. Eventually, it made sense to go long on the common, once it stabilized. Once the conversion rate was set, there was a lot of upside in the common because it had been oversold.

So that was kind of the first time a special sit occurred to me and I figured it out on my own. I remember I had a lot of pride in being able to explain it to the other people in the office, saying, "You know, I think this is what's going to happen and here's why." It was my first example of an open-ended capitalization. It was a lesson I've never forgotten. Any time you have a company that is in a situation where they have to issue more shares subject to where the price is of that security, it just gets worse. It's like a spiral.

Interesting. So you started right off the bat with hedging principles or learning some hedging principles.

Yeah. I think I was at First City for two or three years. So I don't know where along the way that happened, maybe halfway through.

How about the letters on the wall here?

I was trying to get a job in Toronto. I sent out a hundred-something letters to very important people that I had looked up from Halifax in some book I got. They were CFOs and CEOs of all these financial institutions. I think two gave me a chance for an interview. One was Sam Belzberg, so that's how I ended up there.

Were they mostly brokerage firms?

It was a mix—trust companies, money management firms, and brokerage firms.

Did they ever give reasons as to why?

No, I was just another kid with a B.A. in economics who hadn't even done his M.B.A. yet. I ended up never doing an M.B.A. because I ended up working in the business and doing my CFA instead. So it made sense not to go, but at the time, I wouldn't have stood out to anybody.

Well, it's interesting because people who don't necessarily fit in with the norm are the people that are successful.

I think there are a lot of people who do fit in with the norm who do pretty well, but I think you're right too that they don't do spectacularly well. There is a whole level of people who have great incomes and they are people who are good at fitting in. I've never been good at fitting in that way.

When did you work with Sprott Securities?

That was right after First City, and that was for about three years.

There were twenty-six people, and I was the twenty-seventh employee. I was brought on as an analyst—a special-sits analyst—and I wrote reports, trying to come up with ideas both long and short. That was one thing that separated Sprott from the other firms at the time. He was willing to write up and talk about short ideas.

What years were they?

I joined Sprott some time in '90. So between '90 and late '92.

At the time, I was very impressed with him, and I still am. I have a tremendous amount of respect for Eric. At the time he had a certain technique, which started with every day scanning the papers for earnings releases. Anything that had a pretty big jump in earnings he'd go take a look at it. What I liked about it is that he rolled up his sleeves and he looked. He was always on the lookout for another idea. So that was kind of cool to see that in action. I already had more of a value bent, and I think I would describe at that time, certainly, his style as much more of a momentum or growth-oriented style.

Why did you come up with the value bent?

Just stuff that I had read.

I think a lot to do with your personality type too, right?

Yeah, I think that's very true. The value thing just sticks with you, and with other people, it doesn't. It's really hard to know who it will or won't in advance. It just happens that way. I'm more comfortable buying something that I think I'm getting really, really cheap and being patient and waiting. I'm comfortable with that, and I don't mind taking quotational losses while I wait. I know that I'm eventually right and I've built up a lot of knowledge around it. I'm very comfortable with that. I'm not so comfortable buying something that has to keep growing. But let's face it, they're really all part of the same spectrum. If you know something's going to grow and you have conviction in it and you know it's going to grow pretty fast, you should be willing to pay more for that, obviously.

Value stocks turn into growth stocks sooner or later, and they flip back and forth too.

Absolutely.

Right? So really it's just a matter of when you decide to get into it, right?

Totally. Totally. It's really all part of the same spectrum.

Why did you come up with the idea of starting your own firm?

After Sprott, I had an institutional brokerage firm, which had done pretty well, called Puccetti Farrell Capital. We raised money for different special sits. Clearly, our investment ideas as opposed to our capital-raising ideas were very strong. We made a lot of money, and we looked at a lot of special sits, a lot of reorgs and restructurings, and things being spun out. I think I needed to mature a bit and figure out after a while exactly where in the investment business I wanted to end up and somewhere along the way there with Puccetti Farrell it became obvious what I needed to do was to set up a fund where I could just do my investment ideas, where I didn't have the pressure of trying to sell ideas to people all the time on the phone. I can just focus on my own ideas, and they've worked out pretty well. "My investment ideas have been great. Let's go start a fund and let's get a performance fee." So that's how it all started.

As an analyst at Sprott, were you responsible for that? Were you responsible for kind of selling your ideas to people on the streets?

Sprott was very horizontal. It wasn't like a traditional firm. When I joined, it was twenty-something people. When I left two and a half years later, there were sixty-some people. Instead of one office in Toronto, I think there were three offices. So it had grown quite a bit. The stuff that I was doing was more value oriented and more special sits. I had some sort of buy-in from other people in the firm, but not a lot. So a lot of what I was doing was vertically integrated. I was generating an idea, I was taking it to clients that I had started to develop on my own, including some U.S. hedge funds. It occurred to me, "Gee, why don't I just do this on my own?" I mean, it's not like the rest of the firm was buying into this approach. That's why I started Puccetti Farrell. But then it became obvious the best way to do this would be actually to have a fund. It was a better business, with leverage and scalability. If you're actually good at picking stocks, if you have a good track record long term, you can't beat the business. It's fantastic.

And why did you decide to start up long/short? Because most people at the time didn't even think of that.

You had a choice. Originally, for regulatory ease, my fund was a mutual fund. Shortly, within about nine months, I got it set up so that it was a long/short fund. I wanted to be able to have the flexibility to at least know that I could make money in any environment, but there's always been a long bias. It's just a lot easier to buy stocks than it is to short stocks. You can make more money on a buy. You've got everybody pushing for the stock to go up, management included. Shorts are great when you get those few situations just right and you nail them and you can make a lot of money. But the longs are a lot easier.

The shorts have unlimited loss potential and limited gain potential, right?

Well, that's true. You can only make 100 percent on a short. You can reload constantly, it's absolutely true.

Did you like being a sell-side analyst.

I just didn't like the idea of always having to sell my ideas, to convince people that I was right on something. After a while, it gets a little tiring. You're one of eighty people trying to reach a senior portfolio manager on Bay Street who's being called by seventy-nine other people. Sometimes it's tough to stand out. I was pretty good at it and I raised a lot of money because we had some great ideas. It wasn't something I wanted to do for the rest of my life—being a phone jockey.

Do you ever use analysts' reports today?

Yeah. Absolutely.

For information or for their recommendations?

It's a quick and easy way to get up to speed on a particular industry or a particular company. We make use of it, but then if it's going to be a core position with us, we go well beyond what the analyst typically has time to do. There's only a few situations in a year that we'll do that, that we'll get to that level of knowledge. This firm is much more than Peter Puccetti now. My partner Cam is a very capable investor and a very smart businessman. He is a great partner to have, and we have a division of labour. He focuses on running the business, and I focus on running the money. We've got guys like Rob Kittel— Rob's a CA, CFA. He is an extremely bright, talented individual who is hardworking, intense, and focused. He has added a lot of value to this firm over the last four years.

We've got Blake Sumler, who also is a CA, CFA. He's newer with the firm. He's only been here about six months, but, again, a very talented analyst. He has a lot of U.S. experience, so as we sort of migrate more and more into stuff into the States, that's helping out. We also have Thomas Hawkins, who's a junior analyst here. He runs a lot of screens and does a lot of backup research for us. The firm has become a lot more than Peter Puccetti, and I suspect more and more we're going to be moving in that direction.

The name Goodwood—how did you...?

That's where I used to live. It's just outside Stouffville, which is just outside Markham, which is just outside Toronto. It's a little town. If you drive too fast, you'll miss it.

Any other money managers that have influenced you over the years?

Oh, tons. Marty Whitman at Third Avenue, originally M.J. Whitman. I have a good friend who works and runs the international fund down there and used to work with Marty when it was a brokerage firm only. I've always been a fan of Peter Lynch, Warren Buffett. I've tended to gravitate towards stock pickers; those tend to be my role models, if you will.

Graham was deep value and that was it. Buffett said he was 80 percent Graham and 20 percent....

Fisher. Phil Fisher.

Fisher. Right. How would you look at your style?

Every situation calls for a different set of analyses. Sometimes something can be so statistically cheap that you can kind of plug your nose, and even though it's a lousy business, you can buy it because it's that cheap. I'd say we're probably around 50/50 qualitative versus quantitative.

Obviously, I would think that when you're putting in new positions or looking for new positions, it's going to take a while for the positions to come to fruition.

Absolutely. I think this is where having more than just Peter Puccetti able to contribute to the portfolio helps a lot. What tends to happen, if it's one guy, you tend to have a batch of ideas that tend to mature at the same time and then you go through that fallow period. But if you've got Rob contributing ideas and you've got Blake contributing ideas, then there's a bit of an overlay happening. So some of the ideas that these guys are contributing happen on a different cycle than mine, then hopefully our returns can actually smooth out. Now, that remains to be seen, but I think it's actually happening.

So you almost kind of buy the stocks that you wouldn't buy now but you bought a couple years ago and say, "Well, now we'll get the rotation."

You know what? I have a good friend who is utterly convinced that he will have a huge rate of return if he only buys names that I started talking about two years ago. He's probably right.

Maybe talk about the process of how you would find a long position, how you would build a position, what percentage you'd have that in the portfolio.

Yeah, sure. Before I do that, though, I have to say something before I forget. When you're comparing our returns to others, keep in mind that in our almost ten-year history, I believe that something like 90 percent of our month-ends or more we have been below 100 percent aggregate invested. This means the market value of the longs plus the market value of our shorts divided by the equity of the fund has been below 100 percent as it is now.

For example, right now, it would be about 67 percent. That means that the net return that we've generated has really been done with excess cash and no leverage. Also keep in mind we're prohibited from derivatives. So this is really just a stock-picking fund, and it has not generated its returns from leverage. A lot of the guys that we get compared to—I think almost unfairly—are typically 2-to-1 or 2.5-to-1 on equity. They're levered up the yin-yang. They'll tell you that they're hedged—they're long this and they're short that. But, listen, I've been at this long enough. I can say one thing categorically, which is there will be periods of time where your longs—regardless of how well hedged you think you are— your longs go down and your shorts go up. On a 2.5-to-1 gearing ratio, it's not pretty. So I think there's an embedded risk in those other strategies that we get compared to on a return basis, but we're not getting any credit for the fact that with us, you don't have that leverage risk.

The most we've ever been is 120 between longs and shorts. Maybe 80 long, 40 short, but that's been rare. Usually it's 60-ish, 70-ish of equity long and 20 to 30 short. That's a typical stance.

So you had asked how do I accumulate a position?

How do you come up with an idea, build it, and sell it?

Okay, the first part of the question: Ideas come up really from a whole bunch of different ways. Whether it's reading something in the paper that piques your interest and makes you think about something or running screens. We're regularly running screens, looking for cheap stocks on an EBITDA basis—stocks with high free cash flow yields, which is free cash flow divided by the market cap of the stock. We look for stocks with a lot of excessive cash versus the share price. We do all sorts of stuff, reverse for the short ideas. Also we get ideas from other guys in the business. I've got contacts that stretch back seventeen, eighteen years in this business with a lot of smart guys who run money now. We share ideas as much as possible, where it makes sense. A few of them I'm particularly close to. We have a lot of respect for their opinions and they've helped us a lot over the years.

And Rob's got contacts up the yin-yang that he's developed and have generated a lot of ideas for us that way. Cam, the same thing again, and Blake I'm sure is the same way. Blake is newer, so I don't know his net worth like I know Rob's. Blake came from a private equity background. So they come from all sorts of ways.

In terms of how we accumulate a position, the typical core weighting is anything over a 5 or a 6 percent weighting on the long side. We've had some core short ideas, but they've been far less frequent than the longs. That core position is something where we have a lot of conviction, we've done a lot of work on the name, we feel the timing is right, and so we're adding to the position more and more.

A typical situation will take us a year or two. We start out really small. A half a point here, a point there. It builds up, and as we get more comfortable, sometimes we'll trade it. If it runs on us and we think it's gone ahead of itself, we'll sell some and try to buy it back later. We did that with Creo, for example. During the first two years, we bought and sold it a number of times in various sizes. Then once we got serious, once we had Bob Burton with us, we really loaded up. The attitude is all about knowing enough about that file or that industry or that company so that it becomes very obvious to you when you should strike, when you should go big. That takes time, you have to do a lot of reading, and you have to visit the company.

Can you discuss how you came up with the idea for Great Atlantic & Pacific Tea Company?

That was through one of Rob's. It was a behind-the-scenes, and we wrote about seven letters to the board. That was a case where a contact of Rob's, an analyst who he's friendly with who knows the industry very, very well, mentioned the name to Rob. We ended up owning it in a smaller size for about two years. We knew there was value there, but until we felt that they were going to actually sell Canada and unlock some of the value, there was too much risk in owning it in a big size. They had operating losses with a lot of debt.

So for the first few years, we just had a 4 percent weighting, a 5 percent weighting, a 6 percent weighting, back and forth trading it. Then once we started getting all the way along we were writing letters to them. We told them that they really should sell Canada, and we very logically laid out our argument. We wrote very well structured letters to the board and to management explaining why we thought now was the time to sell A&P Canada.

What percent of the company did you own?

Before we went big? It was because somewhere after that two-year period when we finally started saying we knew the file well enough and we knew management well enough, we started getting the vibes, "These guys are now thinking seriously about it," because they had no other option. The debt was killing them. If they sold Canada they could pay down a lot of the debt and eliminate a lot of the negative cash burn.

Once we started getting a warm fuzzy feeling, that's when we took it to a big weight. At that point, I think we owned about 6 percent or maybe 6.5 percent of the Great Atlantic & Pacific Tea Company.

I think that was probably the biggest position in your fund you ever had on a percentage basis, is it?

The first one was Sun Life that got into the 20s on the IPO. That was the first time that on a cost basis I went close to 15 percent, which is the most we're allowed to go to in the fund. In ten years, we've come close to 15 percent four times. The first one was Sun Life on the IPO. It was an absolute lay-up. It was clearly a cheaply priced IPO. I think six months later, it had doubled, and we had been selling through the piece. It got into the 20s as a percent of the fund. I can't remember right now whether it was 24, 25, 26 at the peak. That was the first time we went big. The next time would have been Creo once we got together with Bob Burton, and we could see how we could own a lot of value. We took a 13 percent weighting and then it started to run.

You must have owned quite a bit of Creo.

Well, between us and Bob, we owned 6 percent of Creo as well—2 percent by Bob, 4 percent by us. We filed jointly in the Schedule 13D. Then the next one was A&P, when we started getting the vibe they're serious about selling Canada. It sounds like they're going to do something now. Again, I think we took it to 13 and change, and then it started running. That weighting at the peak would have been in the 20s somewhere. I'm not sure where exactly.

We tend to sell, if anything, too soon, historically.

Value managers tend to buy early and sell early. Have you ever thought about that or struggled with that?

We try to get better at it. Then sure enough, every once in a while you get socked with something that you should have sold more of, right? So you're never going to get it right. Good luck. I mean, what are you really there for? Your job really is to get sort of the meaty low-risk part of the move as a value investor. You really want to say, "Okay, I really bought this well, and I know for sure it's going to go to at least this. So I want to lock that in." You miss a little bit here and you miss a little bit there.

How do you make that sell decision? Do you calculate an intrinsic value, as they say, for the company?

We do. We constantly roll it forward because new information becomes available. A&P Canada, for example, is a classic example—what they sold it for. I think originally the analysts in the States were expecting it to sell for

$400, $500 million U.S.—eventually, it went for a billion. We were thinking maybe $700, $800 million U.S. This was a company with only 38 million shares outstanding. Every 100 million was four bucks on a stock where our cost was originally eight bucks. They talk about torque, which is an Eric Sprott expression. This thing had torque.

So we try to be realistic about those intrinsic values. We try to be conservative. We're all too conservative here, is the truth. Rob's a conservative guy, I'm conservative, Cam's conservative. We sit there with something that's tripled and we kind of get anxious to get out. The fact is often you should sit with it. If the situation gets better, sit with it. I've noticed after seventeen or eighteen years of watching things, the expression "when it rains, it pours," is very true. It works both ways, right? When things get bad, they tend to get worse first before they level off. When things get good, they tend to get really good before they stop. Things happen in bunches.

If a stock has already moved up, the growth managers are going to get all excited about it. I guess that's why it gets that push.

With A&P Canada being sold, they start factoring in what that might go for. They start doing the math and saying, "Okay, I'm going to buy this because I see a 20 percent return in two months." You've raised, actually, a very interesting point because I've thought about this a lot. You look at our rate of return on the first dollar that we invested in Creo, and we sold it two and a half years later for approximately a 90 percent return. The first two years, we were down 10 percent. You compare our rate of return on a time-weighted basis to one of the guys in the States, let's say an arb fund, who picked up our Schedule 13D filing the next day and bought the stock 30 percent higher than where it was the day before we filed the Schedule 13D. But then he or she was able to get a 50 or 60 percent rate of return in three months when Kodak came along and bought it. Their rate of return was far better than ours on a time-weighted basis. The only problem with that analysis is it assumes you can always find and jump into new situations at the right time like that. We're much more comfortable as a firm in getting to know a company really well and being patient. We're shooting for a double or a triple on some of these names or more. We're going to have a couple years where nothing happens.

You can't help but think about it and let it influence what you're doing. If you're focused on a company, on a business, like a business-by-business approach, that does tend to take you away from the macro thinking. You look at something like a Laidlaw and you worry about fuel prices and you sort of assume, over the intermediate term, Laidlaw will be able to pass on some of these fuel-price cost increases and/or fuel prices will level off. Plus they've got some hedging. You don't spend a lot of time worrying about that one potential macro factor. It's all about, "Gee, is Laidlaw a private equity candidate? Can they buy a bunch of stock back here? How clean is their balance sheet? Can they take on leverage to buy back stock?" That's the kind of analysis you end up doing. It's very stock specific, very business specific, very balance-sheet specific. It moves you away from these big macro thoughts.

So you would say probably that the average stock you buy isn't affected very much by market fluctuations. It's more …

Oh, it is.

It is, but it's more affected by company events than the average stock.

Yeah, that's what we're focused on. We know it will go up and down with the market, and if fuel prices go through the roof again, Laidlaw will probably suffer as a result. People who are much brighter than we are have proven that a bottom-up approach, which tends to minimize the macro-economic concerns and sort of maximizes the specifics of that business, tends to do well over the long run. Things sort of level off over the long run, these big macro concerns.

Have you had any resource exposure in the past?

Oh, sure. I think we're as good as anybody else at valuing a company within the industry and whether or not it's cheap against the industry. That's really what you're trying to do when you're focused on special sits. So the resource stuff we've done historically has been special sits. For example, we did Paramount Energy.

This is going back about four years ago or three years ago. There was a decision by the Alberta regulator that was going to restrict the amount of production that some of Paramount's fields could take out, so the units got hit. That's a classic special situation. That's the kind of thing we like to go look at. We bought some because we figured out that it's probably overdone. The regulator would probably have to back off a bit. There would probably be some sort of a compromise. So I think we made, 20 or 30 percent on a kind of small-ish position because we didn't have time to really get into it big.

So, yeah, we'll do any industry. The angle is a special-sits approach. If you're talented as analysts, I think you have a bit of an edge when there's noise and confusion because you're willing to spend the time to roll up your sleeves. That's where the bargains are.

Do you short index units?

Yeah, we shorted XIUs, spiders, diamonds, and the Qs. We did a lot of the Qs in 2000 and '01. We prefer though to have a good fundamental short idea.

Bankruptcy candidate?

Sure. That's one area. That's become virtually impossible with all the liquidity that's around right now. It has been for the last few years.

Some people have come up with the idea of shorting income trusts, and I think it's hard to borrow there.

It's just a business. You've got to pay the yield. If it's going to stop paying a yield or a distribution, then you're okay.

Have you ever invested in trusts before?

Sure. Yeah. Superior Propane was a big win for the fund years ago. We'll do anything. It's a business. Whether you structure it as a trust or a corporation doesn't matter. It's a business.

Well, one of the risks when you're short a stock that's going down and down and down is that it becomes cheap. Somebody comes in and decides to buy the company and it jumps up 30 percent. Have you ever had that happen with a short?

Absolutely. Part of it can be short coverage. That's a serious problem now. A name like Ballard is something that everybody wants to short or a lot of people now want to short. Air Canada was the same thing. There's not enough borrow around to do it, so you pay a lot. You've got to pay a borrow fee when you do it now, right? On a popular name, you can be paying 20 percent to short the stock a year.

Vertex was doing that. They were getting paid 20 percent to lend out Martha Stewart stock.

Great for them, very smart. So all they had to do was somehow hedge off the risk while they own the stock that it might go down.

How active are you managing your long/short ratio? Give me a time when your net has been the lowest that it's ever been and why ?

Well, we've been negative before. In '98, we were negative for a good part of the year. I think we had 20-something percent long as a percent of equity and around 30 percent short. We were net short for some part of the year. It's really, for us, we try to let it be a function of idea flow. If we have a whole bunch of great long ideas, we'll end up more long than we otherwise would have been. If we end up having a bunch of good short ideas, then naturally we're going to be more net short. We just let it try to percolate from the ideas.

In '99, tech was the big thing, and presumably you weren't in that area. But what did you do in '99 to…?

I did find a great way to play tech—a value guy's way to play tech. I was very happy about our idea, which was DataMirror. DataMirror will go down as the stock that I have traded the best in my entire career. I just got lucky. In and out at the right time, I think three times, as it went from 4 to 20-something. I maxed out. It was beautiful. Not tax efficient, but beautiful. It was a great way to play tech because at four bucks, you could make an argument that its interest in a private Silicon Valley company was worth more than four dollars. It was a legitimate business, and in that time and space, it had a tremendous value that exceeded the four bucks a share. So you were paying nothing for DataMirror's own business. I'm trying to remember now, but I think that interest in the private business you could say was worth, like, twelve bucks and the stock was at four.

There are ways even in the middle of a ridiculous bull market, whether it's oil and gas or technology, to find a value special sit within that. That's a great way to play it because you're going with the trend. You're probably not going to suffer early losses. I love doing those sort of things, looking for a big bull market in an industry and then trying to find something unusual within the space.

We talked about this a little bit ago, but all value managers kind of say the same thing, about how they buy stock. Obviously, you've been more successful, especially since you've been less than 100 percent invested on average. If there was one thing that's been responsible for you being different than others and getting better returns, what would it be?

Very, very selective on what becomes a core weighting. It takes a lot for a name with us to get above 5 percent. It doesn't happen often.

I think Cam said that a stock over 5 percent has very rarely turned out badly for you, if ever.

I don't think it has. How do you define that, though? Great Atlantic was over 5 percent a little bit on a couple of occasions during the first two years where we were down. At one point, I think we were down 40 percent.

Yeah. So if you're buying at 30 percent, 40 percent below what you think it's worth, that's what gives you the margin of safety, and I guess helps you feel comfortable.

It makes you feel comfortable, but, quotationally, let's face it, they still go down, they still hurt. You can't get away from that.

Like they say, if there's one cockroach, others come out. In other words, the growth people say when a company comes out with bad earnings, they usually come out with worse and worse and worse earnings for the next four or five quarters.

Yeah, I believe that.

If they beat the market in earnings, they usually beat it for four or five quarters.

Well, when it rains, it pours. It's the same argument. Things happen in batches.

So that's where you just accumulate on the way down?

I think so. Conviction's a funny thing. Maybe that's part of what we're saying here with these core ideas. Conviction is something that you get by doing a lot of work, a lot of digging. It's amazing, for example, what you pick up when you actually go visit the factory or the plant versus just reading it in text. I'm always amazed at the number of guys that we compete against who've never gone to visit the company. Just recently, for example, last week I made two visits, one out west and one in around the GTA, Greater Toronto Area. I was amazed at what I learned on those two trips. I've done a lot of reading on those companies, but you just can't get it by reading. You have to go see and touch and talk to the people on the floor.

It's amazing. You start to realize it's not just a share, it's a friggin' business. So you start to get more comfortable that it isn't going away. It's a bunch of people out there struggling every day to make sure things are produced properly, and they actually have a real business and they've got customers from all over the place and there's an infrastructure. It's kind of neat. It puts meat around the bones that you get by reading.

So that's where the 50 percent qualitative comes in.
Oh, yeah.

You don't buy something just because it's cheap. You go and see what's going on.
The light bulb goes on. For example, in Creo's case, the light bulb went on for us. The defining moment was when I went to Germany for a trade show. Rob was going to come with me but he couldn't because his wife was pregnant and she was due that week. That six days of that German trade show, which is a once-every-four-year event, was so educational because I got to see everybody in the industry all under the same six or seven roofs. It's a huge trade show. All of a sudden, the light bulb went on. Oh my God, if these guys do what they're talking about, they're going to be killed. It was that moment that we said, "We better either sell the stock or find a solution."

How important is management, then, in a company?
Oh, it's critical. But as Rob has pointed out, there are some businesses where you can have an idiot running it and it still does well, right? That's less and less. Buffett will tell you the same thing. In today's environment, with the Internet—technology in general—a lot of those competitive barriers to entry have been eliminated. Things have gotten a lot of more competitive. So probably to make the argument that management is more important now than it ever has been.

There's a good question. What's the biggest win you've ever had on a stock?
Biggest percentage?

Biggest percentage, yeah.
Which is different than dollars. Probably the biggest win…so ignoring time? Sun Life was pretty tough to beat because it doubled in six months, right? No, actually, you can beat Sun Life. That's where it gets tricky because Sun Life doubled in six months or five months, whatever it was. A&P quadru-

pled over a two-and-a-half-year period with a lot of going up and down. The biggest percentage gain, I guess, would be something like an A&P or…DataMirror. Extendicare would probably be tough to beat. Extendicare original stock was bought at $2.40. The stock, our final sales, were done up in the $20s. Canadian Medical Lab—the original stock was bought at $5, and four years later, we were selling it in the $30s. So we've had a number of five-baggers, four-baggers.

A lot of managers would say that out of ten stocks they buy, three of them are big winners.

We run a tighter portfolio than most guys, so it's probably we miss more stuff but we probably don't lose as much on other stuff as well. So there's pros and cons.

Is there any sector that you have made more money on than others?

We're very comfortable with media, and we like media. We think we understand them. It's newspapers, TV, and radio.

That gets hit hard in a recession, I presume. People aren't going to advertise as much.

Yeah. That's typically the thought process, although radio tends to be fairly sticky. We like plain old industrial businesses, where guys make things and assemble things. We like consumer products too. Although there's more fickleness there, especially if you get into retailing with fashion and stuff. Thomas here has been doing work on Abercrombie & Fitch because he loves the company and he thinks it's cheap. I don't think we have a special sits angle on it yet, which is a bit of a problem, so it probably won't be a big position.

So you've invested in technology before, but it's a fast-moving, hard industry to figure out, right?

Yeah. Our angle was very much an unusual situation, a special sit. We wouldn't have done it just to go buy Cisco. That's not us.

Did you just wake up one morning and say, "Gee, I should be an activist investor"?

We'd read about other guys, such as Carl Icahn. I've been a big fan of Carl

Icahn for years. In fact, I've probably read and reread a book that was written—a biography on him. I think it was an unauthorized biography. I think the guy's name was Mark Stevens. It was written in the early '80s or mid-'80s called *King Icahn*. I find it fascinating how small he started. His first activist proxy fight was Tappan, the stove maker. I read about how he had to work the phones at night, calling shareholders, retail mom-and-pop shareholders, trying to get them to move. Who was Carl Icahn at the time? Nobody knew him.

So we knew that activism was always out there. We'd seen other guys do it. But part of it was getting big enough, too. The fund, our position size, had to get big enough so that we could do it. If you're running $50 million, you can't do it, but at $200 million, you could probably have some effect.

Was Creo the first one?

Yeah. Although there's always been behind-the-scenes encouragement and talking and, "Hey, why don't you guys think about doing this, and why don't you do that?" But we're never going to do what you see out of the States with some of these really....

Pirate Capital?

Well, yeah. See that hat on my shelf? I was asked to speak at a seminar in New York, and Pirate was one of the speakers.

The fund's called the Jolly Roger Fund.

They've got a bunch of them, Jolly Roger and a couple others. They're very methodical. What I like about their approach is it's very mechanical. For us, we're value investors in special sits first, and then if there's an opportunity to unlock the value quicker through activism, yeah, of course we'll do it.

You don't mind the confrontation with management?
No.

I'm sure management's never happy, ever.
No. But in this new environment, they're much more compliant.

They have to do what's in the best interests of shareholders, too.

Yeah. Three years ago, or four years ago, they would have fought you tooth and nail on everything you tried to do and called you names in the paper and whatever. Now it's like it's practically they roll over. It's changed a lot, and it's almost like these hedge funds have too much of a say now.

Right. How about the relationship with Bob Burton, the printing industry investor? How did you meet him?

Well, we cold-called him. We did have a slightly warm introduction from a Canadian fund manager that had dealt with him on Moore Corp. So we called him and had a forty-page presentation on Creo. You can't go see somebody and try to get them interested in something by phoning them up and saying, "Gee, it would be a great idea for you to buy Creo with us." He's not going to take you seriously, right? We had a very well-researched forty-plus-page presentation where we went through the business in detail and we went through what we saw as the opportunity in detail. We did analysis like if Creo's costs as a percent of revenue were more in line with these other guys, here's what the earnings would look like. What a steal. It's that kind of stuff. That's how we approached Bob, and he very quickly got back to us and said he would be interested. I think he was in between things, so the timing was lucky. Then he brought us in after Creo into Cenveo.

Okay. I know it's a really long story, but maybe you can give us a synopsis on Dofasco.

The quick *Reader's Digest* version is we made an unsuccessful foray into Stelco. That led us to talk with one of our friends that we hold in high esteem about Dofasco. He brought it to our attention. We quickly did some work. We saw what he was talking about in terms of the quality of the business and how Hamilton was probably an income-trustable business. Then shortly thereafter, they announced the acquisition of QCM, a controlling interest in Quebec Cartier Mining. I was flabbergasted when I saw the numbers in terms of what that meant and how cheap they were buying QCM. I called the CFO and said, "Are you sure? Am I getting this right?" He said, "Yeah, but remember it's a cyclical business." I said, "Yeah, but still," you know. We compared valuations with Labrador Iron Ore Income Fund and some other comparables and quickly realized we've got to ramp this up.

So Dofasco was our fourth time that we got close to a 15 percent weighting at cost, 12 and change. We did it at an average price of about $37 a share.

Other than the Sun Life IPO, it was the fastest accumulation because we had bought it at a 2 percent position over a couple months, and then they announced QCM and it was like, "Holy mackerel, they got this cheap." We went to 12.5 like that. Over a two-day period, I think we went from 2 to 12.5 weighting in the fund.

What was the liquidity on Dofasco?

No, 77 million shares outstanding, I think, trading post the QCM news.

So no problem accumulating it in a short period of time?

No. It was about a $2.8 billion market cap. We started realizing that there was a real activist agenda. We prepared a forty-five-page report on how we could actually get to $100 of value per Dofasco share by following a series of steps of activism. By then, we had developed some relationships with some larger funds in the States, and one in particular who was anxious to work with us let us run the show and they would contribute capital. We weren't big enough to do Dofasco on our own, so we went to them. We showed them the presentation, got them in, and then they started buying with us.

But then the proverbial you-know-what hit the fan, and the company warned about the September '05 quarter. It was the first quarter in. I don't know how long, a long time, that Dofasco's main Hamilton operation was going to have an EBITDA line that was below $100 million. That was a very rare event, so it got us worried. There was a perfect storm happening for Dofasco's main Hamilton operations. Then Ralph Goodale made the bombshell announcement that income trusts were going to be no longer given any advanced tax rulings. So now we thought, "Oh my God, QCM income trust fund is not going to be able to done possibly." Hamilton as an income trust fund is not going to be able to be done A) because it's got fundamental problems that never existed before and B) because Ralph Goodale's just made it more difficult. So we sold down some of our position, not realizing that the board had been approached on multiple occasions by big steel companies elsewhere, like Arcelor, starting in May.

Were you up or down in the stock at that time?

Oh, we were up—up small. I think it was in the low 40s or mid-40s that we sold a good chunk of our position, only to find out afterwards that there were multiple bids happening. It's pretty ugly.

And you didn't find out about those till later.

No. So a board of directors and management team that owned 0.2 percent of the stock made a decision that the rest of us shouldn't know that offers were being made by big steel companies for Dofasco. They decided on our behalf that we didn't need to know.

You and your partner, how much did you own?

Oh, by then we owned just around 4 percent of the company.

Right. They owned 0.2, but they owned more after they issued options.

Yeah. Yeah. True.

All right, 2002; obviously what happened in 2002. It's nice to go through a bad time and see what happened or how that changed your style.

Just about everything that could go wrong did go wrong. Yes, we questioned ourselves. We did a lot of hand-holding with clients. We are actually surprised in retrospect at how little of our client base left. We're quite happy about that, how sticky they were. A lot of the credit for that goes to Cam for all the hand-holding he did. Also the monthly e-mails in general, which was Cam's idea again, have been a great way of keeping people educated about what's in the portfolio. We had a couple of mistakes that really hurt us that were permanent losses of capital. They were never more than 3 percent of the fund, but I made the mistake of averaging down. So in one case, the total capital committed between '01 and '02 was somewhere around 7 percent of our equity between those two years, and it went to zero. In the other case it was about 5 percent total capital committed. So there was 12 percent of our capital blown away on two situations that if WorldCom and Enron hadn't have happened, I think we would have been fine. But they did happen. Then the rest of the portfolio at the same time, of course, went down in value. All that stuff came back and we made money on it the next year. Of course, it hurt us in '02. On the shorts, as we've always done, we took profits on the first big drop on our short positions. The first 15 percent drop roughly we covered and we looked for a chance to reshort, but instead the market kept going down. So just about everything that could go wrong did go wrong in '02. I do think, though, that we'll be better next time for a bunch of reasons.

Did you change anything about your style because of that?

I think we're smarter now. We're older and we're wiser. You asked the question earlier about macro thinking. If we had been giving more credence to the macro environment, I think we would have understood better what the WorldCom and Enron situation meant for our company that was in restructuring. In both cases, these were companies that were in the process of restructuring their balance sheets. In one case, we bought bonds and expected to get equity. We wanted to get equity and enjoy the recovery. Then in the other case, it was, we thought, a straightforward extension of the credit and the problem would be solved. I mean, it was remarkable. Mosaic was the company. It was quite remarkable that here we were six months after Prudential Insurance out of the States had put a huge preferred share into Mosaic. The five banks in Canada—one of the five banks was getting cold feet and basically kyboshed the whole deal. But now that you look back at it, you say, "Well, shit, with Enron, and WorldCom, the banks were scared. They had a lot of credit outstanding in this space." Now I can understand why the top-down decision was made not to extend credit.

Now, if we were a bigger fund at the time, I think we probably could have done something to Mosaic to provide extra capital, to take out the banks and orchestrate something. We just decided, "You know what? We're having headaches left, right, and centre. We need to stop spending time and effort on this. Enough is enough. Let's move on."

So how do you control the emotions? Obviously, it wears on you in years like 2002. You had to stick to your guns.

I think you get tougher and your skin gets thicker. You get more used to it. Let's face it, the rewards during the good times more than compensate for it.

What kind of advantage is it to be a discretionary money manager rather than, let's say, a retail broker, where you have to justify your decision on each stock to retail clients. There's no way you could buy most of your stock. I don't think people would go along with it. People want what is hot.

Yeah. A) they would have a problem buying what I want to buy, B) I would have to spend so much time on the phone talking them into something. There's not enough time in the day now to get everything read. You've probably noticed this office is pretty quiet. It's like a library. We do a lot of reading. We listen to conference calls. We don't have a lot of time to talk to people about what we're doing, you know.

All right. Do you pay attention to the index makeup at all? Your correlation is 0.3 to the index.

No, we don't. What index? Our stocks are off the beaten track.

Yeah. That's the problem in the fund industry. Eighty percent of mutual funds give you index returns minus 2 percent. Why is that? Why won't they leave the index?

Well, you know the reasons as well as I do, right? It's the institutionalization. There's too much business risk to let your portfolio managers stray too far from the index. It's better to get mediocre performance than to try to shoot for superior performance, because if you mess up, you're out of business. It hurts too much. Blah, blah, blah.

So how do you find institutions? You have a defined style, I guess.

Yes, we do. They actually come to us seeking volatility. Typical fund of funds or a pension fund that allocates money to Goodwood is doing so because that group has 90-something percent of their money in market-neutral strategies. But they want to get a little zing. They want to try to find some alpha and some value add by some managers, so they consider us because they think maybe we're okay stock pickers. So in the context of an overall portfolio where it's heavily market neutral, they're throwing us some capital to get a little extra zing.

Now, avoiding big losses I think is a key to winning over time, right? I mean, if you lose 50 percent of your money, you have to make 100 percent to get back to where you started.

Look at '02; '02 hurt big time.

But your down-market performance is really, really exceptional in most markets.

Except for '02.

Why is your down-market performance so good?

I think the two big reasons are, one, the longs have historically been beaten-up situations that they've tended not to sell off with the market, although I find that that applies less and less, I think. It's almost like we're in a cycle where value stocks, if they disappoint, they go down worse than the index. But historically I would say that it was the other way around. They were stickier. Secondly, we've always had some shorts. So there's probably three reasons. The third one is that we're typically not 100 percent invested, so that gives us a cushion.

Why did you increase your shorts dramatically in '98? It was just a function of the stocks that you found you could short? Markets dropped a lot in the third quarter.

The timing just felt right at that moment to be shorting more and more names. It was easier to look at shorts. We were in the middle of the Russian crisis, then you had capital blowing up because of the Russian bond yields going up.

And all the spreads widened.

Yeah, all those spread trades got killed. Polar Capital got hurt. It was an ugly time. It's easier sometimes just to go with the flow. So if you're going to, you come in here every morning and you say, "Okay, what am I going to work on today?" Because you usually have too many things to work on. If the world is falling to bits, there's a natural inclination to say, "Why don't I go work on some of my shorts?" You know, that is what happens.

Have you ever done pairs trading within an industry?

Yeah, but there's a very low return. Guys who are very good at that, and even them with leverage, they're earning, like, 8 percent a year, you know. That's not what we're about.

You've got to be more directional to make money, right?

Yeah. That's our whole niche, you know.

I've always said that the only hedge funds that are really blowing up tend to use a lot of leverage. Illiquidity on top of that is the death blow. The only hedge funds that need to use a lot of leverage are the least risky strategies, the arbitrage strategies, right?

Exactly.

Because you're picking up nickels. So the least risky strategies are actually the riskiest strategies.

I know. There's no free ride in this business. Absolutely. I totally agree with that.

Concentration in the portfolio. Why do you think concentration's important instead of the spray-and-pray approach?

Because you and I, if we were pretending that we're going to buy the whole business instead of just a couple of shares, that means we have to do a lot of work. There's only a few names a year that you can really do that to. It just takes too long. You can't own 100 names and do that kind of research. That's why with portfolio managers, their diversification is their excuse for not doing in-depth work and getting conviction. Let's face it. I mean, that's honest, right?

You ever found value in large cap stocks?

Oh, for sure.

You've invested in large caps in the past? Sun Life, Dofasco. Sure. If you're only sticking to large caps it's going to be hard to beat the index probably again too because you're missing....

I don't think so. No. Let's say you put 15 percent of the fund into Dofasco and it doubled because it got taken over.

If you're concentrated, then, right, obviously you can still....

Concentration is the key, I think. Intelligent bets.

George Soros once said, "You have to bet very large on your best ideas, or you're not going to make money." Is that how you feel too?

But his very large might be three or four times my very large. Not just in dollars, but as a percent of the fund because he's got leverage. What's interesting about George Soros? I've read a lot about him. I've got all his books, all his biographies, all that stuff. I read *Alchemy of Finance* when I was in university. So let me just say that the interesting thing to me about George Soros is that for about the first ten to fifteen years of the Quantum fund, there were long and short stocks exclusively.

Same with Julian Robertson. Yeah, and then they all went to....

It was Jim Rogers and George Soros trying to find stock ideas. Somewhere after that first fifteen years or roughly fifteen years, he morphed into something beyond that because he got bigger. He brought people in to do different strategies. It is way too early for us to consider that. There are now hedge funds in the U.S. that are $8 billion or more who do our sort of thing. So you could actually run serious capital doing what we do.

Have you ever had trouble finding ideas where you just said, "There's no ideas and we're going to cash?"

No. The trouble is always the prioritizing. That is always my problem. I always keep a sheet nearby, where I try to rank what's next important. Remember, this isn't just Peter Puccetti.

That is a very high-tech sheet.

[Peter pulls a sheet of paper with several stock names scribbled on it.]

Yeah, you like that? It's constantly changing because I scribble. I used to keep it on the computer, but that was stupid. The other guys have ideas. Some of them are in here, some of them aren't. So this is the toughest part. It's a chicken-and-egg thing. You don't know what you should go work on until you go work on it. So you've got to take an intuitive guess.

How many stocks would you buy out of ideas that you get? One in ten?

You mean the ones that go to core positions? I'll put it to you this way: Usually we'll end up buying a little bit in a name that we think is interesting. So we'll end up with a bunch of small weightings at the bottom half of the long side of the portfolio. Out of those names, I'd say one to two out of every ten end up being above a 5 percent weighting. That is probably a good guess.

What is your target rate of return over a market cycle?

Well, the thing we've always said in all ten annual reports is the exact same paragraph. We're hoping to average 20 percent per annum or more. So that's the only thing I can throw out there, I guess.

Late 2007 and early 2008 have been tough for value investing and your fund.

I've been in the business since '87. I actually started in the business shortly before the crash, so I was a witness to guys panicking right around the crash, and that came back in very quick period. I think that in three months or four months, the index was right back. Somewhere centered around '91 was tough. Real estate and all sorts of issues out of Japan were affecting the market. I saw '98; I went through '98 with the fund. We had a flat year that year, but it was only by because of being heavily in cash through most of that year and having the same number of shorts as we had longs. I think for most of '98 I was 30 percent long and 30 percent short or close to it, and ended the year up 2 percent or something. If it wasn't for one particular short idea, I would have been down 7. Ninety-nine, 2000, and even 2001 were good.

In '99, a lot of value managers did poorly because there was the whole tech thing going on. You did fine, however, but if you look at a lot of value guys, they were really struggling through. People have short-term memories, right? That was only ten years ago and people don't remember.

Yeah. But then the '02 and early '03 was tough for us. That was the last time we've gone through this kind of pain. It sure set up for a good '03, '04, '05. We sort of look at it as three-year runs. So after '98 we had a very good three-year run. I think it was 190 percent net returns on the A units. Then in the three years after '02, even though we started '03 negative, negative 8 percent by the end of March, and I think we got down to negative 12 or something in April, we finished the year up net 30. The three years, '03, '04, '05, essentially doubled on the net basis, the B units. So this period, maybe I'm just not remembering it clearly, it feels like it's been tougher faster. It's just brutal, brutal, brutal.

Why do you think your style of investing is having a rough time at this point in the cycle? Is it because if you have any sort of catalyst at all, the market doesn't really care? Do you think that RIM is going to continue to do well? It's got the 50 P/E and the whole deal, right? So I think RIM has a larger market cap than Royal Bank now.

Yeah? You're probably right.

RIM will misstep at some point. We all know that. It's too big of a market cap. To answer your question, though, this seems to be in the last six months, a mix of a bunch of different things. First of all, it was brought on by a credit cycle that very few of us could have predicted was going to be this tough. It turns out the bankers were doing some really, really, really stupid thing. I don't necessarily buy the argument that it's the fault of the housing industry in the States, if you will. To me, it's the structured products that bankers let themselves get totally out of control. They did not have risk control, so they've blown up their balance sheets. If it wasn't for those structured products, the housing bubble in the States would not have been as bad as it was because you would not have had these packages of residential mortgage backed securities. Clearly in retrospect, to me, it was a structured credit product problem that made the bubble worse. So the banks—unbelievable in retrospect, how little control they had over it.

The credit crunch was much worse than anybody expected. It shows up in terms of equities. First of all, the small caps get crushed. The small and mid caps have been much more badly mauled than the big names, I think, for a couple of reasons. One, they tend not to have any international exposure. So if they're a North American small cap, chances are their business is in North America. If there are concerns about a U.S. economic recession, and China might still be okay, it doesn't matter, the small cap is going to take it on the chin because all of its business is in the U.S. or Canada, and so that's problem number one. Problem number two: When investors get nervous, they want liquidity, they sell things, and a small cap doesn't have the depth of trading to absorb that selling easily. You tend to get stocks gapping down. I think also the third problem is that you get this lack of international earnings, which is sort of a version of the first problem. That currency, the U.S. dollar weakening, was a great offset for a company like IBM that gets 70 percent of its earnings from outside the States. When it repatriates earnings back into U.S. dollars, it shows a bump in its U.S. dollar earnings. Their balance sheets tend to be pretty strong. The big large companies tend to have significant free cash flow and big strong balance sheets. So if you were in anything that did not have a rock-solid balance sheet, you were in trouble.

How about Cenveo? The market is completely overlooking the restructuring and this sort of thing. It's just looking at its printing operations being in recession.

It's very worried about recession. We know Cenveo management met with a number of investors at a brokerage conference in the States recently. We hear that in almost every single one of those meetings, guys were asking about the bond covenants on Cenveo's bonds. Even people that don't know anything about Cenveo's business, that's the first natural question that comes out in the environment that we're in now. Let's face it, Cenveo does have debt. It's our one holding that has debt, which we overlooked first of all. We're up in a major way because we had purchased mainly with Bob Burton on that proxy contest. Our original cost was $7, and the stock went to $26. Our biggest problem was we didn't sell enough above $20. We kept it because Bob's got this program of making acquisitions, and we could see the stock going a lot higher.

If he's buying....

He keeps buying stock personally, but there is a lot of fear that he's got too much debt. He's reiterated his guidance as recently as a week and a half ago, that they will do $300 million of EBITDA. He's got a number of backup plans. If he has any issues in any particular part of the business, he'll tell you, "I've got Plan A, B, C, D, and E if anything starts screwing up." The family owns $60-odd million dollars worth of stock, and he continues to buy. He's publicly stated now, a week and a half ago in the last conference call, that his family will go from 10 percent ownership over time to 15 percent ownership. I can tell you he is beside himself with the current stock price. This drives him nuts because he's got all these people in the company that are loyal to him who have bought stock. Most of them are still up because they bought below $10, but there's a number that joined more recently who'd be on the wire right now, and he does not find that acceptable. So there are a number of strategic transactions that he might be able to pursue, and we know he's got some acquisitions lined up. Our sense is the market will like it if he makes an acquisition because that whole synergy game will start up again, and cost savings. Bob will buy somebody for four times EBITDA while he's trading at six times EBITDA, and that can get kind of sexy, but the stock for sure has been killed. It is small cap, and has a leveraged balance sheet. To make further acquisitions needs access to more credit. So I would say we're pretty stupid not to have sold more, in retrospect, of that stock because we're sitting on such a huge gain. In fairness, we did sell a bunch.

You could have sold it at $14 and it went to $25, so you never know, right?

Yeah.

You would have been kicking yourself at $25. It's tough, right?

Let me paint you a scenario, though, which is really hard to imagine right now while we're in the throes of this negative psychology. Let's say the financial system stabilizes—and I'm not talking about all of a sudden these banks starting to make the kind of ROEs that they used to—but if they just stabilize and things go back to kind of like a normal environment where there's not a crisis every quarter and there's no worry that UBS and Citicorp are going to have to write off another $10 or $20 billion. If we just go back to a normal banking environment, and you ask me to pick what stock would most benefit from that other than a financial, I'd be hard pressed to find a better one than Cenveo. You've got the best management team in the printing industry by far, and they are personally committed. They continue to buy stock. They have acquisitions lined up subject only to financing, and they're going to buy guys at a discount to where they're trading. So you're going to get that synergistic earnings accretion. Here's a guy that you can bank on. If he tells you there's $50 million in synergies, chances are there's $100 million in synergies. So we can actually still see an environment. I don't know if it's a year out, I don't know if it's two years out, but we can see $30 on this stock easy. It's trading at a 22 percent free cash flow yield now, so that's significant. That means he can pay down debt at a pretty rapid clip. As he pointed out to somebody on a conference call recently, when somebody asked him, "What about if there's a recession, Bob?" Bob said, "What, recession? The printing industry has been in a recession since 1979." It's true.

There's so much fear out there. The last time we've had a point in history in the U.S. where there was this much of a gap between three-month T-bills, U.S. government T-bills, and the S&P dividend yield was 1960. That's just striking; that's a long time ago. It's forty-eight years ago. That's pretty unusual. That's fear.

Your style is very defined. Do you have to modify it at all?

Yeah. You can sort of tweak it. The kind of thing we're finding the most interesting now is going higher up in the capital structure. You can get equity-like returns without taking the risk, which is great—15 to 20 percent without any risk or perceived very low risk, that's hard to beat. Then the other side is that we've got Jean Coutu as almost our biggest position. ATS and Jean Coutu are our two biggest. I would submit to you the drugstores, and in particular Jean Coutu in Quebec, with a 44 percent market share, that nobody comes close to it. It has been operating for fifty, sixty years, however long it's been, and it produces free cash flow. The demographics are such that with the aging population, people take more and more prescriptions, and prescriptions tend to be 60 percent of a store's sales. They are very high margin; hence the large free cash flow. That is a great business that has no exposure to U.S. sub-prime or the consumer or economic sensitivity. It's demographically driven. It's got barriers to entry in the form of an iconic brand in Quebec, as well as real estate. Finding all those choice spots for the stores that have been accumulated over decades is hard. That's not an easy thing for Shoppers to come in and do.

I find it very interesting in the last couple of years the number of Canadian family public businesses that have been sold, most recently CHC Helicopter. Not that long ago, the Waters family, when Allan Waters died, CHUM got sold. You look at Jean Coutu. Mr. Coutu is eighty-plus years old. He's got two sons that are active in the business, but they actually own half the stock. That's about 125 million shares of a stock that's trading on a very depressed basis of ten bucks a share. I got to believe the two sons look at themselves at some point and say, "Do we really want to run this business? Like try to step into the shoes of our dad, or how about we sell it and invest in hedge funds?" That's got to be tempting.

How much money do you manage now? I think you wrote recently that your average stock in your top ten is trading 50 percent below your calculated value.

What we do is we take anything that we would consider a core long position, or certainly the top sort of seven or eight, and we calculate what we think is a reasonable one-year out target. So in the case of Cenveo, even though I said to you a moment ago $30 is possible, the number I think we used for Cenveo might have been $20. On that basis, if you add up all the positions, we have upside of almost 60 percent from where we are today. If the world doesn't disappear, things return to normal, lending returns to normal, we feel that we've got that kind of upside in our portfolio.

I think the last time you had numbers like that was 2002, right?

Yeah, spring of '03. It was a good bounce from there. As I get older, I'd like to figure out how to better manage the downside risk, but other than asking our unitholders for permission to regularly buy put options, it's about the only intelligent thing I can think of. The cost would be 2 to 3 percent a year to hedge the entire portfolio, but it might save us from these kinds of downdrafts. It's not a perfect hedge for us; we're down worse than the index. Russell tends to be the index that we most closely associate. It's about a 58 percent correlation last time we looked. So maybe we could do something down the road, but we're real hesitant to ramp up the shorts because it's tricky, and as we said, "Look, this is not a market neutral fund, and we're not trying to hedge our positions, per se, on the long side. We'd just like to do the occasional short position where we think we could make some money and actually have it as a profitable endeavour." But it's not a focus.

Your types of stocks that you would own are contrarian, out of favour, etc. Are those the sorts of stocks that very active hedge funds are going to short heavily?
Sometimes.

Has that kind of pushed it down maybe this year?
Yeah. Something like a Cenveo, yes; something like a Jean Coutu, no. I don't think so.

There are a lot of interesting things right now. In addition to being able to go up the capital structure and look at bonds, you've got a number of situations. I've got other situations that are fascinating that could have significant upside, but it's too early to comment on them. One in particular that I think would be right up our alley is sort of like what we saw happen with Extendicare. This company may be able to put a ring fence around that part of its business that is risky, and you could then isolate their good business. That good business is basically being priced by the market now at about three times earnings. It's a good business and it's a growing business. It's a business where the whole industry of which it's a leader should double over the next decade, in part because of demographics. So we're doing some work on that. So, yeah, there are a number of opportunities. We have a fair amount of cash right now.

What's your long exposure/short exposure here in early '08?
We're 78 long as a percent of equity, and we're about 28 percent short. In that 28 is our version of FX (currently) hedging—15 percent of the 28 is short U.S. T-bills because we're prohibited from derivatives. When I first set up the fund, I wanted no derivatives. I wanted to be plain vanilla, a stock picking focus, and not scare anybody away with any derivatives. This is my own

money as well, and I didn't want to do any. I don't have any experience in derivatives. We're trying to manage our U.S. exposure because it hurt us a lot in '07. We didn't do enough last year.

Right. The Canadian dollar was up 17 percent, I think, last year.
It cost us in Canadian dollar returns. Last year, it was our biggest negative influence. It cost us about 9 percentage points. So we would have been up....

You would have been up 6 or 7.
Up 6 and change.

It's interesting because if you look at the Canadian dollar, it has a 90 percent correlation to commodity prices going back fifty years, right? The last time it peaked was in the mid '70s when commodities were going through the roof, and here we go again. Australia too—exactly the same right?
In the U.S. the population is 300 million. What percent do you think have no mortgage at all?

I thought it was pretty high, higher than people thought, 50?
Fifty-seven. Fifty-seven percent have no mortgage at all. All we hear about is sub-prime this, sub-prime that, and the world's coming to an end. I don't know where people are going to live if they don't buy a house. You've got to sell newspapers. You've got to talk about the worst.

Dennis Gartman said one time—obviously, he's a real trader sort of guy—but he said, "Markets move and problems happen in markets based upon the 2 percent margin on the side." He said, "The 2 percent, whether it's the excess margin debt or whatever it is, that 2 percent wags the tail of the 98 percent for a while."
For a while.

Do you remember two years ago there was a Playboy Bunny—she was May of 2006 or May of 2005 Bunny or something—I saw it in the paper; she wrote that she quit being a model because the real money was to be made in Florida real estate.
Florida? Condos?

That's right. So she moved down to Florida, and she started specu-

lating in Florida real estate, and we knew that was the top right there when she quit being a Bunny.

Aw, you could find so many examples.

Allan Jacobs
Hold onto Your Winners

"One of the biggest mistakes investors make is selling their winners and holding onto their losers."

Immigrants from South Africa are not normally huge baseball fans, but, then again, hugely successful money managers are not like everyone else. Allan Jacobs moved to Toronto in 1989 with his wife, and ever since, he has been regarded as one of the most successful Canadian equity managers. He loves baseball because of all the fascinating statistics and the fact that he proclaims it to be a "thinking man's game." Coming over to Sprott Asset Management in 2007, he spent the previous fourteen years running the Sceptre Equity Growth Fund, and for the four years before that, he ran a small cap pension fund for Canada Life Investment Management. What was his performance, you ask? With Canada Life, his fund averaged 26 percent a year, while the index did less than 4 percent. With Sceptre, the Equity Growth Fund compounded at approximately 20 percent over the fourteen years he ran it. This track record resulted in his fund being awarded the Best Canadian Small Cap Fund over one, three, five and ten year periods at the 2007 Canadian Lipper Fund Awards. He was also rated the 2006 Fund Manager of the Year at the Canadian Investment Awards for his work at Sceptre. A better track record through good and bad markets is hard to find, especially since while running the Sceptre fund, his consistency was unparalleled!

Allan, trained as an accountant, considers himself to be a numbers guy, so how is this for a number? A 20 percent annualized rate of return gives an investor about 6 times their initial investment in 10 years, 36 times in 20 years, and 216 times their money in 30 years. He talks a lot about the power of compounding earnings growth with the stocks he owns, but obviously the same applies with the fund. The style is decidedly "GARPy," meaning that he likes to own great growth companies trading at great valuations. This is easier said than done, but the manner in which he buys stocks has generally cushioned the fund in bad times and allowed it to excel in good times. Growth managers are usually credited with having fairly high turnover, but he has bought and held many stocks for years, including several for eighteen years. The most common mistake investors make? Holding onto their losers and selling their winners. Allan has no problem doing exactly the opposite.

I can only imagine the numbers that Allan is capable of putting up with a small fund like the one he now manages at Sprott Asset Management. The depth at Sprott is incredible, and with some of the brightest minds in the small cap arena sitting around the table for the daily 8:15 a.m. Sprott meeting, the exchange of ideas is unparalleled. One caveat: Allan doesn't attend every morning meeting. Luckily, his right-hand man and idea generator, Peter Imhof, is there on the days Allan isn't. We actually held our interview in the main Sprott boardroom during market hours. It was just like a fancy restaurant with a waiter-type guy coming by every few minutes, serving us non-alcoholic drinks and a huge tray of fresh fruit and desserts. With the service, the fitness centre, and the fact that Allan goes around the office entertaining Sprott staff with his jokes every day, it sounds like a great place to work. Maybe I'll enquire whether they have an extra office I can work out of. Jokes, you say? Allan is a huge fan of British comedy, and in particular the Goon show, a wacky BBC radio production. He was actually a member of the Goon Show Society. That's not very accountant-like, but Allan is not your normal money manager either.

Bob:

When you were a teenager, were you always interested in stocks? Or interested in business? Warren Buffett used to deliver papers and that taught him a lot about business.

Allan:

I've always had a passion for the stock market, which started at an early age, maybe 10 or 11. My family had a couple of stocks and I was always really interested in it. When I was at university, I did a thesis on the impact of dividend policies and share prices in South Africa. Dividends were kind of a percentage of earnings, so you could almost say it was the impact of earnings, earnings prices, and earnings growth that affected share prices. Dividends were generally a fixed percentage depending on what kind of company you were. I qualified as a chartered accountant in South Africa, but I was always really interested in moving into the stock market. As I said, I had a passion from a pretty early age. I actually took a pay cut to get into investments. Eight months after I finished three years of articles, and I qualified as a chartered accountant, I moved to the Old Mutual, which was the largest investment company in South Africa. It's actually in the FTSE 100 today. It was a really good training ground. It actually was written up in the London *Financial Times* twenty years ago as having world-class systems. There were five computer programmers who just wrote investment programs, and a huge research staff. So the first year and a half I worked as a research analyst and we spent about a month on each company. It was exhaustive research; you had to build an economic cycle based on the economists' forecasts and how cyclical the companies were.

So I then became a small cap portfolio manager, and in South Africa, there were almost no small mining companies because the mining companies that everyone knows about internationally were all owned by the mining houses, and they weren't small. There wasn't really an entrepreneurial class in mining at that stage. The vast majority of companies were actually industrial and commercial companies, and a lot of them actually did very well in South Africa. The foreigners always invested in gold and diamonds, but in those days, the domestic non-mining companies actually did better, because not only were commodity prices not that high but they had big market shares and duopolies and stuff like that. They were protected because the currency was very weak from foreign competition.

So I did that for a year and a half, and I ran a small company portfolio.

Then for about the last eighteen months before I moved to Canada, I ran the largest fund in South Africa, which was about $5 billion equivalent. In South Africa, because inflation was double digits, the life companies used to invest predominantly in equities, not in bonds, because equities did very well with inflation protection and bonds did poorly. It was a very big fund; it was a bit of a super tanker. So it sort of ran itself pretty much, but I was the fund manager for what was then the largest fund in South Africa. Then I moved here in early '89.

The fund was all South African based?
Yeah. It had to be.

So $5 billion is a lot of money? I don't know what the size of the market is.
Yeah, it was the biggest fund in South Africa. The market there even then was significant; there were other big investors as well.

That was in the late '80s?
Yeah. I came in February '89. So I worked in January '89, and then I came here. I actually came on a work permit. Then I guess I've been here for eighteen and a half years managing Canadian small cap stocks on a full-time basis.

The Canadian market is heavily resource based. Was the South African market the same?
It was, but not in small cap. There were quite a few mining analysts as well; we had a huge investment team. In South Africa, you didn't buy stock that lost money and you didn't buy companies that had a lot of debt. People didn't bother with them. There weren't that many like that anyway that were listed, because there were only a few hundred stocks listed. It wasn't that easy to get a listing in those days. You had to be of some substance. It's interesting. When I came here, I didn't know any of the companies, but I was involved in running a portfolio pretty early on. The similarities are that if you are familiar with value stocks or you've got a good feel for numbers, you know the relationship between the income statement and the balance sheet pretty well. I know what deferred tax is from auditing for three years.

You get a feel for how business works pretty well. There were a lot of differences. Like the disclosure in South Africa was actually much more than it was here. You had unconsolidated financial statements and you didn't have any here. There were a lot of differences. If a small company here bought a bigger company, you didn't really know what the bigger company had. If the bigger company was private, you didn't have to send tons of financial information on the bigger company. A year later, you get an annual report and you don't really know how the old company did because you didn't actually get their financial statements. There was a lot more disclosure in South Africa at that stage anyway in many ways. Then there were some new industries here like cable and airlines. There were a few differences—obviously a reasonably significant resource base. In '89, I guess Canada was still booming and the housing market was booming. Then in 1990, the TSX actually lost money when interest rates went sky high and commodity prices were very low. That was a tough year. I think the TSX did lose in 1990, but luckily I was doing small caps, and the fund did 26 percent a year for the four years I was there. It was called the Specialty Growth Fund. It was the Canada Life small cap pooled pension fund. It was actually the best-performing small cap. The four years I was there the TSX did only 4 percent a year and the BMO small cap index also did 4 percent a year. They weren't great years for Canadian stocks and they were really tough times with high interest rates and low commodity prices. The dollar was also at that stage pretty high—$0.85.

Do you remember any names of those years that did really well for you? Or stocks that you had bought at that time that helped your performance a lot? Were they industrial names or research names?

There were a couple. I remember Pine Point—did pretty well on Pine Point. Sprott Securities recommended that stock. It was a zinc stock, but they had a huge stockpile and the cash just poured in, not because zinc prices were high but because they had this massive stockpile of zinc. The company got taken over; I had a lot of industrial companies, like Unican, also.

These were world-class companies, and quite big players in their industries even if they're the niche industries. But who cares if the industry's not the biggest in the world? If you're number one or number two in a niche and it's profitable, that's fantastic. I don't remember a lot of the other names, but there's a few stocks that I owned then and that I still own, eighteen years later. Reitmans, I don't own today, but I guess I've owned it for most of the time. I owned CCL, and I remember I owned Doral. There were less companies to choose from then than there are now—way less. There were so few companies and they've all been taken over now. The number of companies that have started in Canada because of a better economic environment and the fact that lots of entrepreneurs and people are leaving bigger companies—it's huge. Whether it's in mining or technology, there's so many more companies to choose from today. There was a fair number, but there were only a certain amount that were really growing well. I remember we owned Uni-Select and we did really well in that stock. There were a few others. I remember I owned Leon's furniture. There were some pretty good companies.

It was a pretty small team. I basically was running the small caps for four years. There were four people on Canadian equities.

Now, money management, as we know, is half science, or number crunching, and the other side is the qualitative factors. Everybody can crunch the numbers and see what they are, but I think it's that qualitative, or art side, that sets people apart. How much does each role play a part for you?

Well, that's a good question. Because I have an accounting background, I am very focused on numbers. On the other end, I don't need to spend days looking at it. I can go through the numbers quite quickly. I'm not a great believer in having forecasts that have little thought given to them. I find forecasts are too driven to the consensus. The good companies do way better than analysts think and the bad companies do way worse. Sometimes people will crunch out numbers and they come out with some fair market value and what the stock should be worth. If the assumptions are wrong, you get it wrong. I would say as much as I focus on the numbers and on the history as opposed to how people are going to do, I really think the qualitative thing is really important. So try to back management teams that are good, and use your investment judgment. I think you don't need to know 300 things about every company. Do you know the five things that are really important? Do you know if four of them means it's good and one means it's bad, or four are bad and one is good? That to me is the key. What are the key things, and where do you come out? If you know everything about it and you get into the minutiae, you definitely don't need to do that. I don't think you need to necessarily understand all the technical aspects of it, whether it's technology or metallurgy. It helps to understand that stuff, but I don't think you need to be an absolute expert on every industry.

You need to understand the numbers, you need to understand the basics, and I think you've got to have a good feel for how the stock market values things. Is this a tech stock or manufacturer? Is it a gold stock or is it a base metal? They tend to get different valuations, and some of it's the way people perceive things, and that can also change dramatically. There was a time you could buy copper/gold stocks at four times cash flow because the company wasn't an operator. This was because there was more copper than gold and gold analysts didn't like it. To me, that's the way I understand the market works; I take advantage of it. I buy copper/gold companies that may not be operators when they do it cheap, because people don't like them. When they become real gold companies, then they get a higher valuation than they had as a base metal company. That's kind of the history.

It's the same as when people didn't like Reitmans because it had two classes of shares, it didn't trade a lot, it had a lot of cash. You can go on and on and on. It traded at a ridiculously low valuation, not because it's a bad company, and not because it hasn't had decent growth.

So you have these real value situations, but they're not deep value. They're value situations, and they're undervalued for reasons that you can easily change. You can go to one class of shares, do some marketing, pay a big dividend. You can do all sorts of things if you have a ton of cash and you can make acquisitions. Then the valuation suddenly changes. If you can buy up really good value really cheaply, and then, for example, you get good earnings growth for a couple years, those are the kind of stocks that go up explosively and dramatically. They can be really sort of boring companies. The qualitative thing's really important because you've got to use your investment judgment. I don't want to call it "gut feel," but you kind of get a feeling about the company and the management. I think people don't pay enough of a premium for really good companies, and I take advantage of it. I find people underestimate the power of compounding, big time. If you tell someone you've done 20 percent a year for eighteen years, they can't figure out what that compounds to. A lot of people sell their winners and buy the losers because they think they were right on day one. Well, it doesn't work like that. Small cap stocks go up for a good reason, and they fall for a good reason. It may be commodity-price-related, but often it's because they're winning or they're losing. For example, I don't buy junk below book value because to me, book value to some extent is an accounting fiction. But it's got two components, right? I'll pay a discount for share capital because what it means is that they raised money at a price, maybe twenty years ago. Maybe it hasn't made a cent since then, and the assets are worth much less than the book value. There's nothing magical about book value. You can't break the company up at book value necessarily, whereas companies that have a lot of retained earnings means they made a lot of money and they haven't paid it out as a dividend. That means the assets make money. There's an ROE which hopefully is reasonably good. If you buy a low price to book and it doesn't have a high ROE or it's a minimal ROE, it's still going to be a low price to book in five years and the book hasn't gone up. If you buy a very profitable company at two or three times book, hopefully it'll still be at two or three times book in five years but the book value will maybe go up 20 percent a year. I really think you've got to pay a bit of a premium for very successful companies and for growth companies.

The other thing is, I do think investment judgment is really the key. Everybody can read the book and know what Warren Buffett does but how many people have Warren Buffett's judgement? To tell people that you build a moat around every company and then you buy junk companies is kind of nonsense. You have to have good judgement on average over time. From experience, hopefully you get that. It's not something you can learn. Personally, I think some of the best investment people have not only been interested in investments for a long time, but they have a good gut feel and an instinct. You only have to be right two-thirds of the time to do extremely well. You don't have to be right on every stock—no one ever is—and you shouldn't be scared to be wrong on something. The problem is if something goes down a lot for good reason, and then you buy more because you thought you were right and the market's wrong, you've got to admit your fault.

That's a good point. Out of ten stocks that you buy, if three of them are really big winners, they're going to account for most of your performance. Is the majority of the performance due to a minority of the stocks?

Not in the way I run money. The last six years that Pete and I were together, we had fifty-plus stocks. We had over seventy at the end. We had many, many winners in many different sectors. We haven't had twenty- and forty-baggers. Even if we did have a ten- or fifteen-bagger, it's over ten or fifteen years. And guess what? The fund went up thirteen times over fourteen years. I can think of a mining stock that we bought for $3, and it's now $100. But we sold a lot of it at $15 and $20, and it was a smallish position through the piece. It's been a big win, but it's not like it's again 8 or 10 percent of the fund. We always kept a pretty diversified portfolio. I think to that extent we've had quite a lot of winners and relatively few losers, especially in the last six years.

Sprott Asset Management is known for its top-down macro calls. I don't think you've done that in the past. Now that you're at Sprott, are there other influences that could detract you from what you're really good at?

Okay. We might tweak it a bit, but I found the big-picture call pretty tough to do. It just so happens that some of my colleagues have been extremely good at it. I guess if you're really good at it, it makes your job easier to the extent of, "Oh, this is a great industry and a great thing. Let's buy a whole bunch of companies." I bought manufacturers for $0.65, but I didn't say, "Let's choose all the manufacturers." So we'll tweak a little bit what we do, but I don't want to be too reliant on getting the commodity price forecast correct. Will we be influenced by our colleagues that have excellent track records? The answer is at the margin, yeah, we will. When I say we don't overweight or underweight or haven't, it's true, but it's not entirely true. The reason it isn't entirely true is when copper was $0.80 and stocks were unbelievably cheap.

Oil at $10. Did you buy oil stocks?

I didn't buy tons of them. With oil at $10, the oil companies weren't making any money. With copper at $0.80, big companies were just giving things away. HudBay started five years ago as a public—or three years ago—as a public company. Inmet was $3. It's now $100.

Did you ever own Eurozinc?

Yeah.

That was a little $0.80 stock that was good.

We bought it at $0.60. But here's an example: at $0.25 we didn't look at it because it was too small for the funds we ran. We bought it at $0.60 and it was probably $3 or something when it got merged. That all happened in three years or two years. We'll probably tweak what we do a little bit, but we're not going to change our style, I don't anticipate. At the same time, it's a Sprott fund and there's fifteen or sixteen people who do small caps. We get lots of ideas, and are we going to use other people's ideas? Well, obviously, and we've already done that. Are we going to take big overweights and underweights in sectors relative to what we used to do? I'm pretty sure it's pretty unlikely. I have more of a comfort with being well diversified and relying on superior stock picking rather than getting the sector call correct. I think that's hard to do, but Eric obviously has a great record with that.

So you'd buy companies based upon good ROEs and good cash flows and good management rather than buy a uranium company because the fundamentals for uranium are good? Or do you look at the fundamentals of the supply and demand?

Well, we hear about it a lot now. All of a sudden people say, "Do you have any uranium stocks?" I got that question yesterday. I said, "You know, we missed it." We didn't look at them and decide, "Oh, this is no good." We just missed it. If we'd been here and we heard every day about uranium and how great it is, we would have bought two or three. There's no doubt we would have. We would have tried to buy what we thought were the best ones or the ones that were closest to production or the ones that were producing. That's kind of our style.

Yeah, I've thought about that. That's something that I guess you have to be careful with. You want to use what you have here to enhance your returns but not to detract from what's been your success.

We have our collection of companies that we've owned for many, many years, whether it's Melcor, Gildan, Dundee, or CCL. They're not going to go up 100 percent a year, but if they go up 25 percent a year like they have for ten or fifteen years, what difference does that make? I think that's great. I also think they're proven performers and they're fairly low risk. They don't come out with rotten quarters. If they fall 20 percent, I think it's usually because the market's down 20 percent, not because the company's bad. They're not high-risk companies; they're low risk.

I've said it before, in small caps, in many cases, the lowest-risk stocks have given the highest returns. That doesn't mean utilities; it means buying boring companies that make things. People say, "Oh, you know, how are they going to grow much faster than 3 percent a year or 4 percent because it's dependent on retail spending?" I don't look at retail spending, and I don't care if retail spend's up 1 percent or down 2. That sounds ridiculous, but it's not ridiculous because if you have really good companies, if times are bad, they'll get better one day. In the meantime, the competitors are doing really badly. They'll be able to buy things for next to nothing, and companies will go bankrupt. They'll come out way better than their competitors. Sure, the stock's on the fly when retail spending's bad for two or three years, but why is it going to be a worse company versus the competition? It'll do better in good times, it'll do better in bad times than its competitors, and it'll outperform. That doesn't mean retailing's a great business, but that's not where we've done well. We've done well saying, "This is a really good company. We know the management." In the oil patch, you get these companies and they say, "Oh, the company's only got six months' track record." Well, no, it's got a fifteen-year track record. It's the same ten guys in the same area that built up three or four companies, sold it in the good old days to a U.S. company or a trust or whatever, and then started again. People say, "Oh, we don't know the name." Well, they just changed their name, but it's the same people.

It's like your fund.

It's like, "Oh, well, let's see a three- or five-year track record." I don't change jobs that often, but I have a track record. It's not much different, because I always say I'll back really good managers with a proven track record. I always say, in funds, you're buying them at NAV. You're not buying them at a premium or a discount, whether the person has a good or a bad track record. You're buying them at full value every day. The fees may be higher or lower. People aren't paying a premium for Eric's fund because he has 28 percent per year for ten years. They're buying it for what it's worth today.

What word would you use to classify your style?

It's a GARP approach. Growth at a reasonable price.

What do you think your average turnover in the fund is?

Historically, it's been about 40 percent. It's very much a buy-and-hold thing. I don't trade a lot. Now, I'd say of the 40 percent, at least a quarter of that, at least, is takeovers. Some of it is when you have a lot of inflows or outflows, some of it is sort of somewhat....

Cash management.

Cash management. Some of it is selling losers, some of it is trimming winners. It's not buying the stock today, the results come out next week, hoping the results will be good, and then if it goes up 5 or 10 percent, selling what I bought. I don't do that. I'm not saying there's anything wrong with it, but I'm just saying that's not what I do. I try to buy and hold, and if it doesn't work out, I sell. I often don't buy enough. I mean, I often buy stocks only at one price, and I buy at 1.5 or 2 percent at $3, and if it works, great. In five years, the stock's $20 and the cost is still $3.

Do you scale into your stock, usually?

Sometimes I buy a half and then a half a week or two later. Sometimes I buy the full position. The reason's quite simple. If you're going to have, let's say, fifty stocks and the average position's 2 percent, why are you sort of scaling in? If you're going to put in 2 percent, are you going to put in 1 percent and if it goes down are you going to be more sure? Are you going to start thinking you may be wrong? What happens if it goes up? Are you going to say, "Oh, yeah, it was a good pick." Maybe you should have bought it all two weeks ago. So if I scale, it's more that I'll buy it over the next couple of weeks or I'll buy half now and half in a week or two. I don't buy a half position and then wait for the quarter in two month's time. The reason again is that I think having fifty names and an average of 2 percent is diversified enough. It's not like I'm taking 5 percent positions and therefore maybe I'll only buy a half in case it doesn't work.

Do you average down? Do you buy a stock and they come out with a bad quarter, and you say, "Well, this is a good price. I'm going to buy more"? Would you be more apt to say, "Well, this one didn't work," and sell your loser?

If they come out of a bad quarter, I'm much more likely to sell. Way more likely to sell. If they come out of a bad quarter, why is the next one going to be good?

They tend to get worse for a few quarters before things get better.

Well, yeah, if you have a growth stock, and "growth" doesn't mean technology. I have made tons of money on Metro and it was trading at eight times earnings with 15, 20 percent earnings growth. In that case, I'd rather average, but not if it's after bad news. I don't assume that if the market's down 30 percent that there's no good reason. If it fell so much, sometimes someone knows more than you. I'm not going to sell if it's down if I still think it's a great company. If they come up with a bad result, there's not a lot of things that fall because of bad results and then turn around. There are things that fall because tech's hot or it's cold or mining stocks are very popular or unpopular. The sentiment changes so quickly in the market.

You've got to keep your head with the way things change. When the market's really bad, people don't want to look at IPOs. You can't even get a meeting, and that's the best time to buy IPOs. When Rona became public, it was a bad time and people were just buying income trusts. Rona was begging you for an order. The issue got done at a couple of dollars lower. It was a great company, and it has been for a very long time. Of course, today it's not growing that fast right now, but that's okay. To me, that's a great opportunity.

I love buying IPOs of great companies in really bad times because if the market's down 5 percent, IPO price is down 20 or 25, and guess what? They're begging you for an order. If it's a really hot market and you cut back and they raise the price, big deal. You'll make money for a day or a week and then you should just blow it out because it was a frothy market. A month or two later, if it goes to a discount, no one will buy it. It's hard to stand back with fear and greed, but people do stupid things because the front page of the paper tells you how bad things are after they've fallen and it tells you how great things are after they've gone up.

I know it's difficult to be a contrarian, but I try to stand back from that. I'm not saying I buy when things are down a lot. It's a bit like a growth company. Do you sell it when the stock's still flying because the valuation's getting up a bit, or do you wait for the first bad quarter or for it to start tailing off? For example, think of tech. JDS went up, I think, 100 or 200 times before it collapsed by 98 percent. Sometimes it's better to wait for a growth company to falter, because it could be five years after you sell it. If it is, you'll make a lot of money.

Stocks usually run much further than the numbers say they should, right? Because people jump on the bandwagon.

Well, it's momentum.

They go down much further than the numbers say they should go down, right?

Stocks are outrageously volatile. The market goes up nowadays 1 percent a day and it falls 1 percent, and people have a big reason why it did that. Guess what? At the end of the month, it's flat and every day was very volatile with big news. You sort of say to yourself, "There's a lot of noise." So why did the market fall so much in August? Well, maybe it's because it went up a lot in July and June. The stocks that go up the most sometimes fall the most in the short term, and people get so hung up on what's wrong with a company. There's nothing wrong with it. It wasn't spectacular just because it went up 5 percent the previous week, with no results. It's just there was a lot of buyers and then people were taking profits. There's a lot of noise in the market, and I think you sort of have to stand back. It's a pretty stressful job at the best of times. You've got to try and keep your cool and keep your head when people are panicking, and not get too carried away with things either.

Value investors say, "I buy a stock with a low P/E that has horrible expectations anyway." They get the one-two punch when it goes up because suddenly the expectations are better, but then the P/E expands. So you get both of those factors. With a higher price growth stock, it might work the opposite way. The earnings go down, so the expectations get worse, and then the P/E gets compressed also. You have to manage that risk somehow?

Okay. I try not to pay very high multiples for anything. That's the first point. We buy techs as well, but mostly we buy sort of mundane companies. You tend not to have to pay too much for them. So that's the one way to do it. The other way to do it is to buy some sort of value stocks. I think we try to buy decent companies that have a low valuation for spurious reasons, like they don't market, they're not that liquid, they've got two classes of shares, or people think the CEO pays himself too much. There's all sorts of reasons. You can actually do away with some of those things by making an announcement one day. If they have tons of cash, people say, "Oh, what's cash worth?" It's not worth the cash. It's worth a discount. What return are you getting on the cash? Well, you can buy something or you can pay a fat dividend.

There's lots of things, so we try to get a bit of a mixture. What happens when you get a sort of value stock that suddenly has decent earnings growth? You get outrageously high returns. If you're a real deep value investor, you'll probably sell the stock when it goes above your target, which may be 50 or 30 percent higher than the cost. The problem is the stock's going to go up severalfold because it's got real low valuation and low expectation and suddenly they're doing better. Reitmans is a good example, or Inmet. Expectations were nothing when the stock was $2 or $3. Now it's $100. I try not to sell it, because I've learned. When things are going in the right direction and you start off with a low value, then it doesn't have to be a growth stock. If it's a value stock, it's becoming a growth stock. You get this massive multiple expansion from a miniscule valuation, to a bit better, to getting more coverage, to getting into the index, to being compared to medium cap stocks. If the company's then growing quite well, all the fundamentals are improving. Stocks go up way more than you think. With growth stocks, as I said, we try not to pay too much, and we try to buy fast-growing companies that people don't necessarily think are fast growing. They're not like technology stocks that people think, "Well, it's in a fast-growing business." They think, "Oh, it's in the food business or it's in the clothing business, big deal." Home Capital's gone up over a hundred-fold in twelve years. Unfortunately, we haven't made great money, but we've done okay on it. We haven't done great on it.

People are so excited on the big picture that they kind of miss the point. If you're the best in an average business and the valuation's ten times earnings because you're small or not that well known, and you only have three people covering you, then you become a growth company, those are the kind of growth stocks that we look for. We don't buy at thirty or forty times earnings, where the possibility of having a bad quarter and the stock falling 30 or 40 percent is obvious.

As you said, when people appreciate these as growth companies, the multiple keeps going up. We like ones that go from eight to ten to twelve to fourteen to hopefully in the high teens. They don't get into the twenties. Why? Because people don't expect miracles. They always say, "Oh, it's a growth company, but it's going to slow down." The food or the clothing businesses, look how big they are. I can think of a few companies where they became medium caps and their growth rate actually accelerated. Not because it should have but because there were fewer operators. They may become one of the few suppliers to Wal-Mart. They got bigger market shares in what they do. They made acquisitions of competitors that are lower valuations than they trade at, and then they added value to what they bought because they've got synergies. Guess what? They have a clean balance sheet, so they use debt. They borrow money at 5 percent and they got a massive return, and then they pay down the debt, and a year or two later, they do the same thing. People say, "Wow, how come their earnings per share went up 50 percent for a medium-sized company?" It would have only been up 15 without the acquisition. They made this acquisition that transformed the company.

So those are the kind of things we're looking for. They're companies that are really good—good organic growth—and have smart people. They make acquisitions at the right time and don't overpay for things. They add value to what they buy because they're smart. You're not paying thirty or forty times earnings. So the risk of massive decline because of an earnings disappointment is less. That doesn't mean it doesn't exist, but it's much, much less. With tech stocks, they're in growth industries. If the multiple gets too high, you get a really nasty surprise. Someone comes up with something better than they've got, or their new product isn't as good as the competitors. Then people can say, "My God, this thing's now going to be a twelve multiple on much lower numbers instead of a thirty multiple on higher numbers." The stock's down 60 to 70 percent in a day or two. I mean, that can happen. We try to avoid those kinds of growth stocks.

The key is you have to see some growth or something about the company that the consensus doesn't see, right?

You've got to have a lot of patience too. Reitmans was $18 forever, for five or six or seven years, and I actually owned it. We don't own it today, but it's now $19, except that it's done three two-for-one splits. Not everybody understands that that's eight for one. So it's gone up eight or nine times in six or seven years. Yeah, it's partly because the dollar's gone up a lot and they buy in U.S. dollars. Everyone says, "Oh, it's very tough for exporters." Well, how about importers? They're buying things cheap every day, so their margins go up and they've had good earnings growth. The valuation was so bottomed out just because it was boring and didn't trade. It wasn't covered. They had too much cash and two classes of shares. A whole bunch of things, all of which may have been true. It wasn't a bad company and it didn't have a bad record, and yet it had a bottomed-out valuation. So the minute that the earnings growth started, the stock was going to go up by a multiple of the earnings growth because the valuation was so low. Those are the kind of value situations we look at. I don't like buying stocks because they're below book value if they have accumulated losses in ten years. I think those are just awful companies, and people raise millions of dollars for them just to keep them going. I can think of stocks that are less than 10 percent of what they were when I came to Canada. The forest products industry's a typical example. It's such a tough industry. People who buy stocks below book value sometimes fall into the trap. The problem is the book value often gets written off. You've got to look at earnings much more than book value—much more.

I've always noticed that analysts cover the sexy industries and sexy stocks. Have you bought a lot of stocks that were not covered? For example, with HudBay Minerals, nobody covered it at $3, but now they all cover it now that it is over $20.

Yeah, it was $2.25 with warrants. The thing was dirt cheap—that's a good example—and nobody covered it.

Well, then it was a shell. It was like a $10 million shell. You're paying $10 million for nothing. They're making an issue for $200-something million, and they're going to the street, so they're trying to sell control of the company to minority people, in a tough environment. Well, of course they're begging you for orders. So they sell it at a low price, and then they throw in warrants, not at a huge premium. I've seen it so many times. You sort of get to know which brokers tend to price issues for people to make money on because they want to come back to you the next week or the next month with another issue. Sometimes there are firms where they don't want the stock to go up 30 percent after day one on an IPO because they're paying off their loans. Sometimes they tell a company, "You're worth X," and they're trying to get X, and they don't want to lower the price too much. In a tough environment, you have to.

I think you have to be open-minded and opportunistic. People do have these models that it has to meet these ten criteria. Every stock you buy doesn't have to have earnings. Timminco doesn't have earnings, and we own a couple of exploration companies. Do they have a proven track record to get this exploration going? Has the guy run three companies before? Do they have guys that found four mines before, as opposed to, "Oh, we've got a concession somewhere and we paid $100,000 and the market cap's fifty million and we need money to draw." Well, it might be good, but it might not. I like to buy stocks that if they fall 20 or 30 percent, they're better value. If you buy a biotech, for example, it makes you feel good, but it's a tough business. So when they fall 20 or 30 percent, is it better value? Who knows? These things take ten years to be successful, assuming they are, which they usually aren't. Then they run out of money. There's certain industries that I tend to be underweight because they don't make money and they're tough businesses and there's only a chance in ten or twenty of a massive win. Otherwise, it's a battle.

Which industries over the years have you found that it's tough for you to make money in?

Forest products are just a very tough business to make money in.

A lot of the value guys own forestry because they're below book value, right?

Yeah, but the book value's always getting written off, so they're always below book. There's a lot of the stocks are at twenty-, and thirty-, and forty-year lows, with no dividends. It baffles me. They have terrible balance sheets, obviously, because they don't have an ROE, so the debt grows just to stand still with biotech.

I used to have CML, and it has a lab business. It makes money and maybe it has a biotech on the side, but I haven't done well in biotech. I think it's a very tough business. When you buy biotech at $150 or $200 million, that's not much different to what it was when the market cap was $20 or $30 million a year or two earlier. Maybe they'd come up with good phase one or whatever results. Often, with biotech, the stock's gone up because the sector's somewhat hot, and they all go up, but it's still speculative. When you should buy a biotech is probably when the market cap's $5 or $10 million and there's a decent guy running it, because when they get to $200 million, it's not like they've discovered some major cure. They're making progress, but it could be because biotechs are all hot. When they get cold, my God, they all collapse. They can't raise money and they run out of money. So that's a couple of the businesses that we haven't done well on. Building construction is another one. The other one is, what are they called? Alternative....

Energy.

I battle with those type of companies. They're difficult. I have a lot of patience with companies that are good value and that are doing okay but not necessarily spectacular, and people find them boring. Others get fed up with them because they haven't gone up for a while. As I said, when they fall 20 or 30 percent and the market doesn't fall, that doesn't make you feel like you want to buy more because it's still very speculative. It's not like the P/E became 10 and it was 13 because they're burning cash. If they don't raise money soon, it'll be crunch time. I have a real problem with those types of companies, but everything doesn't have to fit the mold of having a growth rate of 25 percent and a P/E of 15. It doesn't have to, but on average it should.

Peter Lynch used to talk a lot about PEG ratios: price-to-earnings growth.

I pay tons of attention to that. I think if your growth rate is in excess of your earnings, those stocks will outperform over time. They won't every month or every quarter, because sometimes small caps are totally out of favour because no one wants to put money into small caps then. I think over time, it's just the power of the numbers. If you're growing at 20 percent and you're trading at fifteen times earnings, if the stock doesn't go up, the P/E will be 12. Another year and it'll be 9 or 10. You can only keep growing and have the stock not go anywhere for a while. In '99 and 2000, lots of stocks went from fifteen times earnings to six or seven times, and they weren't tech. Everything was collapsing. I remember the one day NASDAQ was up 11 percent and the S&P fell 3 percent in one day. It's the most bizarre thing imaginable that techs went up 11 percent and yet the S&P fell 3 percent. Everyone was just selling everything and buying techs. Not just for that day but every day for a year and a half. It was quite phenomenal. Of course, you felt like an idiot if you were underweight tech because your clients weren't very impressed with you and your performance was rotten.

That gets us into your returns in 1999. You were up about 4 percent. Did you have a lot of tech? Probably not.

No, no, no. We were way underweight. We did poorly. One of the problems was we had a lot of microcaps in that day. We used to cut off the cap number at 150 million on the TSX. Subsequently, we changed it to number 100. What happened was medium caps got moved to the large cap fund. I ended up having over a billion under management and I was buying microcaps. It wasn't because I really wanted to, but I had to. During the Asian crisis, you couldn't sell Contrans, a trucking company, at five times earnings. If you owned companies like that, you were losing assets, and the people who owned them were losing assets. The people who were winning money had large cap funds and they had tech funds. I owned a stock that was trading at half its cash with no liabilities, and the stock kept falling. When you think about it, it was for logical reasons. Everyone that owned it was losing assets, and if they were losing their whole portfolio, the person who inherited it didn't own it. In fact, they won the account because they didn't own those types of stocks. They were just blowing it out at half cash. Who cares? "We don't own it in our other funds; we own tech stocks." Why would you even bother looking at it? In fact, you'd rather just get the cash when an account changes hands, like in pension funds. Things go on way too far because of momentum and, of course, because the trend is your friend. Then, one day it changes.

What hurts you one year helps you the next, and I think if we look at 2001 or 2002, you made money in those years but the tech guys and the indexes were getting killed.

Sorry. You're talking about '99. Okay, we were way, way, way under-weight in techs and way overweight in everything else. Way under.

What hurt your performance in '99 obviously helped in 2000 to 2002.

That's true. The large cap guys were buying medium cap stocks and I was having to transfer them because our cut-off was number 150. So what happened was the TSX 200 had 200 stocks. From 100 to 150 was half value of those 50 names, the biggest 50. Instead of being able to own 10 or 12 of those names, I ended up owning none of them. I owned way too many small caps, so we had a couple of rough years. I said, "Well, hang on. You mustn't buy stocks with market caps of $50 or $75 million. The minimum is 150." At the top end, the minimum's not number 150 on the TSX. It's number 100.

The top end raised dramatically, those 50 names was a huge increase in the market cap. Instead of owning 80 or 90 names, we sold down to 50 names. We had a mandate to do that. At the same time, we bought some good companies. We sold a lot of companies, and a lot of them were maybe companies that weren't quite as good, and they were much smaller companies. The other thing that changed was, subsequent to those years, we didn't sell stocks that got to number 90th or 80th largest on the TSX just because they got into the top 100. Before if we bought 160 and it went up to number 130 or 140, we would sell it. The large caps guys would take it off us, so it was a bit of a problem. Microcaps were bad in '98 with the Asian crisis and the Russian debt problem. Microcaps were a disaster from the third quarter of '98 till the second quarter of 2000 or end of the first quarter. Everything other than tech fell, and we were way underweight. Techs were a huge percent of the index, I hate to tell you.

Is that happening with mining stocks, or are the fundamentals better?

No, I think there's still value. I think the stocks are getting revalued because people have more comfort that commodity prices can stay up. Also because a lot of the big cap stocks have been taken out, there's more demand for the HudBays and Inmets and Lundins to fill in the vacuum. I think it's a harder call. Personally, I'm not overweight in mining stocks, and I find that a hard call. I'm trying to buy the best companies. That's part of my caution and why I'm well diversified. I don't have a good enough feel for the big picture. Personally, I have a view, but I prefer an oil company that I can use a 10 percent discount rate and buy it, rather than a gold company which may be at NAV or I have to use a 3 percent discount rate and try and buy it below 1.5 times. Gold trades at higher valuations, so to that extent, I may be bullish on the gold price, but I don't think about it a lot. It doesn't mean I think that gold stocks are really cheap, but I did think mining stocks were really cheap four, five years ago.

Today, I think it's a difficult call. I don't think you can compare it to the techs. The techs were a complete mania, 200 times earnings for companies. Companies trading at 30 times sales, doing web design and losing money. Of course, you thought you were wrong because they kept going and going and going, and then maybe you should cover your bet more. I think that is a risk of being not in a sector. For example, if you had no golds and all those golds were 5 percent of the index, it's not an issue until they double and they go to 10 percent.

I try not to be caught too offside by the big sector moves that I don't have a lot of expertise or experience in. I haven't really tried to call them that well, but here's what I'd say. If you need tons of companies, the industries where there's great value do stand out. It's easier to be an oil company than a mining company because the oil company only needs $1 million. You open an office and you go drill a well. It's not like you need $500 million to build a mine.

Today, for mining companies, it's been easier to raise money, but it's not a simple business for a tiny guy. At the same time, it became easier because the big guys five years ago said, "Hey, the copper price is $0.70 and the gold price is $250 and we've got all these mines; just take them off our hands, you can have them. Give us half a million and a royalty of 1 percent and you can have them." Smart guys and entrepreneurs went and some of the great companies were built from nothing.

There's a lot more to choose from, and you can still buy base metal companies at fairly low valuations. Those are the ones I'm trying to buy, like Blue Note and Quadra. Maybe they're not the top quality, but I think they're okay companies and I think they're really good value. I don't mind buying what's not the top quality company if as a second-best quality, the valuation is significantly cheaper. I'm not going to buy junk, especially where the company has a record of being a disaster and you say, "Well, to me the stock's never really cheap enough. I'd rather just avoid it."

You talked about PEG ratios and so did Peter Lynch. Have you been influenced or emulated by anybody else?

Well, not really. That's not being arrogant. I've read Warren Buffett. But I've never been down for the annual meeting. It's not because I don't think it's not worthwhile.

I do like Peter Lynch. I believe in keeping it simple and I think people complicate things too much. People used to ask us, "Which of the small cap guys do you think are really good?" We always used to say, "Well, Sprott." That was the first name that always came to mind. I do think that good stock pickers recognize other good stock pickers. There are a lot of people who aren't good at picking stocks who always decry what good stock pickers do and say, "Oh, he's taking too much risk. He's so different from the index." Well, sure. That doesn't mean you aren't going to do really well most of the time. The winners way compensate for the losers when you hold your winners. I believe in watering the flowers, not the weeds. I think that's how you make money, especially in smaller companies.

Watering the flowers, not the weeds. That's good. I've never heard that one.

That's a good one. The other one I like to say is we try to find potential gems before they become household names. We use a wide network of brokers. The bigger the choice, the more the great companies and the really cheap ones stand out. Also doing your homework helps, rather than relying on third-party research. We listen to the conference calls ourselves; we ask the questions ourselves. I think after a while, you get experience. I don't prepare for a meeting necessarily with the company. There are just obvious questions that come up as they go through things. You get the flow and you know what's important. There are some things that don't get shined on. I don't talk to a lot of analysts, but occasionally I'll say, "Which stocks don't you cover because you don't like them?" It's like, "I wouldn't touch these three." To me, those kind of things are more valuable.

I also really think it's very valuable meeting companies and getting a good feel for the management. Some of these management teams I've owned for many years. I don't worry about them on a daily basis because they've proven to be successful. So I'm less worried about the stock being ahead of itself. What happens if I'm right and it goes down 15 percent in the next three weeks? Am I going to remember to buy it back? It's not my style. I try to ride my winners, but I try to sell the losers and the ones that aren't working.

Do you bank ideas? Do you say, "Here's a great company that I like. I think it's a good business, but the valuation's too high, so we're just

going to watch it for the next year and see if it hits a price that we think is appropriate"?

Sometimes. Yeah. I don't want to pay too much for a company. The other thing is to say, "It's growing at 25 percent at the moment." Well, it doesn't mean it's sustainable and you've got to be careful. It's amazing. There's quite a few companies that just keep surprising us, and some of them, unfortunately, we don't own. They have such good track records. You do have to keep an open mind. We owned Geac at $5 at six or seven times earnings. People hated it because it used to be a high flyer. Stocks don't become gems overnight. I love buying issues. You meet a company because they're doing a road show. We like the company, and the stock's $2.50. They're doing an issue at $2.20 with or without warrants. Why? Because they've got price protection. They're only raising $15 million, and they only spend three days on a road show. The order book's $15 million, and guess what? The stock goes up because everybody gets cut back. Some people come by private placement, and some people got way too little. It's a good story, so the stock goes to $2.80 and the issue was at $2.20. I liked it at $2.40 or $2.50, and I can buy maybe a decent size on the issue at a discount. Okay, so maybe there's a four-month hold. If it's a really hot IPO I don't mind buying it. That doesn't mean I'll hold it for five years. I'm just being opportunistic. In the old days I bought Leech on IPO. I bought Rona on IPO and I've done quite well on IPOs. For example, late in the cycle you find the companies that have good balance sheets go public. The ones who've got rotten balance sheets have gone public early in the cycle because the bank's waiting to get their money back. They're pushing the company. So I find private guys that don't really want to go public because they have to open themselves up. Then someone eventually says, "Well, if you really want to keep growing, maybe it's good." I found that especially in '94 and '95. There were some great IPOs of good companies, and late in the cycle, of course, people are getting jaded, right?

But don't most IPOs come out at exactly the right time for the company and exactly the wrong time for investors? You didn't see any mining stocks become public in '98 or in '99.

They wouldn't have been able to. It is the same as the big companies giving them away for nothing. It's a good point there. I point out Rona. They became public when there were very few IPOs of corporations, because people were looking at trusts. It's a good point you make. Let's say Canadian oil stocks are totally out of favour in Canada. Do you think they're going to be able to do an issue at a low price? The answer's no. So you make a good point.

Over the years, what's been your biggest mistake that you made? It could have been an individual stock. It could have been an industry sector.

Okay. In some way, I'm sort of wondering if maybe one of the things was being too much underweight techs early on when they were running up. I probably was too underweight when they were just starting to run, because they weren't crazily valued at that time. It's just that they went up so much. There were a lot of people who did poorly who had really good track records until the tech bubble. It really spoiled people's good ten-year numbers, people who added some value every year, and then suddenly it just got wiped out in six months. That doesn't mean you should have been market weight, but if you at least had exposure, you could have been taking profits along the way. When you're behind and it's getting more and more and more and a bigger percentage of the index, you kind of know it's going to change because things are really getting crazily valued.

The problem is that I think one's got to be careful where a sector is significant because that kind of thing can happen. You can argue the same can happen with gold stocks. There have been times historically where they went up a lot when the market was very weak. To that extent, I don't like getting hurt by the big picture when small caps do really badly. That's one of the reasons why we own medium caps because I've been in microcaps where you can't buy them and you can't sell them. It doesn't matter that they're trading at eight times earnings. You can't sell them at eight times earnings and at seven times, and the reason you can't sell them at seven times is because they wouldn't have got there if anyone wanted to buy them. There will be a day that there will be no sellers. I think to that extent I don't want to get hurt too much by being very, very different from a big picture sort of sector thing. That's the first thing. That was a really bad period because it was bad for small caps. I got wiped out by techs. I'm just saying the thing kept going and going, and I think it would have been better to have some exposure earlier on. Unfortunately, people panicked and said, "Wow, it's a new world. It's the Internet." When Nortel was 35 percent of the index trading at 100 times cash earnings and CCL was six times cash earnings, no one looked at it because it wasn't a tech. It was bizarre, right? Anyway, I think that sometimes you can get horribly offside for quite a while.

You have to decide whether to stick with your style or change, right? That's the hard part.

It was such a rough period. I sort of thought afterwards, "Oh, I'm stubborn and I'm sure I'll be proved right in the end." As we know, tech collapsed in the end, but if you had no techs or very little in those few years, my God, you would have got so wiped out that your business would have suffered. People don't have the patience. Every month, people judge you, and you do have to have an open mind.

What do you think the biggest win that you ever had was? It can be a stock or an industry. The best thing that you ever did which has helped your performance?

It's probably from having very, very few mining stocks five and six and seven years ago, because they made very little money. Then we bought a few, especially base metal or copper gold stocks right at the bottom.

Would that have been '98 that you would have bought them?

No, like 2000.

The bids dry up.

When you want to sell them. Why that happened wasn't because they were necessarily bad companies; it was because of the Long-Term Capital blow up and the Asian crisis. It was all sorts of stuff. It was things out of your control.

Do you read the daily newspapers? What is your average day?

Yeah, I read the business sections. We get a lot of internal e-mails besides all of the brokers' stuff that we get. I deal with all the voicemails and try to meet at least two companies a day. That's what Peter and I do. There's a whole bunch of other companies that come in, so we probably get three company visits a day. There's more than three companies that come in here, but I probably meet at least three a day. I put in a couple of trades, but I don't do tons of trades. We do some broker research, but you get so much stuff. There's a couple of brokers that are checked every day. I actually don't answer my phone. I tell people to leave a detailed message because I don't want to get in a twenty-minute chat with everything I'm doing. The reason is because I've got stuff to do and I read tons of quarterlies and I read the analyst stuff and I read through other lumps of papers that I go through. I don't pretend to do modeling and financial forecasts. I can do it in my head, and after a while, you can sort of figure it out. So it's kind of a mixture. It's a passion of mine and it is my hobby.

The normal day is a hodgepodge of things, but my day is really focused on Canadian small cap stocks and some medium caps. I don't spend a lot of time worrying about what happened in retail sales in Canada or the U.S. or what happened in some big stat in the U.S. It might move the market in the U.S., but I really focus on companies and the results that come out. I'm going through annual financial statements, going through quarterlies, being on conference calls when they have them, reading analyst stuff, and listening to brokers. There's a few brokers that I listen to everyday. It's kind of a hodgepodge and it's sort of frenetic. The other thing is I actually jump around a lot. I don't need to spend hours looking at things. I always think if you're analyzing a company and you're an analyst, that's fine. But you've got to have some judgement after a while. You don't have to spend two days on it.

Keep it simple.

You should know what's important. And guess what? It doesn't mean you're going to be right. If you're right, a few things at a time to do extremely well. It's amazing how some stocks do really well and some do really badly. They're just very good or they're not very good. I look at what people have done and what they tell you, because everyone can tell you they will do well. I try to buy companies that have support. If they fall, it's because the market fell but not because they have rotten earnings. Not because management says, "Guess what? We're still looking for something, people haven't paid us yet for our latest invention, but we're probably going to come up with something spectacular." To that extent, we only had one down year in the fourteen calendar years that I was at the old place.

Your fund usually does much better in the up markets and actually better in the down markets than the index. This is unusual because a lot of times, if you're doing better in the up markets, you'll get crushed in the down markets.

It's probably because of our style. Me and Peter buy lots of boring companies like CCL Industries and Kingsway.

You owned Kingsway?

It's a tough one. It always looks cheap.

It always looks cheap. Is that…?

They never do as well as they should.

No.

It's a bit of a battle, but I've got a lot of patience. I don't mind even having a few companies like that. It's okay. It's not spectacular, but that's fine. The other thing is, in reality, attack is the best form of defense. What are you going to buy? If you buy stocks that are growing earnings, they can't fall forever, unless you're paying $100 for $1 of earnings. Then, of course, they're going to fall forever. If their earnings are up 20 percent, and it doesn't go up, then the P/E's come way down.

Right.

It's not that easy to grow 20 percent a year for four years, you know? Those are the kind of companies we try to buy, and backing management teams that have proven it before, whether it's an oil patch or mining or anything else. To me, it just seems like the power of compounding growth. I really like to buy big fast-growing companies. They don't have to be really fast, but they also need reasonable valuations. When I think back, Home Capital's gone up more than a hundredfold—it's remarkable. Not for us, it hasn't, but it has in the past twelve years. The last few years, it hasn't done anything. It's the power of compounding growth. It's like when people show, what, 20 percent or 30 percent a year is for ten years. It's remarkable. There's a whole bunch of people who just don't get it. They're selling their winners and buying the losers, as if there's something magical about the stock price.

Another one was Stantec. It's just amazing what these guys do. It used to trade at five or six times earnings. Now it's sixteen times—much higher numbers. It's no wonder it's gone up so much. Then you figure out how many times all these stocks have split—whether it's Gildan or Reitmans—it's amazing. One stock we have owned for fifteen years, and it's gone up twenty-four-fold. I've never sold a share. Now why would I sell something that is not expensive?

We've had pretty good results in down markets as well. We have also had a very high information ratio in the past, which is then excess return over your benchmark. It's kind of the tracking error, how different you are to the index. Our information ratio numbers were huge, over two at times. That's the other thing, we're buying all sorts of stuff. I love retailing and specialty retailers. There are great companies in Canada.

Let's just talk for a second about your hedge fund versus your mutual fund.

Sure.

How's that going to be different? Are you going to short individual stocks or are you going to short indexes against your positions ?

We were probably 10 percent short at the end of '07. For example, we bought more mining stocks than I would've been comfortable with. Why? Because we thought we were buying them pretty cheap. What happens if the commodity price falls a lot? So we shorted a couple of the mining indices. We added Horizon BetaPro....

Right, HXD....

We've also started shorting a couple of stocks. Now if you said to me, "What experience do you have?"

You can draw upon the experiences at Sprott?

Well, these guys at Sprott short hundreds of stocks. The old company was odd. They pride themselves on this ranking system. Basically, we had to rank 100 stocks, 25 best second best, third best, second worst, and the worst, every month. We had to rank them every month, 25 here, 25 here, 25 here. Our best picks in this period did extremely well. Our worst picks did nothing in a bull market for six years. Do we have the ability to pick the winners and the losers? Well, yes, and guess what? We didn't change our ranking so much. Are there stocks there that we could have shorted in that five or six year bull market? Well, for sure. We have experience in a theoretical portfolio of being able to differentiate between our best and worst. That's one of the reasons we started the hedge fund. Do we have a lot of experience in shorting individual stocks? The answer is no. We've done some of it. You do it a couple of times and you get more comfortable. We work with J.F. [Tardif] and he has shorted hundreds of stocks.

I asked J.F., "What's your number one rule in shorting?" He says, "I never short based on valuation. I short based upon deteriorating fundamentals." Because the valuation can go sky high forever, right? Julian Robertson did that with the Tiger Fund and he collapsed his fund in March of 2000.

I'm well aware of it. If you're good at picking on the long side, hopefully you also know what you haven't bought. So we're moving into it and we will be shorting more in the fund. The hedge fund is $40 million, and undoubtedly it'll be much smaller than the mutual fund. The mutual fund is easier for the masses to buy and the money's flowing in, but we'll be able to buy many more microcaps in the hedge. I want to emphasize that because in the mutual fund, we bought only a couple of microcaps. The point is, if you find a Wi-LAN or Pacific Stratus, like we found a year or two ago that were dirt, dirt cheap, we weren't supposed to look at them because they were around $50 million market cap. We did and bought 9.9 percent. Instead of having a 0.3 or a 0.5 or a 0.8 in something that went up six- or sevenfold, we'll be able to put in 2 percent or 2.5 percent or 3 percent. When they double or triple, we'll take profits. That's the advantage of what we'll be able to do. I think we'll able to do significantly more in the hedge fund, and hopefully we'll be able to add value from the shorts.

When we used to see companies, we would come back from lunches and say, "Oh my God, that's terrible." We just used to laugh it off. Now we can at least consider, "Can you short it?" If you buy a private placement and it goes up a lot, can you short the common? You buy their P/E stock at $0.80 and it goes to $1.90 and then it falls to $1.30. Oh my God, it's coming off restriction next week. Guess what? It's $1.15, it's $1.10. Now there's tons of shares for sale. It's still up 25 percent, but it's not up 140. Those are things that obviously in the hedge fund we'll be able to do some of. In a $30 million, $40 million, or $50 million fund, there's money to be made, and if it's a hot IPO, we're going to do things. If we can make money on the shorts, we're definitely going to do more than we've done. It's a matter of getting a bit more comfortable with the idea of doing it. I'm very well aware that you can get wiped out, not because you're wrong three years later, but because you're too early. I'm very well aware of it. You can be right in the end, but you're still going to be wrong. You're going to be wrong for six or twelve months, and guess what? You're going to panic because the thing's doubled or tripled and you're short. We're going to be very, very judicious and go slow.

Tom Stanley
Against the Crowd

"It's important to remember that if you don't stay humble, the market will make you humble."

Rarely have I interviewed a money manager that is as proud and excited about what he has done for his investors as Tom Stanley. It was refreshing to find someone who seemed to have one thing in mind in his money management career: doing the best for his unitholders. As with many of the other Stock Market Superstars, Tom doesn't fit the traditional mold of what you think is a star money manager. I don't know how far his offices are from downtown Toronto, but I do know it was a $25 taxi ride straight out of Yonge Street. The area was definitely not the centre of Bay Street, but it doesn't have to be to generate good returns. Just look at Warren Buffett in Ohama, Nebraska, probably the greatest investor of all time. Do you think it is a coincidence that Tom is located way off Bay Street, when one of his heroes just happens to be Warren Buffett? Tom said it isn't a coincidence; it's by design. I also suspect nothing is accidental about his performance: $10,000 invested in the Resolute Growth Fund at inception, Dec. 3, 1993, and converted to the Resolute Performance Fund on June 14, 2005, would be worth $336,430 at the end of the first quarter of 2008. This is a combined compound rate of return of 27.8 percent since late 1993.

When Tom became an investment advisor, he didn't know much about the business, so he read everything he could about some of the greatest investors: Warren Buffett, John Templeton, and Peter Lynch. Over the years, Tom then developed a set of principles that rule his investing discipline.

I have also rarely interviewed a money manager that is as secretive about what he does as Tom Stanley. Don't get me wrong; this is not a bad thing. Small cap stocks can be illiquid, and when you only own possibly eight stocks as Tom does, you don't want copycats. Portfolio concentration is a Tom Stanley strategy, as it is also of Buffett's, who once said something like, "Diversification is for people who don't know what they're doing." Tom justifies this strategy by saying, "Card players don't show their hand." Now, with concentration comes volatility, and Tom has had several instances over the years where the fund has dropped by 25 percent or more. It doesn't bother him; it only creates more opportunity. Tom isn't shy about taking a position, and this sort of portfolio would make the traditional money manager's blood curdle. Ah, but maybe this is why the traditional money managers don't even come to half of what Tom's returns have been. He doesn't do things the same way as everyone else. You can't do better than others if you don't do things differently.

More about the office. You have to be directed to the suite by Tom or a staff member, as there is no reference to the company on the building directory. When you get off the elevator, there is no fancy office, oak-panelled walls, or chic reception area. Oh, there's a frosted door at the entrance and big, old, open space when you walk in. It is very nondescript with an empty office or two filled with used furniture. I probably would not have noticed, but Tom mentioned it to me.

There were a couple of nice charts in plain view. Tom took me to see these as soon I entered the office. They were charts of the performance of the Resolute Growth Fund and the Resolute Performance Fund. At one point, this track record put Tom's fund at the top of all North American equity funds. You notice that his starting point is $10,000, not $100,000, as Tom believes in giving great performance to the average person, not limiting his expertise to the already wealthy.

If you want some detail, take a look at the website for the company: www.resolutefunds.com. It explains much of the philosophy and is generally very informative. Tom has posted his eighteen principles of investing on the site, of which he added three just before my interview. I have included these at the end of this chapter. He was very clear that these were the backbone of his investing discipline. He was also very clear about going over some ground rules for the interview—in other words, things he did not want to talk about. Luckily, these weren't on my list of items I wanted to discuss. He even showed me the latest book by Charlie Munger, called *Poor Charlie's Almanack*. At first glance, it looked like a great book, and the further I got into it, the better it was. In case you don't know, Charlie Munger is Warren Buffett's business partner and right-hand man.

Being a retail broker until 2004, what's admirable about Tom is his candor, his eccentricities, his humbleness, and his ability to relate to the average investor.

Tom:

I do not give investment advice; I'm not licensed to. I want to make sure that any statements I make should not be construed as giving investment advice. I simply manage the fund. I'm prepared to answer your questions, but for legal reasons, I do not want it to be construed as making recommendations or giving advice. That's just the way the world is these days. Do you agree to that?

Bob:

Yeah.

Your undergraduate degree is in psychology. Considering that psychology is a big part of the market, do you think it helps your investing process, or does it have any effect on how you manage money?

Sure. Psychology is very important. Generally, I would say people's brains are not wired to be good investors, so it's important to understand the psychology of investing because it's important to think rationally when you invest. Psychology was an enormous help to me, and I've read a lot about the psychology of investing. There have been many good articles about it through the years.

Value investing is built upon the premise that people are going to be irrational and that you can find value in that. I guess if everybody were rational and everything were priced the way it should be, you'd never find anything of value.

I don't believe in the efficient market because people do not always invest rationally. To paraphrase Warren Buffett, it was something to the effect that Mr. Market can be manic depressive. He can be a raging bull one day and a raging depressed bear the next day. That creates opportunities. I very much believe that.

You were an investment advisor up until 1994, dealing with regular clients?

No. I was an investment advisor from 1980 to 2004. I was an investment advisor at many different houses. You say, "How did you have time to research your ideas and stay on top of them and also deal with clients?" I was a lot younger then and I had a lot more energy. I personally did most of my research. I would say I certainly used some of the research of my employers, but I think trying to get information from as many sources as possible was very helpful.

I certainly wouldn't want to do that now because it was a lot of work. It's really having three jobs: being a broker, doing all the research, and managing the money as well.

Yeah. I have dealt with retail clients a lot. Not many money managers have ever done that. It's hard to deal with retail clients, because they are emotional. How did you get people to stick with things?

A couple good points you're alluding to here. First of all, it was a great education for me being a retail advisor because I got the opportunity to see over 1,000 investors, some very spectacularly successful and some unsuccessful at investing. I tried to study and learn and say, "What were people doing that worked and what were people doing that didn't work?" As an advisor, you do the best you can. Certainly, it was a lot of work when you're doing something that might in the short term go in the wrong direction. It's a big challenge trying to get people to do things that are unpopular, such as buying oil at the bottom of the cycle back in 2000. It's easier in a fund where I can just do it. With the retail investor, you have to persuade them. What I try to do as an advisor is just have an overwhelming arsenal of facts. I think through the years I developed a very loyal clientele who would listen to the facts and invest with me accordingly. I've had retail clients who joined me in my first year in 1980 who were in the Growth Fund and who are now in the Performance Fund. They have been with me now for twenty-six years.

Fantastic. That's loyalty! You've gone through rough patches and usually a lot of money flows out. I think you alluded to that fact in '99. It's unfortunate because if people believe in you and what you're doing, they should stick with you.

At the end of the day, enough people did. At the end of the day you have to invest in what you think is right even though it may be temporarily unpopular. I would certainly say that if you saw my four-page history of the fund. I'm just simply saying a lot of people called me in, like, '99 or 2000 and said, "Hey, I like what I'm seeing on your fund. It seems to be doing pretty well, and I'm so excited about getting into technology stocks." I'd say, "Well, we're not in any computer stocks. We're in a lot of oil stocks." I remember one person hung up on me. So you don't invest just because it's popular. You invest in what you think is going to give a good return for your investors. I think that's something I've tried to train myself to do over the years.

Once something becomes popular, basically the opportunity to make profits is limited because everybody's already talking about it. But when people think you're crazy for getting into uranium, four years ago or three years ago, I would suspect that would be the opportunity set that is going to create more money.

Yeah. When I went into the uranium market in 2004, it certainly was not a popular investment theme at the time. I certainly was questioned about it. People were saying, "Well, don't you know that uranium is dangerous? Don't you know that they haven't been building nuclear power plants in the United States for, like, twenty years or twenty-five years?" I just said, "Well, here's the facts as I see them," and that's it. I want to maybe address some of these points because I think I've really tried to strive for effective rationality. Do your homework, know the facts, and make decisions based on the facts. So maybe prevailing sentiment was to say, "Why would you buy uranium?" On the other hand, these are the facts.

You do all your own research. Do you use any analyst information at all?

Of course, yes. Absolutely. I also do a lot of my own homework and I like to check facts directly. Back to my investment philosophy, I read a lot of reports and try to learn from where I can. I think it's important to try to learn as much as you can from as many sources as you can. It only helps you make better decisions.

I understand that your first couple years of running money, you used other people's information or other people's informational sources and you learned that maybe it wasn't the best idea to do that.

I think it's important at the end of the day, as I said in point four, to be skeptical. Check facts directly if you can. It's very important to try to understand the biases and potential conflicts of interest among the sources that provide them. So it's important to try to check facts directly. That's one of the reasons why I prefer to invest in Canada. Occasionally, I'll go into the United States, but it's very unlikely that I would ever invest elsewhere. I won't say "never," but it's unlikely because it's much easier to get good sources of information and understand things better when you're investing here. You just get better information sources. It's easier to kind of understand the politics in Canada than trying to understand the politics or the rules inside the middle of China. So it goes back to investing close to home.

You should diversify throughout the world, but obviously you've found a tremendous amount of opportunity to make money in 3 percent of the world's market. That just shows you can find opportunity anywhere.

I think there's a lot of merit in investing internationally; I just don't think I can do it. Warren Buffett always said, "Know your limits; draw a circle of competence around yourself." I'm paraphrasing him—I'm not saying the quote exactly right. I'm just saying know your limits and stay well within your limits. I don't think that I'm smart enough to be able to invest in a European manufacturing company or a Chinese manufacturing company and be able to have a competitive edge in understanding what's going on, so I prefer to invest in things that I'm comfortable with. What I found over the years is that Canada's a wonderful place. It's one of the bigger economies in the world and we're blessed with tremendous resources here. I've found enormous opportunities in Canada, and being closer to the story, I think I have been able to understand the story a bit better. I've not had a strong motivation to go too far from home.

I think something you have alluded to is staying humble. I heard in 1999 a fund manager called himself the best money manager in the U.S., and obviously it didn't work out too well for him when he was down 50 or 60 percent in 2001 and 2002. Your track record is phenomenal, one of the best in the country. How do you stay humble?

I've had numerous and frequent setbacks throughout my career. A couple years ago, the Performance Fund dropped just over 25 percent. When I was running the Growth Fund, in our history, we had three down years. It's important to remember that if you don't stay humble, the market will make you humble. I've seen this happen to a lot of people. Success can be very dangerous. It can corrupt. I've got a long-term vision of trying to continue to serve my unitholders for as long as I can. I try to view myself as a marathon runner, not a sprinter. Hopefully, if my health stays good and the regulations allow it, I'd like to serve investors for at least another twenty years. It's important to keep your methodology and do what's worked for you. I've tried to outline them in the eighteen principles of my investment philosophy. As I said, the market can make you so humble so quickly. I just find that all the time we are facing setbacks.

You've got a great website.

Thanks. Once we closed down the Growth Fund and we became a non-reporting issuer, we put our website back up. The purpose of the website is just to let people have a little bit of insight into what I think and what our values are, and to tell people a little bit about what we did with the Growth Fund. If you want to use something on the website, if you want to reproduce it, just quote it exactly as it is and you're welcome to use it. We worked on it pretty carefully.

You have eighteen secrets to success there. But if you had to tell me one....

Well, not secrets. I've got them on the website, so they're principles.

If you had one thing you think that's been a reason for your success, what would it be?

One reason? You have to try hard.

Now, you studied Templeton and Buffett and Lynch.

Don't forget Charlie Munger, I have tremendous respect for him.

Yeah, he's a common-sense guy, isn't he?

Tremendously. He's been a very, very good teacher as well. I just love that book he put out, *Poor Charlie's Almanack*. I'll show it to you before you leave today. It's a wonderful book. Charlie's in his '80s now and he basically tried to put all of his collective wisdom, I guess, in a book. It's very humorous. There's good investment advice in there, but it's also good worldly wisdom and it's just an incredible book.

Benjamin Graham had his own philosophy, and then there was Dodd, and Buffett just changed that a little bit, and Templeton did something else, and Lynch did something different. So how have you used what they do and related it to your own style?

Well, my primary investment vehicle has been Canadian stocks and particularly Canadian small caps. Their teachings weren't just for U.S. stocks, so I've taken wisdom from all of them. It's hundreds of things; I can't list what I've taken. But maybe it might be easier to try to tell you what I don't take from them, okay? I don't think I have the brains or the resources to be like Templeton and to invest internationally. I'm not going to be investing all over the world like Templeton was so good at doing. I also don't think I have the resources or the brains like Peter Lynch to be able to invest in so many stocks that he did.

He had hundreds of stocks.

Hundreds and hundreds of stocks in the Fidelity Magellan fund, but he was running a much, much bigger fund. I don't think I'd do that. Again, it's knowing your limits. I invest more like Warren Buffett; I run a concentrated portfolio. Then again, though, I often will buy things when they're unpopular or unfollowed, which is certainly very, very much a hallmark of what Sir John Templeton did. It's almost easier to say I try to emulate what they're doing, and I've got a library on all four of these investors. They're all excellent, and they've all had distinguished track records of investing and they've all been very generous on sharing their wisdom. So you can go get a book and read about—read Charlie Munger's book, or read Warren Buffett's annual reports, which have had a lot of wisdom in them. You can also read Peter Lynch. He has some great books out, *One Up on Wall Street* and all the rest. I've read all of them, and Sir John Templeton's had a lot of books about himself as well.

All of these investors have been extraordinarily generous in sharing their wisdom. There was an institutional investor poll done at the end of the century on who were the best investors in the second half of the 20th century. It came up Buffett, Templeton, and Peter Lynch. I think it's eminently rational to say if these three guys were considered by many to be the best, why don't you try to understand what they're doing and study what they're doing? I was also fortunate to have some mentors in the Canadian market. Some of them are private investors, some of them are in the investment business. They mentored me and taught me as well. I didn't learn just from the masters, but I've had some individuals who've been an enormous help to me through the years as well who are private investors. I think part of humility is trying to learn from whoever you can learn from, because there's a lot you can learn from a lot of different people.

If you take a look at Brandes, who is a deep value manager, or a Templeton, they very rarely have resource stocks because they don't fit into what they look for. So how do you value a resource stock versus value a consumer products company or a retail company?

It's difficult to do so, and there's no easy answer.

Is it more a supply-and-demand equation that you are looking at?

It's a very complicated question. I'm not a naturally good speaker and it's hard for me to try to put it succinctly in one sentence. One of my eighteen principles is to have a flexible approach. I have bought value stocks, price to book ratio, price to sales, price to earnings, price to cash flow, which were very, very cheap. I have bought growth stocks. I have bought resource stocks that were not producing yet. It's very important to have a flexible approach depending on the market. I think if you use one kind of rigid approach all the time to investing, you're foregoing opportunities in the marketplace.

So back to resources, I certainly have a macro opinion about these resources. I think you actually asked me a bit about uranium....

Yes. What was the rationale for getting into that?

There are many reasons, but I will give you half a dozen just off the top of my head. There has been a shortage of production of uranium since 1985. We're looking now at over twenty years where there has been a shortfall of uranium mined versus uranium used in the world, which is extraordinary. You can get the exact numbers out of the Cameco annual report, but in real rough figures, the world is using now about 180 million pounds a year and I'm plus or minus 10 percent. My numbers will be off. I'm not a detail person; I'm more of a big-picture guy. The world is producing about 110 million pounds a year.

So, at this time there remains, as there was in 2004 when I started buying uranium, an ongoing shortfall of production. There continues to be a huge ongoing shortfall of production.

There's not much inventory either.

Well, there were obviously big inventories of uranium back in the '80s. The inventories are being used up. When you have a shortfall of production for twenty years, the inventory gets used up.

Where was the inventory?

Certainly, the Soviet Union and the United States had big inventories. At the end of the Cold War, they were reprocessing nuclear weapons. That put a big supply on the market for a long time.

Obviously, I don't think the inventories were infinite. When I came into the market in 2004, everybody was saying, "Oh, but there's these huge inventories overhanging the market. Russia has all this uranium." Then I'd look and see the Russians are investing in new mines, and they were looking for uranium. That kind of bothered me. I said, "Well, if they had enormous stockpiles of uranium, why were the Russians investing in new uranium mines? Why are they looking for this stuff?" So it suggested to me that we're coming to an end of these massive inventories. There's still inventories, but I'm just saying they're obviously a lot smaller now.

I read a while ago that the Saudis are desperate for drill rigs and they said, "Why do the Saudis want a lot more drill rigs to go search for new oil if they have unlimited supplies?"

Well, the Saudis were looking for drill rigs. They bought some drill rigs—I don't know the exact category of them—but they were deep-water drill rigs. They were looking in the water and for very expensive oil in the deep ocean. If they've got all this available oil on land, why are they spending huge amounts of money to go drill in the deep ocean? It's important to try to get information from as many sources as possible. With uranium, we have a shortage of supply, a massive shortage, which has gone on now for over twenty years. It's a massive gap. Can you think of any other commodity where they're producing less than two-thirds of what the market actually needs every year? What happens when you have such a supply shortfall? You'll use up the inventories, and when the inventories start getting very scarce the holders of the inventories are going to realize that. Uranium, generally speaking, is an essential material. It's used to make 16 percent of the world's electricity.

I was surprised that 80 percent of the power in Western Europe is nuclear.

I don't think those facts are correct. I question those facts. It may be in certain countries like Latvia or France, but I do not think it's in Europe. There's a couple Western European countries. There's a good site—World Nuclear Association—where you can look at it. Some countries are a lot more nuclear than others. Back in 2004, to finish off your question, there's a huge supply shortfall that was continuing. Demand was growing, in spite of prevailing opinion in North America or even Western Europe, nuclear was a growing option. There's five countries in Asia in particular—India, China, South Korea, Japan, and Russia—are all building new nuclear reactors. Most of the building of the new nuclear reactors is still in Asia. Then you have issues such as global warming, which is becoming of increasing concern to the world. One of the beauties is that nuclear creates very little new greenhouse gases. Many environmentalists have started to come out in favor, but every way of producing electricity has its own problems. I notice that people in Massachusetts don't want wind turbines and I read that the Kennedys don't want wind turbines in Massachusetts.

Coal is cheap, but it's got its issues.

Coal creates greenhouse gasses, and it's dirty. I'm just simply saying that nuclear is a viable option for so many people. I was at an environmental conference in Toronto, listening to Tim Flannery, who wrote *The Weather Makers*. He said if China's going to build new power plants, would you rather have them be nuclear or coal? He said he'd rather have them as nuclear. So the environmental movement itself is starting to wake up to the potential. At the end of the day, when we look at supply and demand, every time you build a new nuclear power plant, it requires a lot of uranium just to get it going. I think it takes about a three-year supply. There's some other interesting factors about uranium, which is inelasticity of supply and demand. It's not too easy to find a new uranium mine and put it in. You have to find the stuff, you have to get it permitted, you've got to do an environmental assessment, you've got to build a mill. It takes several years for these things to happen. So supply just can't be turned on with a switch.

U308 to UF6. You've got to convert it and process it.

Well, the CANDU process is different. Demand is inelastic and it's growing. Supply is inelastic. It was a great vehicle for us over the last few years.

There's only a few companies in the world that actually are producers, right? There's Cameco. In small cap land, there's hardly any, right? There's also Paladin. Many other ones are finding uranium, but I don't know how many years it's going to take to get it out of the ground.

We do buy juniors where we look at what we think the reserves may be and you try to get some estimate of asset value. So we're not valuing them based on current earnings. We're not valuing them on current cash flow, because they don't have any. If you are sitting on a lot of uranium and the price is going up, or with a reasonable assurance that the price of uranium is going up, it could be tremendously beneficial. One of the vehicles we owned was IUC, International Uranium. One of the reasons why I bought it was because it had a lot of what I would say were proven uranium mines that had closed down because of low prices. So if they had some higher-cost producers, if prices went up, they stood to benefit a lot if prices recovered.

I've never seen core samples like UEX took out, either. If they keep coming up with those, that's fantastic. I bought it for a buck or something. I don't know whether I was lucky or smart.

We were in some of these ideas fairly early, but we're long-term investors.

Is it hard to pigeonhole your style?

It really is. I think as markets change, so do I. Back to my history again. For example, back in the late '90s, you say, "Well, how did you make money?" Carefully doing a lot of bottom-up stock picking on a lot of what I think were mispriced Canadian small caps. I was in Cangene, a biopharmaceutical company. It was an eclectic mix of small caps. That's what we were doing a lot of in the '90s.

Your style is more contrarian. Is that right or not?

It's not only unpopular, but I would say it's sometimes just unknown ideas or unfollowed ideas. Again using the example of uranium, there wasn't a lot of coverage of uranium stocks in 2004 or enthusiasm for uranium stocks. Now there's been a lot more coverage over the last few years. You can't keep a bull market a secret, and, of course, you're going to get more people coming in. At the end of the day, you find great bargains because they're unfollowed or unloved. So I guess you'd say, yes, contrarianism is definitely a part of the buying. It's one of my eighteen points, so I agree with you. It's not the only all-consuming thing, but it certainly is an important point.

There's something called the value trap. A stock's trading at a low price because it deserves to trade at a low price and it's going to do nothing. You can buy a value stock and hold it for five or six or eight years. Do you look for some sort of catalyst with a stock?

Well, if you're looking for an undervalued stock, it's one of the factors I would consider, trying to think about, "How is that value going to be unlocked?" It's not absolutely critical, and sometimes I do, sometimes I don't. I found many junior oil and gas stocks in 2000, 2001, 2002, 2003 that were just too cheap. They were trading at two or three times cash flow, and they were growing, and the underlying commodity prices were going up. So what's the catalyst that makes them get their value? The answer was that income trusts seemed to have an insatiable desire to take these companies over. So the catalyst for realizing the value of many of my junior oil and gas stocks from the 2000 to 2004 period was income trusts taking them over. Subsequently, when I went into uranium, I felt a catalyst would be a continuing good supply demand. I think in the long run if uranium prices go up, it will help uranium stocks. I know that sounds pretty simplistic, but sometimes investing is that simple. If uranium prices skyrocket, it will help good uranium stocks.

The second thing is that the environmental movement gets more and more concerned about greenhouse gases and the effect on the environment. I spent a lot of time thinking and looking at the alternatives; I just don't think that wind can make 20 or 50 percent of the world's electricity. There's a place for it, but the place is going to be somewhat limited. The same thing applies to a lot of the other alternatives. So I thought at least in this generation, nuclear was one of the most viable alternatives through creating power that's not going to make the greenhouse gas situation worse. So, yes, thinking that the environmental movement will change its mind over the years is one of the triggers. As I said, one of the founders of Greenpeace has gone pro-nuke.

Right. He made a speech that nuclear power was the cleanest form of energy. I guess if we can figure out the nuclear waste, how to dispose of that or reprocess it, it will solve all the problems. How do you keep your patience?

It's very important to try to learn from your mistakes. Back in 1981, I believed that the use of the computer was going to become much more widespread. I believed that computers would communicate with each other somehow. I went into a little Canadian technology stock called Nortel. Nortel went up, I made some money, and I sold it and it just kept going up and up and up. The lesson I've tried to learn is that, as Warren Buffett says, you're not going to get that many good ideas in a lifetime. So when you get a good idea, try to have the patience to enjoy the full benefit of the cycle. People who bought Microsoft in the early '80s when it came out, or Wal-Mart back then, would have done enormously well. But you would only have done enormously well if you stayed with the stock for a period of time. I think it's a natural tendency, going back to the first part of our discussion when you were talking about psychology. It feels good to take a profit. I'm sure as a retail guy you have retail clients. The clients say, "Hey, we've made money," and they feel good to take a profit, particularly during a correction in the market. They say, "Let's take a profit before our profit disappears." If you have a very good idea that's working, you need the patience to let your winners run. I agree. Patience is extraordinarily important because if you get a good idea, you want to try to benefit completely from it. I'm a long-term investor, and in the short run, you will get too many young people getting too enthusiastic about an idea, and they'll get into too much leverage, for example. From time to time, markets have corrections. You mentioned UEX had some tremendous drill holes. Your facts are correct. This is good news; this is materially good news. But corrections will be going on. I found that short-term fluctuations, trying to anticipate the short term, just doesn't work very well for me. So that's why I said principle number one: Be a long-term investor.

That's fighting normal human thoughts which are emotional—fear and greed.

Probably the fear comes from when we were cavemen, you know. When you're facing a threat or something scary, you run. Sell out and get out. The other thing is when you're dealing with the market, it is comforting to have a lot of people agree with you. As people, we like to have support for our opinions and our ideas. So when a large number of people agree with our point of view, that is comforting to us. It's not necessarily good investing, though. If everybody's doing something, as you said, then it's probably or possibly overvalued. The easy money has at least been made. So going back to my whole original premise, our brains are not wired typically for good investing. We have to understand that and understand the pitfalls. It's important, as I said, to just strive for effective rationality.

That was the one thing that John Templeton said, right? Buy at the point of maximum pessimism. He said that over and over and over again, and it takes guts to do that.

Yeah. I remember the quote. It was, "Buy at the point of maximum pessimism and sell at the point of maximum optimism; it requires the greatest of fortitude and gives the greatest rewards." Yeah, I actually had that quote up for a while.

When things have gone poorly for the fund in the past, did it make you

question what you were doing?

I question what I'm doing virtually every day of the year. I think part of humility is figuring out if I'm going to be wrong—why am I going to be wrong? You try to assign the probabilities of it. It's my job to second-guess myself every day that I'm here. If you just get arrogant and say, "I'm right," and put blinkers on it, you can get yourself in trouble. It's important to test and retest—and retest again—your underlying assumptions and say, "Have the facts changed? Has the situation changed? If so, what are we going to do?"

Even Sir John Templeton said, "If you're doing things the same way now as you were twenty years ago, then you won't be doing things correctly." Even coming from somebody who's very disciplined like that, he said things change and you've got to be adaptive.

As I said, in the '90s, I was looking at a lot of what I'd call value small caps. There were some growth ones in there. Certainly since 2000, I've been very, very overweight energy. From 2000 to 2004, it was basically junior small caps in the energy market. As I found many of my ideas just kept getting taken over by income trusts, I started switching to finding uranium because I thought there was good energy value there. Then, of course, we started finding what I thought was great value in the oil-sands stocks.

Losses kill, right? If you take a 50 percent loss, you need 100 percent gain to get back to where you started from. If you ask 90 percent of the population, they think if you lose 50 percent, you need to make 50 percent to get back to where you started from.

In 2001, 2002, when things weren't very good, a big part of doing well over time is not losing big amounts of money in bad times.

In 2001, we returned 24.4 percent after management fees and 2002 was 40.2 percent. I'm not sure what you mean when you say it was bad years.

It was bad years for the market, I meant. Good years for you. How did you do that? The only way most people could have done that is to heavily short.

The predominant part of our portfolio was junior small-cap oil and gas stocks. We were buying a lot of them. I remember ones that were trading at two times cash flow, and the underlying commodity was rising. It was a very, very compelling story. We weren't trying to invest in the market per se. John Templeton said that very succinctly. We can outperform by being different. If you want to mimic the market, you can simply buy an index fund. To outperform the market, you should try to do something that's different from the market. Our mandate was to try to outperform, to make people money and outperform the market. We have been positioned during our entire history quite differently than the market. We're not trying to be an index fund, and we're certainly not what you would call a closet index fund. We were in a lot of junior oil and gases in 2001, 2002, which in my opinion represented tremendous value and tremendous risk reward, and it served us very well.

You'll never outperform if you're going to look like the index. You hear most managers talk about "I'm overweight" banks or something. The index is 35 percent and they go out on a limb and go 38 percent. Mathematically, you take away 90 percent of your opportunity to outperform the index when you do that. I don't know why that's done. Maybe it's because of fear of being wrong, or fear of going down when the index goes up. I'm a huge believer in that. It's unfortunate. That's why 80 percent of mutual funds give you index returns minus 2 percent, because they've got that mentality that they cannot stray from the index very much. It's refreshing to see somebody like you. With everybody that I've interviewed, none of their portfolios look like the index, obviously because they can't.

Well, I guess you're getting a very strong message there. I guess the facts are it's pretty obvious then. These are not secrets because I've put them on my website. These are my principles. I thought very carefully about all eighteen of these points because I think they're all very important and I wanted to share them. I simply say outperform by being different.

The principle is logical, but most people still don't do that.

Well, I can't speak for other investors. I can't speak for other managers. I can only speak for what we do. We don't always outperform the market. There have been many periods where we've underperformed. If you want to have a chance of outperforming, you really have to do something that's different than the market.

Why do you concentrate so much of the portfolio? You said you look at Lynch and you look at Templeton and they had hundreds of stocks.

Well, first of all, Buffett did concentrate. Number one—I can quote Buffett; I have a great quote:

We think diversification as practiced generally makes very little sense to anyone who knows what they're doing. Diversification serves as protection against ignorance. If you want to make sure that nothing bad happens to you relative to the market, you should own everything. There's nothing wrong with that. It's a perfectly sound approach for somebody who doesn't know how to analyze businesses. But if you know how to value businesses, it's crazy to own fifty stocks or forty or thirty stocks, probably because there aren't that many wonderful businesses understandable to a single human being, in all likelihood. To forego buying some super-wonderful business and instead put your money into number thirty or number thirty-five on your list of attractiveness just strikes me as madness.

I'm quoting Warren Buffett in the August 2006 issue of *Outstanding Investor Digest*. It was so important I put that on my wall because he says it better than I can. Number one, if you want to try to pick good stocks, you want to have a stock idea that's meaningful. If it's a 10 percent weighting in your fund and it triples, then you're going to have a meaningful effect. If you've got a 1 percent weighting or half of 1 percent weighting in your fund and it triples, it is not so meaningful. Number two, if I have a good idea, I want it to have a meaningful impact. Number three, one of the most important things to do in a fund for managing risk is knowing what you're investing in. It would be very difficult to really know and understand 200 ideas very well. I don't know how a person could physically do that. I think knowing what you're investing in is very important for controlling the risk. Those are the reasons that I concentrate.

The index has, I think, become riskier and riskier as time goes on because they don't put the worst-performing stocks in. They don't put the out-of-favor stocks. It's the stocks that have grown the biggest. I wish that they had no index, because if they had no index, they would say, "Tom Stanley did 12 percent last year. That was a good return." They wouldn't say, "The index did 20 and Tom did 12, so he underperformed."

By precluding yourself to buying just the index stocks, how many stocks are on the index in Canada? The answer is: I don't know—220, 230, something in that range. I've lost exact count. How many stocks are on the exchanges in Canada? Probably somewhere around 4,000, give or take several hundred. By simply looking at stocks that are on the indexes, you're precluding yourself

308 | Tom Stanley

from the vast majority of stocks and opportunities in Canada.

Those are heavily followed by analysts, too.

I want to make something clear again going back to the point about flex-ibility. We believe in having a flexible approach. I've often found many of my best ideas in small caps because they may be underfollowed and ignored. How-ever, I would not hesitate to buy a larger stock if I felt it met our criteria. I have been in larger stocks both in the uranium and in the oil-sands space.

If you find value, you'll buy it.

If I find the opportunity, our mandate is to try to make money for people. I don't want to make too many rigid restrictions on what we're doing. We do not seek out institutional investors who typically need to have a more rigid and quantifiable investment approach because they want to know exactly what you're going to do and what your limits are. We do not seek out that business. We have chosen instead to try to just serve people. A lot of them are just reg-ular people. We have felt that what's worked better for us is just to have a flex-ible approach. So we've invested in a lot of small caps over the years, but am I strictly small cap? Not a chance. Are we an energy fund? Not per se. We're trying to make people money. Energy has served us well. If I decided that en-ergy was no longer the place to be, I wouldn't be in energy stocks. There were times in the '90s when we had no energy stocks in the fund at all.

I might have the facts wrong here, but I think you said in one of your letters you couldn't get hired to manage money in the '90s, so you just did it on your own.

The funniest question I get is I've had a lot of young people phone me up and say, "Gee, Tom, you've done well. How do I get hired in the business? How do I get hired to run a fund?" I said, "Well, you're asking the wrong per-son because I was not successful in getting hired." I don't have an answer for that. What I actually did was I had some managed accounts that had extraor-dinarily good returns. Close to quadruple-digit returns over a four-year period. I had them accounting-reviewed in four managed accounts. I thought with a good track record and a portfolio manager's license it would be a shoo-in to get hired. I guess I just didn't fit the mold. I don't know. I put my own money in and some of my long-term unitholders said, "You know what? We'll just start a fund and we'll run it part time. If it grows, that's great."

There was an article about me in the *Globe* which was quite true. It was called "Midlife Crisis Fund." The point is that I saw a great movie one time about people at the end of their lives talking about their lives. The greatest regret that people had about their lives were not necessarily their failures or their mistakes, but it was the opportunities they never tried. I felt as I was approaching 40 and I couldn't get hired to run a fund—I always dreamed of running a fund—and if I didn't try to do it, I would always regret it. I'd say, "What would have happened if you could have run a fund? Could you have been able to serve people well?" When I couldn't get hired, I said, "You know what? I'll run a small one." I was fortunate to have employers in the brokerage business who allowed me to run the fund while I served my retail clients. We never got into trying to heavily market the fund or sell it. We just thought, "Let's try and do a good job for investors, and if we do a good job for investors, the results will speak and people will find us." As the fund grew over time, it was quite apparent I needed to do it as a full-time job, so I retired as being a retail broker.

There was a fund at Canaccord that was run by Chan Buckland called the Multiple Opportunities Fund. It did a very, very good job over a period of time.

I had been at several firms running the fund, so when I started the fund, I actually had my own little firm, Stanley Investment Management. I cleared it through my former employer, which was Deacon. Business was slow in the first couple of years, and I was very cautious with the growth fund. It was a lot of work. I was invited back to join Deacon Capital Corporation, and they ended up being taken over by Dundee. Before they got taken over by Dundee, I moved to Thomson Kernaghan, and it had well-publicized financial problems. I was recruited to join Yorkton, then Yorkton ended up with their problems, and they got hit with a lawsuit. They sold off their retail to First Associates, so I moved. The point being is I always ran the fund wherever I was; I ran it under several different umbrellas at several different places. I was always trying to focus on doing the best you can to make your investors money. In hindsight, I'm very glad that as I get older, and as I do have less energy now than I did ten years ago, that I'm just running the one fund. We have our own investment council portfolio management license by the OSC. That's why it's a small office. We don't sell the fund directly. We have a limited number of what I'd say is dealers that we're very comfortable with. That's what we're trying to do. We keep ourselves pretty low key and low profile. There's only about twenty individuals, retail dealers, individual retail dealers who sell it, and they're at a variety of different houses. A lot of the dealers are people who've followed me for a long time. I've known them ten years or longer and they are comfortable with me and I am comfortable with them. It was never our goal to try to be the biggest fund in Canada. It was just our goal to try to be the best we could be.

You see a lot of great money managers start managing too much money and then have to diversify and own 200 stocks. Obviously, you take your opportunity set away. Is that right?

Well, that goes back again to one of my points. I have to just go back to my principles because that's why I put them on the site. Being small is an advantage, number twelve. I have to agree with you. It's easier to outperform by being small. We run somewhere between half to two-thirds of a billion right now, depending on the day. It moves around. I don't think I would be as effective running $25 billion.

A lot of your growth has been growth of assets, not necessarily new money coming in?

Well, obviously, if you look at the chart. We started from a very small base, and, as I said, we don't make any real effort to advertise or aggressively promote ourselves. We from time to time have done a couple press articles, but, you know, I didn't call you, you called me. As I said, my goal is simply to try to serve my unitholders as best as I can over the long haul and keep our business structure simple. As you can see, we don't have a very fancy overpriced office here. Some of our furniture here is used. I have a couple of very good people I work with, and that's it. We don't sell the fund directly, so there's no big dealer-servicing network. I like not being right downtown either. There's a lot of noise downtown and it's a little quieter here to think. That helps.

Can you still make money in a stock after it's widely followed by analysts?

Well, I'll never say never. What I'm saying is that typically a lot of the easy money is made before it becomes widely followed. Once a stock gets widely followed, it can still do well. A lot of my experience has shown that a lot of the greatest successes I've had have been stocks that have been very underfollowed or unknown when I bought them.

Did you ever question your discipline when tech stocks went up and up and up, and say to yourself, "Maybe these valuations are right for tech stocks?"

No, it was a bit frustrating. I certainly was criticized a lot for, "Why aren't you in tech? Why aren't you in tech?" At the end of the day, you have to look at the facts. I looked at these companies and they just made no sense from a valuation point of view. I actually wrote some very strong letters, which, if you read my history, I have quoted. That was the most common question I was getting in 1999 and 2000, "Why aren't you in tech?" Because that was the most common question we were getting, I did feel the need to address it fairly strongly. What I discussed was the bubble and the greater fool. Read "The Bubble and the Greater Fool." It was a tough time to keep up to the market because we avoided Internet and other high-tech computer stocks. We discussed this in our April 13, 2000, letter. I just said, "A bubble is not too strong a word to describe this phenomenon, and we will not pay for it." I got even a little more feisty, "We will not buy an overvalued stock on the theory we can sell it at an even more overvalued price to a greater fool." I just said, "Fine. No." I dug in my heels and said, "I'm not buying tech. If you want to buy tech, you buy another fund."

It was a difficult period, dealing with investors. I was shunned by many investors in 2000 for not buying tech, but it's my job to do what I think is right, it's not simply to do what is popular. I made it very clear to our investors that I thought that tech was in a bubble, and I put it in writing at the peak. If you want tech, we're not the fund for it. The valuations were lunatic. It was a mass dementia. I wanted to make it very clear that's what I was saying. If you need to, I can probably pull out a copy of the actual article, but I quoted it exactly verbatim on that.

So we talked about how you made money in the late '90s without investing in tech stocks. What five rules would you never break? You've got eighteen rules there, right?

These are principles—I will emphasize flexibility. Do I only buy unpopular stocks? Not always. I've got to emphasize the flexibility. So these are principles. You've got to use a bit of flexibility with these principles and actively look for ideas. Many of my best ideas, I find them. They don't find me. I have bought ideas that were presented to me, so these are not absolutely rigid rules. These are just the general principles which I go by.

I use the analogy of adaptability and the fact that the dinosaurs all died out. They were the biggest and the strongest. The cockroaches survived because they were adaptable to a new environment. We still use that to this day. "This stock is a dinosaur."

I'll have to remember that one. That's a good one. The dinosaurs died out, but the cockroaches survived.

That's right. They adapted to the cold winter or whatever happened. What has been your biggest regret?

What I would simply say is my biggest regret? I don't want to phrase it as a mistake. My biggest regret was selling Nortel in 1981, taking profits too soon.

John Templeton said when you're a value investor, you tend to get into things too early and you tend to get out of them too early. It's interesting because many managers have tried to fix that, but I don't know how you fix that.

What I want to say is I do not have any crystal ball for short-term timing. One of the biggest hits my fund ever took was the summer of 2001. The fund was weak in the summer of 2001, the events after 2001 took it down. It dropped just over one third. It was painful, but for those with a long-term perspective, it didn't matter because if you just simply held on several months later, we were back to new highs. Was I able to forecast that something horrible was going to happen on September 11, 2001, and the market would react? Of course not. We don't hold ourselves out to be short-term market timers. It's just too hard to do. We had actually faced in our Growth Fund more turnover than you would have expected because in early 2000, 2001, 2002, our companies kept getting taken out by income trusts or turned into income trusts, which in effect meant that there was turnover. That's beyond my control if our company gets taken over for a big premium. We will try to invest based on long-term observations. Sometimes if there is panic selling of something or other, we will try to take advantage of that. If the market's going to give you particularly good opportunities every day, you try to take advantage of it. My basic principle is, be a long-term investor. We try to educate our investors to be long-term investors as well.

Is technical analysis something you've ever looked at?

I've looked at technical analysis; I just don't know how it can make me money.

As Warren Buffett said, there's no rich technicians in the world.

It goes back to trying to make rational decisions. Go and get that chart book that's published every month and take out 100 charts. Then you cut the charts in half so you don't see what the second half is. You will just see the volume and the price movement of the first half. Then try and forecast the second half. I'd like to see some technical analyst have great success doing the second half. I do not use technical analysis.

That's a great point because when you look at the chart going back, you can always justify it by saying, "Oh, yes. See, here?" It is the ultimate 20/20 hindsight.

Let's take the name off the chart, rip the chart in half. Here's the back half, here's the volume and the price. What happens going forward? I'd simply say that would be a very interesting experiment. I try to make decisions based on rational business decisions, not what a chart says. I don't understand how it would be a benefit to forecasting.

Everybody always looks for the magic pill, and what you've said over and over and over again, and Warren Buffett says, is there's no magic pill. It's common sense and discipline and sticking to your guns.

You're making a good point. I think that goes back to human nature. So people like to have a magic pill, but then again you look at it and say, "Who are successful investors?" Templeton, Buffett and Munger, Peter Lynch. They're saying, "This is what we do." Certainly I think it would serve any investor well to read as much as they can about these investors. There are a lot of books out. I've got a whole bookshelf full of stuff about these three guys, and it's worth reading. Just plotting some little chart on a piece of paper might be fun, but I'm not sure how that's going to necessarily make people rich.

The average investor—they want to hear about five hot stocks to buy now, or five hot mutual funds to buy now. When you say, "Patience, discipline, stick to your guns," etc., they say, "Oh, that's boring. I want to hear five hot funds to buy now." It's too bad, but it's human nature.

It worries me when we have good periods of time. We tried in our letters to unitholders to caution people not to expect too much. It's invariably, as night follows day, that every manager gets cold periods and hot periods. It's just reasonable to expect that. We tried to be very, very careful to say, yes, over the long haul, we've been able to serve people, but in the short run, anything can happen. I can't make any guarantees about the future. We'll just try to do the methodology that's worked for us in the past and hope it keeps working.

You've heard of Hubbert's peak and the peak oil theory. From a supply-and-demand basis, do you believe in the peak oil theory, or that maybe the world production has peaked or is starting to peak and demand's going to continue to increase?

It's common sense that the amount of oil in the world is finite. We do not have an infinite amount of oil, so of course there has to be a time when oil peaks. I can't forecast when it's exactly going to happen.

When an oil field gets down and you've taken more and more oil out of the field, production is going to decline. You just can't help it in that field, right?

There's a lot smarter people than me in this field, like the guy from Texas.

Henry Groppe?

No, the guy who talked about *Twilight in the Desert*.

Matt Simmons.

Matt Simmons has done a lot of very good work on this matter. I've certainly read a lot of him. I do believe in Hubbert's peak as it pertains to light sweet crude. They may be finding ways to make synthetic crudes, however. I bought oils, if that's what you're addressing, for many reasons. One was there is a finite amount of production, and I don't know exactly when oil's peaked or if it already has. I believe that there's a lot of growth going on in Asia led by China and India. I referred to that back in 2000, which was a tremendous benefit to us. A lot of oil is being produced in places where there's a lot of political leverage being used. With strikes and terrorism, there's potential for political problems. When I was buying oil, the valuations looked pretty reasonable relative to the price of the commodity. The last reason I believed in oils is that in the long run, I believe that we will have inflation. As the value of money goes down, the value of commodities, be it uranium, oil, gold, copper, whatever, will go up simply because the value of money is going down. They look like they're going up, but it's actually more of a reflection of the value of money going down. I've given you five reasons why I liked oil, and these were reasons that I used back in 2000. As you can see from the economist's chart, oil was not a popular investment to make in 2000. It was a lot of negative sentiment, which I discussed extensively. I just thought there were great opportunities there.

Interesting, because John Embry, who has said gold is going to the moon, said recently, "I don't necessarily say gold's going to go up a lot, but if the U.S. dollar goes down and gold's valued in U.S. dollars, then gold will go up."

I cannot disagree with that statement. So the fifth reason for me being in energy was the value of money depreciating. There was very good work done by Sprott and I do read his website. There's some very good work done by a lot of smart people, talking about the level of U.S. debt. As Sir John Templeton said, throughout history, governments have almost always preferred to lessen the burden of their debt with inflation. In the long run, I think inflation is going to be a serious issue.

Templeton said that?

Well, he said that in the past at certain times, but I believe that at this time. I certainly have been striving to try to keep my investors' returns ahead of inflation.

Just to give us another context, we've talked about uranium and some other industrial product companies. What was the big thing you saw with UTS Energy in 2004? People thought it was crazy four years ago to say that Canada had an oil deposit as big as Saudi Arabia.

Well, again, this wasn't rocket science. UTS had proven recoverable reserves. I started buying it back in 2004. When I was buying it a few years ago, I started buying it in the neighborhood of $0.70. At that price, based on their proven reserves, you're buying oil at $0.08 a barrel. I was bullish about the price of oil, so I thought oil prices are probably going to go up. I also thought that this was a very cheap way to buy oil. It was that simple. It had proven oil reserves, and it wasn't maybe. I just thought as oil prices went up, the market would recognize this value at $0.08 a barrel. I want to talk on another one of my points here, which I think is very, very important. There is too much emphasis placed on precision. I don't need exact numbers to make decisions. Now, was it exactly $0.08 a barrel? No. It might have been $0.06 a barrel, it might have been $0.09 a barrel, but it wasn't $5 a barrel. It just looked so outstandingly cheap that, yes, I did take a big position in it, and it served our investors very well. I just said, "Here are the assets. Here are proven reserves, and these are what the proven reserves are."

In the big picture it didn't matter if it was $0.08 or $0.09.

Well, yeah. The big picture is I thought oil prices were going to go up. It would seem to me that if you can buy oil at $0.08 a barrel and it looked like a pretty good management team running the company, then it looked to me like it would be something that could do well.

Let's discuss the difference between the Resolute Performance Fund and the Resolute Growth Fund. There's administrative differences and there's investment differences?

The Resolute Growth Fund was a public mutual fund offered by prospectus and subject to the rules and regulations of a public mutual fund. The Resolute Performance Fund is a private fund offered on a very restricted basis by offering memorandum. The Performance Fund is run in a pretty similar fashion. In other words, we have a separate custodian who's Royal Trust. I do not short sell in the Performance Fund, and the Performance Fund is also RSP eligible. I'm simply trying to continue on doing the job that I started in 1993; to run a fund as best as I could with a moderate cost structure to investors.

Do you ever wish you took the opportunity to short?

Shorting is a very, very hard business. It's a very stressful business. You can face theoretically an infinite loss when you short something, and it also relies on short-term timing. You can short something and it can go up a lot before it ends up going bust. It's not what I like to do; I guess I like to sleep at night. I'd rather make a long-term investment that may go up or down, but it's got a finite risk to it because if you buy something, it can only go to zero. As I said, it's more of a game I think for young people, but I like to go home and sleep at night, and it's too much stress and too much risk. I have shorted successfully and unsuccessfully in the past when I was younger. It's a very tough business that requires short-term stuff, which is really, really hard to do. It's one of the toughest games. Let me just make one other point on this. Again, I'm paraphrasing Warren Buffett. He made his billions not by finding eight-foot bars to jump over, but finding one-foot-high bars to step over. In other words, there's many, many ways to be successful in investing, and short-selling is one of the toughest ways, and you need to be very smart, very skilled, and have very good nerves. It's just not something that I'm comfortable doing. So no, we will not, and short-selling is not allowed in the Performance Fund. I have no desire to do it.

Without stop-losses, when you're short, your maximum gain's 100 percent and your maximum loss is unlimited. That's not a very good risk reward.

I actually disagree with your statement. You cannot be guaranteed that a stop-loss can be executed—or a stop-buy. Technically, it's a stop-buy. For example, what happens if the exchange halts trading and something happens? It's just not my game. I'm quite happy to let other people do that business. You don't have to be in every business. All you have to do is find a business that works for you. You don't have to try to do everything. In the past, we found we were able to be successful with our clients without investing directly in Asia, and we don't have to short sell. The Growth Fund's never short sold, and Performance has never short sold. We don't have to do that. There's lots of ways that are less stressed to try to make money.

In the Performance Fund, because it's an OM product, you're allowed to lever. Would you ever do that?

We gave ourselves provisions to leverage, and I will never say never. My preference is to pay for what we have. As I said, when you start getting over-levered, you're relying too much on short-term fluctuations. I would suspect that some players in gold or silver in recent correction who were overlevered got shaken out and lost a lot of money. They may be very well right and the long-term prognosis for gold and silver is very good, but they turned out to be very wrong because by getting overlevered they were shaken out in a short-term correction. I'm not comfortable using a lot of leverage and I prefer not to use it. We gave ourselves some provisions in the fund to use some leverage, but we have not used it. I don't want to make a forward-looking statement, but I'm just saying it's not something I'm comfortable using. We get enough volatility without having to borrow money.

With eight stocks?

Yeah, without borrowing money.

You looked at the supply/demand picture outlook for oil and also for uranium. What do you think for gold or base metals?

In the long run, I believe that the value of the U.S. dollar will drop considerably. So I'm generally positive about the value of most commodities. There may be a specific commodity that I'm not an expert in. I think it's important not to try to hold myself out as being an expert in everything. I don't know a lot about a lot of the base metals, so I can't speak for every base metal because I don't understand them, nor am I well read on the individual supply/demand functions. As a general statement, I would feel that in the long run the price of commodities will generally go up because I feel the value of money will generally go down. Of course there will be corrections all along the way.

Analysts like to call it "performance attribution," but where have you achieved your performance over the years? Obviously, it's been commodities for the last few years, but it was pretty mixed in the '90s.

Yeah. We were an eclectic mix of small-cap stocks in the '90s. We were in a lot of junior oils from 2000. We started getting the junior oils in 2000 and were pretty heavy in junior oils till 2004. Then we started shifting our emphasis to uranium and oil sands after 2004. It's laid out in that letter. As I said, we put a lot of stuff on our website that I think that might be helpful.

Is there some way you can say how much of your research is quantitative versus qualitative? How important is management?

To answer your question, all are of critical importance. Quantitative, qualitative, and management are all of critical importance. All three are. I'm not trying to be obtuse, but it's being flexible in different situations. As I said, it's hard to pigeonhole me. Different situations, qualitative is more important than quantitative. In other situations, quantitative is more important. All three items are of critical importance in every idea that I make.

I made up the cockroach one, too. I thought that was an interesting view compared to the dinosaur.

Yeah, it is a very good one. I don't know if I want to compare myself to a cockroach, but it is a fun metaphor, yeah. Nice one.

Have you ever been running the fund and not been able to find stocks that fit your criteria? If that happened, would you just say, "We'll sit on cash for a while?"

Absolutely. Yeah. If I felt I needed to, I would not hesitate to go to 100 percent cash if I felt that was what the appropriate thing was. There's no mandate in the fund that says we have to be 100 percent invested or we have to look like the market. I just try to use my judgment and do the best I can, and I don't want to put on rigid constraints on what we're doing.

Were you fully invested in 2001 and 2002 during the general bear market?

I was heavily invested. There were tremendous opportunities at the time. It was a wonderful market for us. I was quite heavily invested, maybe 97 percent. It was a wonderful time to be invested. I remember 2001 and 2002 obviously a little bit differently than you remember it because they were great years. They were great years for us. As I said, it was bad years for large parts of the market, but large parts of the market we just weren't in. No one held a gun to my head and said that I had to be in tech stocks in 2001.

You become more confident over time. Say you wanted to invest in oil in 1994 when you first started—people said you were crazy, and it was against the herd mentality. Would you have been as confident at that time as you are now?

I don't know if I would use the word more *confident*. *Confident* is almost a synonym for *cocky*. As you get older, you have the benefit from more experience. Certainly I've been investing for investors since 1980, and having experience has been tremendous. This time we've seen rampaging markets where people were euphoric and very scary times when people were absolutely scared silly. The day after the crash in '87, I remember it like it was yesterday. I remember panic when the first Iraqi war broke out. I remember the panic after September 11th. You'll have periods where people are very euphoric. You have periods of time where people are very despondent. You learn to keep your head about you and be rational.

Well, that's what creates the opportunity, right?

Exactly. That's what creates the opportunity.

Being concentrated in your positions, how have you been able to be relatively consistent? You say, "Gee, we lost money in three years," but three years out of twelve when you have an extremely concentrated portfolio is fantastic, really.

Well, in fairness we did have blowups. About twice, the Growth Fund declined by about a third. A couple of times, the fund declined by about 20 percent. Now, that wasn't over the year, but they are reflected in those numbers in a calendar year. Both funds, Growth and Performance, on a day-to-day level, have been quite volatile. Every week, we're in the top ten list for stocks, going up or going down.

Not to equate investing and gambling, but some of the same attributes make us successful in both. Have you had a few big winners out of all the stocks that you've bought which have been responsible for a lot of the performance?

No. Let's put it this way: I don't play poker, so I can't comment on your poker analogy. With the performance of the funds, it's been a relatively few ideas that have made us a lot of money. I haven't had thousands of good ideas. I haven't. It's been relatively few.

If you're wrong on something, do you average down in it a lot of times? Or do you cut your losses quick and get out?

What do you mean by "wrong"? I don't understand that.

You think the management's good, you think the prospects for this company are good. The stock price goes down and the fundamentals of the company change. Maybe the management changes, whatever the case. Are you going to take that as an opportunity to buy more stock and say, "I'm getting it cheaper?" Or are you going to say, you know, "Things have changed...."

What do you mean "changed"? Changed for the better or changed for the worse? I don't understand the question.

Changed for the worse, fundamentally. Are you going to say, "This is a short-term blip. I'm going to bring down my cost," or do you say, "Let's get rid of it"?

Okay. Your question's still unclear, so let me try to answer what I think you're asking. First of all, we're looking at facts about the company. If facts about the company deteriorate, will you sell? Of course. If the price rises, would you say, "If I buy a good company and the facts remain intact but the stock goes down, will I buy more?" Yes. If the stock simply goes down because the stock goes down, it may create a buying opportunity. If it goes down as a result of deteriorating facts, I might just sell and take a loss. It depends on the rational facts. Let's give you an example. When I had some extremely good news about my uranium stocks and the price went down, I used that as an opportunity to buy more. In another situation a few years ago, I had an extremely good price movement in a stock when the fundamentals did not reflect it. In other words, they were not hitting what I was hoping them to achieve, but the stock went up a lot anyway. I sold. You have to distinguish between the things that are happening—the material things that are happening at the company that are relevant to the valuation of the company and the price. So if the market is going manic-depressive in its valuation of the stock because people are happy or people are sad or they read an article in the *Globe* today and they get nervous or excited, that is one fact. If I hear some material bad news about a company and the stock goes down, will I take a loss? The answer is: of course. I want to tell you something. It's important to take losses because part of humility is saying you're not going to be right all the time. So if you've made a mistake, your original premise is wrong, take a loss and move on. Does that answer your question?

It does. "Material" was the key. If the company has a bad quarter and the stock is down, would you look and say, "The bad quarter was not a material event here which is going to change the future of the company." Obviously, you'd take that as an opportunity to buy.

Strive for effective rationality. Do your homework. If you buy a stock and the company is not working out for your original premises and you're losing money, and the prospects don't look good, sell it and move on. I've taken many losses over the years—many important losses. If you've bought a stock and it's gone up a lot but the prospects still look good, you hold them. The implication there is that I don't make decisions based solely on price cues, and that's what a lot of people do. That's going back to being a technician or a chartist. Just say, "What has materially happened to the company? Is my whole basic premise wrong?" For example, when uranium stocks correct, does that mean the uranium story is finished? Not if the price of uranium is going straight up.

I once heard somebody say, "When do I decide to sell?" They ask themselves, "Would I buy the stock with the fundamentals that it has today at this price today?" If I would buy it based upon that, then I con-

tinue to hold it. If I wouldn't buy it today, then I get rid of it."

That was one of the questions that you had for me, and that's just as good an answer. I agree with that statement. You just constantly revalue it.

One of the most important decisions that I learned as a retail broker is that you sometimes have to take losses. I learned that very early in my career. If you're wrong and you now have new information that you're wrong, you take your losses and move on. I would suggest to you that it's harder for a retail broker to do this because then you have to deal with the client. There's a bias there I think when you're dealing with retail clients. Retail clients love taking profits and they hate taking losses. It's hard to do that as a retail broker, and that's what I endeavour to do. It's easier to do it in a fund because there's not someone looking over your shoulder on every trade. It was a discipline that I had to learn as a retail broker, and it's much easier to do when you're running a fund.

The average person wants to hold on to their losers and they want to sell their winners.

That's one of the most common mistakes.

So ultimately you end up with a portfolio full of losers. You can't help it. They're all losers and there's no winners.

I inherited over the years client portfolios with a whole bunch of dead stocks. I'd say, "Where did these come from?" They just hold onto the stocks forever that are going down.

It's going to get back to the price you paid, right? If you paid ten bucks and it hits $9.90, we're waiting for ten.

So this goes back to our whole original theorem about the brain. The brain is not wired to make good decisions.

What events would make you re-examine your thesis?

Anything and everything. Anything and everything could happen, there could be a thousand events. I'm constantly testing and retesting my thesis.

Were you interested in investing as a kid before you got into the business?

No.

Did you have any jobs before the investment business?

Well, I had a lot of jobs but nothing to do with investing. I would say that I spent a lot of time when I was a kid playing games such as chess, cards, Monopoly, and I think they certainly were of help.

Do you remember the first stock you ever bought for yourself?

Yes, I do. It was Mitel. I made a very small profit on it, and I sold it. After I sold, it just went up and up and up and up. I sold it way too soon. I bought 100 shares of Mitel and I think it went up close to 50 times after I sold it. So I sold it way too soon.

When do you see yourself retiring?

Hopefully not for a long time. I love investing and I enjoy it very much. Hopefully, if my health stays good and, the regulatory environment allows me to, I would like to continue working for at least another twenty-plus years.

If you love it, then it's not a job.

I enjoy it very much. It's wonderful and I'm blessed to have some very good unitholders, many who've been with me for a long, long time. I have tremendous friendships with a lot of them. As I said, my goal in life wasn't to run the biggest company in the world and to have a gigantic family of funds, trying to be all things to all people. We're just trying to run a good fund and keep our unitholders happy and serve them well.

Thank you, Tom.

The Resolute Way: Tom Stanley's Investment Philosophy

Be a Long-Term Investor

Too much emphasis is placed on short-term fluctuations. It is easier to anticipate long-term trends.

Have a Flexible Approach

Change is the only certainty, and as markets change, one should change as well.

Actively Look for Ideas

I find many of my best ideas; they don't find me.

Be Skeptical

Check facts directly. Strive to understand the bias and potential conflicts of interest among the sources that provide them.

I Eat My Own Cooking

My only stock market investment is the Resolute Performance Fund. This aligns my interests with the rest of the unitholders.

I Buy My Best Ideas

I prefer to buy only my best ideas.

Filter Out the Noise

One of the greatest challenges is to filter out the noise and use only what is relevant.

Be Thrifty

Moderate costs facilitate moderate fees. Moderate fees facilitate performance.

Outperform by Being Different

To have a chance of outperforming the market, invest differently than the market.

Know Your Limits

It is just as important for me to know what I don't know as it is to know what I know.

Stay Humble

Stay humble or the market will make you humble.

Being Small Is an Advantage

It is easier to outperform being small.

Apply Spiritual Principles

An important measure of one's success is how much he benefited his fellow man.

Investing Is Not a Team Sport

The best decisions are rarely made by committee.

A Good Card Player Does Not Show His Hand

Confidentiality is essential for successful small-cap investing.

Too Much Emphasis Is Placed on Precision

I don't need exact numbers to make decisions.

Be a Contrarian

Being a contrarian is harder in practice than in theory.

Strive for Effective Rationality

Do the homework, know the facts, and make decisions based on the facts.

Herb & Randall Abramson
A High-Wire Value Act with a Safety Net

"If you can get somebody who's a good value manager and also is better at timing the ins and outs of those value stocks, then you're going to do better. I think that sort of describes us."

I set up my first meeting with Randall Abramson on a trip to Toronto. I confirmed the time but not the place. Relying on an old address I had been given for Trapeze Asset Management, I showed up on time, finding a vacant building that was obviously deserted, with a broken window or two. I thought, "Wow, I've seen some simple offices and even a couple that are a bit tattered, but this is a doozy." Calling my assistant, I was relieved to find out that Trapeze had recently moved locations, and was pleasantly surprised when I finally arrived at their offices.

The firm is run differently than most, not having a particular product that they manage. Instead, they have private clients, with a series of portfolio managers who run managed accounts from Trapeze's model. The portfolio managers manage individual client relationships and come up with ideas for the model portfolios. It is a system that works, as a 23 percent annualized return since October 1998 for the Long-Only Composite portfolio are numbers that most others only dream of. As you may recall, 1998 was a horrific year for small cap stocks in general. Small stocks went down more than the overall market in the huge corrections caused by the Russian debt crisis and the ensuing debt market deep freeze, but they didn't recover like the rest of the market. Needless to say, starting a fund in mid-1998 was a dicey proposition.

How did a firm get named Trapeze Asset Management? Simple: their investment process is much like a trapeze act. First, a trapeze artist looks down on the world, having a top-down perspective. Second, investing in the market is like walking a tightrope at times. Third, the firm's value discipline tends to give it the safety net needed to avoid disaster, when a mishap happens or a sudden gust of wind blows things around. I conducted the interview with Randall Abramson, co-founder and CEO of Trapeze. Randall explained that the firm used a proprietary model that was developed by Dr. Verne Atrill, whose work has been carried on by Ross Healy, someone I have met with many times. Basically, it looks for several variables that are identified to be determinants of stock pricing. One of the most important intricacies of the SVA (Structural Valuation Analysis) process is finding companies with so-called efficient balance sheets. I call it the "Goldilocks" approach to balance sheet analysis. Remember how Goldilocks tried the three bowls of porridge that belonged to the bears, finding one too hot, one too cold, and one "just right"? Well, the SVA methodology identifies balance sheets that are underlevered, ones that are overlevered, and ones that are "just right," effectively using the most efficient amount of leverage or debt. So I guess if you think of Goldilocks swinging on a trapeze, you will understand the investment process of Trapeze Asset Management.

If you want to read what I consider to be some of the most informative and most hilarious quarterly newsletters in the business, make sure to go to www.trapezeasset.com. Whether they talk individual stocks or a top-down perspective, you will be laughing all along the way, and then you will get to the end and say, "Wow, that was also chock full of valuable market information." Who said money managers have to be boring?

Bob:

How did you originally get involved in business, and how did Herb? Was there always an interest in the stock market?

Randall:

He was the corporate lawyer for Goodman and Carr. He was counsel for Connor Clark before they were even Connor Clark. They were Bayshore, or something like that, and he was a corporate lawyer for about thirteen years. Then he got into the business and spent almost seventeen years, just over that, at Connor Clark, and then we started our own shop.

I was in investment banking and became a portfolio manager with Hodgson Roberton Laing, which, funny enough, is where Irwin Michael also came out of, although he was on the fixed income side. I started right in the equity side and spent five years with them and then joined my father, and we've been at it ever since—ten years together now.

What was Strategic Advisors?

We started with Abramson Partners Inc., and then we started Strategic Advisors, and then it became Trapeze Asset Management.

Why the name change to Trapeze?

The original Strategic name came about because we wanted to affiliate ourselves with Ross Healy. Ross is where we've licensed our timing methodology from. The name Strategic was generic, and we were getting sort of lost in the shuffle with all the other Strategics of the world. We wanted something that would really stick out, particularly in the U.S.

There's a SAC in the U.S. too right? Steven Cohen?

Steve Cohen's company, yeah.

He gets 3 percent plus 50 percent of profits as his performance fee.

Yeah, whatever he's got—3.5 and 35 over nothing, I believe. It's crazy stuff.

And yourself, were you in law? Was your dad in law?

He was in law. I was not.

What was your undergrad?

I skipped right to B.Comm. I went to U of T into the B.Comm. and CFA, and that's all I thought I needed.

I'm giving you a revisionist view of the planet. I knew I wanted to be in the business from the get go. I was one of those guys who were in the finance club in high school and watching *Wall $treet Week* with my father—watching it from when I was a young lad. So I always knew I wanted to be in the business. I didn't know what I wanted to be in the business, but I always knew. It was my hobby from when I was a kid. So I knew I wanted to go to business school, and when I came out, I knew I wanted to be involved. I summered at Merrill Lynch in the mailroom as a kid and I loved it. I would sit there reading the research reports.

In the mailroom?

Yeah, and on the subway home.

Did you invest in stocks when you were young, when you were a kid?

Yeah. Yeah. A few things. I didn't....

Do you remember the first one you ever did invest in?

No, but when I joined Hodgson Roberton Laing, they had a portfolio of these companies. They had Royal Trust, they had Trizec and Trilon. I came and I said, "These might be good values, but I don't understand them, and I don't understand the values." We had to bring in another expert, Tom Jarnay, who was fabulous, from First Marathon and another fellow who's also a terrific investor. We were able to convince them to take them out of the portfolios, and it was a good thing because they all went to nothing. Dylex was the other fabulous one they held.

You started the firm in September '98. At that time, I think you had a couple of different mandates. You had long-only, and did you have the long/short mandate at that time?

The long/short didn't really start until '99.

So the long only record is since '98?

It was both, but we didn't really have shorts in the long/short accounts until then. We had accounts that were long/short accounts because even back in the Connor Clark days, Herb laid in the odd short. He was short for various different companies over the course of time. But it wasn't the sort of a normal course—let's do it all the time and range it between X percent and X percent.

At the time, there were not many long/short equity funds around.

Certainly not in Canada. Even in Canada, we'd do it a little different because we were running separately managed accounts. I don't think there's anybody else in Canada running separately managed long/short accounts that I know of. Funds, yes, but not separately managed accounts.

There was one fund called the BPI Global Opportunities Fund. It was run out of New York and then Orlando, Florida. At the time, in 1996, I said, "This is a good way to run money." I mean, if somebody is skilled enough to figure out how to do it, long/short equity can be superior.

Well, the shorts are a lot harder. I was just reading a piece in a value magazine I subscribe to where the fellow shorted a stock at $8. He rode it all the way to $100. He covered at $30. So he still lost a lot of money. Ultimately, it went to $2. So he was right in the end, but he lost a hell of a lot of money along the way. And his point was they don't teach you at business school about how to take pain on the short side. Your timing has to be different. Our trader here, his adage is "shorts are for renting, not owning." Usually when we get into a long, it's with a three-year horizon. When we get into a short, I'm happy to make my money in three weeks.

Well, yeah, losses are unlimited in shorts, and your gains are limited.

Which is why Buffett says, "Don't do it because the deck is stacked severely against you." In fact, he said something recently which really struck a chord. It was perfect. He said that "if you're brilliant at picking shorts, you're wasting your time 'cause you're obviously good at what you do. You should be plying your trade to the long side." It makes perfect sense because you could be making manyfold on your money instead of 100 percent every time.

Interesting.

Use the math. If you're good at what you're doing, use the math and probability is for you. Having said that, the goal in this game is to make sure the compounding continues through good times or bad.

Right. Well, the losses kill. If you take a 50 percent loss, from a portfolio perspective, you have to make 100 percent to get back to where you started from.

Correct.

There's a big team of professionals that you have here at the company. You don't get a lot of them at other places—it's one guy sitting there at a computer. How did that build out?

The team of professionals works insofar as we are set up sort of the same way Connor Clark was set up. It was basically a RE/MAX model. There were two or three models that they had, and then each PM sort of subscribed to that model. They had X percent of that model and they had a little bit of leeway. Then they had their own clients. RPMs are sort of the same, except they all climb onto our model. So we have essentially one model, and all the PMs subscribe to that model. The money is managed centrally, and the PMs act as two things: client servicers to generate more business and service the existing clients and asset mix. At the same time, they will give periodic ideas for us to put in the portfolios and act as a foil as well to make sure they're keeping us honest.

Right. So you have people servicing the clients and also giving you some research ideas?

Absolutely.

Now, let's just get into the strategy again. Not to pigeonhole you, because you can't pigeonhole strategies, but I think you consider yourself to be more value-oriented investors.

I don't mind being pigeonholed into value. But I do come from the Warren Buffett school, again, where he argues, "There's no such thing as value and growth. Is it valuable if it isn't growing?" Right.

I do come from the school of, "We don't like this cigar-butt approach of value," meaning you're never going to find us picking up that little piece of cigar butt to take that one last puff and make 25 percent. Our typical purchase is where we're finding something where it's a discount to fair market value, but that fair market value is going to be that much higher two or three years down the road. So even if the market at large doesn't recognize the disconnect between fair market value and market price today, we at least get the growth, hopefully, along the way. When we get the narrowing of the discount, ultimately we get the double whammy.

Right. Is another term for *fair market value—intrinsic value?*
Yeah. It's interchangeable.

Now that's the trick because how do you figure out that intrinsic value number? Warren Buffett says it simply. Just buy things at below intrinsic value, hold them, and you make $50 billion.
But what is intrinsic value?

That's where his expertise comes in. He's figured out the intrinsic value of companies and other people can't because it's not book value. It has something to do with the future, so I guess that's what we'll talk a little bit more about. How do you define value investing, if you were to give it one sentence?
But it can be many things. The one sentence is, "Buying something below intrinsic value." That's it. The bigger the discount, the greater of margin of safety.

Is there a percentage that you're looking to buy below intrinsic value—30 percent?
Typically, it's at least 30 percent below, but it depends on how quickly the company is growing. In other words, if it's a big cap U.S. healthcare name or something like that, that's a pretty steady ship, you're not going to worry about getting 30 percent. First of all, you're not going to get it at more than a 30 percent discount unless it's, like, Union Carbide with some Bhopal incident, and that's a once-in-a-blue-moon-type thing. Typically, you're going to not get much more than a 25 to 30 percent discount on those types of names. But if it's growing by 25 percent, you're already going to get 25 percent a year and the narrowing of the discount is going to give you that 30 percent over a two- or three-year period. Annualize that out and you've got a wonderful return. It depends on the market cap too. So if we're buying a small cap company, you don't want it to just be ten or eleven times earnings. You want that small cap company to be seven times earnings or below, because if you're wrong, you're stuck.

You look for an optimal balance sheet. But a lot of people say they look for something like a very strong balance sheet. I noticed you described it as, "Strong is important, but optimal is most important to make sure they're using their cash properly." Can you highlight that a little bit more? Because that's a great point.

The SVA methodology is balance-sheet driven. The SVA methodology was originally derived or created by Dr. Verne Atrill before Ross Healy partnered up with him. Ross has taken over the work since Vern died many years ago. One of the concepts behind the work is that you have to have an efficient balance sheet. An efficient balance sheet, according to the actual curve, means that you have to have an optimum use of leverage. We all know what an insolvent company is, one with a lot of leverage. None of us think about the fact that you can have a super-solvent balance sheet, somebody who is like a Microsoft, losing $30 billion of cash. Or in yesteryear in Canada, we had Moore Corp that lugged around a lot of cash.

Cisco and Intel—they're all the same.

You can be in an optimal point, but if all of a sudden you lever up, you're going to have the law of diminishing returns set in. If you get super-solvent, you also have diminishing returns, but not to the same extent. So what you want to have is make sure you're at the most efficient point. If you're de-levering, like GM perhaps selling off GMAC or what have you, you're going to get fabulous rates of return. If you're Microsoft, divvying out their special dividend, it's not as pronounced as a de-levering company. But all of a sudden, your ROE is turned back to normal. If you're wielding all this cash, especially in this day and age where you're only earning 3 percent on your cash, better off that cash is in somebody else's hands. It's all about having a high, stable, repeatable return on equity.

Okay. Then we'll get into the SVA a little bit more because it's obviously something that is proprietary to you, and whatever you can tell me, fine. Whatever you can't, that's fine too.

Yeah.

Benjamin Graham had his style. Warren Buffett used a little bit of Benjamin Graham and a little bit of Dodd. Then there are people like Bob Krembil, who was growth at a reasonable price, which was kind of value. I guess of those ones, would you look at yourself as similar to any of them? Do you need a catalyst when you buy stock?

No, we're not catalyst-type guys at all. We sort of snicker when we see people say, "Oh, they won't touch this stock because it's dead money." For the next six months, how does anybody know that something is going to be dead money? We always talk about up cards and down cards. You know what the up cards are. You have no idea what the down cards are. How can anybody know that there is or is not a catalyst? Sometimes things are very visible, and, yes, it's much better if there's going to be a catalyst. But if you're buying your thing at a good enough margin of safety, cheap enough, the catalyst can often just be a disconnect between fair market value and the market price you're paying for it. So that can be a catalyst in and of itself. That's usually our catalyst, and if the business is growing, and the numbers are going to be good, then it will be fine.

How is the market like a trapeze act?

Yeah. Well, let me answer it in another way, not to skirt around it. We chose the name Trapeze because the market is like walking a tightrope sometimes. First of all, our catch line is, "Higher Perspectives." We do a lot of macro work to emphasize certain sectors and to make sure when we're short and when we're not short. Most value guys will tell you, "I don't know where the market is going." We believe we can, to a large extent, time the market, and that's through macro thinking and, as importantly, the use of the SVA methodology.

Right.

That's a big deal. So that's the trapeze, you know. You're up above looking down on the planet. The other part of it is we're dealing with risk, and it's about how you deal with those risks. Unlike lots of investors out there, we don't believe in high risk, high reward. What they taught you at business school that you have to unlearn when you get out of business school is that risk and reward are always positively correlated. We believe that they're often in an inverse relationship. So what did I mean by that? I mean things can have fallen already, have already had their own bear markets, but intrinsic value may not have fallen. Or maybe it fell a little bit, but the stock market price fell a lot. There's a difference between perception and reality, and we play off of that disconnect. If that disconnect is really large, then we see that it's only a temporary thing, not a permanent thing, then that's a fabulous thing for us, and we'll try to play that.

Now, does your SVA process involve some macro, or is it separate?

No, it involves that as well.

Can you discuss how that works, in a nutshell?

In a nutshell, the SVA methodology is a timing methodology that breaks stocks down into price to adjusted net worth. Based on mathematical constants that are embedded in the methodology, we basically break down a stock into price to book value. We end up with a bunch of floors and ceilings, and those floors and ceilings are the same for all companies. So when we see a stock come down to a floor and inflect up, that's a good thing. It's a buy signal. When we see a stock go up to a ceiling and inflect down, that's a sell signal. Sometimes something will come down to a floor and fall right through it on its way to its next floor. That's also a sell signal or vice versa, a state transition up into the next zone, that's a buy signal. At the same time, if we can do it for an individual stock, we can do it for an aggregation of stocks, call it the Dow 30 or the TSX 60. We can aggregate all of the balance sheets as if the TSX 60 was one company or the Dow 30 was one company, and then we have a view of the overall market.

If we have the market go on sell, we can raise our shorts, raise cash, maybe buy some more golds or be more defensive with the kinds of things that we're buying. At the same time, if the markets are bottoming, we can buy more market type stocks less what I call non-market, smaller cap stocks that may march to their own drum and so on and so forth.

Do you always have longs and shorts in the portfolio?

We always have longs because there's always going to be something in the thousands of stocks out there that we like, that we think is cheap or undervalued. We've virtually always had shorts as well for the same reason, though we know that when the market is going up, a rising tide lifts all boats, and, therefore, we want to have fewer shorts on the way up.

Right. Do you do any pairs trading at all? Would you go long Royal Bank and short CIBC or something like that?

Generally not, because we're not a hedge fund per se like that. That's probably the safest thing to do with your money. You're generally giving some back because it would be unusual, very unusual, for the Royal Bank to go up and CIBC to go down. You might have the Royal Bank go up and CIBC go up less or vice versa. I'd rather go with: If I think the banks are going up, I'd rather be long the banks and short oils if I think the oils are going down.

Right. So you're definitely shorting to make money on the shorts rather than just for risk control?

It's a combination of the two, but it's not just for risk control. Otherwise, what's the point of doing it? You may as well just go long things and then shrink your longs as a risk control rather than going short and losing money on shorts. Our long/short portfolio has outperformed our long-only portfolio.

Exactly, which means you've....

That means we've added value. We've also made some mistakes on the short side, which have hurt us as well—which we're now trying to rectify.

Many managers on Bay Street have proprietary models that they use. Why do you think yours works a bit better?

Let's move away from the methodology for a second. I want to answer it this way. The markets typically give you 8 or 9 percent a year. If you get a good value manager, you're going to beat that by a little bit too, call it one or two points, and now you're 10 or 11 a year. If you can get somebody who's a good value manager and also is better at timing the ins and outs of those value stocks, then you're going to even beat that. I think that sort of describes us.

Sure.

Most of what we do is not necessarily driven by the work. The work comes in at the end of the process. Let's time our entry and exit. Here's an idea, and this is why we think it's cheap. This is what we really think it's worth. Here's the 50 percent disconnect because we're buying that proverbial $0.50 dollar. We think that dollar is going to be worth $1.50 or $2.00 in three years. That's a wonderful return potential, so we're interested. Now, if we're buying it at $0.50 today, where's that break point? Is it $0.42? Is it on sell? Is it on buy? Oh, it's on sell. Well, let's wait a few cents until it gets down to our floor. Now go and buy.

Right. Okay. Does the system look at some normal technical factors?

No, but it is a chart. Ross Healy, who we licensed it from, calls it true technical analysis. We're not taking out the pencil and the ruler and charting the point and figure or the 200-day moving average or any of that wonderful stuff. We do look at relative strength and some of those things from time to time, but they have tended to be noisy. I've tried to overlay our own individual work because the SVA work on individual stocks is about seven out of ten, in terms of the computer calling the buy-and-sell signal. On sectors and stock and markets, it tends to be eight or nine out of ten. So I like to increase that seven out of ten to something else. I've overlaid it with all these technical tools, but I've never really found anything that has done it yet.

Once the SVA model says the stock is at buy, do you look at the company's management?

Yes, it is very important. We're business owners before we're stock owners.

So there's qualitative and quantitative factors?

Absolutely. This happens to be a stock market, where things trade every day. At this auction market of ours, we can buy something today, and we can change our mind tomorrow. That's the beauty of investing in public companies.

Is it about a 50/50 breakdown of the qualitative and quantitative factors?

It's hard to say because the cheaper something gets, the more important the quantitative becomes. That's the best way to put it. The less important the qualitative becomes because, as Buffett said a few years ago when he was buying Korean stocks at two times earnings, he went out and bought ten of them: "I didn't need to know management. I needed to read the financial statements. How do you screw something up like that when it's that cheap?"

Does the system look at all the stocks in the TSX? Most screening systems will look at the top 500 stocks or top 800 stocks or whatever? But when you put a stock like Connacher Oil and Gas in the portfolio, it wasn't covered at all.

Well, that was an example of something that we didn't buy based on the work. That was a different thing when we bought that at something under $0.50. The company's land package was probably worth $0.90, and there was, at the time, a great potential for having an oil sands play there. Based on the fact that we had nothing to lose, it was a double based on just the sheer land. It had this tremendous upside from what they were about to do with the land. That was why we invested in that one.

It would be hard for a system to value a stock like that. There's got to be some intuition.

Correct. There was a different way of valuing that one at the time.

Most of what we do, we want to make sure that a company has earnings. We have been burned in the past by investing in too many names where there were no earnings. We will make that exception only if we're investing in a company that has hard assets like a land package, a mill, or a mine.

That was the question: As a value investor, how do you value companies like that?

We don't like things that are cyclical. We like things that are stable. We own one stock that is in the nickel and copper business, but there is nothing else that we'd consider terribly cyclical. The golds, I would say, are volatile but not necessarily cyclical. They're more secular. You will have a secular down trend with disinflation, and then you'll get a secular uptrend with inflation. You try to get those macro things right and get the commodity cycle right in terms of supply and demand of gold. Gold should have moved a long time ago, but there was an overhang from central bank selling and hedging and the carry trade. That now mostly is all evaporated, allowed the price to go back to its equilibrium. Therefore, it's allowed us to play it. But we think gold is a defensive play and not necessarily a cyclical commodity. Same with oil, we have to heat our home and drive our cars.

Do you believe that we've reached peak oil or that we're getting close?

Yeah. I think you're seeing it right now in the price. We just had a major correction in the price of virtually all commodities but oil. Oil was the one that was supposed to have this $15 to $30 terrorist premium or whatever in there, right? Well, where was that premium? It never came out of it, right? It's hung in beautifully. I believe that you're seeing right now the criss-cross between the supply and demand lines. I took Economics 101, and they don't teach you what the equilibrium price is when all of a sudden supply gets ahead of demand. What happens is the demand has to come down too so that your supply and demand equal at some point because your consumption can't exceed what is out there in supply. So I don't know where the price is going to have to go to get that to knock back that demand.

Well, it's interesting. The Saudis were desperate for drill rigs so they

could go find some oil. Why are they desperate to go find more oil? I thought they had hundreds of years of cheap oil there under the ground, but maybe that isn't the case.

You found a lot of stocks that were not covered by analysts. It seems like when stocks become popular and they have a big run, then analysts start to cover them. When that happens, a lot of the opportunity set for gain is gone. Can you comment on that?

Yeah, I've always had a theory. You asked me earlier about what was the first stock I ever bought. I don't remember how old I was when I bought this one, but I bought Meridian Technologies back when it was about $1. It was a die caster in the automotive business, and I sold it when it got to $11, which was nice. But it didn't make its real move until it sort of tootled between $1 and $4. At the $4 mark or so, all of a sudden, five analysts covered it, and then it took off from there. I always thought, and to this day, once the fifth analyst comes aboard, that's when the thing starts to move. Pan Ocean, which we owned, had, I think, four analysts. It moved very nicely, but I waited for that fifth analyst.

How important is insider buying or selling of the stock?

It can give a very good clue. We subscribe to a firm out of the U.S. that does insider buy-and-sell analysis. Anything less than 0.9 something, I believe, is a buy for the overall markets over a number of weeks. You can't read too much into it because, with managers, that's how they make their money and their livelihoods. The real good managers seem to be ones who don't take tremendous amounts of salary but are owner-operators and live for the appreciation of the stock price. You can't blame anybody for taking profits from time to time. When you see a person sell the brunt of their position or a disproportionate amount, especially when your view is the thing is really undervalued, then you really have to start to wonder.

Yeah, that's why some people say that the buying is more important than the selling.

Have you invested in large caps in the past?

Yeah. Our adage around here is "bigger is better." First of all, we can use our work more effectively to get in and get out. Also, if we have the story right on a large cap stock, the time value of money is on our side. We may not have the same discount from fair market value, although it happens. Sometimes, you get a real cheap large cap stock. But certainly you're going to make your money faster because there are thirty-two analysts instead of three to five analysts, and they're going to come around real quick once the fundamentals change.

Is there one large cap stock that stands out in your mind?

Well, I was just going to give you an example of a company, Nextel, that acquired or merged with Sprint. Nextel we were originally looking at because we were going to go short. It is a perfect example of something that happened very quickly, but we looked at it and they made $500 million free cash flow. We said this doesn't really look like a short to us. In fact, oh my gosh, if you multiply that out by four and divide it by the number of shares outstanding, and the stock was trading at $6 and change at the time, this looks awfully cheap. So we called the company and said, "Can we multiply this by four?" and they said, "Yeah." Well, why aren't the analysts doing that? Well, it's only one quarter. They want to see another couple of quarters before they come out in print and say anything. Well, we didn't wait for them. So we loaded up our position there, and it went up manyfold after that. It was a terrific one and we were able to use our floors and ceilings to get out and get back in.

Are there stocks that you have done that they call round trips? You go up, you ride it, and then you notice that they're overvalued or they're a good short candidate, and you short them?

I can't think of one at the moment because usually the companies that we're buying have tremendous fundamentals. Therefore, not really the short candidates. We have shorted, like back in 1999, 2000, good companies, that were ridiculously overvalued, like Cisco, Juniper, and these were pretty good companies but they had ridiculous valuations. Typically, we're trying not to short really good companies. I shorted Wendy's, which is a company that I have owned from the long side in the past. But it's not like we stopped, sold it, and then we turned around and shorted it. There was, you know, two years in between, or four years in between, where we watched the thing go to the moon, like Tim Hortons.

I think that was kind of overhyped though, Tim Hortons.

I think it was probably overhyped. Not necessarily Tim Hortons, because Tim Hortons is a very valuable franchise. The Wendy's franchise, it's a terrific well-run company, but it got overvalued based on the break-up value and the amount of Tim's in there.

Back to the shorts again. One of the risks of shorting is somebody is going to come in and pay 30 percent more than the market just because it's cheap. Do you employ stop buys?

Yeah, if something moves against us, we have these floors and ceilings, and we're trying to do our buys at floors. We're trying to do our sells, our shorts, at a ceiling. So if something starts breaking out to the upside from a ceiling, we get a buy signal in the work. Again, it's seven out of ten stuff. The computer, which tells me every day out loud because I've programmed it to say, "Buy, Sell, Short." If it says, "Cover," I better cover because, most likely, I'm going to be wrong. I've overruled it too many times, probably, to my chagrin.

Value managers tend to get into stocks early and get out of them early. Is that what you've tried to fix with the SVAs?

Yeah. One of the things that I like to say about the work is that it gets you out by giving you a sell signal. If there's no sell signal, it keeps you in, which, I think, was what you're getting at. In other words, we might play portfolio manager, so to speak, and if we've backed up the truck to an 8 percent weighting, which is typically the largest weighting we go to on book cost, and if all of a sudden the thing goes up 50 percent, well, we're going to have a 12 percent weighting. Now that may be a little bit much, so we want to start cutting it back even though the thing might be undervalued. Depending on the magnitude of how undervalued, we might let something run even from that standpoint. But the larger it gets in the portfolio, the more interested we are in shrinking it back.

That was the next thing, it's concentration in the portfolio. Do you believe in having a more concentrated portfolio?

Correct.

Right. How many? Twenty-five?

It could be anywhere from twenty to thirty names. Our typical weighting is about a 4 or 5 percent weighting, you know. Toe in the water would be 3 percent, and then 8 percent usually, but we've eclipsed that a couple of times.

Capacity is always a bit of an issue when you want to have some smaller cap names.

Bill Miller wrote a book recently, and he had an interesting point in his book. He said that your median market cap should be approximately the size of the assets under management. If you think about that mathematically, it kind of works. You don't end up too big. I think that's what's going to happen to us more likely than having too many names. We want to know the names really well and not have too much on our plate. I still want to be able to go home every night and have dinner with my family.

How do you define alpha, and why should somebody look for alpha?

The point of hiring a money manager, if you're going to pay them fees and not index, is to beat the market. Otherwise, you may as well do the low MER thing and get market results. So our point is to give an above-market result. If the market is typically 8 to 9 a year, then we ought to be 10, 11, 12 plus. If we're not that, there's no alpha. How do we achieve that alpha? Well, it's everything we've been talking about in terms of low risk, high reward, those types of things.

You mentioned here the long/short funds outperform the long-only fund?

When I look back, about 40 percent of the time, the shorts are going against us. We're trying really hard to diminish that. But then, 60 percent of the time, hopefully, it'll be working for us.

When stocks get down to very low valuations and everybody hates them, you would think it would be a little more difficult to make money on shorting them.

It's not as much about multiples as it is about the fundamentals of the business, because you can have something at a low multiple. Well, when do you buy the TSX? Usually, you buy the TSX when it's at a high multiple because the earnings are crap. Once you get to the low multiple, you want to get out.

Right. Right.

My father wanted us to short a ream of auto parts companies going back about two years ago, Ford and others. I looked, and I went, "What? They're just so cheap, such low multiples." But, boy, was he right. You know, if the fundamentals are souring, normally it doesn't matter what multiple it's trading at.

What is your max net long? Do you lever in the portfolio, or will you be over 100 percent net long?

I'll give you our max net long, yeah. We would go to 115 to 120 odd percent on the long side.

Have you ever been market neutral?

Not in the last few years. The largest short exposure we've had is 40 percent. So for every million bucks, we may have been $400,000 short, and we may have been maybe 80 percent long and 40 percent short. So we would have been 40 percent net long. That might have been our lowest exposure.

When was that? Before the Gulf War?

That was probably in 2000, the middle of 2000, and just before the Gulf War as well; we were pretty negative.

How did you get through 2000, 2001, 2002? How did things work out during that time, and what did you short?

Well, in 2000, we were short anything with a dot-com, I think because we were pretty fussy about what we picked. But as I mentioned a few names before, we were short in Canada names like Bid.com. It went to something in our work called the conservation limit, which is over fifty times adjusted book value. You cannot sustain a valuation above that, basically because you can't generate an ROE large enough to sustain that premium to book value for a period greater than a few months. Juniper was a perfect example. It actually went above that. We felt some pain for a few months, but, ultimately, I think we shorted at $160. It went to $220 or higher, and we ultimately covered at $50-something. We were short Nortel on three separate occasions. We had nothing against the company per se the first couple of times. The third time we actually thought, boy, the balance sheet looks particularly ugly.

Do you regard this as a North American portfolio? Or is it mostly Canadian?

We can go anywhere on the planet—go anywhere, any security, to make the client money. Having said that, because of time differences, language barriers, accounting standards, quarterly balance sheets versus semi-annual, I rely on balance sheets, timely information, and press releases to use our SVA methodology. Therefore, we've stayed close to home. Your best ideas tend to come to you randomly—the newspaper, clients, business contacts, and ours are mostly Canadian. So our portfolio has always been disproportionately populated with Canadian ideas. The Canadian market is also less efficient than the U.S. market and, at the same time, the U.S. has the best companies in the world still. We don't have the equivalent of Johnson & Johnson here in Canada unfortunately. Therefore, we love to play those companies when they become bargains. That's our favourite thing to do because I like to call those "lie on a beach" stocks. I don't have to worry about the portfolio. I know that Johnson & Johnson isn't going anywhere.

They treat the stocks like stocks.
Sometimes, yeah, that can happen.

Would you ever own bullion or certificates in the portfolio?
It's not our game because we want that double whammy. We may be wrong about the gold bullion. We think we're going to be right about the gold stocks. In gold, like an oil rig, now we think we're set up for the triple whammy because we're going to get the growth of the production of the company. We're going to get the narrowing of the discount from intrinsic value and market price, and we're going to get potentially the commodity price going up. Pan Ocean, our largest position at one time, was a very valuable stock sitting at $44-odd dollars. We thought it was worth $60-something, based on $50 oil. But at $75 oil, they make $15 earnings per share.

Now maybe we'll talk about emotions and investing. The average investor is wired up incorrectly. How do you get over that with people?
You don't. You have to politely brow beat. You have to be strong with your convictions, be firm. What drives me crazy is the client who comes in for the minimum and says, "I'm going to test you out." Well, as I said, "Okay. Well, let's follow this through. Now I'm up for you a lot of money a year down the road, or two years, or whenever that period is. Test is over. It has been successful. Now you're going to give me more money. Let's say I'm down. Is that an unsuccessful test? Because if I'm down, you should definitely be giving me more money."

The fact that you're giving me the money to manage is not the test. The true test is for you to ask me all the questions that you can to study us to make sure that we're the right fit for you. We have a discipline here about how we invest. That's not going to change. These are businesses, and businesses get better and worse, and people analyze them, and there's true values for them, and those things will never alter.

When you look at your net long exposure, for example, do you do a beta adjusted net?

Not quantitatively but qualitatively. We've had periods before where we wish we had done that quantitatively, because the big dot-coms of the world are going crazy against us, and the small cap stocks are being ignored. That's how we were able to find tremendous value on the long side in 2000, because everyone was playing tech and ignoring everything else. Companies that we could never touch before, like Abercrombie & Fitch that had 30 percent comps and spectacular and enormous returns on capital and great balance sheets, all of a sudden were trading at twelve times earnings. We ended up buying Abercrombie & Fitch, probably one of the twelve times, and we averaged down. It got down to five times earnings ex the cash they had on their balance sheet. It was ridiculous.

So you will average down on stocks if they still fit your parameters?

We may, if it gives a sell signal. If it's cheap enough, we may stop buying because it's on sell, and we'll wait for the next floor to start buying again, another advantage of ours.

What do you consider your biggest mistake in the portfolio?

It's probably on the short side. It was not covering some of the shorts quick enough, thinking that we were right on the overvaluation and the fundamental souring. It was either waiting until it was too painful to stick with them or just not acknowledging that the market sometimes wants to take things on a frolic of their own for longer than any human could possibly withstand it.

How about on being right? Do you know what your biggest win on a stock was?

Yeah. We've been around Pan Ocean for a number of years, which before that was Ocelot. Actually, in between it was Pan African, and they've spun out Lynx, and so we've been there for a long time. But I think we started buying it at $5 initially. We loaded up at $2.50 on an average down basis. It spun out a company that's trading at $5 now. It spun it out, so our cost is $1 and change.

If you add the East Coast, which is $5 to the Pan Ocean, you got almost $50 for our $1 and change. That was pretty good, in about seven or eight years.

In April of 2000, you wrote about the danger in the market and the fact that things were going in the wrong direction. Was that something that the computer brought up, or was it qualitative?

It was both. It was three things. Macro told us that it couldn't continue. It just smelled bubble to us. People still say, "Well, there was no bubble." Oh my God, I don't know what they're smoking. The second part of it was from a strict SVA break-point perspective, floors and ceilings. It had given a sell signal; therefore, it was on sell. Finally, from a valuation standpoint, we were not only with most big cap stocks, but the markets as a whole were way above fair market value, and particularly the NASDAQ, which had to have been the leader. So that was the wicked combination, all of those factors.

How about the people that say there's a commodity bubble?

The commodity prices might be high, but if China implodes and the developing world implodes, which I don't think, then Armageddon is going to happen there. I suppose if you had a flu pandemic, you could have a multi-year problem. But I think we're into something that is multi-year—democracy, global village. This is something that we're all going to be telling our children about that is pretty exciting.

We don't use $175 oil in our budgeting purposes. We use $50. If it works at $50, my gosh, it's really going to work at $100.

You have a hurdle rate of 8 percent. Is that right?

Yeah. Sorry. I want to complete one thought on the bubble thing before I forget about it. In the bubble, you had NASDAQ stocks selling at, as we discussed before, fifty-odd times book value. That was insane. These were multiples of earnings that were crazy, and multiples of revenue. These were nonsensical valuations never seen before. That fifty times book value, which we called the conservation limit, we saw at least a dozen companies. Priceline.com, Bid.com, AOL, Dell. Before that, we'd only seen a couple, like in the previous ten or fifteen years. That was a bizarre period. You're not seeing that in commodity land at all now. I'm buying companies at three, four times earnings—six times, seven times. This is ridiculous.

So this is very different. Now, commodity prices may come way off. I can't tell you that copper is not going back to $1.50. It could even go lower. I mean, it bottomed at $0.50 a few times. That's where it normally bottoms. Will it revert the next time we get a recession, a global recession? Maybe.

When you didn't cover the shorts fast, did you change the system at all, or did you modify it?

Who wants to keep making the same mistake over and over again?

Even John Templeton said, "If you're doing things the same as you were twenty years ago, you're not going to be doing it right."

He also said something else, which is, "The best investors are the ones who screwed up early on in their careers." We went through an awful period in 1998 when we were invested in a few too many concept names. A couple of these names ended up making us a gob of money later on. In the meantime, we lost money for clients in '98, then lost too many clients and said we would never do that again. So we went out, and that's when we sought the methodology, and that's when we said we're only going to invest in things that have earnings to make sure that we were doing it better.

Do you have any role models in the industry other than your dad? He'd like that?

All the value guys like Buffett and Phil Fisher and Ben Graham.

It's funny because value investing seems to be sustainable. You see very few growth guys that over twenty years continue to put out good numbers. It happens. They can do it, but there's more value managers.

I think Bill Sands is his name, who was a great value guy. He had a line, which was great, and his line was that "value investors spend 80 percent of their time depressed and 20 percent euphoric." He said, "Momentum guys spend 80 percent of their time euphoric and 20 percent looking for a job." I think growth comes in and out of vogue. So does value. If value is defined as buying cheap stocks that are under their true intrinsic value, how can that ever go out of style? Like if you're going to go buy groceries, that's saying to someone, well, you shouldn't go buy something cheap. Always go to the most expensive store and buy it there. It's illogical, right?

Any books that you think are good books for people to read?

I think reading the Warren Buffett annual reports is fabulous. I think that reading the two Peter Lynch books, the *One Up on Wall Street* and the sequel to that one, are both terrific books.

Your system is sustainable, and that's important.

Correct. We did make a couple of great calls. We were invested in Petro Kazakhstan from $3.50 through $45. That helps. We've also made it in Ambercrombie & Fitch, in Bristol-Myers, in Honeywell and Kimberly Clark, and other names along the way too. So I know that the work works in all sorts of ways, and value is never going to not work. There might be periods where growth outperforms the way we're doing it because people decide to take momentum in a completely different direction. Or we'll underperform because, all of a sudden, technology will do well and go to the moon. You know, people might say, "Oh my God, I got to get into nanotechnology. It's the place to be," and all those stocks go sky-high.

Pfizer, Merck, Bristol-Myers have just been doing nothing for years.

The fundamentals are in retreat because there are threats from generics. Nobody's been coming out with new blockbusters. You've had margin erosion. You've had governmental pressures on pricing, both from Europe, from the U.S. at large, from individual states making preferred lists for various drugs. We've tried to make one pass at Pfizer and did it unsuccessfully. We did make a successful pass at Bristol-Myers, but that was before most of these headwinds. But some of them are getting cheap enough now, like Pfizer. Another couple of dollars and we'll likely have to invest there again because it's just getting too cheap. Eleven times earnings for that kind of franchise where they literally spend almost $8 billion a year on R & D—that's cheap. My goodness, they got to find something for that amount of money.

Have you ever looked at what I call the bachelor's stock, Philip Morris?
Yeah.

Beer, cigarettes, and Kraft Dinner. What else is there, right?
It's the one thing that we don't buy around here. I can buy a gambling stock. I can buy a defense stock, and I can buy plenty of different things. I find it very hard given the number of people who have been around me—family members

that have passed away from cancer—to buy a tobacco stock. I just find it a very difficult thing to do. You can make the arguments that people can do whatever they want with their own lives. That's fine, and I don't disagree with that. I mean, now you're hearing second-hand smoke stories. There are arguments against that too. But I don't have to profit off of it. I know it's zero-sum game, and whether I own the shares or someone else, the share still exists out there. From that perspective, it's a zero-sum game, but it just doesn't feel right to me. I wish cigarettes didn't exist.

Well, maybe we can get to the point where the stocks are overvalued, then you can short it.

Maybe. You'd think they would be losing some litigation one of these days. I heard the other day that light cigarettes are actually worse for you.

Really? Is that right?

Because you smoke more. You're less likely to give it up, and you think you're treating your body better when you're not. I don't know.

Sentiment is terrible here at the beginning of '08, and value investing has gone through a rough patch.

There was a stat from the AAII survey. You had 2.4 bears to every bull. You're back to that exact same stat again, jumping back above the 2 mark. Anytime you get below 2 or above 2, as the case might be, you're into a territory where it's uncharted. Every time you've gone above 2 bears to every bull, you've had a bull market ensue. The average up is 24 percent with no instances of decline in the following twelve months. So, this is the point of maximum pessimism. It's just that we keep bouncing off of it. Every day they take out another one, and it's a take-no-prisoners approach. We had one today where one of our retailers announced that they weren't giving guidance for the following year. They missed earnings. Instead of doing $0.06 they did $0.02, sort of who cares? The long-term outlook for the company, such as earnings power is completely intact. But they took the stock down by 23 percent nevertheless. It's just crazy stuff.

I think it was Rohit that mentioned to me that 97 percent of the return in 2007 was in six stocks in the TSX: Agrium, Potash, RIM, Alcan, BCE, and Petrobank.

Yeah.

That happened in '99, right? It was a very narrow focus, and it pushed the market up in value.

It has to come back because you can't have things that are trading at half off for this long. We went through a period in 2000 where the big cappers were twenty-five and thirty times earnings. The small cappers and the value line index, which is 1,700 equal-weighted stocks, was twelve or thirteen times back then. So it was pretty easy pickings to pick your average stock, but difficult to pick something that was bigger cap.

What happened is the big caps came down, and then started tracking fair value because they came down from twenty-five to thirty multiples to fifteen, sixteen multiples. Only recently, they've come down to ridiculous at thirteen times, right? Now all of a sudden, for the first time in ten years, we can look at a big cap stock because it's trading at 25 to 30 percent off. You have to be careful what you're getting into because we're into an economic malaise here. Suddenly, you've got discounts, which we didn't have before. At the same time, small cap went from that thirteen times earnings in yesteryear all the way up to nineteen times in the middle of 2007, so they were at a premium to big cap. So, that had to adjust back down. We missed that here, right? We were in our small caps because ours weren't at nineteen by any means. But the nineteen times P/Es came down and took everything else with it. We've now had a 30 percent correction into the Venture Exchange, which is Canada's proxy for small cap, and in the Russell 2000 Value Index.

Right. The Venture corrected in August 2007 and hasn't come back yet.

No. But it's off of its bottom. Its bottom was January 19th. It's off of its bottom as is the whole TSX, but from peak to trough, it was bloody ugly. A case in point to showing you how value isn't working, particularly in small cap land, is that we've made a great call here. We called bullion. We called oil, right? They're up ginormously. Had we played Newmont and Barrick in the last six months, we would have done really well. But our tiny little names just as well could have been selling widgets, not barrels of oil or ounces of gold.

There was a huge divergence between bullion and gold stocks, or small cap gold stocks, in early 2008. That'll fill in sooner or later.

Correct. I'm surprised you haven't seen the bigger companies taking over the smaller companies yet. Maybe it's because we're in this credit crisis. In gold land, you've got some companies that are trading for $600 an ounce. Then you've got these tiny little companies that are trading for $25 an ounce. I mean, that's just too big of a disconnect.

The costs are so high to go out and drill your own property. It's much easier to go and just buy some assets.

It's way easier now. I'm sure you could win these things for less than their 52-week highs, because they're so far off. People would be saying, "Okay, now." But companies are afraid to make boo-boos, so they don't necessarily go out and make a bid for an entire company.

Banks aren't even lending to each other in late 2007.

I've read though, recently, that you've even seen a couple of major company CEOs disposing of shares of their own companies and going out and buying a diversified pot of juniors. People in the know, the smart money, are buying the juniors now. They're so cheap.

Yeah, with the Venture down 30, there's going to be lots of stocks that are down in the 60, 70 range for that to happen.

I think there's unbelievable value in oil and gas. It's still the cheapest sector in the S&P in the U.S., oil and gas.

Is it because analysts don't believe that oil's going to be $100 a barrel?

Everybody's afraid this is a commodity oil bubble, and that there's a speculative development in the commodity prices.

Oil, base metals, etc., are not usually at highs if we're going into recession. Usually, you're going to start to see those commodities weaken because they figure the demand's going to be lower.

Well, it depends what's going in a recession. The argument is that, is this a U.S.-centric world anymore or not? So, the U.S. is having a slowdown, clearly. Canada isn't so much, South America isn't. The rest of the globe isn't, but Europe has slowed. Asia is still going gangbusters, and China's been growing at 9 percent for twenty-five years now? So it might slow from its new current 11 percent pace. But it's not going to go negative or a recession.

How in this environment do you avoid catching a falling knife? With U.S. financials, for example.

We haven't really been playing any of those because it's too tough to analyze both sides of the balance sheet. You're not sure how to value the assets because of the mark-to-market issues. There's off-balance-sheet stuff on the liability side that you don't quantify. I just don't know what's there. So we say, "Yeah, it looks cheap, but there's other stuff that looks really cheap here."

I think you've increased your U.S. exposure, right?

Yeah.

What sectors?

It's not as much of a sector thing, although we do have a penchant now for retail. Like the financials, the retails have been creamed.

You had Abercrombie?

We had that from yesteryear. We sold that. We've owned that five or six times in the last seven or eight years now. We sold that at the high $70s, a number of months back. I wish I had bought it back on that January 21st day, because it got all the way down to $68 again. In early '08, we were buying things like Office Depot. Office Depot fell all the way to its book value. It's only been there three times before, within the last twenty years. That's a thumbprint valuation. The company should have the ability to gain Staples-type margins. Staples now earns in excess of 10 percent operating margins.

The magic of value investing is that the companies that are going through trouble, the expectations become so low. Then the P/Es get compressed, and then when it comes out the other side, suddenly everybody's realizing that they beat expectations, and you get the P/E expansion too. You get the double whammy.

People talk about how you have to buy cyclicals when they're trading at huge P/E multiples, and sell them when they're selling at low multiples. We look at it the other way with some of these values, particularly in retailers. If we can buy these retailers at ten times trough earnings, and earnings are going up, it's pretty hard to go wrong when they've got good balance sheets. The companies are doing all the right things, and they're not terribly cyclical. We own another one today, DSW, which is the shoe retailer. It fell in the 24 percent range today. If we hack the numbers to bits here, it's a $13 share price. It's got $2, almost $3 a share in cash and no debt. Call it $10 ex the debt, and it's got $1-plus of earnings. So it is around ten times earnings for a company that's got a clean balance sheet. At the moment, traffic stinks, but if they just got back to where they were, margin-wise, in a normal operating year, like they did in '06, we think they can get a lot higher. If we get them back to $2-plus of earnings, and we think they can actually make $3-plus of earnings, that is going to get us a $40, $50 stock price. You're looking at a potential three or four times your money over the next two or three years, and with pretty low risk. We look at our upside over a three-year period. Ours is over 40 percent per year over a three-year annualized period, which is higher than it's ever been on a portfolio-wide basis. I don't know if we're going to get 40 percent a year, because we're going to make some mistakes along the way. In terms of expectations, it's as high as we've seen it.

You said with large caps, obviously, there's more value there. So would you move up the scale there?

Yeah, if we can, absolutely. Bigger is better. If you get it right, it happens faster. We bought United Technologies recently. We bought Walgreens recently. The businesses are steady ships, but they tend to get undervalued less frequently because the market is more efficient. As Ned Goodman pointed out in this morning's paper, you want to find something that's not just underloved but underowned. The big caps can be underloved, but they don't tend to be underowned.

Everybody that I talked to for this book were small cap managers, generally speaking, over the long term. That's where you're going to get the push for your dollar. So, you'll be back there, I guess.

The problem when you're owning small caps is even if you see a correction coming, you can't get out. That is fine if you're there for the long term and we make our decent returns, but you end up with a very volatile experience along the way.

I was listening to somebody a while ago, and he said, "You know, value investing underperforms for a period of time, and it only does it for about a year. You then see it bounce back pretty fast. It doesn't go on for years and years and years."

There was a great chart in *Investor's Digest* recently. It went back, I think, forty years. Value stocks were defined as the cheapest quintile of the S&P 500—you know, the lowest price to book values. He took those 100 stocks and how they performed over time. Basically, you made 200 times your money over a forty-year period, which nicely outperformed the S&P 500 itself. I don't remember if it was four or five periods, including this one, in early 2008, where you were down 20 percent. On a chart, that looks like a little blip. When you're going through it, it doesn't feel like a blip.

Yeah, investors always look at the chart and say, "Oh, that's no problem," because they see the end of the line.

Right. When you're in the middle of it, they extrapolate on that 20 percent, "Oh my God, what happens if I lose another 20 percent?" But we're seeing things now that are just shocking to me in terms of value, just shocking.

So you haven't seen this sort of thing since 2000?

In five years. I say it comes every five years. I try to warn the clients. As much as you warn them, they don't remember.

The money all flows in at the top, and out at the bottom.

People keep saying, "If you guys come out of this, I'm going to introduce you to all my friends." It's like, "Why? When we get back to our highs? Send them in now. This is buy low, sell high!" Buffett always talks about how perverse it is that value managers get hit with redemptions at times when they should be buying for people, not selling. That's because when Coach purses go on sale, everybody flocks to the store. Stocks go on sale, and everybody goes, "Oh my God, I got to wait for tomorrow. Maybe there'll be a better sale." You just close your nose and you buy it.

I think somebody mentioned to me today that Buffett's top five stocks in 1973-74 were down 65 percent or something like that.

That could be, that was a horrible hideous period. That's why he always says, "If you can't stomach a 50 percent decline in a stock, you ought not to be in it." He also gave out the stat that I think the average New York Stock Exchange stock in any given year fluctuates 50 percent from its 52-week high to its 52-week low.

Do value stocks tend to do well and come out of the bear better than anything else? Going into the bear, they get hit harder because people are worried if a business is having trouble.

I argue that value doesn't go out of style. It's just every once in a while everything goes down, including value. I don't know if the momentum is down any worse than value now. The stat that I see thrown about is that as you're going into a recession, momentum tends to do well and value gets creamed. That makes sense because companies where there's big fat earning streams, and revenues that are still growing nicely, hold up because valuations don't matter. People aren't dumping the stock because the business is still doing well, right?

It makes sense.

Then, as the bear market is culminating, my father-in-law likes to point out, "I remember the last one to fall in yesteryear was Koffler Stores," the former Shoppers Drug Mart. They take the best ones last and kill them, which is exactly what's happened this time around.

That happened with the tech stocks too.

Yeah. Well, that's right. They got killed at the end. That's just happened now, where the last ones to get hurt were the S&P. The Russell 2000 and the Venture Exchange started going down in May of last year. The NASDAQ 100 didn't peak until October. It didn't have its material fall until January of this year, the same for the S&P.

That happened in the Nifty Fifty stocks, right? In the early '70s, they went up.

Finally they had to at last give up, because there's a flight to quality, and then there's a flight from everything. There's a flight to cash. Right now, the stat is there's 20 percent cash in the average American's mattress. They've got, whether it be cash or money market instruments, 20 percent. We've only seen that go above 17 to 20 once before, which was the start of the whole bull market in '80-'81. It hit above 17. On two other occasions, that happened: at the end of the bear market in '90 and at the end of the bear market in '02. Just to finish up on your answer there, the value stocks tend to lead coming out of a recession. As soon as the recession starts, that's when value starts doing well. The average outperformance of value stocks is up 24 percent during that period.

All the growth guys say it's justified that Research In Motion has the same market cap as the Royal Bank. What do you think about that sort of thing? I have a BlackBerry, and it's a nice little thing. Should the business be valued the same as the Royal Bank?

No. Royal Bank looks attractive. It could still be a little bit overvalued here because there's stuff that we're going to still find out. They may be a little bit behind the U.S. in things that have gone on in the planet.

I don't think they've let everything out yet.

Perhaps Canada's banks are going to come apart a little bit, but not big time, I don't think. But we could have some problems here that you've seen in the U.S. Our housing market is still booming; maybe it slows down. Research In Motion is definitely a phenomenal company with good profit margins, but it doesn't deserve the multiple that it's got. That's got to come in, unless they're going to grow into it over time, which is possible.

I guess that's the beauty of value investing. Expectations are really low. It's not really hard to beat the expectations. Whereas a momentum stock, you set those expectations, and they keep raising the expectations. Sooner or later, you're going to disappoint.

It might be later. That's why momentum can often work for a long time, because those stocks keep going and going and going and going.

Let's talk about the shorting in the past year or two. What worked and what didn't?

It was very difficult as you came into the period of early 2007, because you had private equity at its heyday, and that whole thing turned on a dime. We had things that we were short that were vulnerable or rumoured to be private equitized, and we had to get off of them because we didn't want to take that risk. Those things are now way down from where they were. I wish we had remained short them, but it wasn't worth the risk of being there at the time. We gave up all of our shorts in November of last year because we believed the market was bottoming. It looks like it was three or four months too early. All of our shorts now are sitting at a floor. I think the whole market's at a floor, as I've said. To me, even the bad companies should go up in this intervening period. I think it's dangerous to be short things at this time. We are now long-only in our long/short....

Right. So, you have the flexibility to do that?

Yeah, we're not a hedge fund; we're not market neutral. If we don't think it's the right time to be short, we won't be short at all. We were short 40 percent of our portfolios going back into the bubble, and a couple of times in and around that as well, just before it and just after it. Coming into last year, into early '07, we were about 15 to 20 percent short. That's where we'll normalize again when the market runs back up another 20-odd percent here, closer to fair value.

I'm talking about the big cap markets, yes. I'd even make the same argument for the various indexes. I mean, the S&P on an equal-weighted basis, the S&P 500 in the U.S., is sitting at one and a half times book value, which is as cheap as it's ever been.

Earnings yields are way higher than ten-year bond yields?

Correct. What I like to look at is the earnings yield, which is now 7.1 percent. The cap rate on stocks is very attractive. It doubled that of the bond rate. Mr. and Mrs. Pension Fund ought to want to put their money into equities versus bonds once they stop being scared of their shadow.

When the market's up 20 percent, then they'll feel more comfortable.

They might do it then. That's when we'll start shorting again, because things will have run to nonsensical levels. You do have pockets of the market that are crazy now, like some of the solar stocks and some of the NASDAQ stocks.

When would you decide to short a way overvalued stock? When the fundamentals break down, but not just based on value?

No, you want to do both when the economy is coming off. I remember we were short Cisco back through the bubble. It was one of the later ones to fall. Everybody kept saying, "Oh, you can't do it just based on valuation." It got so far ahead you could do it just on valuation, but it didn't roll over until the whole economy started floundering a bit. Then it just got pushed into oblivion. That was probably a lesson that we should have extrapolated into the most recent period because things were flying. As soon as you got wind of the recession coming, it was easy pickings to short. When something goes to two times its fair market value, that's a good point to get off the short.

I remember being short Whole Foods at $55. I got off of it at $60. It went to $80 and I didn't revisit it. The fair market value was around $40, it went to $80, so it got to two times. It's now back at $38, a fabulous short. With Apple, we did make a little bit of money shorting, because we traded off of our SVA work. But Apple went to whatever the peak was, $200 and some odd dollars. Our fair market value was like $110 at the time. Then the fair market value grew nicely. The stock fell all the way back virtually to fair market value.

We did go through the bubble where you saw things go to three or four times their fair market value. So, you've got to be very careful if you're in that environment. In normal times, you can have a company, go to two times valuation and still short it on valuation alone because, ultimately, they're going to miss something. I mean Whole Foods hasn't gone off the rails. It had a little thing here, and a little thing there, and boom.

So, that's what you look at is two times fair market value?

On a momentum growth stock, that's typically not what we're looking to short. We're looking to short the opposite of what we're looking to long, something that's maybe got a levered balance sheet or something that has an anemic growth in their business—that just the valuation is too high for whatever reason. There's no momentum in the business. The balance sheet and the income statement aren't growing like stink. They're growing nowhere. That's what we'd prefer.

What's your average hold time on a short? Is it a function of the market?

It's a function of the market. We don't hold a short for more than a year or six months at a time.

On the long side?

We're just looking to make 20 percent on the short. A long has been probably in and around three years because we're looking to make 100 percent on the long.

Yeah. If the cards are stacked against you, as Buffett says, "Your maximum gain on a short is 100 percent, and maximum loss is unlimited."

Correct. That is true. Those are awful probabilities. Having said that, he also points out the fact that he and Charlie have been right on every single short they've executed. He says, "We've made some very good calls on the overwhelming majority of our shorts." It's just that the mathematics are stacked against you. If you get one wrong, you can offset a whole bunch of your winners.

So you have to have stop-losses?

You have to have stops. One mistake that we made in the past that I will try not to make in the future is shorting things that maybe were a little too small. So when they did go up, they didn't go up slowly, they went right up. When we were short First Solar, and it went against us, it went up 30 percent in an afternoon, after hours. How do you have a stop there? It goes right through your stop. It opens through your stop versus a bigger name that moves at a slower pace. Now, there's certain markets where you can short names like that where the market's collapsing.

Do you see a lot more competition these days on the short side just because there's a lot more hedge funds in the U.S.? In Canada, there's not a lot of money here that's shorting, I don't think.

I don't really see it that way. People are making a stink over the fact that you've got the rule change on the….

Uptick?

The uptick rules. I don't think that makes a difference. People can maybe manipulate the stock down, and people can manipulate the stock up too. What's the difference?

The only difference with competition is that you can get involved in situations where an extreme amount of a float is sold short. If it goes against you, it can really go against you because the short interest is so high. You've got to be wary of that.

Delta Petroleum had 10 million, 12 million shares short out of 50 million outstanding. I think some of that's gone because Kerkorian came in with $650 million.

Yes.

There's something going on there because when you add up all the shares, it was way more than they had outstanding.

I'm convinced there's naked shorting going on. We own another company called CompuCredit, where the volume in that stock has just been too high given what the float shares are. Management owns 60 percent of the company, and we own close to 10. There are another couple of groups out there that own a big chunk too. So it doesn't add up. There's got to be some naked shorting going on still. I don't know how people get around it, but they somehow are.

You are heavy on gold, and you are heavy on energy. We obviously know why you're heavy on energy. For gold, is it because the stocks are cheap in relation to the price of gold, or is it because you think the supply/demand equation for gold is going to push it to $2,000 an ounce?

Yes and yes. We won't play in a sector of the market unless we both have a bottom-up and a top-down call. In other words, we want a tailwind from the macro environment. We want the supply and demand fundamentals in our favour, which we do believe are both there for gold bullion and for oil and gas. At the same time, we won't play unless we can find stocks that are cheap no matter what. We believe our oil stocks, for example, work at $65, $70 oil. Over $100, or wherever we are today, is just icing on the cake.

Why do you see gold going up in price? Is it just because there's a lot of supply problems in the world? The uranium demand was a lot greater than supply, but it stayed at $9 a pound for a while because you had the Russians dumping their uranium from nuclear weapons. With gold, you had demand a lot greater than supply, but you had central banks dumping gold. The magic question is, when will the central banks stop dumping gold?

That's part of the magic question. There were three things that held back the supply/demand deficit on gold. You had central banks selling. That created an artificial supply for more than ten years now. I remember reading Peter Lynch's *One Up On Wall Street,* which was written in the 1980s or something. He talked about the supply and demand deficit of over 1,000 tons in gold. So you had central banks selling and you had hedge books from the various major producers. At the same time, you had a carry trade. The carry trade's basically gone. The hedgers aren't really hedging anymore because nobody wants them to, with gold going up. The central banks have, to a large extent, stopped selling. Canada's devoid of the stuff. As of last year, I read that individuals around the world now own more gold than the central banks. If you don't have the artificial supply anymore, and if you do have a belief that gold, as it has been for 5,000 years or so, behaves as the ultimate currency, and is the ultimate store

of value, then it should go up. Currencies around the world are debasing because money supplies are growing at double-digit rates. The U.S. money supply is growing at almost 17 percent a year, and various other countries around
the world are also growing at double-digit rates. That debases the currency
and gold goes up. South Africa, on the supply side, produces less, even though
it is the world's largest producer. It produces less gold now than it did in the
'20s. It's staggering. It's going to get worse there because they've got all these
power problems.

Right, rotating power outages. Chile's got their water problems....
It's a scarce commodity, not easy to find. The costs have gone up to find
it. I get visited by lots of companies and I always say, "Where are the guys who
look like you and don't have gray hair on their head who work at mining companies?" They don't exist. Mining engineers aren't coming out of schools in
droves anymore. So you've got a bunch of white-haired guys in the industry,
which is fine, but it's hard to find people to run your business. People like
Minefinders, which has an interesting property in Mexico right now, have out-
sourced everything to contractors. You have had skill costs escalate and power
costs escalate. That all causes a pressure on the ultimate price to go higher
over time.

Gold has to go up because the input costs are going up?
The marginal cost of production is going up. You've had the supply/de-
mand deficit forever. All three artificial elements of supply are now gone.
You're into a reflationary period for the first time in many years. We were
going through a disinflationary period from the early '80s. That's difficult right
now because you've got housing prices coming down, and you still have a foreign effect with people moving offshore to produce things—that is deflation-
ary, or at least disinflationary. Now you've got this whole reflation going on
with the central banks printing money. That cannot be good for inflation.

Some people say that inflation is really 7, 8 percent, or 9 percent.
It could be. I find it hard to believe that every government around the
world is cooking their inflation books. Housing is coming down now, not here
in Canada, but certainly in the U.S., and the car prices aren't really going up,
and computer prices aren't going up, and all your big-ticket items aren't really
going up.

How many positions, approximately, on the long side?

We probably have about fortyish.

You're all long. About fortyish?

Fortyish. The top ten positions, though, probably represent about half the portfolio.

Okay. So, 5 percent positions approximately?

Yeah, we've got a few, 6 or 7s now. We've only gone to 8 percent or more on about a half dozen occasions in the last 10 years, and they've all worked out really well for us.

Your long position is 100 percent?

For accounts that have been with us for a while, we're about 115 long on average now simply because we didn't have the dry powder to buy the cash in this environment. We've added an itty-bitty leverage amount where people have allowed us to.

Because you deal with separately managed accounts, how do you calculate the return?

A composite. We follow the rules for composite.

Okay. I don't think there's really anything else.

Great. Thanks.

Normand Lamarche
Mining for Golden Stocks

"I think the big distinguishing thing is not so much seeing the opportunities, it's having the nerve or the conviction to follow through."

The *Globe and Mail* has called Normand Lamarche the best mutual fund manager that nobody has heard of. His track record with the Front Street Special Opportunities of 30 percent annualized over the last nine years puts him in the top echelon of all Canadian money managers. What does this type of return give an investor over ten years? Only about ten times their money. Not bad for your retirement savings! This track record included eight positive years and only one down year, and a 121 percent return in 2003! His Front Street Mining Opportunities has tripled since its inception in January 2005. How do I know? Because I invested my own money in it right at the beginning. Sure, resource stocks have been the place to be over the last few years, but even resource stocks have not had nearly the performance that Norm has chalked up. Hired at Altamira to be "an analyst," he reported to Frank Mersch. Getting frustrated with spinning his wheels, he told Frank he wanted to manage money. That was 1991. Norm got two funds to run, and the rest is history. Frank and Norm actually run money literally side by side on the trading desk, on an equal basis. Front Street Capital has quite the one-two punch with these two running the investment side of the business.

After Norm took a sabbatical from the money management business, he later started up Tuscarora Capital. It was primarily a resource firm specializing in small cap resource stocks, flow-through shares and the like. Surprisingly, he and Frank got together again and Front Street Capital was born, this time with them as equals. Being a self-proclaimed bit of a loner, Norm is regarded by many as one of the "hardest guys to get a hold of on the street." It's not that he is on the phone or busy. He just doesn't want to talk to analysts or sales guys. He would much rather sit up in the loft at Front Street's offices and read reports. Don't get me wrong, I have spent some time sitting in the loft, talking with Front Street's boss, Gary Selke. It is a very comfortable place to while the time away indeed.

I actually interviewed Normand Lamarche in my office in Vancouver overlooking the North Shore Mountains. He was out in Vancouver doing some of his own research and doing some branch presentations, discussing his outlook. Norm was reserved, and came across as very humble, not at all like the impression you may have of a cocky hedge fund manager full of hubris. Being wealthy enough not to have to work, Norm still has a reputation for being frugal, down to earth, and humble—traits that I saw as common among the best investment managers in the country.

Bob:

I think the first thing is to go way, way back. How did you first get involved in the money management business? Or was it kind of in your family?

Normand:

Certainly not in the family. Complete different direction than my folks. But I had studied economics at Carleton in Ottawa for a number of years, and as soon as I graduated I was able to get into the central bank as sort of a junior economist. I was working with their research department. They called it the Projection Coordination Unit. They had a large team of analysts, pretty much similar to what Bay Street and Wall Street has in terms of having analysts identify and follow a research model. I was part of the unit that put everything together and made sure that the economic model properly kept hold. So when consumption goes up, you want to make sure GNP goes up. I realized pretty quickly my interests were always closer to here, closer to Bay Street. I liked the idea of investing in equities, and for me, the central bank part was a stepping stone to get into this kind of business. So even while at the bank doing research, I did my securities course, my CFA, which was pretty difficult to do when you're not really working in the environment. So a lot of it was kind of new. I bumped into the guys at Altamira when I was in transition. I was leaving the bank to pursue a master's in finance degree in Montreal. I had given myself some time off to relax before the next thing. I bumped into Ron Meade and Otto Felber who were at the time reorganizing Altamira management, which had been a fixed-income firm forever. They basically wanted to rejig it. They were bringing in Frank Mersch, Will Sutherland, and Philip Armstrong. It was a Quebec-based organization and they wanted me to run the office, in Quebec, and the money market operations.

I figured that there was a lot of risk in that organization. It's not a company that I really knew. They made me an offer that I just couldn't refuse, and I figured worst-case scenario I can always go back to school and do my finance degree—best case-scenario I'll get to know the business a bit, get to know some people. I landed up with Frank, and Will Sutherland, and started working basically with Frank, more as his assistant in the earlier days, doing grunt work. He would send me off to visit companies that had issues and things like that. He would want me to report to him, but he never really listened to me anyway. That's typical Frank. I'd be sitting across from him waiting to report on what I had seen and the phone would ring and he'd pick it up. It would be one of those things over a three-hour period, and then finally I'd just get up and leave—to a point where I got really frustrated and where I wanted to run money. It's one of those things where it just sort of simmers forever and you worry. Finally, one day I just went up to him and said, "We're going to have lunch today." I didn't really give him an option. He kind of just looked at me and said, "Okay." He asked me what was up, and I said, "I want to run money." He said, "Okay. So here are two resource funds." The Altamira Resource Fund had $3.2 million at the time in it, and we had an offshore version of it called Orbitex, which had, I think, $13 million or maybe less. He said these words exactly: "Go hang yourself with it, and here's your rope." That would have been probably in 1991 when I would have started actually physically running money.

Did you actually invest in stocks for yourself when you were at the Bank of Canada?

No. I mean, I have had some ugly investing stories as I was growing up. Judging from those results, I probably should have stayed far away from the money management business. For example, I would have gotten caught up in the massive gold and silver rush in the '80s. Was it the '80s when gold prices sort of went up to $800 or something like this? I remember I was in grade 12 economics, and the economics teacher told me that silver would be heading a lot higher. It did for a short while, and then it kind of gave everything up, along with my wealth.

That's when they cornered the market.

That's right. That's when the Hunt brothers cornered the market. I think one of the important lessons there was to pay attention to or to really refine the information flows that you get. This guy was basically just an economics teacher in a small town that didn't really know anything about silver. That's important. I think in our business, especially in an environment where you're just inundated with information and with opinions, you really need to ratchet down and to upgrade the quality of that information very selectively. Everyone has an axe to grind in business, and that's the quickest and one of the toughest lessons to learn at the end of the day.

Do you remember the first stock you invested in? I think the worst thing is if you make a lot of money on your first investment, because you don't really learn anything.

That's right. Then you lose sight of what can go wrong very quickly. There was a little tiny copper company—the name escapes me. It was a tiny little acid leach company out in Arizona. Arimetco, that's it—its symbol was ARX and it traded for about a dollar, or something like that, a share. This guy basically had a small deposit in the U.S. and he was applying acid leaching, which was relatively new back then. He was into production very quickly. I was very excited about that. I remember being at a Midland Walwyn luncheon where he was presenting the story. I was already a shareholder and he was updating investors and basically announcing that he had growth opportunities with more deposits that they would be putting into production. I remember running from the meeting to the office so I could buy more—I literally ran. I was so excited that I just ran to the office to buy more of the thing. Ultimately, the thing didn't perform as well as expected, largely because of management execution. That's another thing that you sort of learn over the years, that management is extremely important, especially the smaller the companies are.

From your experience with the Bank of Canada, where you learned more on the economic side, what do you think is more important, looking at the big picture or looking at the stock-by-stock basis? Do you consider yourself an investor or a trader?

Again, you learn over time. You learn from your experiences. You learn from your mistakes. You learn from the opportunities that you've had in the past. The more that I've been developing as a manager over the years, the more top-down that I've become. In fact, so much so that I don't really talk to a lot of people anymore. I don't talk to analysts. I read their things and I have access to all the information. I don't talk to sales guys, for the most part. A lot of guys have labelled me the hardest man to reach on the street. It's not because I'm terribly busy away from the phone; I just don't want to talk to them. I would rather hide in the loft area at the office and just quietly read.

It's one thing that the experience at Altamira gave me. We became so large, so fast, that the assets that I ran individually were certainly well through $2 billion at the peak. It just put a lot of time pressures on me, and I was invested in too many companies. My office door was a revolving door. I had five, six, seven companies a day coming in through my office. You just didn't have time to think. The best thing that happened between Altamira and the new entity is a time-off that I took—a one-year sabbatical—to basically relax and spend some time with the kids. That's one thing that I kept on doing afterwards. I don't want to be caught up in the noise thing. What was important, I think, is a realization that I don't have to own everything, all the successful stocks. I can let other people own them as well. I don't have to own them all. I don't have to compare myself. I don't have to be number one in the industry. I don't have to beat Rohit. I don't have to beat Tom Stanley. All I have to do is worry about my portfolios and my clients, and hopefully I can deliver for them. I think that's the main friggin' thing that I've learned.

In the energy patch, I spent all of my time, for the most part, on information sources like Bloomberg, following what the industry's doing. I may not be interested in investing in Exxon, but I'm interested in knowing what they're doing, where they're investing, what kind of deals they're structuring in the Middle East and Africa and all those things. It gives me a greater sense of what the total industry cost structures are and what the return opportunities are that ultimately will sort of phase itself into my reality. So where I spend most of my time is just worrying about industry conditions and what the players are doing.

What do you think your turnover is? Do you trade quite a bit or do you think of yourself more as an investor?

I probably put myself in the middle of the pack. I'm certainly not a buy-and-hold guy. My groups are very volatile, and I think you always have target values in mind, although you need to re-evaluate those almost on a daily basis. But I trade around the core positions pretty aggressively. My turnovers would be as much as two and a half times, three times for the hedge funds.

Do you ever find ideas outside of Canada? I mean, Australia's big. Paladin Resources is in Namibia.

For the most part, there's a very high correlation amongst the players. The Canadian companies have always had a tremendous amount of leadership. Capital markets have always been at the forefront where they've actually attracted a lot of foreign players to be listed here. It's always liquid, so our preference—and, for the most part, our weightings—have been in Canadian-listed companies that do business internationally. When we don't have access domestically, we go elsewhere. For example, we're big fans of infrastructure, energy infrastructure companies. We're in a U.K.-listed company that does just that. They build offshore platforms. But you're not going to see us in really foreign markets, in the Russian stocks or in Chinese-listed companies. I think those are just more layers of risk that I don't understand, that I can eliminate easily.

Do you ever use technical analysis at all?

No.

To decide when to sell or buy? Not really? Nothing?

Never.

Do you see this going on for quite a long period of time just because of the lack of capital expenditures that was put into that sector?

I think there's certainly the possibility of that. The elements are in place for a much more secular, longer move. Those conditions are largely on the demand side, driven by what you see in the appetite coming from the emerging world, which has very high basic-materials intensity in their GNP growth. At the same time too, we just think that times always seem to catch up to you when you're not paying attention or reinvesting. I think if you listened to the State of the Union Address, they mentioned the need to basically rebuild our energy infrastructure domestically. I think that's going to require a massive amount of capital spending to do just that. It's not just the demand. I think what's really interesting, which is really catching up to us, is a realization that we have an inability to reinvest sufficiently to meet the kind of demand that's growing at a decent clip. It has everything to do with who the players are.

In the oil patch, the production and the reserves more importantly are in difficult hands. They're with guys who are inhospitable, where access is difficult, and if you do get access, the terms are very expensive. So it boils down to being where the companies will take all of the risks to have a smaller and smaller piece of the opportunity. The mining side, as well, is turning into that, quite frankly. You look at what's happening in Latin America—it's got tremendous left-leaning tendencies. Governments are thinking of nationalizing a lot of their natural wealth, which are resources, and they're making it very difficult and expensive for the likes of Western companies to invest. So all of that is going to boil down to a slower reinvestment rate cycle. So I think you've got the elements for a much longer powerful cycle in this thing than we've ever seen.

Do you remember what your biggest win on a stock ever was?

Biggest win on a stock. I think when you're in the resource sectors, there are some mammoth wins from a price appreciation side, given the leverage that you get in that kind of group. One which would line up quite handily is a company called Profico. It's run by Clayton Woitas, who built Renaissance Energy into one of the fastest growing, more efficient oil-and-gas companies that was later sold to Husky. He created a new company about five years ago. I think in total, he would have raised a total of $50 or $60 million of equity. That's all he's raised. No other equities raised since. Today, he has cash on the balance sheet. He's cash taxable. He's producing around 18,000 barrels a day of oil-equivalent, which is mostly gas. The company's actually being sold now, but most people think that this thing will sell for about $1.5 to $1.6 billion. Tremendous. When the share—the initial share tranche—was at $8, thinking as it goes for and it's trading in the marketplace around $155, a lot of guys think that it's going to go for $170, $180 a share.

Twenty times. You had that in the Energy Growth Fund, right?
Yeah. It's in our Special Opportunities Fund as well.

Bre-X—did you ever invest in it? Were you able to make any money off it?
No. Never touched it. It was probably more luck than anything else. Yeah, Bre-X was unfolding when I was leaving Altamira—the time when the story was just becoming known. I had handed the portfolios off to Dave Taylor, and then I went on sabbatical. I was away from the market. I was away from the fundamentals, so I just didn't play any story like that. You're investing in very aggressive groups and I have a tendency of not chasing the ridiculous stories that move, whether for right or wrong. I just got totally lucky on this one. Quite frankly I'm not sure how I would have played it had I been there. As I said, I don't have a habit of chasing things that are just rocketing.

People who built big companies, sold them off and went and started up little companies. So do you look a lot at the management when you invest in a stock? Is that really important?
One hundred percent. I mean, the smaller the business is, the greater the influence of management, both good and bad. They're very dynamic companies where discovery can have a meaningful impact. So you really have to follow them attentively. I would sit down with them maybe six to seven, eight times a year, just to get a solid update operationally. I never keep notes in any of my meetings, but I try to see the companies often enough so that I just keep not only reminding myself but also updating myself as to whether it's good or bad.

Sometimes you just collect those little red flags along the way. You have things that you don't like, to a point where you make the decision where you want to dispose of the stock or whether you just want to accumulate more of it.

So management's the most important, definitely, in the small cap area?

Absolutely. Although in this environment today, where it's very difficult—expensive—I would go beyond that. It's more difficult for even the good management teams to acquire a large opportunity base cheaply. It's very expensive in the oil patch. So we're not really funding a lot of what we call the blind pools: good management team, no opportunities, but with the idea of farming in. We haven't been doing that for years.

How do you short in the resource sector?

It's an adjustment because you've been trained to always head into a story with the idea of buying it or not buying it. You have to be a bit more open-minded with the greater tools that you have because you're not taking any new information from the meeting. You simply have greater opportunities to deal with that same investment. You can either buy it or not buy it. You can actually sell it or pair it up with something else. Over time, you just develop a skill.

Would that be something you'd do, go long on stocks that you like and then short the oil-and-gas index or the mining index? The idea with hedging is you want your returns to be attributable to your skill instead of to the market.

There are lots of different strategies that you could use. For example, you're into an environment right now where the commodity prices will be higher for longer. You're into a growth phase here; you want to be with the companies that have a greater ability to grow than Exxon would, or even a lot of the super majors would. One strategy, and they're not hedges, is to be long a lot of these well-managed growth vehicles. If you didn't want to really add that much more exposure to the portfolio, you may want to short some of the seniors against it. It's not a perfect strategy. Over long periods of time, it works. Short periods of time, it doesn't work. You can be offside for liquidity reasons and things like that. But that's creating a new vehicle, a growth vehicle, without the commodity exposure or the beta exposure that it comes with.

I don't know if you can rattle these off the top of your head, but if you could give three or four rules that you always go by when you look at a stock or when you manage the portfolio?

Well, if you're looking at the whole process, I think trusting your instincts. We all have tools that we sort of develop over time. I think a lot of the great managers that are on that list, like Mersch or Rohit and guys like Sprott, will take different bets relative to the average investor. That's because they believe in their skills, and they're willing to make the unpopular positions and they stick to them. I think that's important. A lot of people have the same gut feel about situations or about companies, and yet they're afraid of being too different. They're afraid of being wrong; a lot of these guys on your list are not afraid of being wrong. I think common sense goes a long ways in our business, like it does for any other business. You've got to do your work, obviously, and you stay disciplined about it, and you stay realistic about opportunities and risks. Trust what you've been trained to do—that's really important. Think, and have time to think and reflect.

Are there any books that you just consider the best books around?

I'm not one to read much other than the boring. I'll even read research material when I'm on holidays by the pool or on the beach with the kids and stuff.

You managed a lot of pension money at Altamira?

It was a big part of our business. I think we had anywhere from $8 to $10 billion at the peak in the pension area. There certainly is a familiarity with us and the consultants and the pension industry itself. Having said that, we haven't found a real need to go and chase that subgroup yet.

Fund of funds isn't really sticky money. They'll take their money out quick if you're not performing, which is unfortunate.

Yeah. I find that the trend has been to be less sticky no matter who you are, whether you're a retail or institutional client, fund of funds or a pension fund. Everyone is watching the clock and they're watching short-term performance a lot more than they used to.

Wayne Deans said he was looking at firing some of his pension clients because he's getting paid a quarter of a point or half a point on pension

assets. He says, "I can make 1.5 percent off retail clients and they don't complain every quarter if I don't perform."

Yeah, I share his views.

Let's talk a little bit about the differences in the funds. The mining opportunities, the special opportunities, and the small cap Canadian.

Okay. There's two small cap funds that are kind of broad-based small cap funds. There is a small cap fund, as you say, in the Special Opportunities, and I've been managing those for many years. They're different in style and in philosophy. The Small Cap Fund is a thematically driven fund, where you're looking at identifying those themes that will propel the economic activity that will drive growth in sales and margins. It's very much a top-down fund. Our firm is very much like that. I am a top-down guy. I spend most of my time worrying about what's happening and the forces that are at play. If you can identify that it just makes the stock picking a lot easier, because when a tide sort of comes in, it lifts a lot of things, which makes the stock-picking job a lot easier to some degree.

For example, I may not like Exxon because it doesn't grow on its own. I do pay attention to what they do and how they invest and what it costs them because that gives me an indication of where I think my prices probably should be longer term. I use a lot of those observations from industry, governments, to set the tone for the opportunities and give me a sense of what the supply/demand situations are and, most importantly, what the cost structures are looking like. Once you've got your sights set on those opportunities, the bottom-up work takes place. Then that's where you go hunting. For example, if you like the nat gas sectors we do in North America, there's definitely a preference for companies that have what I would call deep-basin type of opportunities or sale plays. A company like Duvernay, for example, has a lot of visibility in spending where there's less of a geological risk and more of a completion situation facing the company. Alberta to me is out of the question. If I'm going to invest in nat gas I'm going to look at producers that are operating out of B.C.; Saskatchewan, if there are any; or in the U.S. There are some great companies that are chasing the deeper shale plays in Texas, Oklahoma, Louisiana, and you name it. The top-down sort of picture identifies the opportunity and themes that develop.

There are some sub-themes that can originate from there as well. For example, I think there's a lot of interesting technologies that are being developed that are creating tremendous opportunities for the oil patch players. I like that, so I'll chase the guys who are very much involved. If a lot of the gas opportunities are deeper that require intense frac services, I see a lot of longevity in that kind of business. I want to be associated with the service companies that provide that service—companies like Trican, Calfrac, and the companies that are drilling horizontally, or the guys that are providing engines for horizontal drilling. So those sub-themes are something I focus on, and then I just home in on it.

Everything's pretty much unconventional in that area, oil and gas exploration. All the conventional stuff is pretty much done, right?

Absolutely. I think the conventional stuff in North America and for the most part in many of the basins is a tough business. Technology does evolve, increasing your odds and increasing your opportunities. At the end of the day, there's a lot of resources in North America alone in the oil sands. It's very unconventional, but it's there in a plentiful way. So you want to own the resource, number one. And two, pay attention to the emerging technologies, whether it's a company like Petrobank, for example, which I think has a smashing opportunity here with their THAI technology—Toe-to-Heel Air Injector thing—that they're deploying in Fort McMurray. I think that could be revolutionary on a cost basis for the deeper-site new players. I think in a sense it's a *Mad Max* world. You want to own the resource. You want to own that supertanker because without it, you can't operate your vehicles. In a case of resource companies, you need the resource in order to fuel growth, and that's the object. One of the themes that's driving our portfolio is to be resource rich, whether it's in basic materials or energy or things like that.

The International Energy Agency in the second quarter of '08 came out and said that maybe supply won't be able to keep up with the demand in oil. They've always been saying, "Oh, it's no problem. We'll get up to 116 million barrels a day in the next ten or fifteen years." Now they've suddenly said, "Oh my God, maybe that isn't going to happen." Why did it take them five years to see the light that other smart people saw a few years ago?

Well, because they've seen evidence. They haven't seen a growth in extraction, number one. I don't think they believe the original thesis themselves. There's some guys in your group that are talking peak oil theory. I don't quite buy that myself, but I think it's true for different reasons. The end result is the same. The end result is that supply isn't growing as fast as it should. It's not because of geological issues as some of our friends talk about. The argument is that we've found largely the easy oil deposits and they're declining. There is some element to that, there's no question. The bigger element that I think is driving the energy prices to where they are today is not a geological issue, it's a geopolitical problem. We need to look no further than what's happened in Venezuela.

When Frank Mersch and I were at Altamira, Venezuela produced twice what they produce today, and we've had nothing but one of the greatest commodity boom cycles on the planet. Venezuela, if you would add their heavy-oil assets, would rank second in the world in terms of oil resources behind Saudi Arabia. So why, in the greatest boom in energy in our lifetime, is it that their production has been cut in half? Why is it that Indonesia has now turned into an oil importer when they are very rich geologically? The answer is governments. The answer in Indonesia is that twenty years of Suharto has done nothing but discourage investment. The answer in Venezuela is Chavez, over ten years, has done nothing but piss off all the executives and nationalized people away from it. You're seeing the impact in Russia already from all of this screwing around by, again, quasi-nationalizing Exxon, BP, Shell out of their interest after having spent real good money developing reserves and assets. They're now coming in and changing the rules. That's happened in Argentina. It's happened in Alberta. Now you're seeing Alberta investment decline. Why? Because the government's taking the entire uptake. In Alberta, you're seeing money flow out of it into B.C., into Saskatchewan, and into internationals. Why? Because the government is screwing with the companies, and their net take out of the oil patch in Alberta is now equal to what Middle Eastern nations are. So the reinvestment by Exxon in the craziest commodity world that we have today is difficult for them. It's not because of lack of reserves.

Is Exxon going to spend $25 billion in Kazakhstan if they're not clear whether the government's just going to take it, right?

Exactly. So are you going to build a $4 billion copper mine in Ecuador today? Are you going to build a $10 billion infrastructure in the Congo today? Are you going to be investing in Venezuela short term? Are you going to be investing in Russia short term? The answer is no. It's not entirely a geological peak oil theory, it's a geopolitical one. That can change, but it won't change until we have a real economic depression that's going to force government changes. It's happening to some degree. The Alberta government's already come back and clawed back to some degree some measures. Even the Russian government is now talking about reducing taxation or increasing domestic prices to attract investment again because production is rolling over. There are rumours that the Argentinean government is looking to relax some of the measures that they imposed last year, which capped companies at $40 a barrel no matter what. Oil can go to $1,000 and companies are still going to get $40 a barrel; meanwhile, their costs are rising every day. We may have overshot from a greed perspective on the government front. So there may be some retracement to come.

Remember all the copper mines in the '70s in the Congo? Then governments started to take them all back.

You bet. You're bang on. Again, the government greed is a function of the economic situation, and that basically troughed, now it's run its peak again. It all came to a head in 1998, '99, when all the emerging nations were effectively bankrupt when you had the currency fiasco that sent oil prices and the economies of the emerging world into tailspins. Oil prices were at $10, and that's when the Venezuelan government was quite open to business. The Russian government had defaulted on IMF. They were quite open to business with the Western companies and offering everything at very attractive terms, and now things have changed. So you're right, that does come in cycles to some degree.

Jim Rogers said that one of the reasons for the fall of Communism was not really because the system broke up but because the commodity markets were so bad they had no hard currency coming in. I think that is why they're becoming strong again and Putin's starting to talk pretty tough again because they've got lots of money coming in.

Well, that's the interesting thing. The mighty oil barrel in our *Mad Max* game is changing the landscape. If you own the supertanker, then you're stronger politically. There's a massive redistribution of wealth taking place from the consuming world to the producing world. They are behaving politically different. You're right, the Russians were economically bankrupt in '98, '99. Today, they're behaving as though we're back in the Cold War era to some degree, some people think. They're behaving tougher with their terms of trade. It's a harsh environment for producers. Opportunities are hard to come by, and as far as themes go, we want to be in companies that not only have resources, but they have producing resources, number one. They are generating ridiculous cash flow levels, and probably for longer because reinvestment gain from the industry isn't sticky. This means that they are going to probably have higher commodities for longer, which means that if you're in the production game, you're going to reap those rewards. Investors don't believe that visibility for longer, yet. They believe that on energy, but they're not buying that on the other materials to some degree.

Rohit said to me, "The stock prices will only go up when analysts start to increase their outlook for these commodity prices in regards to whether they're going to stay high." Has that happened yet? Or is that factored into the base metal stocks?

The analysts are always late, and they always retrace after the fact, and they always uptick. They're always well below what the real industry players know or inherently believe. If you were to ask BHP where they think long-term nickel prices are, analysts are still sticking to some of the low prices of maybe $5.50 a pound longer term or some may have ratcheted it up to $6.00 or something from $3.50 not long ago. Most companies will tell you there's no fricking way they would build green field capacity with a long-term price of $5.00 or $6.00. Just given the cost of building these things, the cost of operating and the energy cost, it doesn't work under those sorts of terms. You do have that big wedge between how the market is valuing assets and production, cash flow, and the cost of bringing on, and what those companies are inherently discounting in the stock market, and what the true cost is of bringing on green field. As a result of that, you're not getting a lot of reinvestment to a degree, and I think that's why you're going to get a lot of M&A activity in the mining world over the next two years. It's happening already. You have the big companies that you would never have thought would be susceptible to M&A—a company like Xstrata—and these are some of the world's biggest resource companies to be the subject of M&A. Who would have thought that? That is going to find its way downstream into the seniors, the mid-tiers, the juniors even before we decide to build mines. It's cheaper now to buy Freeport, which trades at four times EBITDA at today's commodity prices than to go out and build a mine in the Congo, not knowing what the true cost of development will be, not knowing whose government will be in place, and not knowing what will be in place four or five years from today.

Why did Exxon take all these full-page ads saying the price of oil really should be $50? They keep talking down the price of oil and saying the fundamentals don't justify these prices. Why would Exxon do that?

Because they're under the gun from the groups politically. They're having to defend themselves. It's easy right now to point at these guys given the amount of profitability, but the fact of the matter is they don't control oil prices. Then the groups like Congress and the Senate are looking at them, and the general population believes or at least suspect that these guys are sort of controlling and manipulating or driving oil prices higher. But the fact of the matter is they're not. Exxon is making record amounts of earnings cash flow, but yet they'll also tell you that business has never been tougher. Where do they go with the cash flow? Their production is down year over year. In fact, the big group is down year over year in production. A company like Chevron, which is the size of an OPEC nation, has oil reserves that are at eight-year lows. So you can't tell me that things are as rosy for the big guys.

Mexico is panicking now because the Cantarell oil field's declining about 10 to 15 percent a year and they haven't reinvested any money in it in ten years. They're panicking now because their revenues are decreasing. They're going to have to put some more money into that field, right? That's probably happening all over the world with Third World countries.

So is that a peak oil theory or is that a geopolitical problem? In the case of Mexico, you're right. The state oil company, Pemex, gets access to a small fraction of the cash flows. The rest of it goes to the state government. If they had access to all of the cash flow, would they not be reinvesting more, maybe finding more, developing more, offsetting the declines more, all those things? The same applies to Russia. The same applies to the Middle East. The same applies to Argentina. Again, it boils down to the geopolitical peak oil theory as opposed to geological.

The gold price is down a little bit, but it's still around $920. The gold stocks have just been hammered. Why is that? Is it because gold companies aren't really making any money?

That's certainly part of it. Do you ever remember the gold companies making money? [Laughs]

The costs are so high, right?

The costs are rising, and the costs are reflecting energy, materials, currency. They're reflecting all those things which are real. It also should be telling us that the commodity will stay higher for longer because of the true cost of doing business. When you have groups like Barrick that are shutting down developments because costs are running out of control, that's an issue again on the metal side. Investors, on the other hand, are not pricing long-term gold at $930 in their models. They're somewhat lower than that. So there's a bit of both. There's the fear of costs and there's also the fear of lack of sustainability in the commodity. Looking at it from the outside looking in, just looking at the tendencies of supply, there's not a whole lot of reinvestment taking place. Mine supply hasn't grown in many years on the gold front and costs are rising, so what does that tell you about where the commodity's going to be longer term? I haven't said anything about the U.S. dollar. I don't need to. I look purely at fundamentals, supply-and-demand costs, and those I like are based purely from those fundamentals.

Do you see this commodity cycle continuing for another four or five years?

I think so. This whole industrial revolution is not going away. You're going to get some economic cycles within that. You're going to get some hiccups; 2008 is a hiccup that's been prompted by this whole credit issue which is spreading into the real world, and it will probably slow the emerging nations' growth profiles a little bit. You're getting a lot of economic hiccup activity within places like China, for example, whether it's weather related, whether it's hurricane or earthquake related. At the end of the day, you have an emerging world which has a tremendous amount to offer to the world in terms of labour and productivity. I think you'll continue to see a lot of that enhanced economic activity worldwide. The type of growth that they bring is very much still primitive, and they will consume a lot of the basic materials, even though we as a Western world continue to sort of wean ourselves off of it. In Japan, oil demand peaked in the 1970s. Today, they're consuming less than they did thirty years ago, and they are the world's second largest economy. If someone would have told you thirty years ago that the world's second largest economy and consumer of oil was going to have decreasing demand over thirty years, you probably would have sold your crude futures then, worrying about the state of supply and demand. The world has grown notwithstanding that, and I think this is what's going to happen in the future. We're going to become more efficient, and we're going to conserve. We're going to become smarter in a consuming world, yet that'll be offset by some of the growth from the more primitive nations to some degree. If the nations that control oil—which is as much as 80 percent of the oil reserves are in the hands of the Russians and the Middle Eastern and the OPEC nations—don't really change their behaviour, supply isn't going to grow as fast. That's what the IEA is finally sort of catching on to. Oil will probably stay higher because of that.

How do you trade around your core positions? You mentioned that you don't use technical analysis.

I tend to worry about more the bigger picture and the posturing and the positioning. I spend more of my time away from the desk and observing what's happening around me. This is how I would characterize myself.

Do you and Frank exchange ideas quite a bit at the firm?

We sit next to each other, and so it's a lively desk. We're all at the same desk, all the portfolio managers and the traders. We don't always agree on things, but we sure throw a lot of things in the air that we beat about. We have morning meetings every day, where every one of us, analysts, managers, traders, are demanded to speak about at least one thing that they've encountered the day before. It could be a company that they met the day before, had a meeting with, or a situation that's developed or a piece of news that they thought was relevant. We try to enforce that into the behaviour. But we're trying to keep the thing as open as possible. Having said that, then it's up to Frank to manage his fund and it's up to me to manage my mandates at the end of the day. So, yeah, we do talk.

How important do you think is your gut feel? A lot of the people say, "I just have this feeling that is hard to quantify."

I think everyone has a gut feeling, and what distinguishes managers is how they use that. Most of the guys that are part of this group I would characterize as people that are very proactive and believe in their gut. A *gut* is a loosely used term, but it's really a reflection of the years of education and work and history and the pain and the opportunities that they've experienced in the marketplace. That gives them a gut feel when they see situations arise. Guys like Rohit and Eric and the guys that you have on your list here aren't afraid to invest where they see the opportunities. Many are—many are afraid to divert too much in case they're wrong.

Everybody on this list, except for Rohit, run their own company. I've often thought within a big corporate structure, if you go too far offside, you're not going to have a job too long. With a small owner-operated firm, you might have times when you far underperform the index, or whatever the case is, and you don't really care because you're running your own shop.

That's probably one of the main reasons why people just gravitate to their own environments, so that they can follow through with their views. I think you're right. Everyone has a gut feel, and most of the gut feels wouldn't be different, facing a similar series of events. I think if you would ask a group of twenty managers what their gut is telling them on a certain situation, the answer would probably be strikingly pretty similar. The behaviour, though, is the difference. Some people would wholeheartedly move to take advantage of that and some would be quite careful at it, and some wouldn't do anything until they have further evidence. I think the big distinguishing thing is not so much seeing the opportunities; it's having the nerve or the conviction to follow through.

How important do you think is behavioral finance? I saw a hedge fund manager on CNBC a few years ago and it was fantastic what he said. He said, "My job is to take people's money, unsophisticated people's money, out of their account and I put it in my account because they make stupid mistakes." I thought that was pretty brazen, but it's probably true.

There's a bit of that, that's for sure. Hopefully, the individuals have to do some of the work to make sure that they're well diversified amongst the group of managers and things like that. It's hard to compete with guys like Rohit and Eric that do that all day long. If you're an individual or retail investor working full-time at your day job, how can you compete with a guy like that? You don't have the same information base.

Because the market is a big auction, right? If you're buying the stock, somebody else is selling it to you because they think it's a rotten deal.

It's a matter of having that competitive advantage. He who works the hardest and the smartest should have a leg up.

Just to get an idea again about how you go about picking stock, I think Duvernay has been one of your favorite stocks for a long time: What did you like about that company? Why did you buy it? Why do you continue to hold it?

It's a big holding, for sure. It starts with management. I have invested in many companies over the years and have seen many of them fail. The common thread amongst them is management. The management team that can identify opportunities will win. It's the management teams that can bail you out of difficult situations when the time comes. That's the one thing that I've learned over the years, is that you get what you pay for. I'm willing to pay the higher multiples for the good-quality guys. Sometimes along the value chain there's a reason why stocks are cheap, and the quality guys get better value for the money, which means that their cost of capital is lower and it just accentuates the whole game for these guys. That's where it starts. You mentioned Duvernay. It started with them because I knew them and I knew what they had done at Berkeley. They were probably one of the best exploration teams in North America, if not beyond that. The guys are good. The guys are dedicated. They work hard and they throw a lot of their own money into the venture. They're tireless, and they always seem to expose themselves to the great opportunities, years before other guys do. It boils down to management.

[Duvernay was taken over at $80 a share and was one of the best-performing stocks in 2008.]

Let's say the commodity cycle ends in four years and there's lots of supply out there, and it's overcome the demand. You as a resource manager, how do you start to make money, if we go back to 1982?

I think you have to pay attention to that. You always want to be where the economic activity will be, and you worry about that. It keeps you up at night. It's nice to believe that the industrial revolution will last many cycles, but you worry about the supply response as well. Is it sufficient? Will it exceed the demand that'll come from it? Will it depress commodity prices?

It goes back to the big-picture perspective. Where do you want to be as an investor longer term? Just because there happens to be ten sectors within the TSE doesn't mean that I have to own them. I want to be in the ones where I think you will see a proportionate amount of economic activity within that. When I look at this world where we're growing at excessive rates and we're abusing the environment excessively, I see a lot of things developing from this world of ours today, and the oil prices alone are going to create some issues politically, geopolitically, and economically. It's forcing the need for energy security. It's forcing a need for energy alternatives. It's forcing a need for green forms of energy.

Those are all segments that will continue to attract capital. Count on it. If it's greener the better, and I think we as a society are going to entrench in our governments the need to push a Kyoto-type of accord worldwide. Consumers are going to want it, and society needs it. The pollution is going to be something of a bigger issue longer term.

So getting into the carbon space is something that your next book will be talking about, and it's something that's one of the ventures that we're doing today. We've developed a team of carbon originators, for example, that will be investing in this industry, investing in technologies or processes that will reduce emissions footprint, and for the carbon credits that evolve from it. So that is something that we as investors will be talking about openly years from today. That's a theme of the future. Count on it. Water is also an issue.

All of those things to me you can draw from the big picture and you identify as those major themes that will attract capital. That's where I want to be. I don't necessarily care about real estate. I don't necessarily care about the banking sector. You may not see me in those groups. So the portfolio gets concentrated to where I see the economic activities.

In the small cap fund, you've owned non-resource companies before. You had some technology companies. Do you add companies as you see fit, or are you going to be pretty focused on resource?

Well, I hadn't owned banks. I didn't have banking exposure up until recently. I've purchased the Big Five banks, if you can believe that, in the small cap fund.

Really? Okay.

I purchased them on the day when all the central banks worldwide came together with the dual measures of interest rate relief and, more importantly, the non-interest rate relief that provided both the banking and non-banking financial institutions opportunity to bank their paper and borrow against the discount window. That to me was everything I needed to see that would allow the financial situation to fix itself. The credit markets had frozen on all the players, and inter-bank lending had frozen, which was really making it difficult for the whole industry at the end of the day. Having the ability to borrow from the central banks at a very attractive price, by banking your whatever crap paper that they had in inventory, would allow them an opportunity to rebuild the profitability and the equity base that's necessary longer term for them to do business.

So we did get involved in the banking sector recently, a few months ago. Up until then, I had never owned a bank in the group. It's an area that I feel less comfortable with, up until recently.

Since you've been in the business, what do you think your biggest mistake is, either on a stock or a theme?

The list is too long to report. I've had way too many situations that have failed miserably for many reasons. The common thread certainly in the past has been the inability to kind of trust your instincts. When your gut is telling you that things are not as good, you should trust your instincts. In terms of stocks, it boils down to management execution. In the small cap fund years, a big mistake was a private situation called the Indian Motorcycle Company, which had a great, great, great, great concept. In the very strong North American market was Harley Davidson, a strong player, growing regularly every year, beating analysts' forecasts continually with a product that had no competition.

Here a group of seasoned industry professionals from the automotive industry came together with financing to bring back the Indian brand, which, in its heyday back in the '40s and '50s, shared the marketplace with Harley Davidson. It had the brand, and the brand is something that takes generations to build for most companies. So you were starting out with a brand, and the product itself had been off the market for many years because of the bankruptcies. I came about with a group of investors that funded that for the fund, and it failed miserably. It went to zero. At the end of the day, the concept was right. You had seasoned veterans, but the execution killed the company. What we all missed was the difficulty in recreating and building an automotive company. It required not only manufacturing capabilities but working capital to maintain all the parts. You had to build a distribution system worldwide that could support the products and all those things. It was operationally very difficult and it just kept on requiring capital and capital and capital. Finally, we just stopped. Again sometimes the great concepts, the great ideas, the great themes, great products, an icon in the industry, with brand-name people and investors, come together and still don't work. I'd probably make the same mistake today.

Has there been anything in your personal life that has had an effect and made you a better investor? Any business ventures that you did when you were a kid?

I was always pretty business oriented right from ground zero. I think a lot of us had jobs, whether delivering papers or working as a youngster for small little ventures. Whether it was a little Kool-Aid vending station on the street, I was always sort of dabbling with making an extra dollar. Studying human nature comes back in a big way in this business. Everybody has an axe to grind to some degree. It's human nature for most CEOs that come through our offices to want to tell us what we want to hear, whether they believe their own opportunities or not. A lot of guys omit telling us a lot of things because they're afraid to tell us the bad news. Over the years, you tend to understand human nature a little bit, at least as far as the business, and you become skeptical. You're skeptical about everything in life. When someone comes in my office today, I don't believe them. You want to believe, but you need to do the work necessary over time and with confidence that you build in them.

So you're a bit of an investigative reporter, or an investigative detective? Frank never used to listen to you when you were working for him as an analyst. I thought that was one of the funniest stories I heard.

You learn from observing Frank, whether it's in meetings or how he thinks in his investments. That's what you gain the most, by paying attention to not necessarily what he says but what he does and how he does it. Altamira, for example—that all came about in the latter part of the 1980s and early 1990s. There have been some guys that have gone off and did some good things outside of Altamira beyond that.

I think while we didn't really work necessarily as a unit in terms of collectively managing money together as a team, it created an atmosphere of competitiveness and of hard work. That's what people have taken away with them from it.

Barry Allan.
Barry Allan, for example. A great guy. Will Sutherland.

Dave Taylor's done well too.

Dave Taylor, for sure. The list goes on. I think again that was an environment that was quite competitive.

In all your years in the market, what do you think is the biggest mistake the average investor makes?

Always emotions, fear and greed. We get caught up with it ourselves. You've got to trust those instincts. When things look excessive both on the positive and negative side, you've got to leave some stuff on the table. It's painful sometimes. When you're selling things, for example. You look at the uranium environment, up until about a year ago, it was quite fashionable to be invested in this group. It's frustrating because every day you would sell something, the next day it would be up even higher. Sometimes that's what you've got to do. You can't own the final dollar of movement. You're never smart enough to catch the bottoms, so you average down. That seems like a great concept, but it's painful to do because you're catching sharp knives and you're buying them when no one else wants to. It's having the conviction to stand there and having the longevity, and it's not easy to do in this world when investors are not as patient as we think they should be. I think investors in general are short-term oriented.

So you will average down, definitely. When broker firms' analysts report, they print target prices, they're always short term.

I think we all have axes to grind. They want to see activity. That's something that you just observe over the years and you don't really get caught up by that. In my case, I don't talk to a lot of people. A lot of people have sort of labelled me as one of the toughest guys to reach on the street. It's not because I don't want to talk to them but I try to stay away from the noise as much as possible because noise is usually associated with a business proposition on their part. From my perspective, I'm interested in what they have to offer from a news perspective, a research perspective. You take it for what it is and you just sort of shave off what you consider to be the baggage that comes with it sometimes. You use it for the facts, and then you tend to make up your own mind. I tend to do a lot of my own meetings, and I spend a lot of time in the boardroom meeting with companies.

Why did you take your sabbatical from Altamira in '96? Has this already been talked about?

Because I think I needed a break. It was a period of rapid growth at the shop, with lots of success. The firm grew enormously from $200 million of administration, when Frank and I came on in '87, to over $16 billion when I left in '95. The amount of mandates and the funds in administration that I had at that age was a big deal. I didn't really own a big piece of my own destiny. I was a very small shareholder of the firm. The primary reason was the fact that I needed to own a bigger piece. That wasn't going to be happening. The firm took great care of us, but at the end of the day, I didn't own it. So I needed to go where I controlled my own destiny and ownership. That was a great opportunity to take some time off and step away and reflect on all those things.

You aren't an extravagant spender in your personal life. Obviously, you have way more than enough money that you don't have to work, so why do you continue to work? Frank's in the same position, right? Everybody I've interviewed in the book is in the same position.

Yeah, Frank's going to die in front of the screen, and we're going to have to remove him in a casket from the office. A lot of people are like that. Some days, I can tell you, you're feeling differently than that. You're thinking, "What the frick—?" Because it's stressful, and it's not always pleasant. There are periods of time where people question you, you question yourself, things aren't going well, and you're thinking, "You know what? I'm just not up to this thing." Sometimes you wish you were retired and enjoying the fruits of all the prior labour.

But you outlive those things. The net of it all, the good and the bad, is that it's a business that people like and enjoy doing and waking up for. We're all pretty young here in the shop, and I think we have lots to do still.

Rohit said, "This is tough on me, being the kind of manager I am. I'd be retired for two weeks and I'd be happy for two weeks, and then I wouldn't know what to do with myself. So that's why I continue to do it."

He's one of the hardest working guys on the street.

Are there any funny stories that you had along the years that you wanted to share?

If you're investing in this business, then you've been on many trips—mining trips or energy trips in difficult parts of the world. Many of us are still happy to pinch ourselves that we're still alive, given the logistics that were put in front of us. For me, it was a similar kind of trip, in Namibia visiting an ocean diamond mining operation and along the Namibian coast. They call it the Elephant Coast. That's where a lot of ships have come to shore and grounded because it's some of the roughest water in the world. If you were doing a Friedland type of trip, you would have been helicoptered onto the vessel itself, which was the right way of doing it. Our company was a lot more emerging than that, and the vessel wasn't capable of handling helicopters, so we were in a bit of a dinghy. It was one of those things where you'd go up five feet and the next wave would set you back ten. It just took forever to get to the vessel, especially with really rough waters and no life jackets. It was the most ridiculous thing, thinking about it today. That was one of the most dangerous things that we did.

The worst part was embarking on the vessel from the dinghy, and they basically threw a rope ladder overboard. These waves are coming at you, and with every wave, your dinghy would crash up against this vessel and then it would subsequently suck you away from it. So whenever you decided to hang onto this thing, you would look beneath you, and your dinghy's gone. It took three or four waves to catch it. I latched onto the ladder and I didn't let go and climbed up, and the waters just got rougher from there. We ended up spending a whole of twenty minutes because the storm was coming in.

These are things that managers probably shouldn't do for investors.

You put your life on the line for your investors. That's a good thing.

No, it was that proverbial manager getting hit by the bus thing. There are better ways of managing your logistics. We don't do that today.

Did you buy that stock?

No. In fact, the general manager that was responsible for putting the trip together was let go that day. We never bought the stock. I'm just glad I'm back. There's too many stories that aren't worth repeating.

John Thiessen & Jeff McCord
Arb Your Way to Profits

"There are a lot of reasons management sells stock, but their belief that the stock is going higher is not one of them. [...] Not too many CEOs are willing to put themselves on the line."

It was a spectacular day in Vancouver when I strolled the ten minute walk from my office in downtown Vancouver to Vertex One's head office. "Who is Vertex One? Never heard of them." This is the most common response that I get from Baystreeters in Toronto when I mention this company from Vancouver that has one of the best track records in the country.

I chose Vertex One as one of my interviewees for a reason. First, led by John Thiessen, their track record has not only been great over the last ten years, but it has also been relatively consistent. They are a long/short alternative investment money manager, and with a 20-percent-plus rate of return since inception of the flagship Vertex Fund over ten years ago, they put most other investment firms to shame. I was certainly eager to see how they achieved these returns, especially since the return on the S&P 500 over the same time frame was a paltry return of less than 2 percent. An annualized alpha of 22 percent is certainly out of the norm also. If you aren't sure what "alpha" is, suffice it to say that it is their "value added," and 22 percent is a phenomenal number.

Although the firm, as evidenced by their balanced fund, has a decidedly value based tilt, their hedge product, the Vertex Fund, is very opportunistic. Their specialty was merger arbitrage originally, but that is just because they identified a lot of trades that they considered to be relatively low risk and at the same time highly profitable. John saw these trades when he was a long-only traditional money manager but couldn't take advantage of them, for that was not allowed in the investment mandate. That's one of the reasons the team went out on their own. The company started in 1998 on principles that had worked for them at M.K. Wong & Associates. John Thiessen ran U.S. equities and Jeff McCord and Matt Wood took care of private clients. They started up Vertex One, and the rest is history.

When I walked in the office, it looked like a really nice condo. As you enter the front door, the first thing you see is a big, modern-looking kitchen off to the right. To the left are a couple of comfy-looking couches, with a nice coffee table. The openness of the office is very inviting, and it looks like a great place to have a cocktail party. Looking straight ahead as you come through the door, you see the trading desk, where John Thiessen and the team sit. The desks and computer terminals face the window, which, by the way, gives the best view in the city. The office looks toward the North Shore mountains, out over the Vancouver harbour. It just so happens to be the same as the view from my office, just down the street, so I realize how lucky I am to have the view I do.

Sitting in the spacious boardroom with John Thiessen and Jeff McCord, we grabbed some cranberry juice and started the interview. It's funny—money managers aren't often relaxed in an interview scenario. This was not the case at all in this interview. John is young-looking, talks in a straightforward manner, and was very relaxed as we all slouched a bit in the comfortable chairs. The conversation flowed quite easily and the answers were very complete, so the interview was a pleasure. Sitting there for a couple of hours or so on our first interview, we swapped stories about the industry, the market, and strategies.

Bob:
How did you get started?

John:
I always had a fascination with the news. The beauty of this business is that it's always news related. Current events actually always in some manner or respect blow into the actual portfolio, and fold into it. As a kid, I was fascinated with reading the *Winnipeg Free Press,* and Jeff's grandparents actually used to live across the street from me when I was a kid, believe it or not, although I didn't know it at the time.

Jeff:
You knew it at the time. You just didn't know that we were going to come together later on. That's what you didn't know.

Yeah, exactly. If you read the newspaper, half of it is business, really. I didn't really have much interest in sports besides the Winnipeg Jets. So I was interested to see how the daily news on the front ties in to the business section in the back. You always want to see where the linkages came. I ended up with sort of a business interest in university, and I took economics, and then I took the securities course and then I took the options course and then I took the futures course, etc.

When I graduated from university in Calgary, oil was $11, $12, and there were no jobs to be had. So I went traveling around the world and did my version of Jim Rogers' *Investment Biker*. I got lucky because I got a great job when I came out of university, working for the Alberta Heritage Savings Fund as a junior analyst. That was my first job for $5.50 an hour. My student loan and my rent—it was $100 more than my salary.

You were investing all your excess cash? [Laughs]
Yeah, that's right. Yeah.

Do you remember the first stock you ever bought?
Yeah. Blake Resources, 100 shares. I bought it on a recommendation of a Merrill Lynch analyst at $4.05. It went to zero.

Excellent. That is just a common story.

It's funny because I'm thinking of the first stock I bought and I can't remember the name of it. Very similar result, right? Some friend of my dad's recommended this stock, and in those days, the only way you got your stock quotes was the newspaper.

This Merrill Lynch guy came into the U of C. He did a presentation about his job and just worked through a report that he had just written, then straight to zero.

I think if you make money, it doesn't teach you anything. It's only losing, where you say, "What actually happened here? What went wrong?"

I've heard that quite a bit. How many companies in Canada do you think have Triple A credit rating?

I thought two thirds or three quarters were issuing junk bonds on the TSX, so I don't know. How many?

There's only one company in Canada with a Triple A.

Is that right? Is it Royal?

TD Bank.

No. They don't have Triple A.

TD used to be Triple A.

Yeah, not anymore.

Really?

This company has had uninterrupted dividend growth of 125 years. In the last ten years, they've bought back 40 percent of their stock, and you never see research on it.

Imperial Oil.

Imperial Oil? Really?
No kidding.

Yeah. I just looked it up today. No one ever talks about it. I'm long Imperial. They're doing everything right, but it is totally ignored.

You're right. Nobody talks about it.
It's the value name of all time.

It's like Philip Morris in the U.S.—best-performing stock on the Dow, except for Microsoft.
Yeah. We own that one. We don't own it in our own backyard, but we know it's a good smoking stock.

And collect a nice dividend on that one.

So you were in Alberta Heritage, what was your next firm? Was it M.K. Wong?
No, National Trust. Matt and Jeff were also at trust companies. Matt was at Royal Trust. Jeff was at Canada Trust. I was at National Trust. We were just doing small portfolios, which you thought were large at the time, of course. You know, people from $100,000 and up.

Yeah, I know. Some guy comes in with $300,000—you think it's a big account.

Then all three of us met each other from there because that's where Milt's old stomping ground was. We all ended up at M.K. Wong & Associates.

What was the philosophy at M.K. Wong?
The beauty of that firm was the philosophy is based on the employees that work there. It changed continuously.

Yeah. Milt said to me, you know, "Why are you guys leaving? I let you do your own thing." On the personal side where Matt and I were, I remember only once sitting down with anybody in terms of them looking at what we were doing. That was actually what gave us the confidence to go on your own. It's like we're already doing 80 percent of it on our own. We can do the other 20 percent, which is just building the infrastructure of the firm. The money management part of it wasn't intimidating to go on your own.

What was the catalyst that caused you to go out on your own?

Well, there were a number of catalysts. One, it was a bank-owned firm. I looked at working for an independent mid-sized counselling firm where you contribute, help grow the business, and you get equity and you share in it, etc. Once you become a bank-owned firm, two things happen. One, that possibility goes away, and two, early on you know the way they're going to run the organization. One of the things about getting out of Canada Trust was you knew you didn't want to work for the big organization again.

They were great, though. HSBC treated us really well. But just to work there long term wasn't for us. There was the catalyst of wanting to do your own thing and have your own business.

If you look at all the managers that you're interviewing, none of them work for a bank-owned firm. The two will never go hand in hand because it stifles you.

The cycle will happen just like it does with the boutique brokerage shops.

When we just got bought by HSBC, we had small equity stakes, and Milt had 51 percent, so we didn't really have a say in the business. I was reading a *Forbes* article by the chairman of HSBC. The article said, people that work here, they don't do it for the money. I went, "Oh. Well, I guess this is not the place that I want to be if I'm going to be held back just based on that situation."

Well, it's funny. I mean, from John Embry to anybody that excels, they move somewhere else.

That's so true.

Well, he stayed longer than most guys do. There's no question.

So, John, you ran U.S.?

Yeah, I ran U.S. equities.

And Jeff?

We ran high net worth portfolios, segregated portfolios. Matt and I were running those. So we would have our Canadian picks in there. We got our U.S. names from John.

Two questions: When you decided to start Vertex, why did you decide to start a hedge fund? Nobody really did that in Canada in '97, '98. Why wouldn't you just say, "Let's go long"?

Well, it wasn't easy because we had a lot of grief from clients who just weren't familiar with especially the fee structure. There aren't that many original things in life, whether it's building a house or building a hedge fund. You need to take examples. Those people that do well in life learn well from the examples of people who can see that that's the right model. We just basically looked at the U.S. market, which is the leading market. There were maybe six funds in Canada at the time. There wasn't much going on in Western Canada, that's for sure.

They were mostly private, the hedge funds that were in Canada at that time. It was John's idea. You and I talked about doing something with BCE options in our personal accounts. Every once in a while there would be an arbitrage opportunity that would be out there and it would be like, "Wow, what a great way to make money, but we can't do that here." Then there was the fact that even in '97, we thought some stocks' valuations were getting high. We never anticipated it going to the levels it did. So when John had this idea, I remember choking on the 1-percent-plus-20-percent concept of profits. Because where I came from was the seg side where the fee is one on the first million and then it's 25 basis points. When we started our side, we had some seg clients come with us. We had to tell them that it was 1 percent. Then if they had the hedge fund, it was 1 plus 20.

Hard sell.

Well, you know what? It was, but it's an easy, easy sell now. It has been for a lot of years, but it was just getting your own mental self over that hurdle. Once you did that, it was easy.

Yeah. If you realized people are paying for performance instead of just assets under admin, right? Then it's easy.

That's the biggest problem I have too, trying to explain it to the financial press. They're constantly saying, "Well, the fees are high. The fees are high."

Our MER (management expense ratio) goes on Globe Fund.

Yeah, like, 6.5 or something.

Well, last year it was 5.8. This year it's 8.3 or something. People phone up and go, "Eight percent." But that's only if you make money.

It's 1 if you don't make money, and if we lose a lot, then it's 1 for a long time until we get over the high-water mark.

You know what, though, Bob? There's truth in the fact that, if you look at our historical performance, 7 percent in '01 and -2 in '02, you're earning your money big time in those years because you aren't -20.

Absolutely. It's the hedge that provides the advantage in the down times. That's a hard sell because people don't understand that.

Internally, we kind of consider ourselves to be more like equity managers, though.

We use all those available tools that are out there to reduce risk. We love merger arb, if we can do what we call high probability deals—high probability that they'll close. We love to do those kinds of deals. Merger arbitrage is a hedge fund strategy that usually involves buying the stock of a company being acquired and simultaneously selling (shorting) the stock of a company acquiring the target business.

How did you develop the expertise? Because long-only managers a lot of times don't have that expertise.

Merger arb to me has always been a simple strategy.

Yeah, it is simple. The thing was that basically when we ran U.S. equities, we had so many companies, especially at that time with higher valuations where people used paper instead of cash. We'd say, "Wow, we can make 10 to 12 percent and lock it in." Unfortunately, when you're managing money long-only, it was like having one hand tied behind your back. So we figured, if you run a hedge fund using the U.S. format, which you have to study from the first place because you learn more from the losers than you do the winners—once you understand the winner's format, then you have to see where people make mistakes. Like trying to bet on market direction or using leverage. So those are the two things that we said from the outset that we weren't going to do. But then if you could do merger arb and lock in the other side with hedging the purchaser of the asset's share price, you can reduce the risk in the portfolio.

When MacMillan Bloedel got taken out, that was a really good example. I think in that deal there was 13 percent and Weyerhaeuser was buying them. Between the time the deal got announced and the deal closed, the whole forest product sector corrected 20 percent. People ask that question too, like, "How do you guys do all these different things with just such a few number of people?" It's really you're just applying the same investment acumen to different situations, looking at what the risk is, what the downside is, and what the upside is.

The key is because it's such a seminal event for a corporation to sell itself. So when you have a board of directors like West Coast Energy here in town or Terasen, formerly B.C. Gas, or MacMillan Bloedel, as Jeff mentioned, these companies have a very long track record. When you get to that threshold that the company wants to sell itself, then the chance of the probability of something happening is very high. You can ride the cycles out of owning a stock on the high and the lows. We believe there's a probability in excess of 95 percent once a company wants to do something. Event-driven strategies like merger arb, if we do seventy deals a year, on average we have sixty-nine complete. So the returns are lower. The fact is, as John Templeton said, "You only have to be right six out of ten times when you're picking longs." So we're right 99 percent of the time. We take that with a lower return, but we're able to compound that with these deals, which usually get wrapped up over a ninety-day period.

It's always looking for deals where the probability of an action is higher than just owning a stock for value's sake. So you have a probability that an oil and gas company's going to convert to an income trust after they've announced it is very high, so we're happy to own that. Our whole strategy here is just only owning two funds and being focused. I think that's one common concept you see is if you're focused on just a few funds, you do much better than having a little bit of everything for everyone. That focus has worked out well with the strategies of the stocks that we own.

Just to get back on the point, the strategy that we see now for the first time is shareholders—especially in an environment where you have the S&P flat for ten years now—excluding dividends. We know dividends are really the biggest proportion of return for most investors, on a side note. I always say the Dow Jones index is a million if you include dividends. Without it, it's only ten thousand. But we're seeing capital shareholders have a 20 percent interest in names like Hudson's Bay or Wendy's or Time Warner or McDonald's or Creo. They get active in these companies and become the catalyst instead of the board of directors and hotels. So for the first time, the catalyst now is the shareholder instead of the management, and people are reacting to that. It's been a recent and new catalyst event-driven strategy for us.

Just to go back to when you started, merger arb was a big part of your returns. Let's talk about the performance attribution in the late '90s. It's interesting to see how you kind of morphed and changed things around.

Well, you're reacting to it. Like an economic cycle, there's an investment cycle. Three or four years ago, there was a lot of money made in the income trust conversion marketplace. You didn't make money doing that seven years ago. It didn't happen. That's one of the things about our offering memorandum. The way it's written in terms of being opportunistic is that we can participate in these situations as they appear on the horizon. I've looked a little bit at the history of merger arb and the spreads in merger arbitrage and the opportunities tend to increase when the markets are rising. It's because the shift of money goes to the long side. What happened in 2001 was, after the markets rolled over in 2000, everybody was looking for the safe haven, and it just compressed yields on merger arbitrage.

What did you have to do in those years to preserve capital?

We would have done a lot better than we did. A lot of the merger arb deals, like Mario Gabelli, who I think runs one of the best merger arb funds, were on a fully hedged basis. He sort of leveraged an 8 percent rate of return. We could do that, but we're obviously trying to add alpha to that. The biggest thing we're proud of is that our beta is 0.36. We run a very conservative balanced fund with a third Government of Canada bonds and the rest stocks. Its beta is 0.46—and very low rate of turnover.

So on a day-to-day basis, we think our beta's 1.00, but the strategy shows that over time, it compounds to 0.36. The reason we can add value is because a lot of the merger arb deals we look at just from a value perspective, so we've got the synergy from the balance fund. That means we own a lot of deals on an unhedged basis because we're comfortable with it.

Yeah, more than we did in '99, for sure. Because you could lock in bigger spreads back then.

Right. So you're going on an unhedged basis. You have about 26, 30 percent merger arb right now in front?
Yeah.

So how did you generate returns in 2001, 2002? What did you do?
Option writing.

Option writing. Hedged. As you realize the market is just going to be bad for a long time, you end up doing a lot of hedged merger-arb transactions.

There were a lot of the related trades then too.

Yeah, there were. One of our biggest trades was just....

We were into Falconbridge.

Right. Falconbridge.

Weston Loblaws.

We loved a lot of those trades back then. The takeovers were great from HotJobs.com and the small cap merger-arbs base. What happens is especially with stocks under five bucks, the cost to borrow would be so high that people weren't willing to participate in that space, so the returns were much higher. We had a very good prime brokerage relationship at the time with National Bank so that our cost to borrow was almost nothing, and that allowed us to get a really good rate of return for our shareholders.

Which one worked out the best for you? Was it MacMillan?
The best risk-arb deal?

Yeah.
HotJobs.

Yeah. Dot-com. We made 5 percent in December and saved our year.

I remember that. I was just thinking about it. One of the best risk-arbs, though, was when the fund was a limited partnership and it was that technology deal out of....

Veritas TeleBackup Systems?

Yeah. TeleBackup Systems. What happened was the company that was doing the acquiring was up fourfold as was the company being acquired. Because it was a limited partnership, it had this huge income loss that you could flow through your unitholder. There was a big spread in that deal. I think it was, like, 30 to 35 percent. We would have made way more money had we just been long in TeleBackup Systems, but then you would have had the market risk that went with it. From a valuation perspective, it never made sense to own the stock.

But net-net to the investor on an after-tax basis, it was just a phenomenal situation. It really worked out.

Any that didn't work out?
No. Well, that's the beauty of the strategy, because as long as the company's up for sale, usually there's a catalyst, so people still believe that something can happen. So you can walk away with only losing usually 10 to 15 percent of your money.

As long as you stay in the position. Tyson Foods was like that because the deal blew up there and we stayed on the position and took the lumps, and then eventually....

It got taken out, right?
It did, yeah. But the one we've made the most money on a dollar basis, not a percentage basis, would probably be Pan American bought Corner Bay Minerals, and they gave us five-year warrants. So we did all right on the deal, but basically we got five-year silver warrants where we've in turn written call options on a monthly basis of about a quarter million dollars on that for three years. So on a merger arb deal like that, we would have made $10 million easily on a small cap mining deal. Of course, we're bigger, so we did Archipelago and NASDAQ. On those deals which we owned unhedged, we've made almost $20 million. So recently, of course, the numbers are bigger because we're investing more. That was a unique situation of being Canadian, to be

able to look at the value of the exchange versus what the Americans viewed it as. I think the same situation existed with Wendy's. The Americans didn't really understand the franchise value of fat donuts, especially after Krispy Kreme went under.

Did you see this hat that Hudson Bay's made for the Olympic Games? It's the full hoser hat. Have you seen it?

No.

Oh, it's the one with the flaps and the strings on it. My mom bought it. When the Americans see that, they'll realize that donuts and coffee in Canada are big sellers. Wait till they see those hats.

There's got to be a way to profit from that.
They're so bad that they're cool.

What options strategies do you use to enhance value? Covered calls can enhance income.
I think that's true. We deal with some really smart option traders, and every time we do a trade, they just think we're complete idiots because nothing we do makes sense based on their models. It always makes sense to us intrinsically in the deals we do. The old line in options is, "You're always picking up pennies in front of the steam-roller," or, "I got called out of that name and it went up fourfold, but I couldn't wait till next month to redo it." Richard Croft, for example, some of the best articles together in Canada. Unfortunately, we get investors from his fund coming in here all the time going, "Yeah, but we're not making any money."

The theories are great—a lot of the strategies. We can own warrants and then add the money calls each month, just as long as the ball's high and we've taken premium money. For us, it's all about the dollar value that we can take in, not about the model. It's about the dollar value, and if it's less than a dollar, we have no interest. We never do options that cost less than a buck because you just don't make any money in that space. We need to get dollars and we need to get volume. The bottom line is you're usually selling to retail guys. You need to have the ball in the market. So sometimes we're shut out of the market for a year.

Of course, the strategy does not work in Canada. You cannot do options in Canada because we just don't have the market breadth here. Even in the U.S., sometimes we're buttressed against our size versus trying to do it. We basically will write cover calls on names that we like, and we will short-put on names that we like. We never do what the models say.

So you're using your common sense rather than the models, basically.

Yeah. We never even know what the model's supposed to say because the option traders always laugh on the other end of the line. They take us a little more seriously now. We have a golf tournament with a guy who's here in town. We were probably about an $80 million fund and he gave us almost $3 million of option income in one year. Every trade didn't make sense from his proprietary trading desk, but it worked for us because we came from the equity side, from the bottom-up side not the model side.

That leads into the next question. How much of your investment process is based upon bottom-up versus big-picture top-down analysis?

I think 100 percent is bottom-up. People ask us what our interest rate forecast is. The Bank of Canada doesn't know, so we don't know.

We don't know what the markets are going to do. We don't know what the currency's going to do. We don't know what interest rates are going to do. But, damn it, if we know the board of directors wants to sell the company, we're comfortable with that. That's the catalyst and the event that we know for sure, and we're willing to because someone's actually told us something that they're going to do. The other things are all variables. The first thing that you learn in Economics 101, on a macro basis, that you can control interest rates, you can control money supply, and you can control your currency rate, but once you pick one, you lose control of the other two.

Somehow they all want to manage all three at the same time. They say that interest rates are policy in terms of the way they'll run it, but they're concerned about the currency and they're concerned about money supply. We know that every reserve bank of any G8 nation is trying to basically somehow try and look after all three at once.

Wayne Deans started out at the Bank of Canada and he worked there for ten years, and he said, "The biggest thing I learned at the Bank of Canada is they didn't know anything about the economy and what was

going to happen to it." So when he decided to manage money, he said, "I didn't pay attention to that. I just picked bottom-up." Those are basically his exact words. So it's interesting, yeah.

Yeah, he's totally right. I just got that from the newspapers. [Laughs]

So the only way you can do it is to think differently than everybody else?

That is correct. My view is different than others. There's some people who get it and some who don't, that's why I like money management. It will always be more art than science for the bigger numbers.

Yeah. There was an e-mail that was going around. It was a bunch of analysts and it was a bunch of round heads and it was a chart. You moved your mouse and wherever your cursor went, the heads went on the analysts.

It went from a happy face when it's high to a sad face when it's low.

It was something about how analysts predict stocks. If they're going up they just take a ruler and draw the line straight up. And I think, I hate to beat up on poor old Nortel or JDS, but there was a classic example where even PH&N said, "Oh, we have to own it because it's in the index."

If you understand that, you need to understand where the crowd is and where the crowd is going. Why does the crowd shift to the hockey game from the basketball game? Don't fret about the small stuff. People in this business fret 90 percent of the time. I don't. We can talk about any company and we can spend 100 hours of work to get a great file going. If the CEO sold his stock, all the work doesn't mean crap because that one variable unfortunately means more than the other 10,000 that you put together. There's a lot of reasons management sells stock, but their belief that it's going higher is not one of them. Insider buying is so important. Not too many CEOs are willing to put their money on the line.

Now, you have to be careful there because Ray Loewen believed his own BS.

Bernie Ebbers believed his own accounting numbers, but, statistically, you will win.

I don't think Greg Maffei at 360networks dumped his stock, did he?

No, he stayed right till the end. He couldn't read a balance sheet because he came from Microsoft. He was the CFO of a company with no debt, and he didn't realize that the situation changes.

Yeah, debt is what killed him.

Life for us is always the catalyst. So we went with Air Canada on the way down because it's about behavioural shift. It talks about a whole bunch of new shareholders. Nobody wants to own Air Canada when it's going from $3 to zero, so everybody gets off the stock and so you get that great catalyst of bankruptcy. Then when it goes into bankruptcy, usually the restructuring takes a long time, depending on the company. Some are fast. Air Canada was one of the fastest bankruptcies we've seen in a long time. So we also then want to own the bonds because people will buy the bonds in the bankruptcy situation. They're also not interested in being a long-term equity holder, so we want to be there during that change. We wanted to own Air Canada bonds through the bankruptcy, and then obviously our bonds get converted to equity and then we get a great ride just to take up that behavioural shift.

You wouldn't believe how many retail clients that I had phoning when Air Canada was a dollar and bouncing around, saying, "Oh, I should buy a bunch of Air Canada stock." I said, "But the news release came out yesterday and it said it was worth nothing."

The regulators tend to be the big brother and protect the investor. In the U.S., it's just you list it as soon as they go into Chapter 11.

I know. I mean, so many people bought it.

There was so much volume. Well, the thing is it's beautiful because so many guys can buy 10 million shares at $0.10 and sell it for $0.14 a day later. With a lot of those penny stocks, it's more fun than Vegas. As long as you know the parameters, just don't play for more than a few minutes.

One of the places you differ from a lot of other hedge managers is that I think you're limited to 15 percent short. Is that right?

Yeah. Basically what we're trying to do in the portfolio is always take the risk out of it. So we never have more than 100 percent equity exposure or we don't use index options. We don't use futures. Shorts can whipsaw you. So we're looking for bankruptcy targets, the ones we've done are Royal Oak Mines, Loewen Group, most of the U.S. airlines, which most are bankrupt now.

Any steel stocks?
Yeah, we were shorting Stelco for a while.

Yeah, we were short Stelco. We lost the borrow.

Similar to Peter Puccetti, he will only short bankruptcy candidates. He's been short Ballard Power for years.
Where's that stock trading?

Three to five bucks.

What is your criteria for shorting?
Our criteria is that the company needs to be bankrupt within twelve months. The stock's usually below five bucks, so it's no longer marginable. They're losing analyst coverage, and the balance sheet's holding a gun to the company's head. Those are all things that make us happy as well as the bonds have already dropped off. The fixed income guys as a rule are usually smarter than the equity guys because they do more work; they don't really care about the business or the product.

Aren't two thirds of the companies in the TSX issuing junk bonds if they're issuing them?
Oh, yeah, for sure. We know there's only one Triple A. I remember in 1989 there were only twelve companies in the S&P 500 with Triple A. I don't know what the number is today.

I don't think it's very many at all. GE's still Triple A, but I think it's hard to find others.
Even in GE's case, I know a lot of it's syndicated, the debt to equity is massive. It's just good for the issuers to have them at Triple A. Everybody wins, and the insiders gain.

Do you use stop losses at all? Or stop buys would be on the short position.

No, never. No. Unless we figure out we're wrong, like owning the Independent Power Producers, which we owned.

Stop losses wouldn't have helped there anyways.

Yeah. It just goes down so fast.

They were gapping down.

It's interesting because that's the difference between a trader and an investor.

You do have to take a second look, though. That's one thing we've done, and John brings up Independent Power Producers. When some new information came to the surface and we looked at what was really going on, we had to swallow it and take our losses and move on. There's been other situations where we bought Extendicare and a month, or if not two or three weeks later, we were down 25 percent on the position. It was like you've got to go back and look at it. That one beared out, the market was wrong. So you do have to take that second and sometimes third look through at what's going on when stuff starts moving like that.

It says in your advertising literature you look at distressed securities too. What's that?

Well, we want the companies usually within two quarters of coming out of bankruptcy, like Microcell. I hear the cows are coming home. Yeah, Air Canada and Microcell have sort of been our biggest.

How did you come up with the securities lending idea?

I think Matt …

You did it with Martha Stewart?

Oh, yeah. Where it really started was with Fairfax. It is one of our largest positions in our balanced fund. All of a sudden what we were getting on the return to lend out the stock was 15 to 20 percent. Apparently, some guys have paid up to 40 percent to borrow that stock.

Over the short term. But the great statistic with Fairfax was that 20 million shares were held by institutions and insiders, and there's 17 million shares out. Have you ever heard of any such a thing in your life? I don't know where the 3 million shortage comes from.

Well, it says "borrowed," right?

I know, but it's borrow/overborrow. Then there was another. I think it was Decker in the U.S. Matt and Tim came up with that idea where you do the straddles and lend the stock out. The thing is if you do enough of those deals, even if one of those stocks drops and you get hit on it and you have to buy in, it doesn't matter because you're doing it every month and you're collecting the premiums every month. Plus, you're doing more than one deal. There's always more than one that you can find to do. So you only have to be successful at that for a few months and you've taken the downside out of the transaction.

It did happen with one of them, I can't remember if it was Decker or not. This was in our balanced fund where we did get called on the stock. We'd received so much premium income already it sort of just neutralized it. It was zero and now there was more volatility in the options. So we just kept doing it.

Do you believe in a commodity boom that will last? What are your thoughts on peak oil and that sort of thing?

You've already got some great opinions from a couple people who've studied it quite a bit. The biggest thing for us is that these companies are in a cycle, whether it's oil or base metals. Forest products are the one exception to this great commodity cycle. Because the exception proves the rule, as we know. When you have that kind of cash flow, you have a lot of events that drive deals, including spinouts. You couldn't give away oil-sand assets ten years ago. So our key is that the reason we currently have 25 percent of the portfolio in oil is not necessarily because we're believers in it. It's just that these companies that we invest in have such unbelievable free cash flow and hence have such a great ability to drive deals that it means that we're going to be in the space.

The investment bankers are very focused in that sector in terms of driving it. So everything just compounds it.

I guess I should hold on to my oil and gas.

Yeah, exactly. With the base metals, there's a demand and supply imbalance. It takes a long time usually for that to work itself through the system. By the time you come up with the idea, finance, go find a mine, build a road to it, hire people, it's ten years.

Ten years to bring a zinc discovery and bring it into production!

Luckily, Pan American mines have turned their silver mines to zinc because the grades were so low. People said Pan American was really just a zinc miner not a silver miner.

Maybe they should change the name too, like Cartaway Resources. Remember they used to cart away people's garbage, and then the big nickel discovery happened and they changed it to Cartaway Resources and the stock went to $21?

I didn't know that that's where it came from.

It was Cartaway. Cartaway Garbage.

Oh, that's perfect.

Oh, that's good. I didn't know that.

Imagine all the scandals.

Okay, and now the other one is gold.

It's a beauty because Canadian gold is the ultimate behavioural metal. It's like a technology stock: We all believe it goes higher, then it goes higher. We all believe it goes lower—it goes lower. Every single ounce that's ever been produced has never been used. It may sit on your wrist for twenty years or your ring finger for a lifetime, but, at the end of the day, it all gets melted down and reused. So every single ounce has been still on and available for investment purposes at any time for any human being. For the first time in our lives, there's actually a financial buyer through the Gold ETF. You actually now have a financial buyer and you can actually buy the stock now as a portfolio manager without being ridiculed like the Trimark managers were ten years ago for owning it in their portfolio.

Ego.

It cost him his job. But now if you own GLD shares no one thinks the same. So it's okay to think outside the box, but just don't think too early outside the box or people will crucify you and you'll have to pay with your head. Now you have a situation where you have financial buyers for the assets. You have a booming economy where the best part about this economy is that there's no one that thinks better groupthink than the Chinese. So at the end of the day it will probably be a fantastic boom if the Chinese believe in the behavioural buying of it all.

Are there any rules that you always go by when you're making an investment decision that gives you discipline?
Well, for us it's the events and the catalyst. In the old days when we were looking at stocks, it was always about free cash flow. What does it trade at?

It's low price to value metrics.

Yeah. So if a long bond is yielding 5 percent, that means you'll pay up to twenty times free cash flow for it. Long bonds yielding 10 percent you shouldn't pay more than ten times because the earnings yield is the opposite. Plus we're willing to pay some type of growth rate. I think that's probably the most important because, at the end of the day, there's only one factor of all the things that make stocks go up. What is the one factor that makes stocks go up? I always ask the kids at UBC this question. I go, "Hey, guys. What do you think makes stock go up?" You get a million hands from, "Oh, it's quality management, great product, it's margins, it's…."

Earnings.

It's only earnings, and people forget that. But Nortel never had any earnings through the whole cycle. People forgot that as well because it's earnings before charges.

Do you ever watch CNBC?
We only watch Report on Business TV now. We never watch others. We couldn't take the talking heads anymore. It drove us crazy.

You're not necessarily bullish on oil and gas. You just say, "There's a lot of M&A activity that we can see could happen in the sector."

We all have our own personal views, but we don't want them to get in the way of us making money. Basically, we see some fantastic events, and that's what we want to do is look for more of the events. It just so happens that a bull market or a cash flow market brings events. The opposite works as well. With the lack of cash flow and the bear market, it brings events too in terms of distressed securities.

What is your biggest win in a stock?
America Online. AOL.

Oh, really?
Yeah. It ended up that it was a hundred-bagger for us at M.K. Wong.

Is that right?
Yeah. The second one is a stock we own again now. It was a thirty-bagger and it was Chesapeake Energy. AOL was our biggest. We owned 1 percent of the company and it was basically like walking into Starbucks. When we became an AOL user they had 150,000 users at the time—on the way to 20 million plus. That was just a massive ride.

What year, approximately?
Nineteen-ninety-five, '94.

I was with C.M. Oliver at that time, and Rob Millham used to write a little thing called *Equity Search*. He talked about AOL back in '95, and he says, you know, "This could be a good little stock."
That little *Equity Search* was a great little publication because it didn't have anything to do with CM Oliver. It was just a bunch of guys that came up with small cap ideas. They had lots of great little ideas in that thing.
Yeah, we tried to buy the IPO at AOL, but we didn't know the game was rigged, so that's why we never got any stock. We got shut out, then it turned out we just basically bought it post-IPO. Paul Allen, co-founder of Microsoft, had one good trade, and he's had fifty losers since. He owned 10 percent of the company and he sold it all because he couldn't get a board seat, so he missed

a hundred-bagger because of his ego.

I've thought about that with Paul Allen. I haven't seen too many things that he invested in that actually....
Want to know why the Seahawks lost? Because Paul Allen's there, simple.

Paul made money on that trade, though.

Yeah, it's been fantastic. They're no longer called "owners." They're now called "chairman." I noticed that. It must be for tax purposes.

Your track record's been fantastic, but people's expectations get out of line too. They expect 30 percent a year with no standard deviation. So what is a reasonable rate of return you would be happy with when you retire twenty years down the road?
It's just dangerous to throw out numbers because we're all blessed to have the returns that we currently have. There's a fantastic research report written last year in my favourite newspaper, the *Financial Times* of London, that talked about....

Which paper was that?
FT. The U.S. or European edition. It's the pink sheets. Not to be confused with the other pink sheets south of the border. It talked about what the Indians sold for Manhattan. The thing is you say, "Well, you know, if you'd invested that in a GIC and had a rate of return, yada, yada, yada, how much would it be worth today?" But the thing is that no one actually ever looks at the standard deviation of the returns at that time.

So saying to compound your number over a period of time is a very dangerous thing because it's not possible to look at longer-term track records. Over time, the human factor gets involved. The GICs are yielding 18 percent and GICs are yielding 2 percent—it changes behaviour to do different things. When you reinvest—and how often you reinvest—did you lock in 1981 at 18 percent for a twenty-year bond? That whole compounding effect has a massive change on the standard deviation of reinvestment, and it's never accounted into people's returns.

You need to realize the human condition affects all these returns. I think for investors the key thing is that's great for the past, but what about the future?

There's not too many guys you're interviewing that are under the age of 40, that's for sure. You'll get that regression to the mean.

Thanks, guys.

Common Traits and Lessons of the Stock Market Superstars

As I researched some of Canada's best money managers, and subsequently interviewed them, one thing more than any other came to light: What is the biggest thing I learned? It was that there is no best way to manage money. It reminds me of a lecture in university I attended. I studied anatomy and physiology, and in this particular lecture, an MD was discussing knee operations. I remember he said that there were five different ways of doing the same knee operation. He asked us, "What does that tell you about knee operations?" None of knew, of course, but he said, "It tells you there is no best way to do a knee operation. If there were, everybody would use the best method. Further, each knee surgeon uses the method that best fits their training, personality, and all the other factors that make them who they are." I don't think any analogy is more fitting to money management. Each of these managers has his own distinct style that he has honed and developed over the years. No style is best, but the style each uses is best for him. The key is that they do not deviate from their styles, just as surgeons don't change their operating style each time they operate.

This doesn't mean there aren't common traits among the great stock pickers. Interestingly enough, managers with polar opposite strategies often do some of the same things. An example is the way a growth manager and a value investor would control risk. As I sat down at a table with Rohit Sehgal, I asked him if he had an important rule that helped shaped his philosophy. He pounded his fist on the table and said, "Never average down." In other words, he was saying that he cuts his losses quickly if he is wrong, and doesn't try to make a losing position better by trying to catch a falling knife. This is very common with growth managers, because once stocks with high P/E ratios start to fall, they can go down a long way, giving an investor a permanent loss of capital.

On the other hand, value investors may control risk another way, and averaging down is often central to their approach. When I interviewed Peter Puccetti, a deep value investor, I asked him how he accumulates stocks. He said, "We take a 1-percent position, and the stock usually falls after our initial purchase. If we like it, and we become more confident, we continue to average down, and hopefully near the bottom, we have accumulated our full position." They tend to buy stocks at values that are below their calculated intrinsic value. When market value is far below what they think the value of the company is, they buy it. This is usually well in advance of what the market sees in the short run. The end result is that the stock will often fall after the initial purchase. In this case, value managers will average down.

As you can see, averaging down may be a good strategy for a value manager who manages risk through the margin of safety they think they have between their initial purchase price and the "true" value they think the stock is worth. Keep this in mind as you read through the lessons and traits of some of the best stock pickers in Canada.

Having Discipline

Each Stock Market Superstar has his own method he continuously tries to perfect. The key is that they are disciplined with their approach, within a framework that also allows them to be flexible. A recipe for disaster is to become something that you aren't, or lose faith in your style, your process, or yourself. Discipline, while constantly asking questions about your process, is a key.

Thinking Differently (Outside of the Box)

The only way a person can be successful is by doing things differently from others. Investors who are successful in the stock market see things that others don't. They don't follow others, they lead with ideas that the masses may think are wrong or that they are uncomfortable with. They don't follow the index, and they act upon the ideas that they have, completely independent of what the makeup of the market is.

Having Confidence

When you strike out on your own, do your own thing, and dare to be different, you will often be wrong in the short run. All the Stock Market Superstars have enough confidence in their own abilities to stick with something that may be unpopular short term. There is a delicate balance between being confident, knowing when you are wrong, and admitting you have a made a mistake

Capitalizing on Market Psychology

I think that behavioural finance is the most important determinant of success with individual investors. Fear and greed rule the markets, and those who learn to control them or use them to their advantage, have the opportunity to do well. Most value investors rely on the fact that the market is inefficient in the short run due to fear and greed. They capitalize on this by buying unwanted, unloved securities. They then wait for the market to get more efficient and for the "true" value of a stock to be reflected in its price. The trick is to be able to subdue the emotional part of human behaviour. This is why Tom Stanley repeated many times, "Humans are not wired up correctly for investing," and nothing could be truer. Eliminating or reducing the effect of human emotion in the investing process is a key to success.

Management

Every single great stock picker mentioned that one of the most, if not the most important, variable to look for when contemplating the purchase of a stock is good management. The business is built on trust, and management should be trustworthy, competent, and do what is in the best interest of shareholders, not themselves. One of the ways Wayne Deans does this is by looking at the notes to financial statements, in particular how much stock the management has given away to themselves in the form of cheap options.

Tim McElvaine thought that management was important, but that the board of directors was also very important. The key here was that each of these money managers has achieved much of his excellent performance through investing in small cap stocks. With small companies, management is even more important, as companies' fortunes can turn negative on a dime, especially in the face of poor or dishonest management.

Size Matters

Successful stock pickers generally go big or go home. In other words, they know that good ideas are plentiful, but great ideas don't come around that often. When they find a truly great idea, they back up the truck and take a big position. One of the managers said that, in reality, he and others had found many of the same ideas over the years. The key that made him better was that he took large positions in stocks he thought were the best, whereas others didn't have the fortitude to put that much on the line. This was one of the first rules of George Soros. This goes for managers who have a lot of stocks, or just a few.

Furthermore, many of the great stock pickers actually manage a relatively small amount of money. This allows them to be nimble and flexible. This is especially important in small cap land, where a lot of them live.

Small Cap

Every one of the top stock pickers has derived an absolute majority of their gains from small stocks. When you are buying large caps, it is much harder to find the big upside, although it is not impossible. A few of the managers said they had made some significant gains with large cap stocks that were misunderstood by the consensus.

Being Flexible and Adaptable

Although they all have a style that they strictly adhere to, the best money managers also realize that things change. Adaptability to changing circumstances is the key to success. It isn't the biggest or even the best in any particular environment who survive; it's the ones who best adapt to change who survive. As I mentioned in some of the interviews, this is the reason why cockroaches survived the great meteorological calamity that occurred millions of years ago and the dinosaurs did not. We still use the analogy today when we say a particular stock or company is a "dinosaur," meaning it may be out of touch and will not survive.

Portfolio Concentration

This is not a rule, but most of the great stock pickers have a limited number of stocks. This is because they get to know the companies in their portfolio very well, and there is only a small number of companies one can follow in detail. Tom Stanley has as few as eight to ten stocks, whereas a number of twenty is more common. On the other hand, Eric Sprott may have hundreds of stocks, but he also tends to concentrate with bigger positions in a small number of names, with the rest of the portfolio representing a small percentage.

Uncovered and Underfollowed Stocks

This may be similar to the idea of investing in small stocks. Many of the best stock pickers look for something that they can find, that others have overlooked. With stocks that analysts follow diligently, information is disseminated quickly, but it is more difficult to capitalize on little known information. This case can also occur when industries are out of favour. If analysts are not paying attention to a particular industry, there may be gems, even with large stocks, that people are just not interested in. If you can get into a stock when others are uninterested, even if it is a growth company, results can be spectacular when others start to become interested and buy.

Having Patience

Mr. Market was an analogy that Benjamin Graham used to describe the emotion of the stock market. Personifying the market, when Mr. Market gets emotional due to fear and greed, he does irrational things. He is bipolar, and the emotional swings can happen violently, even on a daily basis. With the market telling us the market price of a security daily, it is easy to lose patience and lose sight of the fact that stocks are just pieces of businesses. Businesses grow, and underlying businesses often differ from what their market price is reflecting daily. It is difficult to maintain patience with your stock purchases in the face of all the market noise out there. Many of the managers interviewed, from value to growth to hedge, said that they wish they were more patient, and it was something they were always working on. For instance, Frank Mersch said that his fund at one time owned 30 percent of the company Canadian Natural Resources at about $0.10 per share. If he had held that today, his position would have been worth billions of dollars.

Being Humble

This was common with all the managers. Generally, the impression was that if you don't remain humble, the market will make you humble sooner or later. This is a tricky one, as you must also be very confident and not pay attention to what others are saying in order to be successful. It is a fine balance.

Constantly Questioning Yourself

Each of the managers interviewed constantly questions his decisions in order to justify his positions in his own mind in the face of market noise or to see if he should be changing course.

Not Being Afraid to Admit Mistakes

The "best," whether it is at stock picking, business, or sports, are bold enough and confident enough to not be afraid of being wrong. If you are worried about what others think or get embarrassed about stepping out from the norm and being wrong, then mediocrity is usually on the horizon.

Learning from Mistakes

Mistakes are regarded as a good thing by great stock pickers, as they can learn from them. It was a common question that I asked all of the Superstars during their respective interviews. Most felt they were better investors today than they were ten years ago, largely because they had the opportunity to make more mistakes and learn valuable lessons. I am a pilot, and as they say in the aviation industry, "As long as you survive making a mistake, it turns out to be a good learning experience."

Letting Winners Run

Most people sell their winners and hold onto their losers. This common trait is responsible for many investors doing poorly. All the growth managers interviewed cited this consideration as a key to their success. Interestingly enough, several value managers said that this was important and something they tried to work on. The typical value manager sells early in many cases. Allan Jacobs said that issues with a company are usually worse than people expect, but, on the other hand, good companies are usually underestimated. This is why for him holding onto winners is important.

Looking for the Unusual

Finding things that others have missed is part of thinking outside the box. This goes further however, as Frank Mersch mentioned. He said he saw a small piece in the paper about the Minister of Infrastructure for Alberta going to Israel to learn about how Israel managed its water supply. Why was this the case? As it happens, Alberta has plenty of water, but the oil sands uses 30 percent of the watershed in Western Canada. For every barrel of oil produced, ten barrels of water are required.

Another example is if there is large demand for natural gas, don't just look at the drillers, also look at the equipment providers for the drillers and the people who supply them. These may be overlooked companies.

Trusting Instincts (Having a Good Gut Feel)

The market is a big auction, and it pays to have a good feel for the market. It also pays to have a good feel for the honesty of management and the ability of companies to grow. This is what makes being a good money manager more of an art than a science. I don't know if this skill can be taught or if it can be learned from scratch. One thing is clear, however, and that is most great pickers have a good gut feel. This was highlighted especially by Allan Jacobs, and reiterated by others. Your gut feelings can be improved with experience and with making mistakes.

Owning Your Own Shop

Great stock pickers have traits that don't fit into the norm. This is what makes them great money managers. The problem is that many traditional large money management shops are not set up for this "outside of the box" thinking. If you are going to do things differently, you are going to be wrong from time to time, sometimes severely wrong. This can cause career risk in the form of getting fired. On the other hand, people who work for themselves, owning their own companies, can run money the way they want to, as they are their own boss. This is a key reason that all but one Superstar are independent owners of their own businesses, and the one who isn't, works in a firm that rewards the qualities it takes to be great.